Network Security Management in Heterogeneous Networks

Network Security Management in Heterogeneous Networks

Guest Editors

Tao Zhang
Xiangyun Tang
Jiacheng Wang
Jiqiang Liu

Basel • Beijing • Wuhan • Barcelona • Belgrade • Novi Sad • Cluj • Manchester

Guest Editors

Tao Zhang
School of Cyberspace Science
and Technology
Beijing Jiaotong University
Beijing
China

Xiangyun Tang
School of Information
Engineering
Minzu University of China
Beijing
China

Jiacheng Wang
School of Computer Science
and Engineering
Nanyang Technological
University
Singapore
Singapore

Jiqiang Liu
School of Cyberspace Science
and Technology
Beijing Jiaotong University
Beijing
China

Editorial Office
MDPI AG
Grosspeteranlage 5
4052 Basel, Switzerland

This is a reprint of the Special Issue, published open access by the journal *Electronics* (ISSN 2079-9292), freely accessible at: www.mdpi.com/journal/electronics/special_issues/IL4N9306O0.

For citation purposes, cite each article independently as indicated on the article page online and using the guide below:

Lastname, A.A.; Lastname, B.B. Article Title. *Journal Name* **Year**, *Volume Number*, Page Range.

ISBN 978-3-7258-3318-4 (Hbk)
ISBN 978-3-7258-3317-7 (PDF)
https://doi.org/10.3390/books978-3-7258-3317-7

© 2025 by the authors. Articles in this book are Open Access and distributed under the Creative Commons Attribution (CC BY) license. The book as a whole is distributed by MDPI under the terms and conditions of the Creative Commons Attribution-NonCommercial-NoDerivs (CC BY-NC-ND) license (https://creativecommons.org/licenses/by-nc-nd/4.0/).

Contents

About the Editors vii

Tao Zhang, Xiangyun Tang, Jiacheng Wang and Jiqiang Liu
Network Security Management in Heterogeneous Networks
Reprinted from: *Electronics* **2025**, *14*, 568, https://doi.org/10.3390/electronics14030568 1

Zhimao Lai, Zhuangxi Yao, Guanyu Lai, Chuntao Wang and Renhai Feng
A Novel Face Swapping Detection Scheme Using the Pseudo Zernike Transform Based Robust Watermarking
Reprinted from: *Electronics* **2024**, *13*, 4955, https://doi.org/10.3390/electronics13244955 6

Shan Jiang, Yingshan Shi, Yingchun Zhang and Yulin Zhang
An Improved Retinex-Based Approach Based on Attention Mechanisms for Low-Light Image Enhancement
Reprinted from: *Electronics* **2024**, *13*, 3645, https://doi.org/10.3390/electronics13183645 29

Yinjie Han, Jingyi Meng and Zihang Luo
Multi-Agent Deep Reinforcement Learning for Blockchain-Based Energy Trading in Decentralized Electric Vehicle Charger-Sharing Networks
Reprinted from: *Electronics* **2024**, *13*, 4235, https://doi.org/10.3390/electronics13214235 40

Yong Xiao, Xiaoming Lin, Yiyong Lei, Yanzhang Gu, Jianlin Tang and Fan Zhang et al.
Blockchain-Assisted Secure Energy Trading in Electricity Markets: A Tiny Deep Reinforcement Learning-Based Stackelberg Game Approach
Reprinted from: *Electronics* **2024**, *13*, 3647, https://doi.org/10.3390/electronics13183647 58

Chuhan Gao, Guixian Xu and Yueting Meng
Integrated Extraction of Entities and Relations via Attentive Graph Convolutional Networks
Reprinted from: *Electronics* **2024**, *13*, 4373, https://doi.org/10.3390/electronics13224373 77

Rong Lu, Yong Liang, Jiatai Lin and Yuqiang Chen
Graph Neural Network-Based Modeling with Subcategory Exploration for Drug Repositioning
Reprinted from: *Electronics* **2024**, *13*, 3835, https://doi.org/10.3390/electronics13193835 93

Ning Wu, Xiaoming Lin, Jianbin Lu, Fan Zhang, Weidong Chen and Jianlin Tang et al.
Byzantine-Robust Multimodal Federated Learning Framework for Intelligent Connected Vehicle
Reprinted from: *Electronics* **2024**, *13*, 3635, https://doi.org/10.3390/electronics13183635 104

Jia Zhao, Yating Guo, Bokai Yang and Yanchun Wang
P2P Federated Learning Based on Node Segmentation with Privacy Protection for IoV
Reprinted from: *Electronics* **2024**, *13*, 2276, https://doi.org/10.3390/electronics13122276 119

Haodong Lu, Xiaoming He and Dengyin Zhang
Security-Aware Task Offloading in Mobile Edge Computing Systems via Deep Reinforcement Learning
Reprinted from: *Electronics* **2024**, *13*, 2933, https://doi.org/10.3390/electronics13152933 139

Changkui Yin, Yingchi Mao, Zhenyuan He, Meng Chen, Xiaoming He and Yi Rong
Edge Computing-Enabled Secure Forecasting Nationwide Industry $PM_{2.5}$ with LLM in the Heterogeneous Network
Reprinted from: *Electronics* **2024**, *13*, 2581, https://doi.org/10.3390/electronics13132581 156

Shengyuan Qi, Lin Yang, Linru Ma, Shanqing Jiang, Yuyang Zhou and Guang Cheng
MOMTA-HN: A Secure and Reliable Multi-Objective Optimized Multipath Transmission Algorithm for Heterogeneous Networks
Reprinted from: *Electronics* **2024**, *13*, 2697, https://doi.org/10.3390/electronics13142697 . . . . . **172**

Xiaoming Yuan, Weixuan Kong, Zhenyu Luo and Minrui Xu
Efficient Inference Offloading for Mixture-of-Experts Large Language Models in Internet of Medical Things
Reprinted from: *Electronics* **2024**, *13*, 2077, https://doi.org/10.3390/electronics13112077 . . . . . **196**

Yiwei Liu, Wencong Liu, Xiangyun Tang, Hao Yin, Peng Yin and Xin Xu et al.
CSIM: A Fast Community Detection Algorithm Based on Structure Information Maximization
Reprinted from: *Electronics* **2024**, *13*, 1119, https://doi.org/10.3390/electronics13061119 . . . . . **213**

Weidong Zhang, Dongshang Deng and Lidong Wang
FedScrap: Layer-Wise Personalized Federated Learning for Scrap Detection
Reprinted from: *Electronics* **2024**, *13*, 527, https://doi.org/10.3390/electronics13030527 . . . . . . **232**

About the Editors

Tao Zhang

Tao Zhang received his B.S. degree in Internet of Things engineering from the Beijing University of Posts and Telecommunications (BUPT) and the Queen Mary University of London in 2018, and Ph.D. in computer science and technology from BUPT in 2023. He is currently an Associate Professor with the School of Cyberspace Science and Technology, Beijing Jiaotong University. His publications include highly cited ESI papers and well-archived international journals and proceedings, such as IEEE COMST, JSAC, TIFS, TDSC, TMC, TITS, TCCN, TII, etc. His research interests include network security, moving target defense, and federated learning. He has served as a guest editor for Electronics and the Chinese Journal of Network and Information Security and as the TPC chair and PC member for some international conferences and workshops. He was a recipient of the Best Paper Award from NaNA 2018, IWCMC 2021, DIONE 2024, and ICA3PP 2024, and a recipient of the Outstanding Paper Award from iThings 2023 and SmartCity 2024. His Ph.D. thesis was awarded the Outstanding Doctoral Dissertation by BUPT in 2023.

Xiangyun Tang

Xiangyun Tang received her B.Eng degree in computer science from Minzu University of China, Beijing, China in 2016, and Ph.D in cyberspace security from Beijing Institute of Technology, Beijing, China, in 2022. She is currently an Associate Professor with the School of Information Engineering, Minzu University of China. She has served as a guest editor for multiple journals and as the TPC chair and PC member for international conferences and workshops. She was a recipient of the Best Paper Award from ICA3PP 2024 andIEEE ICBCTIS 2023, and a recipient of the Outstanding Paper Award from IEEE iThings 2023. Her research interests include secure multi-party computation and machine learning security.

Jiacheng Wang

Jiacheng Wang received his M.S degree and Ph.D. from the School of Communication and Information Engineering, Chongqing University of Posts and Telecommunications, in 2018 and 2022, respectively. From 2021 to 2022, he was a Visiting Researcher at the College of Computing and Data Science, at Nanyang Technological University, Singapore, where he is now a Postdoc Research Fellow. His research interests include generative AI, integrated sensing and communications, network optimization, and edge intelligence. He has published more than 40 papers, including in IEEE JSAC, IEEE TMC, IEEE TWC, IEEE TCCN, IEEE TVT, IEEE CMOST, IEEE WCM, IEEE Network, IEEE WCL, IEEE GLOBECOM, IEEE ICC, and IEEE WCNC. He has been a guest editor of IEEE Open Journal of the Communications Society, IEEE Internet of Things Magazine, and IEEE Networking Letters.

Jiqiang Liu

Jiqiang Liu received his Ph.D. from Beijing Normal University in 1999. He is currently a Full Professor and the Dean of the School of Cyberspace Science and Technology, Beijing Jiaotong University. He has authored or coauthored over 200 publications. In recent years, he has been mainly engaged in research on trusted computing, privacy protection, and cloud computing security.

Editorial

Network Security Management in Heterogeneous Networks

Tao Zhang [1,*], Xiangyun Tang [2], Jiacheng Wang [3] and Jiqiang Liu [1]

1. School of Cyberspace Science and Technology, Beijing Jiaotong University, Beijing 100044, China; jqliu@bjtu.edu.cn
2. School of Information Engineering, Minzu University of China, Beijing 100081, China; xiangyunt@muc.edu.cn
3. School of Computer Science and Engineering, Nanyang Technological University, Nanyang Avenue, Singapore 639798, Singapore; jiacheng.wang@ntu.edu.sg
* Correspondence: taozh@bjtu.edu.cn

Heterogeneous networks, as a critical component of modern communication technology, have experienced rapid development in recent years [1]. The emergence of technologies like 5G [2], the Internet of Things (IoT) [3,4], and edge computing [5] has significantly enhanced the diversity and complexity of heterogeneous networks [6], making them pivotal for diverse application demands.

However, the openness and diverse characteristics of heterogeneous networks expose them to serious security challenges [7,8]. Such networks are vulnerable to attacks like Distributed Denial of Service (DDoS) attacks [9], malware propagation [10], and jamming attacks [11], posing significant risks to system stability and data privacy.

To address these pressing security challenges, researchers have developed a variety of defense strategies aimed at mitigating risks in heterogeneous networks [12–17]. Compared to traditional approaches, these strategies exhibit several distinct advantages, such as the ability to efficiently handle large amounts of data while ensuring data security, flexibility in tackling various security challenges, and resilience against advanced and persistent cyberattacks. These approaches provide significant theoretical and practical support for improving the security of heterogeneous networks.

The rapid growth of deepfake technology represents a societal risk [18]. The first contribution to this Special Issue (Contribution 1) proposes a forensic defense method with robust pseudo-Zernike moment watermarks. It employs an adaptive strategy to embed a watermark in the image background, acting as a detection marker. After experimental validation, it was found that the method can effectively improve the robustness of face-switching detection in complex environments and in the presence of disturbances. On the other hand, poor-quality images tend to hamper accurate threat detection, which, in turn, affects the proper functioning of security measures [19]. In Contribution 2, the authors propose an unsupervised low-light image enhancement method using a U-net neural network based on Retinex theory and a Convolutional Block Attention Module (CBAM). The method effectively enhances image details during image decomposition using Retinex theory, while a local adaptive enhancement function is applied to improve reflection map brightness. In addition, the designed loss function addresses the challenges of denoising, brightness enhancement, illumination smoothness, and color restoration.

The growth of low-carbon transport, spurred by environmental policies and technological advances, highlights the importance of energy trading [20]. The issue of energy trading in the electric vehicle (EV) market is beginning to attract attention from researchers. Contribution 3 presents a multi-agent reinforcement learning (MADRL)-based auction algorithm to optimize distributed energy trading in EV charger-sharing networks, enhancing social welfare and efficiency. This approach leverages blockchain technology to ensure the transparency and immutability of transactions, providing users with a transparent and decentralized trading platform. Deep reinforcement learning (DRL) techniques are used to train agents (such as EVs or charging stations) to make optimal decisions in uncertain environments. Contribution 4 presents a blockchain-based framework for secure electricity trading between EV operators and the electricity market. A Stackelberg game model using the Tiny DRL algorithm is proposed to optimize trading strategies, enhancing efficiency in uncertain markets.

Entity and relation extraction plays a key role in real-time cybersecurity monitoring and analysis [21]. Contribution 5 introduces a model for entity and relation extraction using an attention mechanism and a Graph Convolutional Network (GCN). The method uses sequence labeling for entity span detection and employs multi-feature fusion to identify all entity spans and build an entity span matrix. Next, based on the attention mechanism, the authors construct an entity relation matrix to represent correlations between entities. Finally, the entity span matrix and entity relation weighted matrix are fed into the GCN for unified entity and relation extraction.

Contribution 6 addresses the challenge of drug repositioning using Graph Neural Networks (GNNs) to model complex relationships between drugs, diseases, and their subcategories. It incorporates a prototype-based feature-enhancement mechanism (PFEM) along with a dual-task classification head (D3TC) to enhance the representation of these relationships. The proposed method was experimentally validated on four public datasets. The results showed that the method surpasses state-of-the-art approaches, significantly enhancing drug repositioning accuracy and efficiency.

The rapid growth of the Internet of Vehicles (IoV) has led to increased focus on its security challenges [22]. Federated learning (FL) can address security and privacy concerns in the Intelligent Connected Vehicle (ICV) domain [23,24], but still faces challenges like multimodal data integration [25], Byzantine attacks [26], and communication limits [27]. In response to these challenges, Contribution 7 introduces a Byzantine-robust multimodal FL framework to tackle these issues. It counters Byzantine attacks with a gradient compression-based aggregation technique. It incorporates a multimodal learning framework to improve adaptability to complex environments and uses top-k gradient compression to enhance communication efficiency. Contribution 8 addresses the privacy leakage risks associated with model parameter exchange in the peer-to-peer (P2P) architecture of FL for IoV scenarios. To address these risks, a differential privacy scheme is proposed, allowing nodes to dynamically adjust noise levels in their model parameters based on their distances to other nodes. This method balances security and model quality.

In edge computing, security is a key factor affecting system performance and user trust [28–30]. The issue of security in Mobile Edge Computing (MEC) scenarios remains an open challenge [31]. To address this, Contribution 9 presents a DRL-based security-aware task-offloading framework. This framework uses an Advanced Encryption Standard (AES) to secure data during task offloading. Furthermore, the task-offloading process is modeled as a Markov Decision Process (MDP) and optimized with a Proximal Policy Optimization (PPO) algorithm to reduce latency and energy use. Contribution 10 introduces an approach based on a large language model (LLM) called the Spatio-Temporal Large Language Model with Edge Computing Servers (STLLM-ECS) to predict industrial production nationwide $PM_{2.5}$. To address security risks in centralized training, such as data leaks during transmission, the paper introduces an edge-distributed learning framework, STLLM-ECS. The framework uses a novel method, called NodeSort, to divide the nationwide sensor network graph into subgraphs. Data and training tasks for each subgraph are allocated to separate Edge Computing Servers (ECSs), reducing data leakage risks.

To address security challenges in heterogeneous networks, Contribution 11 introduces the optimized multi-objective multipath transmission algorithm (MOMTA-HN). This algorithm integrates multiple objectives into path selection, allowing the calculation of optimal paths. Using these redundant paths, the algorithm provides enhanced protection for communication processes within heterogeneous networks.

Contribution 12 presents MedMixtral 8x7B, a medical LLM using the mixture-of-experts (MoE) architecture and an offloading strategy for IoMT deployment. Using the proposed efficient inference-offloading strategy, the model dynamically allocates its weights between the CPU RAM and disk during run-time, effectively reducing GPU memory consumption. This approach enables the deployment of MedMixtral 8x7B on resource-constrained IoMT devices, thus enhancing user privacy protection.

Community detection is a crucial method for analyzing complex systems and organizational structures [32]. Contribution 13 reinterprets community structure by encoding edge information, highlighting its essence by reducing transmitting edge information uncertainty within community structures. This new definition better captures the intrinsic characteristics of communities. Based on this concept, the community detection algorithm CSIM is proposed, which aims to maximize community structure information as its optimization objective and efficiently approximates optimal community partitioning, with its practical effectiveness validated through experiments.

Scrap detection is key to linking the smelting process with the industrial internet, prioritizing security and privacy [33]. Contribution 14 introduces FedScrap, a layer-wise personalized FL framework that coordinates decentralized scrap data while safeguarding privacy. FedScrap uses a self-attention mechanism to aggregate personalized client models layer-by-layer, prioritizing data relevance. This approach enhances the accuracy of model aggregation while addressing data heterogeneity and protecting data privacy.

Funding: This research was funded by the Talent Fund of Beijing Jiaotong University under Grant number 2023XKRC050; by the National Natural Science Foundation of China (NSFC) under Grant number 62402029, 62302539; by the China Postdoctoral Science Foundation under Grant number 2024T170047, GZC20230223, 2024M750165.

Data Availability Statement: No new data were created or analyzed in this study. Data sharing is not applicable to this article.

Conflicts of Interest: The authors declare no conflicts of interest.

List of Contributions

1. Lai, Z.; Yao, Z.; Lai, G.; Wang, C.; Feng, R. A Novel Face Swapping Detection Scheme Using the Pseudo Zemike Tranform Based Robust Watermarking. *Electronics* **2024**, *13*, 4955. https://doi.org/10.3390/electronics13244955.
2. Jiang, S.; Shi, Y.; Zhang, Y.; Zhang, Y. An Improved Retinex-Based Approach Based on Attention Mechanisms for Low-Light Image Enhancement. *Electronics* **2024**, *13*, 3645. https://doi.org/10.3390/electronics13183645.
3. Han, Y.; Meng, J.; Luo, Z. Multi-Agent Deep Reinforcement Learning for Blockchain-Based Energy Trading in Decentralized Electric Vehicle Charger-Sharing Networks. *Electronics* **2024**, *13*, 4235. https://doi.org/10.3390/electronics13214235.
4. Xiao, Y.; Lin, X.; Lei, Y.; Gu, Y.; Tang, J.; Zhang, F.; Qian, B. Blockchain-Assisted Secure Energy Trading in Electricity Markets: A Tiny Deep Reinforcement Learning-Based Stackelberg Game Approach. *Electronics* **2024**, *13*, 3647. https://doi.org/10.3390/electronics13183647.
5. Gao, C.; Xu, G.; Meng, Y. Integrated Extraction of Entities and Relations via Attentive Graph Convolutional Networks. *Electronics* **2024**, *13*, 4373. https://doi.org/10.3390/electronics13224373.
6. Lu, R.; Liang, Y.; Lin, J.; Chen, Y. Graph Neural Network-Based Modeling with Subcategory Exploration for Drug Repositioning. *Electronics* **2024**, *13*, 3835. https://doi.org/10.3390/electronics13193835.

7. Wu, N.; Lin, X.; Lu, J.; Zhang, F.; Chen, W.; Tang, J.; Xiao, J. Byzantine-Robust Multimodal Federated Learning Framework for Intelligent Connected Vehicle. *Electronics* **2024**, *13*, 3635. https://doi.org/10.3390/electronics13183635.
8. Zhao, J.; Guo, Y.; Yang, B.; Wang, Y. P2P Federated Learning Based on Node Segmentation with Privacy Protection for IoV. *Electronics* **2024**, *13*, 2276. https://doi.org/10.3390/electronics13122276.
9. Lu, H.; He, X.; Zhang, D. Security-Aware Task Offloading Using Deep Reinforcement Learning in Mobile Edge Computing Systems. *Electronics* **2024**, *13*, 2933. https://doi.org/10.3390/electronics13152933.
10. Yin, C.; Mao, Y.; He, Z.; Chen, M.; He, X.; Rong, Y. Edge Computing-Enabled Secure Forecasting Nationwide Industry PM2.5 with LLM in the Heterogeneous Network. *Electronics* **2024**, *13*, 2581. https://doi.org/10.3390/electronics13132581.
11. Qi, S.; Yang, L.; Ma, L.; Jiang, S.; Zhou, Y.; Cheng, G. MOMTA-HN: A Secure and Reliable Multi-Objective Optimized Multipath Transmission Algorithm for Heterogeneous Networks. *Electronics* **2024**, *13*, 2697. https://doi.org/10.3390/electronics13142697.
12. Yuan, X.; Kong, W.; Luo, Z.; Xu, M. Efficient Inference Offloading for Mixture-of-Experts Large Language Models in Internet of Medical Things. *Electronics* **2024**, *13*, 2077. https://doi.org/10.3390/electronics13112077.
13. Liu, Y.; Liu, W.; Tang, X.; Yin, H.; Yin, P.; Xu, X.; Wang, Y. CSIM: A Fast Community Detection Algorithm Based on Structure Information Maximization. *Electronics* **2024**, *13*, 1119. https://doi.org/10.3390/electronics13061119.
14. Zhang, W.; Deng, D.; Wang, L. FedScrap: Layer-Wise Personalized Federated Learning for Scrap Detection. *Electronics* **2024**, *13*, 527. https://doi.org/10.3390/electronics13030527.

References

1. Xu, Y.; Gui, G.; Gacanin, H.; Adachi, F. A survey on resource allocation for 5G heterogeneous networks: Current research, future trends, and challenges. *IEEE Commun. Surv. Tutor.* **2021**, *23*, 668–695. [CrossRef]
2. Zhang, R.; Xiong, K.; Lu, Y.; Ng, D.W.K.; Fan, P.; Letaief, K.B. SWIPT-Enabled Cell-Free Massive MIMO-NOMA Networks: A Machine Learning-Based Approach. *IEEE Trans. Wirel. Commun.* **2024**, *23*, 6701–6718. [CrossRef]
3. Wang, J.; Du, H.; Niyato, D.; Kang, J.; Cui, S.; Shen, X.S.; Zhang, P. Generative AI for integrated sensing and communication: Insights from the physical layer perspective. *IEEE Wirel. Commun.* **2024**, *31*, 246–255. [CrossRef]
4. Wang, J.; Du, H.; Niyato, D.; Xiong, Z.; Kang, J.; Ai, B.; Han, Z.; Kim, D.I. Generative Artificial Intelligence Assisted Wireless Sensing: Human Flow Detection in Practical Communication Environments. *IEEE J. Sel. Areas Commun.* **2024**, *42*, 2737–2753. [CrossRef]
5. Zhang, R.; Du, H.; Liu, Y.; Niyato, D.; Kang, J.; Sun, S.; Shen, X.; Poor, H.V. Interactive AI with Retrieval-Augmented Generation for Next Generation Networking. *IEEE Netw.* **2024**, *38*, 414–424. [CrossRef]
6. Cui, Z.; Zhao, Y.; Cao, Y.; Cai, X.; Zhang, W.; Chen, J. Malicious code detection under 5G HetNets based on a multi-objective RBM model. *IEEE Netw.* **2021**, *35*, 82–87. [CrossRef]
7. Wang, J.; Yan, Z.; Wang, H.; Li, T.; Pedrycz, W. A survey on trust models in heterogeneous networks. *IEEE Commun. Surv. Tutor.* **2022**, *24*, 2127–2162. [CrossRef]
8. Zhang, T.; Kong, F.; Deng, D.; Tang, X.; Wu, X.; Xu, C.; Zhu, L.; Liu, J.; Ai, B.; Han, Z.; et al. Moving Target Defense Meets Artificial Intelligence-Driven Network: A Comprehensive Survey. *IEEE Internet Things J.* **2025**, *1*. [CrossRef]
9. Dey, M.R.; Patra, M.; Mishra, P. Efficient detection and localization of dos attacks in heterogeneous vehicular networks. *IEEE Trans. Veh. Technol.* **2023**, *72*, 5597–5611. [CrossRef]
10. Wang, X.; Zhang, X.; Wang, S.; Xiao, J.; Tao, X. Modeling, Critical Threshold, and Lowest-Cost Patching Strategy of Malware Propagation in Heterogeneous IoT Networks. *IEEE Trans. Inf. Forensics Secur.* **2023**, *18*, 3531–3545. [CrossRef]
11. Sharma, H.; Kumar, N.; Tekchandani, R. Mitigating jamming attack in 5G heterogeneous networks: A federated deep reinforcement learning approach. *IEEE Trans. Veh. Technol.* **2022**, *72*, 2439–2452. [CrossRef]
12. Tang, X.; Shen, M.; Li, Q.; Zhu, L.; Xue, T.; Qu, Q. Pile: Robust privacy-preserving federated learning via verifiable perturbations. *IEEE Trans. Dependable Secur. Comput.* **2023**, *20*, 5005–5023. [CrossRef]
13. Zhang, T.; Xu, C.; Lian, Y.; Tian, H.; Kang, J.; Kuang, X.; Niyato, D. When moving target defense meets attack prediction in digital twins: A convolutional and hierarchical reinforcement learning approach. *IEEE J. Sel. Areas Commun.* **2023**, *41*, 3293–3305. [CrossRef]

14. Zhang, T.; Xu, C.; Zou, P.; Tian, H.; Kuang, X.; Yang, S.; Zhong, L.; Niyato, D. How to mitigate DDoS intelligently in SD-IoV: A moving target defense approach. *IEEE Trans. Ind. Inform.* **2022**, *19*, 1097–1106. [CrossRef]
15. Zhu, X.; Liu, J.; Lu, L.; Zhang, T.; Qiu, T.; Wang, C.; Liu, Y. Enabling intelligent connectivity: A survey of secure isac in 6g networks. *IEEE Commun. Surv. Tutor.* **2024**. [CrossRef]
16. Zhang, W.; He, Y.; Zhang, T.; Ying, C.; Kang, J. Intelligent Resource Adaptation for Diversified Service Requirements in Industrial IoT. *IEEE Trans. Cogn. Commun. Netw.* **2024**. [CrossRef]
17. Zhang, T.; Xu, C.; Shen, J.; Kuang, X.; Grieco, L.A. How to disturb network reconnaissance: A moving target defense approach based on deep reinforcement learning. *IEEE Trans. Inf. Forensics Secur.* **2023**, *18*, 5735–5748. [CrossRef]
18. Seow, J.W.; Lim, M.K.; Phan, R.C.; Liu, J.K. A comprehensive overview of Deepfake: Generation, detection, datasets, and opportunities. *Neurocomputing* **2022**, *513*, 351–371. [CrossRef]
19. Li, L.; Xu, W.; Gao, Y.; Lu, Y.; Yang, D.; Liu, R.W.; Zhang, R. Attention-oriented residual block for real-time low-light image enhancement in smart ports. *Comput. Electr. Eng.* **2024**, *120*, 109634. [CrossRef]
20. Krishnamurthy, D.; Uckun, C.; Zhou, Z.; Thimmapuram, P.R.; Botterud, A. Energy storage arbitrage under day-ahead and real-time price uncertainty. *IEEE Trans. Power Syst.* **2017**, *33*, 84–93. [CrossRef]
21. Wang, X.; Liu, J. A novel feature integration and entity boundary detection for named entity recognition in cybersecurity. *Knowl.-Based Syst.* **2023**, *260*, 110114. [CrossRef]
22. Kumar, R.; Kumar, P.; Tripathi, R.; Gupta, G.P.; Kumar, N. P2SF-IoV: A privacy-preservation-based secured framework for Internet of Vehicles. *IEEE Trans. Intell. Transp. Syst.* **2021**, *23*, 22571–22582. [CrossRef]
23. Manias, D.M.; Shami, A. Making a case for federated learning in the internet of vehicles and intelligent transportation systems. *IEEE Netw.* **2021**, *35*, 88–94. [CrossRef]
24. Chellapandi, V.P.; Yuan, L.; Brinton, C.G.; Żak, S.H.; Wang, Z. Federated learning for connected and automated vehicles: A survey of existing approaches and challenges. *IEEE Trans. Intell. Veh.* **2023**, *9*, 119–137. [CrossRef]
25. Huang, W.; Wang, D.; Ouyang, X.; Wan, J.; Liu, J.; Li, T. Multimodal federated learning: Concept, methods, applications and future directions. *Inf. Fusion* **2024**, *112*, 102576. [CrossRef]
26. Ma, X.; Jiang, Q.; Shojafar, M.; Alazab, M.; Kumar, S.; Kumari, S. Disbezant: Secure and robust federated learning against byzantine attack in iot-enabled mts. *IEEE Trans. Intell. Transp. Syst.* **2022**, *24*, 2492–2502. [CrossRef]
27. Chen, M.; Shlezinger, N.; Poor, H.V.; Eldar, Y.C.; Cui, S. Communication-efficient federated learning. *Proc. Natl. Acad. Sci. USA* **2021**, *118*, e2024789118. [CrossRef] [PubMed]
28. Ranaweera, P.; Jurcut, A.D.; Liyanage, M. Survey on multi-access edge computing security and privacy. *IEEE Commun. Surv. Tutorials* **2021**, *23*, 1078–1124. [CrossRef]
29. Singh, A.; Chatterjee, K. Securing smart healthcare system with edge computing. *Comput. Secur.* **2021**, *108*, 102353. [CrossRef]
30. Xue, H.; Chen, D.; Zhang, N.; Dai, H.N.; Yu, K. Integration of blockchain and edge computing in internet of things: A survey. *Future Gener. Comput. Syst.* **2023**, *144*, 307–326. [CrossRef]
31. Garg, S.; Kaur, K.; Kaddoum, G.; Garigipati, P.; Aujla, G.S. Security in IoT-driven mobile edge computing: New paradigms, challenges, and opportunities. *IEEE Netw.* **2021**, *35*, 298–305. [CrossRef]
32. Su, X.; Xue, S.; Liu, F.; Wu, J.; Yang, J.; Zhou, C.; Hu, W.; Paris, C.; Nepal, S.; Jin, D.; et al. A comprehensive survey on community detection with deep learning. *IEEE Trans. Neural Netw. Learn. Syst.* **2022**, *35*, 4682–4702. [CrossRef] [PubMed]
33. Xu, W.; Xiao, P.; Zhu, L.; Zhang, Y.; Chang, J.; Zhu, R.; Xu, Y. Classification and rating of steel scrap using deep learning. *Eng. Appl. Artif. Intell.* **2023**, *123*, 106241. [CrossRef]

Disclaimer/Publisher's Note: The statements, opinions and data contained in all publications are solely those of the individual author(s) and contributor(s) and not of MDPI and/or the editor(s). MDPI and/or the editor(s) disclaim responsibility for any injury to people or property resulting from any ideas, methods, instructions or products referred to in the content.

Article

A Novel Face Swapping Detection Scheme Using the Pseudo Zernike Transform Based Robust Watermarking

Zhimao Lai [1,2], Zhuangxi Yao [3], Guanyu Lai [2], Chuntao Wang [3,*] and Renhai Feng [4]

1. School of Immigration Administration (Guangzhou), China People's Police University, Guangzhou 510663, China; laizhimao@cppu.edu.cn
2. School of Automation, Guangdong University and Technology, Guangzhou 510006, China; lgy124@gdut.edu.cn
3. College of Mathematics and Informatics, South China Agricultural University, Guangzhou 510642, China; yaozhuangxi@stu.scau.edu.cn
4. School of Electrical and Information Engineering, Tianjin University, Tianjin 300072, China; fengrenhai@tju.edu.cn
* Correspondence: wangct@scau.edu.cn

Citation: Lai, Z.; Yao, Z.; Lai, G.; Wang, C.; Feng, R. A Novel Face Swapping Detection Scheme Using the Pseudo Zernike Transform Based Robust Watermarking. *Electronics* **2024**, *13*, 4955. https://doi.org/10.3390/electronics13244955

Academic Editor: George A. Tsihrintzis

Received: 6 November 2024
Revised: 9 December 2024
Accepted: 11 December 2024
Published: 16 December 2024

Copyright: © 2024 by the authors. Licensee MDPI, Basel, Switzerland. This article is an open access article distributed under the terms and conditions of the Creative Commons Attribution (CC BY) license (https://creativecommons.org/licenses/by/4.0/).

Abstract: The rapid advancement of Artificial Intelligence Generated Content (AIGC) has significantly accelerated the evolution of Deepfake technology, thereby introducing escalating social risks due to its potential misuse. In response to these adverse effects, researchers have developed defensive measures, including passive detection and proactive forensics. Although passive detection has achieved some success in identifying Deepfakes, it encounters challenges such as poor generalization and decreased accuracy, particularly when confronted with anti-forensic techniques and adversarial noise. As a result, proactive forensics, which offers a more resilient defense mechanism, has garnered considerable scholarly interest. However, existing proactive forensic methodologies often fall short in terms of visual quality, detection accuracy, and robustness. To address these deficiencies, we propose a novel proactive forensic approach that utilizes pseudo-Zernike moment robust watermarking. This method is specifically designed to enhance the detection and analysis of face swapping by transforming facial data into a binary bit stream and embedding this information within the non-facial regions of video frames. Our approach facilitates the detection of Deepfakes while preserving the visual integrity of the video content. Comprehensive experimental evaluations have demonstrated the robustness of this method against standard signal processing operations and its superior performance in detecting Deepfake manipulations.

Keywords: Deepfake detection; face swapping; proactive forensics; robust watermarking; image hashing; pseudo-Zernike transform

1. Introduction

The rapid advancement of visual generation models, such as Generative Adversarial Networks (GANs) [1] and Stable Diffusion [2], has significantly enhanced Deepfake technology, particularly in the creation of highly realistic human face images. Face swapping [3,4], a prominent form of Deepfake technology, poses a significant risk to current social governance, necessitating focused preventive measures. This technique involves the high-fidelity replacement of a specific person's face in a given scene, effectively altering the individual's depicted identity. Despite the progress made in passive detection methods, they often struggle with poor generalization and decreased accuracy, particularly when dealing with anti-forensic techniques and adversarial noise. To address these challenges, our study introduces a novel proactive forensic approach that employs pseudo-Zernike moment robust watermarking, specifically designed to enhance the detection and analysis of face swapping.

The fundamental principle of face swapping is illustrated in Figures 1 and 2 provides a detailed comparison of outcomes from various face swapping algorithms. These comparisons highlight the primary strategy of these algorithms, i.e., modifying only the facial region of the target image to minimize distortion and maintain scene coherence, while preserving the rest of the original image. This approach ensures the visual realism of the resulting image, thereby enhancing the deceptive potential of the technology. Existing passive detection methods [5–12], which typically employ a supervised approach to identify face swapping, often face challenges such as overfitting and susceptibility to anti-forensic techniques and adversarial noise, resulting in reduced accuracy. As passive detection functions as a post-event defense, it is unable to proactively prevent the malicious dissemination of forged face images or videos. Moreover, the outcomes of passive detection frequently lack the reliable evidence necessary to conclusively prove face forgery. To address these limitations, researchers have introduced active forensic methods for Deepfake. These methods center on embedding specific digital watermarks into images or videos prior to their online distribution. This proactive strategy aims to authenticate and verify the integrity of images with minimal training costs, thereby achieving higher detection efficiency and providing a preemptive defense mechanism. For instance, Yu et al. [13] pioneered an active detection scheme utilizing Artificial GAN Fingerprints (AFP). They embedded these artificial fingerprints into the training data, ensuring their transferability to the generated model, which resulted in the fingerprints being present in the forged outputs. Similarly, Wang et al. [14] developed a method called FakeTagger, which safeguards the security and privacy of facial images by embedding information into victim images. This information can be retrieved after Deepfake generation to ascertain whether the images have been forged and manipulated by GANs. To offer semantic-level protection for facial images and prevent the manipulation of identity features, Zhao et al. [15] introduced an active defense method based on identity watermarks. These injected tags are intricately linked with facial identity features, making them highly sensitive to face-swapping manipulations while remaining robust against traditional image modifications such as resizing and compression. Furthermore, various studies [16–18] have explored active forensic methods using robust watermarks, fragile watermarks, and semi-fragile watermarks, each tailored to specific application scenarios and watermarking characteristics. Although these methods provide innovative research directions and practical solutions for active Deepfake forensics, their detection performance may vary when confronted with common signal processing attacks, including JPEG compression, noise attacks, rotation, and scaling, as well as Deepfake-specific attacks.

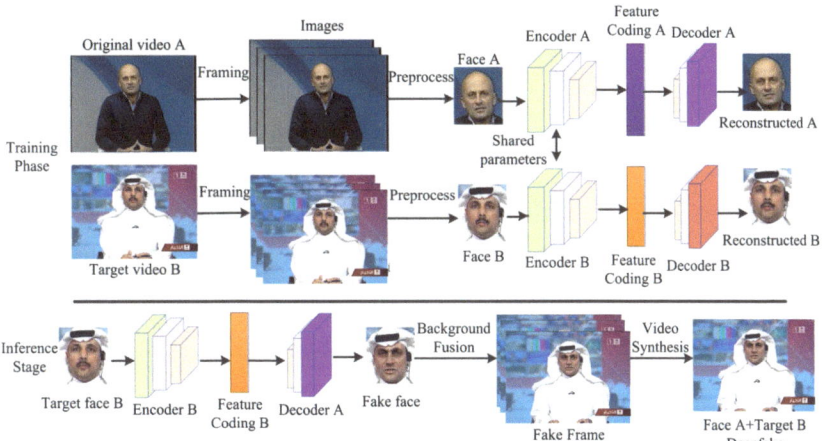

Figure 1. The fundamental principle of face swapping.

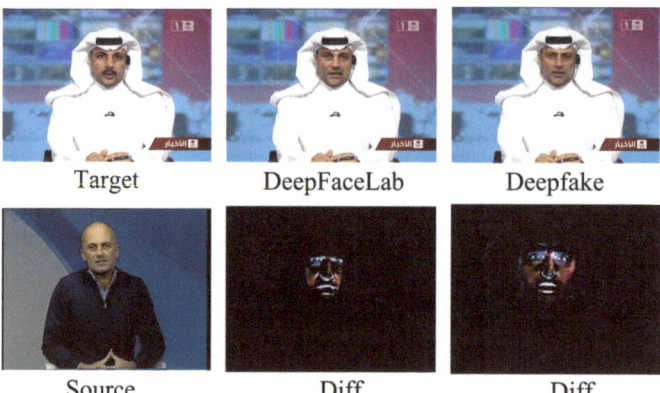

Figure 2. Results of two face-swapping algorithms and difference maps between ground-truth target images and face-swapping images.

The primary challenges in Deepfake detection include the need for methods that can generalize well across different datasets and conditions, maintain high accuracy despite adversarial attacks, and provide robust evidence for forensic analysis. Our approach aims to overcome these challenges by focusing on proactive forensics, offering a more resilient defense mechanism. Figure 3 presents the face-swapping detection method based on the pseudo-Zernike moment robust watermarks proposed in this paper, alongside other active detection methods that utilize watermarks. Traditional active forensic methods for face swapping involve embedding predefined watermarking information directly into the protected face. During the detection process, these methods compare the extracted watermarking from the detected face with the originally stored watermarking information to ascertain whether a face swap has occurred. However, these methods are susceptible to false positives, particularly when exposed to conventional signal processing attacks, as the extracted watermarking can significantly deviate from the original. Furthermore, they necessitate the management of original watermarking information, imposing additional burdens on practical applications. In contrast, the method proposed in this paper offers a more robust and practical solution. It involves embedding a visual hash result, which represents the protected face information, into the background region of the image. During detection, the watermarking information extracted from the background is compared with a visual hash sequence regenerated from the detected face. This approach not only reduces the likelihood of false positives but also eliminates the need to manage original watermarking information, thereby enhancing the method's practicality and reliability in face-swapping detection.

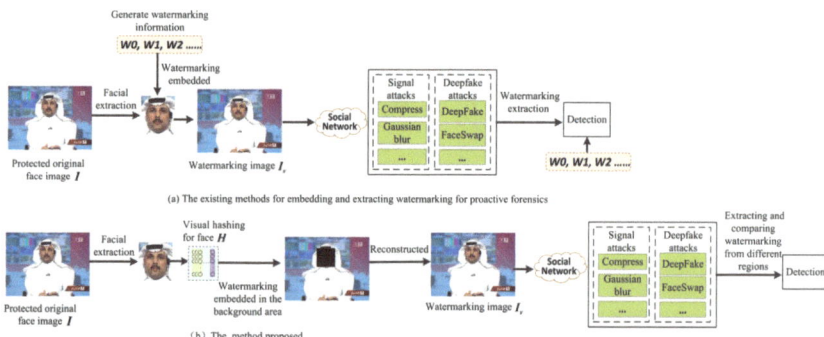

Figure 3. Diagram compares existing watermark-based active detection methods with the method proposed.

Our contributions can be summarized as follows:

- We extend the robust watermarking technique proposed by Tang [19] to the domain of active forensics specifically for face swapping. By integrating adaptive normalization and embedding optimization methods, we achieve an optimal balance between robustness and invisibility. This extension forms the basis of our proactive forensic scheme for face swapping, which utilizes pseudo-Zernike moment robust watermarks.
- We develop a method to generate a hash sequence from the protected face, embedding it into the background region of the image. This region remains unchanged during the face-swapping process, thereby enhancing the watermarking's resilience. Our approach effectively withstands conventional signal processing attacks, including compression, noise addition, and geometric distortions, as well as Deepfake attacks that target facial features.
- An adaptive strategy is developed to determine suitable background regions for watermarking embedding. By dividing the image into blocks and adaptively selecting background regions based on the blocks occupied by the face, we address the challenge of inconsistent face recognition results before and after watermarking embedding. This inconsistency can lead to failed watermarking extraction. Our strategy ensures the successful implementation of the proposed scheme, maintaining the integrity of the watermarking process.

The structure of this paper is organized as follows: Section 2 reviews related work, focusing on active forensic methods for Deepfake, robust watermarking techniques utilizing geometric moments, and perceptual image hashing. Section 3 characterizes the problem and elaborates on the detailed implementation of the proposed method. Section 4 presents the experimental results and offers a comprehensive analysis. Finally, Section 5 summarizes the research findings and concludes the paper.

2. Related Works

This paper examines the detection of face swapping through the application of robust watermarks, specifically utilizing pseudo-Zernike moments. The study is grounded in the background knowledge of active forensic methods for identifying Deepfake, the implementation of robust watermarks derived from geometric moments, and perceptual image hashing. These foundational topics are systematically explored in Sections 2.1, 2.2 and 2.3, respectively.

2.1. Deepfake Proactive Forensics

Active forensic methods for Deepfake focus on embedding specific information during the content generation or dissemination process, which can later be used to verify the authenticity of the content. Yu et al. [13] pioneered the application of image steganography techniques to active forensics for Deepfake by introducing artificial fingerprints into generative models. This innovation enables the identification and tracking of these models. Liao et al. [20] proposed using adversarial learning to simulate various distortion enhancement strategies, thereby improving the robustness of artificial or model fingerprints. In another approach, Wang et al. [14] introduced FakeTagger, a method designed to protect face security and privacy through image tagging. This method employs a simple yet effective encoder–decoder design and channel coding to embed messages into facial images, which can still be recovered after DeepFakes forgery. Despite its effectiveness, FakeTagger is prone to misclassifying real face images that have undergone conventional signal post-processing as fakes. Zhao et al. [15] introduced a tamper-proof label mechanism to provide semantic-level protection for face images, aiming to prevent forgers from manipulating identity features. This approach involves embedding watermarks as adversarial labels into facial identity features. The entanglement of these labels with facial identity features makes them highly sensitive to face-swapping manipulations while remaining robust against traditional image modifications such as resizing and compression. However, the method necessitates high-intensity watermarks to ensure detectability. To address both traceability and Deepfake detection, Wu et al. [16] introduced SepMark, an end-to-end trainable separable watermarking method. This approach employs robust and fragile decoders to extract watermarks with varying levels of robustness, thereby providing a unified forensic framework. Similarly, Liu et al. [17] extended the application of watermarks to various forensic scenarios with BiFPro, a bidirectional face data protection framework where watermarks exhibit either fragility or robustness. Despite the advancements these methods offer in forensic capabilities for Deepfake content, they still encounter limitations when confronted with complex attack scenarios.

2.2. Robust Watermarking Technique Based on Geometric Moments

Geometric moments are a feature extraction method for images, projecting them onto a set of orthogonal basis vectors and exhibiting geometric invariance properties such as rotation, scaling, and translation [21]. These moments, particularly in their low-order forms, are statistically robust, meaning their characteristics remain stable even when image quality degrades. This robustness makes geometric moments a popular choice in the literature for implementing robust watermarks, enhancing the watermarking's resilience. In the realm of robust watermarking design, Hu and Xiang [22] pioneered a method that embeds watermarking information into the low-order Zernike Moments (ZMs) of an image. This approach achieves invariance to image scaling and arbitrary rotations, while also providing robustness against interpolation errors in geometric transformations and common image processing operations. Recognizing that pseudo-Zernike Moments (PZMs) offer greater noise resistance than traditional ZMs [23], Tang et al. [19] opted to embed robust watermarks in PZMs. They utilized an adaptive normalization method to balance invariance to pixel amplitude changes, robustness, and imperceptibility, significantly reducing embedding distortion through their optimized strategy. Building on the robustness of Fractional-order Orthogonal Moments (FoOM), Fu et al. [24] employed FoOM to enhance ZMs/PZMs, thereby improving the numerical stability and computational accuracy of these moments. This advancement further contributes to the development of robust watermarking techniques. Pseudo-Zernike moments (PZMs) are recognized for their superior performance in image reconstruction, numerical stability, and computational complexity when compared to other geometric moments. Leveraging these advantages, Hu and Xiang [25] developed a novel quantization watermarking strategy utilizing Polar Harmonic Transforms (PHTs). By embedding bit information into PHTs, their approach achieved enhanced watermarking robustness and increased embedding capacity.

2.3. Perceptual Image Hashing

Visual Hashing, also known as Perceptual Image Hashing (PIH), algorithms are designed to extract visual features from images, generating unique hash values that remain stable under minor modifications, such as rotation, cropping, gamma correction, and noise addition, while being sensitive to perceptual variations [26]. This technique is crucial in various applications, including image content identification, authentication, and copyright protection. A significant contribution to this field was made by Tang et al. [27], who introduced a robust PIH scheme. Their approach begins by normalizing input images to a standardized size, followed by segmenting them into non-overlapping blocks. The entropy of each block is then computed, and a two-dimensional discrete wavelet transform (2D DWT) is applied for feature compression, resulting in compact hash codes. The similarity between these hash codes is assessed using correlation coefficients, which highlights the algorithm's resilience to common image processing operations such as JPEG compression, watermarking, gamma correction, Gaussian blurring, brightness and contrast adjustments, scaling, and slight rotations. Furthermore, the method demonstrates a strong ability to distinguish between different images, as evidenced by the low similarity scores. Shen and Zhao [26] introduced a PIH method that utilizes color opponent components (COC) and quadtree decomposition (QD). Qin et al. [28] developed a PIH method that employs singular value decomposition (SVD) for preprocessing the original image. Perceptual features are then extracted using block truncation coding, followed by the application of principal component analysis (PCA) to generate the final hash sequence. This method achieves satisfactory collision resistance and security. Collectively, these methods enhance the uniqueness and robustness of hash values by extracting visual features from images.

3. The Proposed Method

Images are frequently utilized as materials for Deepfakes due to their ease of acquisition and transmission. As these images circulate through various social networks, they often undergo a range of intentional and unintentional conventional signal processing, which can affect the integrity of embedded digital watermarks. Consequently, when employing digital watermarks for active forensics, these watermarks are vulnerable to various attacks, both intentional and unintentional, which can lead to their destruction. This vulnerability is particularly pronounced when images are subjected to Deepfake manipulations, as there is a high likelihood that the watermarks will be erased. Therefore, digital watermarks used for Deepfake forensics must be robust against traditional signal processing attacks, such as noise, compression, and geometric transformations, as well as resistant to novel Deepfake attacks that utilize deep neural network content generation. This paper focuses on utilizing digital watermarking techniques to detect and defend against image face-swapping attacks. The proposed method employs robust watermarks based on pseudo-Zernike moments, which are known for their strong resistance to various attacks, including compression, noise, filtering, and geometric distortions [29]. Specifically, the study introduces a face-swapping detection approach that leverages these robust watermarks. To extract semantic features and ensure semantic consistency in published images, visual hash algorithms [30] are used to generate watermarking information from the protected facial data within the images. This watermarking information is then embedded into the background outside the face region, making the method inherently resistant to Deepfake attacks targeting faces. Furthermore, to ensure the embedded watermarking information can withstand conventional signal processing attacks, it is incorporated into the pseudo-Zernike moments of the background region. The face-swapping detection process involves two primary steps. First, the face is extracted from the current image being tested, and the same visual hash method is employed to generate the watermarking information representing the face. Second, the embedded watermarking information is extracted from the background of the test image. These two sets of watermarking information are then compared. If the difference between them exceeds a certain threshold, it indicates that the face in the current test image has been swapped. Conversely, if the difference does not exceed the threshold, the face is considered authentic. The face-swapping detection method based on the pseudo-Zernike moment robust watermarks proposed in this study meets three essential characteristics. Firstly, the watermarking data remain extractable even after the images undergo conventional signal processing attacks, such as compression, noise, and geometric deformations, enabling the detection and verification of Deepfake attacks. Secondly, in cases of malicious manipulation, such as face swapping, the embedded digital watermarks can be used for comparison and authentication. Lastly, the embedded digital watermarks are visually imperceptible and do not degrade the quality of the images. In conclusion, this method provides natural resistance to both conventional signal processing attacks and Deepfake attacks targeting faces, thereby offering robust Deepfake detection performance.

This paper proposes a proactive forensics method named "Pseudo-Zernike Moment-Based Deepfake Detection (PZM-DD)" to enhance the resilience of deep learning-based face replacement attacks against common signal processing attacks, including compression, noise addition, and geometric deformations, as well as Deepfake-specific attacks. Figure 4 provides an illustration of the proposed face replacement proactive forensics method. The proposed method comprises two main stages: robust watermarking embedding and detection. The specific procedures are as follows:

(1) In the robust watermarking embedding phase, several preprocessing steps are applied to the facial image intended for protection before it is uploaded to social networks.

Initially, the face region within the image is identified through segmentation. A visual hashing algorithm is then employed to extract visual features from this region, generating a hash sequence that serves as the watermarking. This sequence is embedded into the non-facial areas of the image, as these background regions typically remain unchanged during Deepfake operations. Embedding the hash sequence in these areas enhances the watermarking's robustness and provides a defense against deep learning-driven face replacement attacks. To ensure the watermarking's resilience against common signal processing challenges such as compression, noise injection, and geometric distortions, highly robust pseudo-Zernike moments are chosen as the carrier for embedding. Once the watermarking embedding is complete, the face region is restored to its original position within the image, resulting in an image that integrates the protective visual hash value.

(2) In the detection phase, the received image undergoes a systematic analysis to ascertain whether the face depicted is original and authentic or has been substituted with another. The process begins with segmenting the face region from the received image. Subsequently, a visual hash sequence is generated using the same visual hashing method employed during the embedding phase. Following this, the robust watermarking is extracted from the image's background regions. The final step involves calculating the Bit Error Rate (BER) between the generated visual hash sequence and the extracted robust watermarking. The BER that exceeds a predefined threshold suggests that the face in the image has experienced significant distortion, indicating a possible replacement. Conversely, if the BER remains below the threshold, it is concluded that the face in the image has not been tampered with.

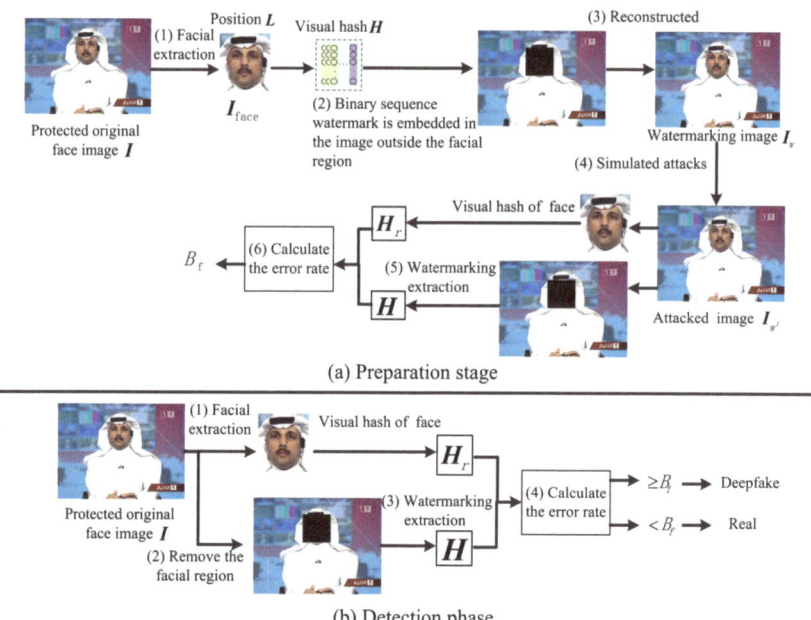

Figure 4. The framework of our method.

3.1. Robust Watermarking Embedding Phase

The robust watermarking embedding phase is comprised of three essential steps: determining the embedding region, generating the watermarking information, and embedding the robust watermarking. Each of these steps is crucial for the successful implementation of the watermarking process. Figure 5 provides a flowchart that visually represents this phase, offering a detailed depiction of each step involved. The flowchart begins with the initial input of the image, followed by the segmentation of the image into predefined regions. It then outlines the extraction of pseudo-Zernike moments for each region, the normalization process to ensure robustness against image manipulations, and the embedding of the watermark information using Quantization Index Modulation (QIM) technology. Subsequent steps include the inverse normalization and the reconstruction of the watermarked image, taking into account rounding errors and compensation techniques to maintain image integrity. The flowchart concludes with the final output, which is the robust watermarked image ready for distribution or further processing.

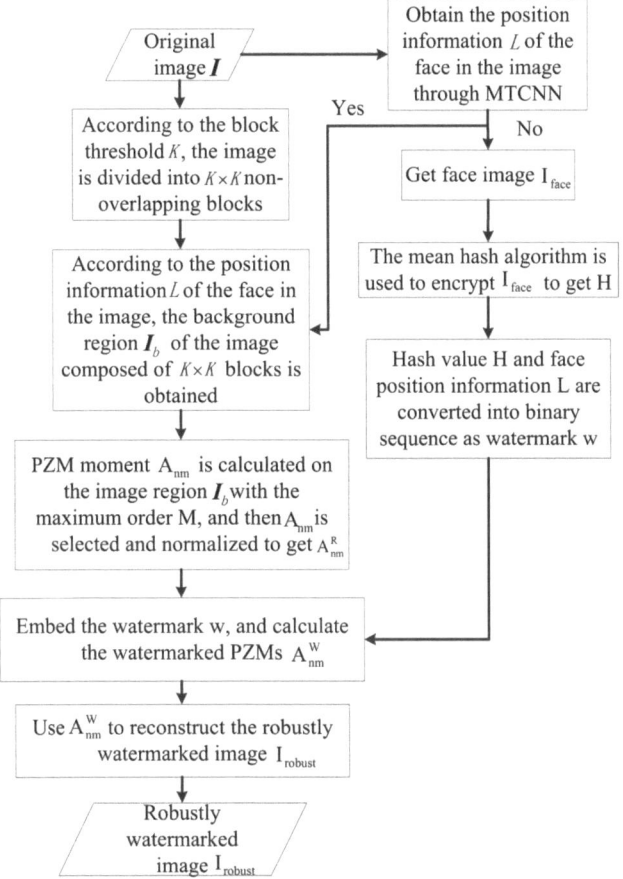

Figure 5. The process of generating robust watermarked images.

3.1.1. Determining the Embedding Region

Determining the location and region for watermarking embedding within facial images is a critical preliminary step. This is essential for accurately comparing the hash value of the facial area in the current image with the similarity of the extracted watermarking information during the detection phase. To avoid interference with the facial area by the watermarking information, this study chooses to embed the watermarking in non-facial regions. Predominantly, deep learning-based facial detection networks, known for their robust performance, are employed to identify facial regions. However, minor variations in the positions of the facial bounding boxes obtained from these networks can lead to inconsistencies between the positions during the watermarking embedding and facial replacement detection phases. This inconsistency poses a significant challenge in accurately pinpointing the embedded area for watermarking detection. To address this issue, this paper introduces a novel strategy named "Adaptive Block Selection Strategy (ABSS)" for selecting the watermark embedding region, thereby ensuring consistency between watermark embedding and detection. The ABSS strategy intelligently selects the most suitable areas for embedding watermark information by analyzing both facial and non-facial regions in the image. This method not only enhances the robustness of the watermark but also increases resistance to various signal processing attacks.

This research begins by employing facial detection technology to identify the coordinates of the facial bounding box within an image. As shown in Block a of Figure 6, the facial image is divided into non-overlapping blocks, each measuring $K \times K$ pixels. The alignment of each block with the facial region is assessed using the facial bounding box data. If a block aligns with the facial region, it is excluded from the watermarking embedding process; otherwise, it is considered a candidate for embedding. As shown in the right figure of Figure 6b locks that overlap with the facial region, as indicated by the black areas in the accompanying diagram, are not utilized for watermarking embedding, whereas non-overlapping blocks are deemed suitable. Notably, the method proposed in this study ensures that even minor displacements in the facial bounding box position do not significantly impact the accuracy of determining block overlap. Consequently, the methodology effectively addresses the challenge of accurately synchronizing the embedding area during both the watermarking embedding and detection processes.

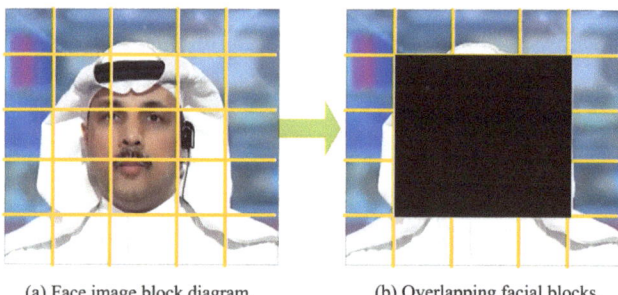

(a) Face image block diagram. (b) Overlapping facial blocks.

Figure 6. The determination of the watermark embedding region. (**a**) The facial region is divided into 5×5 non-overlapping blocks. (**b**) The black areas are not used for watermark embedding.

3.1.2. Generating the Watermarking Information

To verify whether a face in an image has been tampered with using a single image, our approach involves embedding the visual hash sequence of the detected face as a watermarking into a designated area. High-precision face detection is crucial to minimize interference with the visual hash value. Therefore, our method employs the highly accurate MTCNN [31] network to detect faces within an image and obtain the bounding box information of the face. Once the bounding box information is acquired, the face image is extracted, and the mean hash algorithm is applied to generate the hash sequence of the face. This hash sequence is then converted into a binary sequence, which functions as the watermarking information representing the face to be protected.

The inherent randomness of deep neural networks, such as the MTCNN, can result in inconsistent facial bounding box information when detecting faces in the same image multiple times. This inconsistency may lead to mismatches between the facial images cropped during the detection and embedding phases, thereby causing deviations in the facial hash sequences and increasing the risk of false positives. To address this issue, this paper proposes a facial repositioning strategy. The strategy involves embedding four integers, which represent the top-left coordinates, length, and width of the facial bounding box, as auxiliary information into the selected region of the image. This allows for accurate restoration of the facial detection box position during the detection phase. Given the minor fluctuations in facial bounding box positions, only the last five bits of the binary representation of these four integers are retained as auxiliary information to minimize the number of bits required. Upon receiving the facial box information, the recipient can use these 20 bits of auxiliary information to replace the last five bits of the four integers obtained during the detection phase, thereby accurately restoring the facial box information from the embedding phase. Experimental results demonstrate that the position fluctuations of facial boxes detected by MTCNN range from -16 to $+16$, confirming that these 20 bits of auxiliary information are sufficient for accurate restoration. Consequently, the watermarking information comprises three components: the hash sequence representing the face to be protected, 20 bits for restoring the facial box information, and 128 bits obtained by compressing the facial image using the mean hash algorithm, resulting in a total of 148 bits. Our experiments were conducted using the FaceForensics++ dataset, which includes 1000 real videos and 3000 Deepfake videos. From each video, we extracted 8 frames at equal intervals, totaling 32,000 frames for our tests. The dataset's diversity in terms of age, gender, ethnicity, and facial expressions allows for a thorough assessment of the proposed method's performance across various real-world scenarios. Through our experiments, we have determined that 20 bits of auxiliary information are sufficient to accurately restore the facial bounding box information. This quantization level ensures that even minor fluctuations in facial bounding box positions do not significantly impact the accuracy of determining block overlap, which is critical for the synchronization of the embedding area during both the watermarking embedding and detection processes.

3.1.3. Embedding the Robust Watermarking

This section outlines the process of embedding watermarking information into selected regions, as detailed in Section 3.1.1. The proposed Deepfake face detection framework employs the watermarking embedding and extraction scheme introduced by Tang [19]. This approach involves calculating pseudo-Zernike moments for each non-overlapping $K \times K$ block within the designated embedding region, followed by adaptive normalization of these moments. Subsequently, the watermarking information is embedded bit-by-bit into the corresponding moments using Quantization Index Modulation (QIM) technology. Figure 3 illustrates the watermarking embedding process, with further specifics provided below.

(1) Calculation of pseudo-Zernike moments. Consider an image block I of size $K \times K$. The pseudo-Zernike moment, denoted as Z_{nm}, is calculated for order n (where $0 \leq n \leq N$) and repetition m (where $0 \leq |m| \leq n$), with N representing the maximum order. The radial pseudo-Zernike polynomial R_{nm} within the inscribed circle of the image block I is computed as follows:

$$R_{nm}(r) = \sum_{k=0}^{n-|m|} (-1)^k \frac{(2n+1-k)! r^{n-k}}{k!(n+|m|+1-k)!(n-|m|-k)!} \quad (1)$$

Here, ! denotes factorial. Using R_{nm}, the pseudo-Zernike moment Z_{nm} is determined by the following:

$$Z_{nm} = \frac{n+1}{\pi} \sum_{s=0}^{N-1} \sum_{t=0}^{N-1} I(x_s, y_t) V_{nm}^*(x_s, y_t) \Delta x_s \Delta y_t \quad (2)$$

where $I(x_s, y_t)$ is the pixel value at position (x_s, y_t) in the image block, and $V_{nm}^*(x_s, y_t)$ is the conjugate of $V_{nm}(x_s, y_t)$. $V_{nm}(x_s, y_t)$ is determined by the following:

$$V_{nm}(x_s, y_t) = R_{nm}(r) e^{im\theta}, \quad (3)$$

(2) Selection and normalization of pseudo-Zernike moments. While Equation (2) facilitates the calculation of pseudo-Zernike moments for discrete digital images, there are computational challenges associated with the calculation of pseudo-Zernike moments, specifically when the repetition parameter $m = 4j$ (where $j \in \mathbb{Z}$). In these cases, the moments

deviate from orthogonality, which affects the accuracy of their calculation. Consequently, such moments are excluded from watermarking embedding. The selected pseudo-Zernike moments for embedding are as follows: $C = \{Z_{nm} \mid 0 < n \leq N, 0 < m \leq n, m \neq 4j\}$.

Assuming each pseudo-Zernike moment carries one watermarking bit, there are L watermarking bits w_i (where $w_i \in \{0,1\}, i = 1, 2, \ldots, L$) with $L < \text{length}(C)$. Using a key, L moments are randomly selected from set C to form the following: $Z = \{Z_{n1,m1}, Z_{n2,m2}, \ldots, Z_{nL,mL}\}$.

Normalization is employed to address the significant alterations in the magnitude of pseudo-Zernike moments due to scaling operations. The normalization formula is as follows:

$$Z^R_{ni,mi} = \frac{Z_{ni,mi}}{Z_{00}} \quad (4)$$

Normalization ensures scale invariance. Given that low-order pseudo-Zernike moments exhibit greater stability against common signal processing attacks than high-order moments, higher embedding strength is applied to high-order moments for enhanced robustness under the same embedding distortion. An adaptive normalization strategy is thus adopted:

$$Z^R_{ni,mi} = \frac{Z_{n,mi}}{Z_{00}} \times T_{ni} \quad (5)$$

where T_{ni} is an adaptive normalization weight greater than zero, varying according to the order of the pseudo-Zernike moment. Consequently, the range of $Z^R_{n,mi}$ is $[0, T_{ni}]$.

Given the challenge of theoretically deriving the optimal T_{ni}, a heuristic strategy is employed, setting it as follows:

$$T_{ni} = T_{\text{start}} - \gamma \times n_i \quad (6)$$

Here, T_{start} is the initial value of the adaptive normalization weight, and $\gamma (\gamma > 0)$ is a global parameter for adjusting watermarking embedding strength, with n_i denoting the order of the pseudo-Zernike moment into which the ith watermarking bit w_i is embedded. Parameters T_{start} and γ are determined through experimental simulations to adjust the invisibility of the watermarking information.

(3) Embedding of watermarking information. Normalized pseudo-Zernike moments $Z^R_{ni,mi}$ are invariant to scaling attacks. To achieve rotation invariance, the amplitude of rotation-invariant pseudo-Zernike moments $|Z^R_{ni,mi}|$ is used as the watermarking carrier. To balance robustness, invisibility, and embedding capacity, the QIM robust watermarking technique is employed:

$$|Z^{Rj}_{ni,mi}| = \left[\frac{|Z^R_{ni,mi}| - \beta_i(j)}{\Delta}\right] \times \Delta + \beta_i(j), \quad i = 1, 2, \ldots, L, \quad j \in \{0, 1\} \quad (7)$$

where $[\cdot]$ denotes the rounding function, Δ is the quantization step, and $\beta_i(j)$ is the dither value, constrained by $\beta_i(1) = \beta_i(0) + \Delta/2$.

After embedding the watermarking into the normalized pseudo-Zernike moments, inverse normalization is performed to obtain the watermarking-embedded pseudo-Zernike moments:

$$Z^W_{ni,mi} = \frac{|Z^{Rj}_{ni,mi}|}{|Z^R_{ni,mi}|} \times z^R_{ni,mi} \quad (8)$$

(4) Reconstruction of robust watermarked images. Once all watermarking information is embedded, the generated watermarking-embedded pseudo-Zernike moments $Z^W_{ni,mi}$ are used to reconstruct the robust watermarked image I_{intr}. To ensure the pixel values of the reconstructed image are real numbers, the conjugate moments $Z^{*R}_{n,mi}$ undergo the same embedding operation to obtain $Z^{**}_{ni,-mi}$. Since only part of the pseudo-Zernike moments carry

watermarking information, the reconstruction error caused by watermarking embedding is added to the original image to generate the robust watermarked image I_{inter}:

$$I_{\text{inter}} = I + \left[\sum_{i=1}^{L}\left((Z^W_{ni,mi} - Z_{ni,mi})V_{ni,mi} + (Z^W_{ni,-mi} - Z_{ni,-mi})V_{ni,-mi}\right)\right] \quad (9)$$

Since the pixel values of I_{inter} must be integers, rounding operations are necessary, leading to rounding errors. To mitigate these errors, a rounding error compensation technique is adopted. Specifically, the pseudo-Zernike moments $\check{Z}^W_{ni,mi}$ of I_{inter} are recalculated. Due to rounding, $\check{Z}^W_{ni,mi}$ does not match $Z^W_{ni,mi}$. The difference between them represents the rounding error, which can be used to reduce such errors. An error image I_{error} is reconstructed similarly to Equation (8):

$$I_{\text{error}} = \left[\sum_{i=1}^{L}\left((Z^W_{ni,mi} - \check{Z}_{ni,mi})V_{ni,mi} + (Z^W_{ni,-mi} - \check{Z}_{ni,-mi})V_{ni,-mi}\right)\right] \quad (10)$$

The error image I_{error} is superimposed onto I_{inter} to compensate for rounding errors, resulting in the final robust watermarked image I_w. This process is mathematically represented as follows:

$$I_w = I_{\text{inter}} + I_{\text{error}} \quad (11)$$

3.1.4. Watermarking Extraction

The watermarking extraction process, depicted in Figure 7, is essentially the reverse of the embedding process. Initially, the robust image is segmented into blocks based on a predetermined threshold K. The background area containing the embedded watermarking is identified using the face bounding box information. Subsequently, pseudo-Zernike moments are computed for the background image, and the selected moments are normalized to form the set $Z^{Rrw} = \{Z^{Rrw}_{n1,m1}, Z^{Rrw}_{n2,m2}, \ldots, Z^{Rrw}_{nL,mL}\}$. The watermarking information w is then extracted using the following formula:

$$|Z^{Rrj}_{ni,mi}| = \left[\frac{|Z^{Rrw}_{ni,mi}| - \beta_i(j)}{\Delta}\right] \times \Delta + \beta_i(j), \quad i = 1, 2, \ldots, L, \quad j \in \{0, 1\} \quad (12)$$

$$w'_i = \begin{cases} 0 & \text{, if } \left||Z^{Rrw}_{ni,mi}| - |Z^{Rr0}_{ni,mi}|\right| \leq \left||Z^{Rrw}_{ni,mi}| - |Z^{Rr1}_{ni,mi}|\right| \\ 1 & \text{, if } \left||Z^{Rrw}_{ni,mi}| - |Z^{Rr0}_{ni,mi}|\right| > \left||Z^{Rrw}_{ni,mi}| - |Z^{Rr1}_{ni,mi}|\right| \end{cases} \quad (13)$$

3.2. Robust Watermarking Detection Phase

To assess whether the face in the received image I_r has been altered, a detection process is conducted, as shown in Figure 8. This phase incorporates the watermarking extraction process outlined in Figure 7, with the following detailed steps:

(1) Face detection. The MTCNN network, previously utilized during the robust watermarking embedding phase, is employed to detect the face in I_r. This step yields the face bounding box information L_r, which includes the coordinates of the top-left corner and the dimensions of the bounding box.

(2) Watermarking region determination and extraction. The watermarking detection region is identified using the method described in Section 3.1.1. The watermarking extraction process, as illustrated in Figure 7, is executed to retrieve the embedded watermarking information from the designated region. Pseudo-Zernike moments are calculated for each block, and the moments are selected and normalized before applying Equations (11) and (12) to extract the watermarking. A total of 148 bits of information is extracted, comprising the watermarking information H and 20 auxiliary bits embedded during the robust watermarking embedding phase.

(3) Restoration of face bounding box information. Utilizing the auxiliary information, the last 5 bits of the four integers in the face bounding box information of the received image are replaced to accurately restore the face bounding box information from the embedding phase.
(4) Face localization and hash calculation. With the restored face bounding box information, the current face location is repositioned, and the face image I_f is extracted from I_r. The perceptual hash binary sequence H_r of the face to be detected is then generated using the mean hashing method.
(5) Error rate calculation. Calculate the bit error rate (BER) between H' and H_r. If I_r is not under attack, the BER will be 0. If I_r is subjected to typical signal processing attacks such as compression, noise addition, or geometric transformations, the BER will be below the predefined threshold B_f. However, if I_r undergoes face replacement operations, the BER will exceed the threshold B_f.

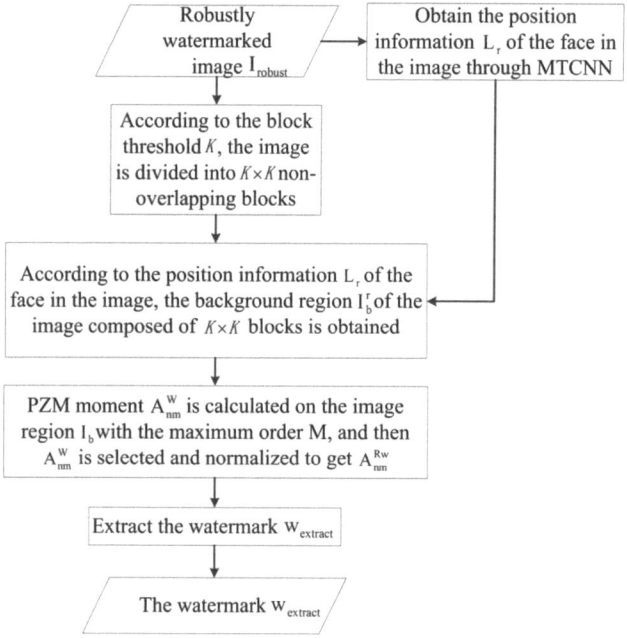

Figure 7. The process of generating robust watermarked images.

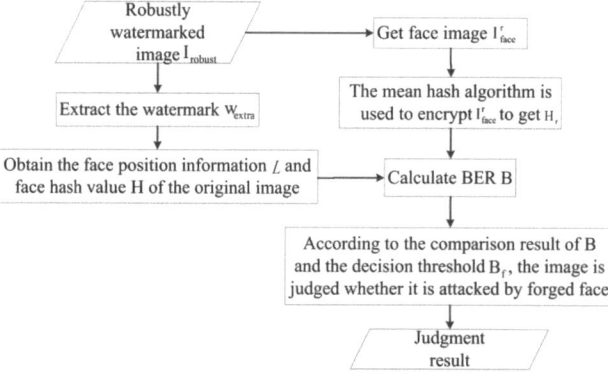

Figure 8. The process of detection for face swapping.

4. Experimental Results and Analysis

4.1. Experiment Setups

(1) Datasets. Following the mainstream methods in face swapping detection, this paper employed the public dataset FaceForensics++ [32] in the experimental simulation process. FaceForensics++ is widely used for Deepfake face detection and contains 1000 real videos downloaded from YouTube. All videos feature a traceable and mostly unobstructed frontal face with a resolution of at least 480p. Using Face2Face, FaceSwap, DeepFakes, and NeuralTextures, four automatic face-swap algorithms were applied to these 1000 real video sequences, resulting in 3000 Deepfake videos. Additionally, the videos were subjected to three different levels of compression: no compression (C0), compression rate 23 (C23), and compression rate 40 (C40), yielding videos with different compression rates, and totaling 3×1000 segments. In the experimental phase, 50 videos from the FaceForensics++ dataset were selected for testing. Given the large number of frames in each video and the high time and computational costs associated with embedding and extracting watermarks for every frame, this study extracted eight frames from each video at equal intervals, totaling 400 images for subsequent experimental simulation.

(2) Parameter settings. The overall scheme can be divided into three main algorithmic modules: a robust watermarking algorithm, an image compression hashing algorithm, and the image blocking algorithm proposed in this paper. This section will introduce the parameters involved in each algorithm, with specific parameter settings shown in Table 1. For the robust watermarking algorithm, this paper adopts Tang's [19] scheme, using pseudo-Zernike moments as the carrier for watermarking embedding and employing adaptive normalization to enhance the robustness of the watermarking while maintaining invisibility. This scheme only uses the robust watermarking embedding strategy from Tang's [19] scheme, omitting the integrity authentication and reversible watermarking parts, involving three main parameters: the watermarking embedding strength parameter Δ, the number of pseudo-Zernike moments n_{max}, and the normalization parameters T_{start} and γ. The parameter Δ controls the invisibility and robustness of the watermarking; n_{max} determines the highest order and number of calculated pseudo-Zernike moments, affecting the number of available carriers and computation time; parameters T_{start} and γ are used to control the invisibility of the watermarking image. For the image-blocking algorithm, the main consideration is the setting of the block size threshold K. Different values of K significantly affect the stability of the scheme's performance, so it needs to be determined through experiments. This paper sets $K = 90$, which was derived from extensive simulation experiments to ensure the maximum accurate extraction of watermarking information in noise-free conditions. These simulation experiments will be introduced in Section 4.2. Additionally, due to the large number of video frames, this experiment extracts eight frames from each video at equal intervals, totaling 400 frames for all subsequent experiments.

Table 1. Parameter Settings.

Module	Parameter Settings
Robust Watermarking Algorithm	$\Delta = 100, n_{max} = 18, T_{start} = 2000, \gamma = 10$
Image Blocking	$K = 90$

While our work involves a number of parameters and design choices, we aim to provide clarity and guidance for future researchers. Here are some practical guidelines for tuning the parameters based on different scenarios:

- Parameter Δ: This controls the robustness and imperceptibility of the watermark. For applications requiring higher security, consider increasing Δ. However, this may slightly reduce the image quality.

- Pseudo-Zernike Moments Order n_{max}: The order affects the number of carriers available for watermarking. Higher orders provide more robustness against attacks but increase computational complexity.
- Normalization Parameters T_{start} and γ: These parameters control the invisibility of the watermark. Adjusting them can help balance the visibility of the watermark against its robustness.
- Block Size K: The choice of block size significantly affects the stability of the scheme's performance. We recommend starting with K = 90 and adjusting based on the specific characteristics of the dataset.

(3) Comparisons. To assess the efficacy of the face replacement detection method based on the robust watermarking introduced in this study, we conducted an experimental simulation phase. During this phase, we selected two comparative methods: FakeTagger, developed by Wang [14], and the bidirectional facial data protection framework (BiFPro), proposed by Liu et al. [17]. FakeTagger represents the pioneering approach in utilizing robust watermarking for proactive forensics in Deepfake detection. It employs an encoder–decoder mechanism to embed watermarking information into the facial region of an image. This mechanism is trained using Deepfake tampering simulations, which enhances the watermarking's resilience against deep tampering and improves the accuracy of forgery detection. On the other hand, BiFPro focuses on ensuring the traceability of protected facial images by embedding robust watermarks. This capability allows for the tracking of fake faces even after facial swapping has occurred. By comparing these methods, we aim to verify the effectiveness of the proposed method in this paper.

(4) Evaluation metrics. To evaluate the visual quality, objective visual quality assessment metrics such as Peak Signal-to-Noise Ratio (PSNR) [33] and Structural Similarity Index (SSIM) [34] were used in the experimental simulation. In addition, to assess the robustness of the proposed method, the average bit error ratio (BER) was used as an evaluation metric; to evaluate the accuracy of face replacement detection, accuracy (ACC) was used as an evaluation metric. The specific definitions of each metric are as follows:

PSNR. This is an objective image quality assessment metric, and a higher value indicates higher image quality. Specifically, for an original image I and a noisy image K of size $m \times n$, the mean square error (MSE) is defined as follows:

$$\text{MSE} = \frac{1}{mn} \sum_{i=0}^{m-1} \sum_{j=0}^{n-1} [I(i,j) - K(i,j)]^2 \tag{14}$$

The calculation formula for PSNR is as follows:

$$\text{PSNR} = 10 \cdot \log_{10} \frac{(\text{MAX}_I)^2}{\text{MSE}} \tag{15}$$

where MAX_I represents the maximum pixel value in the original image I, for example, for a grayscale image $\text{MAX}_I = 255$.

SSIM. Based on the similarity of structural information in the image, this metric better reflects the human visual system's judgment of image similarity. SSIM comprehensively assesses from three aspects: brightness, contrast, and structure. For an original image I and a noisy image K of size $m \times n$, the SSIM is expressed as follows:

$$\text{SSIM} = \frac{(2\mu_I \mu_K + C_1)(2\sigma_I \sigma_K + C_2)}{(\mu_I^2 + \mu_K^2 + C_1)(\sigma_I^2 + \sigma_K^2 + C_2)} \tag{16}$$

where μ_I and μ_K are the average values of I and K, respectively, calculated as follows:

$$\mu_I = \frac{1}{mn} \sum_{i=1}^{m} \sum_{j=1}^{n} [I(i,j)] \tag{17}$$

and σ_I^2 and σ_K^2 are the variances of I and K, respectively, given by the following:

$$\sigma_I^2 = \frac{1}{mn-1} \sum_{i=1}^{m}\sum_{j=1}^{n}[I(i,j) - \mu_I]^2 \tag{18}$$

while σ_{IK} is the covariance of I and K:

$$\sigma_{IK} = \frac{1}{mn-1} \sum_{i=1}^{m}\sum_{j=1}^{n}[I(i,j) - \mu_I][K(i,j) - \mu_K] \tag{19}$$

Additionally, C_1 and C_2 are two stability coefficients, calculated as $C_1 = (D_1 L)^2$ and $C_2 = (D_2 L)^2$. Here, $D_1 = 0.001$, $D_2 = 0.003$, and L is related to the image type. For uint8 type images, $L = 255$.

BER. The average bit error ratio, which represents the percentage of bits that change during transmission due to noise, interference, etc., compared to the total number of bits. The extracted binary watermarking sequence from the robust watermarking image is compared with the binary hash sequence obtained from the encrypted face area, and the percentage of different bits is calculated. Suppose that the embedded watermark is $\omega \in \{0,1\}^{B \times L}$ and the extracted watermark is $\tilde{\omega} \in \{0,1\}^{B \times L}$. Then, BER is computed as

$$BER(\omega, \tilde{\omega}) = \frac{1}{R} \times \frac{1}{L} \times \sum_{i=1}^{B}\sum_{j=1}^{L}|\omega^{i \times j} - \tilde{\omega}^{i \times j}| \times 100\% \tag{20}$$

And the bitwise accuracy is defined as follows:

$$Bitwiseaccuray(\omega, \tilde{\omega}) = 1 - \frac{1}{B} \times \frac{1}{L} \times \sum_{i=1}^{B}\sum_{j=1}^{L}|\omega^{i \times j} - \tilde{\omega}^{i \times j}| \tag{21}$$

ACC. ACC is used to evaluate the accuracy of predictions, and represents the percentage of samples that are correctly predicted out of the total number of samples. The calculation method for accuracy is as follows:

$$ACC = \frac{TP}{TP + FP} \tag{22}$$

Here, TP (True Positives) refers to the number of samples that are correctly predicted as the positive class. FP (False Positives) refers to the number of samples that are incorrectly predicted as the positive class.

4.2. Impacts of the Threshold Parameter on Image Block Size K

To tackle the challenge of inconsistent face bounding box locations before and after watermarking embedding in facial recognition systems, this paper introduces an image tiling method. In real-world scenarios, if the face bounding box at the time of embedding is near the edge of a tile, the bounding box during the extraction phase might extend beyond the original tile's boundaries, causing errors in watermarking domain localization and resulting in the extraction of incorrect watermarking information. Thus, the selection of tile size is critical for the effectiveness of this approach. To identify the most suitable tile size, we conducted extensive simulations across 800 images, testing tile sizes ranging from 10 to 100 pixels, with a step increment of 10 pixels. The results, summarized in Table 2, indicate that a tile size of 90 × 90 pixels achieves the best performance, effectively minimizing the adverse effects of changes in face bounding box positions.

As shown in Table 2, when the tile size K is set to 90, setting the image tiling to 90 × 90 pixels can maximize the reduction in the impact caused by changes in face bounding box positions before and after embedding.

Table 2. Impact of different tiling sizes $K(K \in [10, 100])$ on performance.

K	10	20	30	40	50	60	70	80	90	100
Correct Extraction	530	582	587	611	623	614	628	633	647	643
Incorrect Extraction	270	218	213	189	177	186	172	167	153	157
Average BER	0.128	0.093	0.082	0.077	0.071	0.065	0.066	0.064	0.059	0.061

4.3. Comparison with Other Proactive Forensics Methods

4.3.1. Robustness Against Conventional Signal Processing Attacks and the Determination of Parameter Threshold B_f

The algorithm proposed in this paper aims to identify whether faces in images have been forged while ensuring that the scheme can resist common signal processing attacks. This section discusses the robustness of the watermarking information against various conventional signal attacks and determines the key parameter B_f for proactive forensics.

To verify the robustness of the digital watermarking technique proposed in this paper, we applied common signal attacks to video images with embedded watermarks. These attacks primarily include Gaussian low-pass filtering, JPEG compression, JPEG2000 compression, and video compression in MP4 format. We then evaluated the BER of the proposed watermarking without performing face replacement.

During the simulation, we conducted experiments on four videos, extracting a total of 32 face images. We tested these images with Gaussian low-pass filtering, JPEG compression, and JPEG2000 attacks. The parameters for Gaussian low-pass filtering were set to $[0.1, 1]$ with a step size of 0.1. The quality factors for JPEG compression and compression rates for JPEG2000 were both set to $[10, 100]$ with a step size of 10. We then calculated the average BER for the 32 images under different attack parameters. Tables 3–5 present the experimental results of the proposed method's robustness against common signal processing attacks.

As shown in Tables 3–5, under all attack parameters of Gaussian low-pass filtering, the average BER does not exceed 0.13. For JPEG attacks, the BER exceeds 0.16 only when the quality factor is less than 40; otherwise, it remains below 0.16. Similarly, for JPEG2000 attacks, the BER exceeds 0.15 only when the compression rate is higher than 80. Given that in real-world scenarios, normal video transmission (e.g., on social media) typically encounters attack parameters no stronger than those set in our experiments (e.g., JPEG compression quality factor does not exceed 80), we set the BER threshold for face forgery detection to 0.20. This threshold is sufficient to resist various common signal processing attacks encountered during normal transmission.

In other words, when a receiver receives a video, they authenticate the face information by extracting the watermarking and comparing it with the face information to calculate the BER. If the BER is below 0.20, we consider that the video has only experienced normal channel loss during transmission. If the BER exceeds 0.20, we conclude that the video has undergone more severe attacks, such as face forgery attacks. This method helps distinguish between normal channel loss and malicious face manipulation.

Table 3. Gaussian low-pass filtering attack.

K	0.1	0.2	0.3	0.4	0.5	0.6	0.7	0.8	0.9	1
Average BER	0.03945	0.03945	0.04025	0.07344	0.08840	0.10793	0.11426	0.11307	0.11542	0.10983

Table 4. JPEG attack.

Param	10	20	30	40	50	60	70	80	90	100
Average BER	0.31464	0.20938	0.17690	0.14938	0.15139	0.14111	0.13284	0.12179	0.10040	0.08755

Table 5. JPEG2000 attack.

Param	10	20	30	40	50	60	70	80	90	100
Average BER	0.08579	0.11451	0.11571	0.12911	0.13689	0.14055	0.14861	0.16913	0.17215	0.16909

4.3.2. Robustness Against Face Swapping

For malicious face replacement operations, we selected two representative methods: DeepFaceLab [35] and Deepfake [36]. Using BER as the evaluation metric, this paper performed face-swapping attacks on videos and ultimately assessed the BER of each tampered image using both DeepFaceLab and Deepfake. During the simulation, the face images were cropped to a size of 256 × 256 pixels. In Section 4.3.1, we determined the critical threshold B_{max} to be 0.2. This threshold is lower than the average BER values shown in Table 6 for both tampering methods. Therefore, when the sample size is large, the accuracy of face tampering detection, measured by the ACC metric, can achieve a good level. Table 7 presents the average BER performance under different face-swapping attacks on the FF++ dataset.

Table 6. Average BER under different face swapping attacks on the FF++ dataset.

Face Swapping Method	Deepfake	DeepFaceLab
Average BER (%)	0.267913	0.344242

Table 7 shows the performance of the proposed method compared to other schemes, specifically FakeTagger and BiFPro, in detecting face forgery on images of size 256 × 256 pixels under Deepfakes and DeepFaceLab tampering. It can be seen that the proposed method performs slightly worse than other schemes under Deepfakes tampering but outperforms them under DeepFaceLab tampering. By adjusting the threshold B_f, the detection accuracy can be effectively improved. For example, setting B_f to 0.18 increases the detection accuracy by more than 1 percentage point for DeepFaceLab and nearly 8 percentage points for Deepfakes, as shown in Table 8. However, adjusting B_f comes at a cost; while reducing the threshold significantly improves ACC, it also affects the robustness of the scheme against common signal attacks. This trade-off will be discussed in Section 4.3.3.

Table 7. Face forgery detection accuracy and AUC (%).

Detection Methods	Deepfake		DeepFaceLab	
	ACC	AUC	ACC	AUC
FaceTagger [14]	-	-	87.80	89.90
BiFPro [17]	92.18	93.56	93.75	94.18
Capsule [37]	70.25	73.85	73.75	78.62
SPSL [38]	81.57	82.82	83.84	86.53
LipForensics [39]	86.18	88.56	83.75	84.65
Proposed ($B_f = 0.2$)	72.40	75.68	94.27	96.22
Proposed ($B_f = 0.18$)	80.20	82.56	95.83	97.88

Table 8. Invisibility performance of image frames post-watermarking.

Metric	Watermarked Image	Tampered with DeepfakeLab
PSNR (dB)	40.088	30.773
SSIM	0.98228	0.96448

4.3.3. Robustness of the Methods Are Influenced by Different Threshold Settings

In Section 4.3.2, the impact of different decision thresholds on the accuracy of face forgery recognition is analyzed. This subsection examines how these thresholds influence the robustness of the proposed method. It is observed that as the decision threshold increases, the accuracy of identifying face forgery decreases, while the method's resistance to common signal attacks becomes more pronounced. For example, when the decision threshold is set extremely low, the accuracy of recognizing face forgery approaches 100%, but the method's ability to resist common signal attacks is severely compromised. Conversely, setting the threshold close to 1 renders the scheme nearly ineffective for proactive face forgery forensics. Therefore, the choice of decision threshold critically affects the overall performance of the solution.

The scheme's performance in detecting deep face forgery, with decision thresholds set to 0.18 and 0.2, is analyzed as depicted in Figure 3. The experiment introduces noise using Gaussian filtering, JPEG, and JPEG2000, with attack parameters and step sizes shown in Figure 9. A higher threshold setting significantly enhances the scheme's ability to differentiate between noisy images and face forgery, thereby improving its robustness.

The results in Table 7, which detail the performance of face forgery recognition under various thresholds, support the argument presented in this section. Higher decision thresholds lead to decreased accuracy in identifying face forgery but increased robustness against common noise attacks, and the opposite is also true.

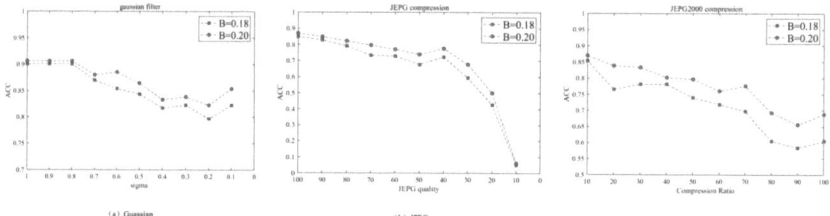

Figure 9. ACC of different thresholds under various types of conventional signal attacks.

4.4. Visual Quality

To effectively address the challenge of face replacement forgery detection through digital watermarking, it is essential to achieve high detection accuracy while maintaining the visual quality of the watermarked face images. This ensures that the embedded watermarking remains inconspicuous, thereby evading detection by adversaries and enhancing the security of digital watermarking-based face replacement detection schemes. A critical aspect of this approach is balancing robustness and imperceptibility, which can be managed by controlling the embedding strength parameter under a fixed capacity. In our experimental simulations, we employed a moderate embedding strength parameter of $\Delta = 100$ to embed a 128-bit watermarking into videos from the FF++ dataset. For each video, eight frames were selected to serve as carriers for the watermarking, and upon completion of the embedding process, the average PSNR value for these frames was calculated.

Figure 10 illustrates the effect of watermarking embedding, with the original image displayed on the left and the watermarked image in the center. Visually, it is challenging to discern any differences between the two images. The watermarked image achieves a PSNR of 38.76dB and an SSIM of 0.97, indicating excellent visual quality post-watermarking and underscoring the high level of concealment of the embedded watermarks. The image on the far right shows the result after tampering with the watermarked image using DeepfakeLab, which results in a PSNR of 33.46dB and an SSIM of 0.96. Despite the noticeable differences in image quality from the original, the tampered face in the watermarked image blends naturally with the background, making it difficult to detect facial tampering through visual inspection alone.

Table 8 presents the average image quality metrics after embedding watermarks in the FF++ dataset and following tampering with the DeepfakeLab technique. This table effectively demonstrates the impact of watermarking and subsequent tampering on the visual quality of images, as quantified by the PSNR and SSIM metrics. The significant differences in PSNR and SSIM values between the watermarked and tampered images highlight the robustness of the watermarking technique against tampering.

(a) Source image.   (b) Watermarking image.   (c) DeepFaceLab image.

Figure 10. The visual effects of watermarking image and Deepfake image. (**a**) Source image: PSNR = Inf, SSIM = 1.0; (**b**) Watermarking image: PSNR = 38.76, SSIM = 0.9710; (**c**) DeepFaceLab image: PSNR = 33.46, SSIM = 0.9680.

5. Discussion

Our findings indicate that the proposed method PZM-DD shows promise in enhancing the resilience of deep learning-based face replacement attacks against common signal processing attacks. The results suggest that our approach is effective in maintaining the integrity of watermarks under various conditions. Despite the positive outcomes, several open questions remain. For instance, the scalability of our method to real-time applications requires further investigation. Additionally, the impact of our method on the visual quality of high-resolution images is an area that merits more research.

This work is pioneering in integrating traditional robust watermarking for active forensic detection of face forgery, thereby introducing a new research direction and framework for Deepfake forensics. While most existing solutions that use digital watermarking for forensic purposes rely on deep watermarking, these approaches, despite enhancing the traceability of Deepfake content, face limitations in complex attack scenarios due to restricted training datasets, resulting in poor generalization. Traditional robust watermarking, with its fixed embedding and extraction parameters, offers superior generalization over deep watermarking. However, this framework, which employs traditional robust watermarking, experiences lower computational efficiency and slower image processing compared to deep watermarking. Future research should focus on optimizing the forensic algorithm's computational complexity to improve real-time performance.

6. Conclusions

This paper introduces a proactive forensic method, PZM-DD, for deep face swapping, employing robust watermarking based on pseudo-Zernike moments. Our method not only enhances detection accuracy but also preserves the integrity of the watermark when subjected to common signal processing attacks. Specifically, our experimental results demonstrate that the detection accuracy rate remains above 90% under standard signal processing operations, and its robustness against JPEG compression attacks has reached an industry-leading level. Despite these achievements, we acknowledge unresolved issues, such as the scalability of our method in real-time applications and its impact on high-resolution images, which necessitate further investigation. Additionally, our study highlights that certain groups, including public figures and politicians, are particularly vulnerable to the misuse of Deepfake technology. To mitigate these risks, we recommend that these individuals increase their awareness of Deepfake technology and promptly notify relevant legal authorities upon encountering suspicious content. Looking forward, we propose that future research should prioritize the following areas: first, the exploration of more efficient algorithms to enhance real-time performance; second, the examination of watermarking technology's effects on images of varying resolutions and finally, the strengthening of legal and ethical research on Deepfake misuse to develop more comprehensive protective measures.

While our study has demonstrated the effectiveness of the proposed method, there is scope for further enhancement. One promising direction is the exploration of dynamic thresholding to overcome the limitations of a fixed BER threshold. We propose future research into context-aware models, such as statistical analyses, machine learning classifiers, or deep learning approaches, that could adapt thresholds based on signal properties or attack scenarios. Additionally, we will employ more standardized benchmarks using curated datasets that reflect real-world complexities, including adversarial and multimodal content, to further validate the robustness and practical applicability of our proposed method.

Author Contributions: Data curation, Z.L. and Z.Y.; Formal analysis, Z.L. and G.L.; Investigation, Z.Y.; Methodology, Z.L. and Z.Y.; Supervision, Z.L. and R.F.; Visualization, Z.L. and C.W.; Writing—original draft, Z.L. and C.W.; Writing—review and editing, Z.Y. All authors have read and agreed to the published version of the manuscript.

Funding: This work is funded by Science Research Project of Hebei Education Department under Grants QN2025025.

Institutional Review Board Statement: Not applicable.

Informed Consent Statement: Not applicable.

Data Availability Statement: The FaceForensics++ dataset used in this work are available at https://github.com/ondyari/FaceForensics, accessed on 20 September 2024.

Conflicts of Interest: The authors declare no conflicts of interest.

Abbreviations

The following abbreviations are used in this manuscript:

AIGC	Artificial Intelligence Generated Content
AI	Artificial Intelligence
GANs	Generative Adversarial Networks
AFP	Artificial GAN Fingerprints
ZMs	Zernike Moments
PZMs	pseudo-Zernike Moments
PHTs	Polar Harmonic Transforms
2D DWT	Two-dimensional Discrete Wavelet Transform
COC	Color Opponent Coponents
QD	Quadtree Decomposition
SVD	Singular Value Decomposition
PCA	Principal Component Analysis
BER	Bit Error Rate
MTCNN	Multi-Task Cascaded Convolutional Networks
PIH	Perceptual Image Hashing
PSNR	Peak Signal-to-Noise Ratio
MSE	Mean Square Error
ACC	Accuracy
TP	True Positives
FP	False Positives
SSIM	Structural Similarity Index

References

1. Goodfellow, I.; Pouget-Abadie, J.; Mirza, M.; Xu, B.; Warde-Farley, D.; Ozair, S.; Courville, A.; Bengio, Y. Generative adversarial networks. *Commun. ACM* **2020**, *63*, 139–144. [CrossRef]
2. Rombach, R.; Blattmann, A.; Lorenz, D.; Esser, P.; Ommer, B. High-resolution image synthesis with latent diffusion models. In Proceedings of the IEEE/CVF Conference on Computer Vision and Pattern Recognition, New Orleans, LA, USA, 18–24 June 2022; pp. 10684–10695. [CrossRef]
3. Chen, R.; Chen, X.; Ni, B.; Chen, J.; Shen, X. SimSwap: An efficient framework for high fidelity face swapping. In Proceedings of the 28th ACM International Conference on Multimedia, Seattle, WA, USA, 12–16 October 2020; pp. 2003–2011. [CrossRef]
4. Zhao, W.; Rao, Y.; Shi, W.; Wang, J.; Wu, X. DiffSwap: High-fidelity and controllable face swapping via 3D-aware masked diffusion. In Proceedings of the IEEE/CVF Conference on Computer Vision and Pattern Recognition, Vancouver, BC, Canada, 17–24 June 2023; pp. 8568–8577. [CrossRef]
5. Miao, C.; Tan, Z.; Chu, Q.; Li, X.; Wu, F.; Wang, X. F2Trans: High-frequency fine-grained transformer for face forgery detection. *IEEE Trans. Inf. Forensics Secur.* **2023**, *18*, 1039–1051. [CrossRef]
6. Yu, Y.; Zhao, X.; Ni, R.; Li, X.; Wang, X. Augmented multi-scale spatiotemporal inconsistency magnifier for generalized DeepFake detection. *IEEE Trans. Multimed.* **2023**, *25*, 8487–8498. [CrossRef]
7. Zhang, D.; Chen, J.; Liao, X.; Li, X. Face Forgery Detection via Multi-Feature Fusion and Local Enhancement. *IEEE Trans. Circuits Syst. Video Technol.* **2024**, *34*, 8972–8977. [CrossRef]
8. Lin, C.Y.; Lee, J.C.; Wang, S.J.; Chiang, C.S.; Chou, C.L. Video Detection Method Based on Temporal and Spatial Foundations for Accurate Verification of Authenticity. *Electronics* **2024**, *13*, 2132. [CrossRef]
9. Alhaji, H.S.; Celik, Y.; Goel, S. An Approach to Deepfake Video Detection Based on ACO-PSO Features and Deep Learning. *Electronics* **2024**, *13*, 2398. [CrossRef]
10. Gong, L.Y.; Li, X.J.; Chong, P.H.J. Swin-Fake: A Consistency Learning Transformer-Based Deepfake Video Detector. *Electronics* **2024**, *13*, 3045. [CrossRef]
11. Gao, Y.; Wang, X.; Zhang, Y.; Zeng, P.; Ma, Y. Temporal Feature Prediction in Audio–Visual Deepfake Detection. *Electronics* **2024**, *13*, 3433. [CrossRef]
12. Lai, G.; Li, L.; Wang, Y.; Xiao, H.; Chen, C.L.P. Fixed-Time Adaptive Control With Predefined Tracking Accuracy for Piezoactuators Subject to Stochastic Disturbances. *IEEE Trans. Circuits Syst. I Regul. Pap.* **2024**, *Early Access*. [CrossRef]
13. Yu, N.; Skripniuk, V.; Abdelnabi, S.; Zhang, X.; Liu, Y. Artificial fingerprinting for generative models: Rooting deepfake attribution in training data. In Proceedings of the IEEE/CVF International Conference on Computer Vision, Montreal, BC, Canada, 11–17 October 2021; pp. 14448–14457. [CrossRef]
14. Wang, R.; Juefei-Xu, F.; Luo, M.; Zhang, X.; Liu, Y.; Li, X. Faketagger: Robust safeguards against deepfake dissemination via provenance tracking. In Proceedings of the 29th ACM International Conference on Multimedia, Virtual Event, 20–24 October 2021; pp. 3546–3555. [CrossRef]
15. Zhao, Y.; Liu, B.; Ding, M.; Wu, X.; Li, X. Proactive deepfake defence via identity watermarking. In Proceedings of the IEEE/CVF Winter Conference on Applications of Computer Vision, Waikoloa, HI, USA, 2–7 January 2023; pp. 4602–4611. [CrossRef]
16. Wu, X.; Liao, X.; Ou, B.; Li, X. SepMark: Deep separable watermarking for unified source tracing and deepfake detection. In Proceedings of the 31st ACM International Conference on Multimedia, Ottawa, ON, Canada, 29 October–3 November 2023; pp. 1190–1201. [CrossRef]
17. Liu, H.; Li, X.; Zhou, W.; Wang, X.; Li, X. BiFPro: A Bidirectional Facial-data Protection Framework against DeepFake. In Proceedings of the 31st ACM International Conference on Multimedia, Ottawa, ON, Canada, 29 October–3 November 2023; pp. 7075–7084. [CrossRef]
18. Neekhara, P.; Hussain, S.; Zhang, X.; Liu, Y. FaceSigns: Semi-Fragile Watermarks for Media Authentication. *Acm Trans. Multimed. Comput. Commun. Appl.* **2024**, *20*, 1–21. [CrossRef]
19. Tang, Y.; Wang, S.; Wang, C.; Xiang, S. A highly robust reversible watermarking scheme using embedding optimization and rounded error compensation. *IEEE Trans. Circuits Syst. Video Technol.* **2022**, *33*, 1593–1609. [CrossRef]
20. Liao, C.Y.; Huang, C.H.; Chen, J.C.; Liu, Y. Enhancing the Robustness of Deep Learning Based Fingerprinting to Improve Deepfake Attribution. In Proceedings of the 4th ACM International Conference on Multimedia in Asia, Tokyo, Japan, 13–16 December 2022; pp. 1–7. [CrossRef]
21. Qi, S.; Zhang, Y.; Wang, C.; Li, X. A survey of orthogonal moments for image representation: Theory, implementation, and evaluation. *Acm Comput. Surv. (CSUR)* **2021**, *55*, 1–35. [CrossRef]
22. Hu, R.; Xiang, S. Cover-lossless robust image watermarking against geometric deformations. *IEEE Trans. Image Process.* **2020**, *30*, 318–331. [CrossRef] [PubMed]
23. Teh, C.H.; Chin, R.T. On image analysis by the methods of moments. *IEEE Trans. Pattern Anal. Mach. Intell.* **1988**, *10*, 496–513. [CrossRef]
24. Fu, D.; Zhou, X.; Xu, L.; Li, X. Robust Reversible Watermarking by Fractional Order Zernike Moments and Pseudo-Zernike Moments. *IEEE Trans. Circuits Syst. Video Technol.* **2023**, *33*, 7310–7326. [CrossRef]
25. Hu, R.; Xiang, S. Lossless robust image watermarking by using polar harmonic transform. *Signal Process.* **2021**, *179*, 107833. [CrossRef]

26. Shen, Q.; Zhao, Y. Perceptual hashing for color image based on color opponent component and quadtree structure. *Signal Process.* **2020**, *166*, 107244. [CrossRef]
27. Tang, Z.J.; Zhang, X.Q.; Dai, Y.M.; Wang, S.; Li, H. Perceptual image hashing using local entropies and DWT. *Imaging Sci. J.* **2013**, *61*, 241–251. [CrossRef]
28. Qin, C.; Chen, X.; Ye, D.; Li, X. A novel image hashing scheme with perceptual robustness using block truncation coding. *Inf. Sci.* **2016**, *361*, 84–99. [CrossRef]
29. Tang, Y.; Li, K.; Wang, C.; Xiang, S. A two-stage robust reversible watermarking using polar harmonic transform for high robustness and capacity. *Inf. Sci.* **2024**, *654*, 119786. [CrossRef]
30. Qin, C.; Liu, E.; Feng, G.; Wang, X. Perceptual image hashing for content authentication based on convolutional neural network with multiple constraints. *IEEE Trans. Circuits Syst. Video Technol.* **2020**, *31*, 4523–4537. [CrossRef]
31. Zhang, K.; Zhang, Z.; Li, Z.; Qiao, Y. Joint face detection and alignment using multitask cascaded convolutional networks. *IEEE Signal Process. Lett.* **2016**, *23*, 1499–1503. [CrossRef]
32. Rössler, A.; Cozzolino, D.; Verdoliva, L.; Riess, C.; Thies, J.; Nießner, M. Faceforensics++: Learning to detect manipulated facial images. In Proceedings of the IEEE/CVF International Conference on Computer Vision, Seoul, Republic of Korea, 27–28 October 2019; pp. 1–11. [CrossRef]
33. Baluja, S. Hiding Images within Images. *IEEE Trans. Pattern Anal. Mach. Intell.* **2020**, *42*, 1685–1697. [CrossRef] [PubMed]
34. Wang, Z.; Bovik, A.C.; Sheikh, H.R.; Simoncelli, E.P. Image quality assessment: From error visibility to structural similarity. *IEEE Trans. Image Process.* **2004**, *13*, 600–612. [CrossRef]
35. DeepFaceLab. Available online: https://github.com/iperov/DeepFaceLab (accessed on 7 October 2024).
36. DeepFake. Available online: https://github.com/deepfakes/faceswap (accessed on 7 October 2024).
37. Nguyen, H.H.; Yamagishi, J.; Echizen, I. Capsule-forensics: Using capsule networks to detect forged images and videos. In Proceedings of the ICASSP 2019-2019 IEEE International Conference on Acoustics, Speech and Signal Processing (ICASSP), Brighton, UK, 12–17 May 2019; IEEE: Piscataway, NJ, USA, 2019; pp. 2307–2311. [CrossRef]
38. Liu, H.; Li, X.; Zhou, W.; Chen, Y.; He, Y.; Xue, H.; Zhang, W.; Yu, N. Spatial-phase shallow learning: Rethinking face forgery detection in frequency domain. In Proceedings of the IEEE/CVF Conference on Computer Vision and Pattern Recognition, Nashville, TN, USA, 20–25 June 2021; pp. 772–781.
39. Haliassos, A.; Vougioukas, K.; Petridis, S.; Pantic, M. Lips don't lie: A generalisable and robust approach to face forgery detection. In Proceedings of the IEEE/CVF Conference on Computer Vision and Pattern Recognition, Nashville, TN, USA, 20–25 June 2021; pp. 5039–5049. [CrossRef]

Disclaimer/Publisher's Note: The statements, opinions and data contained in all publications are solely those of the individual author(s) and contributor(s) and not of MDPI and/or the editor(s). MDPI and/or the editor(s) disclaim responsibility for any injury to people or property resulting from any ideas, methods, instructions or products referred to in the content.

Article

An Improved Retinex-Based Approach Based on Attention Mechanisms for Low-Light Image Enhancement

Shan Jiang [1,2], Yingshan Shi [1,2], Yingchun Zhang [1,2] and Yulin Zhang [1,2,*]

1. Key Laboratory of Ethnic Language Intelligent Analysis and Security Governance of MOE, Minzu University of China, Beijing 100081, China; jshan@muc.edu.cn (S.J.); ysshi@muc.edu.cn (Y.S.); 21302036@muc.edu.cn (Y.Z.)
2. School of Information Engineering, Minzu University of China, Beijing 100081, China
* Correspondence: yzhang@muc.edu.cn

Abstract: Captured images often suffer from issues like color distortion, detail loss, and significant noise. Therefore, it is necessary to improve image quality for reliable threat detection. Balancing brightness enhancement with the preservation of natural colors and details is particularly challenging in low-light image enhancement. To address these issues, this paper proposes an unsupervised low-light image enhancement approach using a U-net neural network with Retinex theory and a Convolutional Block Attention Module (CBAM). This method leverages Retinex-based decomposition to separate and enhance the reflectance map, ensuring visibility and contrast without introducing artifacts. A local adaptive enhancement function improves the brightness of the reflection map, while the designed loss function addresses illumination smoothness, brightness enhancement, color restoration, and denoising. Experiments validate the effectiveness of our method, revealing improved image brightness, reduced color deviation, and superior color restoration compared to leading approaches.

Keywords: low-light image enhancement; Retinex theory; attention mechanism; unsupervised learning

Citation: Jiang, S.; Shi, Y.; Zhang, Y.; Zhang, Y. An Improved Retinex-Based Approach Based on Attention Mechanisms for Low-Light Image Enhancement. *Electronics* **2024**, *13*, 3645. https://doi.org/10.3390/electronics13183645

Academic Editor: Stefano Scanzio

Received: 31 July 2024
Revised: 8 September 2024
Accepted: 10 September 2024
Published: 13 September 2024

Copyright: © 2024 by the authors. Licensee MDPI, Basel, Switzerland. This article is an open access article distributed under the terms and conditions of the Creative Commons Attribution (CC BY) license (https://creativecommons.org/licenses/by/4.0/).

1. Introduction

Low-light conditions often result in poor image quality, hindering accurate threat detection and compromising security measures. Traditional supervised methods require extensive labeled datasets, which are impractical to obtain in diverse and dynamic environments. Unsupervised learning approaches, on the other hand, can leverage abundant low-light images without the need for labeled counterparts, enabling the development of robust enhancement algorithms. These algorithms improve the visibility and detail of images captured under challenging lighting conditions, thus enhancing the reliability and effectiveness of security systems across heterogeneous networks. By ensuring better image quality, unsupervised low-light image enhancement contributes to more accurate monitoring and analysis, ultimately strengthening overall network security. Therefore, improving low-light images is essential for security and surveillance.

Algorithms for enhancing low-light images can be broadly divided into two categories: conventional techniques and deep learning-based methods. Among conventional techniques, histogram equalization and its related methods [1] are the most commonly used. These methods enhance image brightness by calculating the gray levels of the picture and redistributing them evenly across the full range of gray levels. The main advantage of this method is its fast computation speed, which effectively enhances the brightness of general grayscale images. However, it is less effective for RGB image enhancement, often resulting in significant noise, color deviation, and over-enhancement issues.

Researchers have developed various low-light image enhancement techniques [2,3] rooted in Retinex theory [4]. With the success of deep learning in image reconstruction and restoration, neural network-based algorithms like CNN [5] have gained considerable attention. Among them, supervised learning methods rely on large datasets of paired low-light and well-lit images for training. These methods can achieve impressive results but are limited by the availability of high-quality paired datasets. In contrast, unsupervised learning methods do not require paired datasets. Instead, they use loss functions that incorporate illumination smoothness, brightness consistency, and color restoration to guide the network. The unsupervised approaches are more flexible and practical in scenarios where paired datasets are scarce, enabling effective enhancement by training solely on low-light images. However, unsupervised learning-based algorithms still encounter challenges, including significant color distortion and the blurring of details.

Significant progress has been made in low-light image enhancement in recent years. However, in complex low-light scenarios, image enhancement methods still struggle with preserving natural colors and details while dealing with significant noise. To address these issues, this paper constructs a U-net network based on the Convolutional Block Attention Module (CBAM) to decompose images and enhance the brightness of the reflectance map. The attention mechanism allows the network to concentrate on key features and regions in the image. Retinex theory explains that image brightness is determined by both illumination and object reflection. By separating these components, we can effectively enhance image details. In our approach, we divide the initial image into a low-light RGB image and its corresponding brightness values. Since the illumination conditions in different regions of the image may be different, in order to avoid a one-size-fits-all processing method and enhance local details more finely, we propose a local adaptive enhancement function when enhancing the low-light image. Meanwhile, an unsupervised learning loss function is designed for illumination smoothness, brightness consistency, and color restoration, guiding the network to effectively enhance low-light images. The main contributions of this paper are as follows:

(1) Combining the U-net network with the CBAM grounded in Retinex theory to achieve the decomposition of the images.
(2) Establishing a local adaptive enhancement function that calculates the local gray mean of the image through a block operation and adjusts the enhancement effect according to the specific values of each gray block. The parameters within the function allow for the flexible adjustment of the enhancement degree, avoiding over-enhancement.
(3) Designing an unsupervised learning loss function that introduces a color restoration loss term, further optimizing color restoration, effectively improving image brightness and preserving image details.

The structure of this paper is as follows: Section 2 reviews related research. Section 3 introduces the unsupervised low-light enhancement algorithm developed in this study, detailing the design of the local adaptive function and the loss function. The experimental results are presented in Section 4, and Section 5 offers several conclusions.

2. Related Works

2.1. Unsupervised Low-Light Image Enhancement Algorithms

Many researchers have proposed unsupervised learning-based algorithms to enhance the generalization and robustness of image enhancement models. Jiang et al. [6] proposed an unsupervised decomposition and correction network inspired by the Retinex model. Hu et al. [7] introduced a method that first used the traditional retinol-based method to pre-enhance images, and then used the thinning network for additional quality improvement. Shi et al. [8] proposed a structure-aware unsupervised network comprising four modules. Ma et al. [9] proposed a region-based, unsupervised, low-light image enhancement algorithm that utilizes explicit domain supervision to convert unsupervised segmentation into a supervised process, developing several region-based loss functions to establish semantic consistency between regions and daytime. Guo et al. [10] introduced a new hybrid loss function that combines quality, task, and perception to tackle problems such as blurring and unnatural colors. Wang et al. [11] presented a mixed-attention-guided Generative Adversarial Network (GAN) in a fully unsupervised fashion. Fu et al. [12] introduced an unsupervised learning network featuring an illumination-aware attention module and a novel identity-invariant loss.

Unsupervised learning methods leverage loss functions to guide the network without the need for paired examples. By focusing on intrinsic properties such as illumination smoothness, brightness consistency, and color restoration, unsupervised approaches offer greater flexibility and robustness.

2.2. Retinex Theory

An image is decomposed into a reflectance component that represents the inherent color of objects and an illumination component representing the varying light conditions. This decomposition allows for the enhancement of images by adjusting the illumination component without destroying the natural colors and details. Assuming the input image is $S(x,y)$, it can be expressed as follows:

$$S(x,y) = I(x,y) \odot R(x,y) \qquad (1)$$

where $I(x,y)$ represents the image illumination component, $R(x,y)$ represents the reflectance component of the image, and $\odot$ denotes pixel-wise multiplication.

Retinex theory is commonly applied to enhance visibility and contrast without introducing significant artifacts. Wu et al. [2] proposed a Retinex-based deep unfolding network to obtain noise suppression and detail preservation. Zhao et al. [13] presented a generative strategy for Retinex decomposition, casting the decomposition as a generative problem. Jiang et al. [14] proposed a self-regularized method that preserves all colors while integrating Retinex theory solely for brightness adjustments. Liu et al. [15] constructed a deep learning framework, comprising a decomposition network and adjustment networks that address both global and local brightness. Ma et al. [16] introduced a Retinex-based variational model that effectively produces noise-free images and shows generalizability across various lighting conditions. Yang et al. [17] proposed an image enhancement algorithm that integrates a fast and robust fuzzy C-means clustering technique with Retinex theory, producing enhanced images characterized by their rich detail and texture.

Numerous studies have demonstrated the effectiveness of Retinex in this field. Retinex-based methods can effectively improve visibility and contrast in low-light conditions by accurately decomposing an image into its illumination and reflectance components.

2.3. Attention Mechanisms

To further enhance the feature-learning capability of networks and improve image enhancement results, many scholars have introduced attention mechanisms to boost performance. Chen et al. [18] proposed an attention-based network that incorporates Retinex theory, featuring an attention mechanism module integrated into the convolutional layer. Ai and Kwon [19] developed a convolutional network that integrates an attention gate with a U-net network. Lv et al. [20] separated the tasks of brightness enhancement and noise reduction and completed them separately with two attention maps. Atoum et al. [21] introduced a color-wise attention network that identifies useful color cues to assist with color enhancement. Zhang and Wang [22] proposed an illumination attention map to identify areas of different illumination levels, and a multi-scale attention Retinex network. Zhang et al. [23] developed a neural network that incorporates channel attention and spatial attention modules and achieved a positive effect.

3. Methodology

3.1. Neural Network Structure

This paper constructs a U-net architecture in which the CBAM is introduced [24]. The U-net decomposes low-light images and regards the reflectance map as the enhanced image. In Figure 1, the network receives low-light RGB images and the corresponding brightness values, while the output of the network includes the decomposed reflectance and illumination maps. The encoder of the network gradually reduces the size of the input tensor and increases the number of layers through convolution and max pooling. The decoder consists of upsampling and convolution layers, which restore the tensor size through convolution and upsampling. During the upsampling process, the CBAM is employed to assign weights to the extracted feature maps to enhance feature refinement and focus during the reconstruction phase, optimizing the network performance. By applying channel attention mechanisms during decoding, we can selectively enhance important features that are identified during encoding, improving detail restoration. Spatial attention enables focus on relevant areas of the image, which is crucial for accurately reconstructing details under low-light conditions. Meanwhile, placing these mechanisms in the decoder reduces the computational load during encoding, allowing for efficient feature extraction.

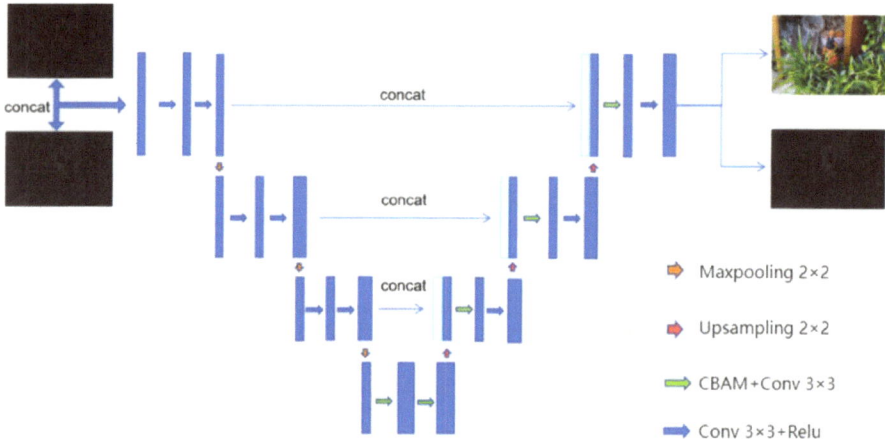

Figure 1. U-net network with attention mechanisms.

The CBAM is a type of Channel and Spatial Mixed Attention (CSMA) mechanism, as shown in Figure 2. The network initially utilizes channel attention, which emphasizes the relationships and dependencies among various feature channels, enabling the network to weigh the importance of each channel differently. The channel attention mechanism can be expressed as follows:

$$M_c(F) = \sigma(MLP(AvgPool(F)) + MLP(MaxPool(F))) \qquad (2)$$

where $\sigma(\cdot)$ is the S-shaped function, $MLP(\cdot)$ denotes the multilayer perceptron, $AvgPool(\cdot)$ represents the average pooling, and $MaxPool(\cdot)$ is the maximum pooling. It then applies spatial attention to emphasize the significance of various spatial locations, allowing the network to focus on the relevant regions of the image. The attention module can be written as follows:

$$M_s(F) = \delta\left(Conv^{7\times 7}([AvgPool(F); MaxPool(F)])\right) \qquad (3)$$

where $\delta(\cdot)$ denotes the sigmoid function and $Conv^{7\times 7}(\cdot)$ refers to the convolution operation through a convolution kernel, sized 7×7. By combining these two types of attention, the network can capture complex patterns and dependencies in the data, leading to improved performance in image enhancement where both channel and spatial information are crucial for achieving high-quality results.

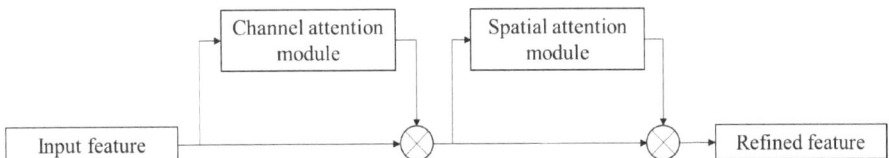

Figure 2. CBAM module.

3.2. Adaptive Enhancement Function

This paper proposes a local adaptive enhancement function that divides a low-light image into multiple blocks and enhances them separately. The mathematical expression is as follows:

$$L_g(x,y) = \min\left(\frac{\alpha + L_{w,max}}{\alpha + \overline{L_w}}, \frac{L_w(x,y)}{L_{w,max}} + \frac{L_w(x,y)}{\overline{L_w}}\right) * \frac{\log(L_w(x,y)/\overline{L_w} + 1)}{\log(L_{w,max}/\overline{L_w} + 1)} \quad (4)$$

where $L_g(x,y)$ represents the corresponding pixel value of the globally adaptive output, $L_w(x,y)$ represents the corresponding input pixel value, $L_{w,max}$ represents the highest brightness value of the input image, α is a constant parameter that regulates the overall enhancement level, and $\overline{L_w}$ represents the logarithmic mean brightness, which can be written as:

$$\overline{L_w} = \exp\left\{\frac{1}{N}\sum \log[\delta + L_w(x,y)]\right\} \quad (5)$$

Equation (4) uses the minimum function to flexibly adjust the enhancement level based on the grayscale values of each block, preventing the excessive enhancement of brightness values.

3.3. Loss Function

By applying the ternary Bayesian theorem, the illumination and reflectance components can be derived from Equation (1):

$$P(R,I|S) \propto P(S|R,I)P(R)P(I) \quad (6)$$

The designed loss function includes an illumination smoothness term, a brightness enhancement term, a color restoration term, and a smoothness term. The reconstruction loss recon can be written as follows:

$$L_{rc} = \left\|S - R \odot I\right\|_1 \quad (7)$$

where S denotes the low-light picture, R represents the reflectance component, I represents the illumination component, and $\odot$ denotes pixel-wise multiplication. The reconstruction loss primarily constrains the decomposition effect of the network, making the decomposed image closer to the real image. The RGB image is transformed into an HSV image and the brightness value V channel can be calculated. And then, the unsupervised learning reflectance loss L_R can be obtained as follows:

$$L_R = \left\|\max_{C \in R,G,B} R_C - F\left(\max_{C \in R,G,B} S_C\right)\right\|_1 \quad (8)$$

where $\max_{C \in R,G,B} R_C$ refers to the maximum value channel of the reflectance component, and $F(\cdot)$ represents the local adaptive enhancement function which can be obtained by Equation (4). The illumination loss L_I is calculated as follows:

$$L_I = \left\|\nabla I \odot \exp(-\lambda \nabla R)\right\|_1 \quad (9)$$

where ∇I represents the gradient variation of the illumination component, controlled by the gradient change of the reflectance, and λ is a constant parameter. The color restoration loss L_C is established as follows:

$$L_C = \sum_{i,j \in (R,G,B)} |R_I - R_J|^2 \qquad (10)$$

Equation (10) expresses a relationship between the RGB channels of the reflectance map, further enhancing the color restoration effect. In addition, the noise issue after enhancement is also considered. Thus, the loss function includes the reconstruction loss L_{rc}, the reflectance loss L_R, the color restoration loss L_C, and the denoising loss, expressed as follows:

$$\begin{aligned} L = &\lambda_1 \|S - R \odot I\|_1 + \lambda_2 \left\| \max_{C \in R,G,B} R_C - F\left(\max_{C \in R,G,B} s_C\right) \right\|_1 \\ &+ \lambda_3 \sum_{i,j \in (R,G,B)} |R_I - R_J|^2 + \lambda_4 \|\nabla I \odot exp(-\lambda_5 \nabla R)\|_1 \\ &+ \lambda_6 \|\nabla R\|_1 \end{aligned} \qquad (11)$$

where ∇R represents the gradient of the reflectance component, mainly used for image denoising. Through the illumination enhancement function, the brightness value of the reflectance map is increased, ultimately achieving low-light image enhancement.

4. Experimental Results and Analysis

4.1. Experimental Setup

The experiments are implemented with an AMD 7945HX processor (Advanced Micro Devices, Santa Clara, CA, USA), an NVIDIA GTX 4060 GPU (Colorful, Shenzhen, China), and 32 GB of memory (Crucial, Meridian, MS, USA). The experimental environment includes Python version 3.9 and TensorFlow version 2.10.0. The training dataset used is LOL, consisting of 500 pairs of low-light and normal-light images captured under various illumination conditions and scenes. In this experiment, LOL contains 485 low/normal-light image pairs for training and 15 pairs for testing. This dataset comprises images from both indoor and outdoor scenes, each with a resolution of 600 × 400. We meticulously examine various hyperparameters, including batch size, learning rate, the number of epochs, and weight decay. The search range for each hyperparameter is specified, emphasizing the optimal configuration that yields the best performance. Ultimately, we find that setting the batch size to 8, learning rate to 0.001, number of epochs to 160, and weight decay to 0.0005 result in the best performance of our model on the LOL dataset. The selection of this optimal configuration undergoes thorough experimental validation, ensuring the robustness and effectiveness of our proposed low-light image enhancement method in various aspects.

The average training duration is approximately 60 min, while the processing time for each image in the test set is 0.465 s. Through many experiments, the values of the six parameters $\lambda_1, \lambda_2, \lambda_3, \lambda_4, \lambda_5, \lambda_6$ in Equation (11) are set to 20, 1, 5, 0.1, 10, and 0.01, respectively. This parameter combination has been validated to achieve the best results on the test set. In this combination, $\lambda_1, \lambda_2, \lambda_3, \lambda_4, \lambda_5, \lambda_6$ control the weights of reconstruction loss, reflection loss, color recovery loss, illumination loss, local reflection component gradient, and global reflection component gradient, respectively. Fine-tuning in different datasets and application scenarios according to actual needs is recommended.

4.2. Experimental Results

To assess the effectiveness of the proposed algorithm, several comparative experiments are carried out with methods like Retines [25], LIME [26], SCI [27], Zero-DCE [28], EnlightenGAN [29], and GLADNet [30]. We also choose the methods of class unsupervised learning, based on deep learning techniques such as RUAS [31] and SSIE [32].

4.2.1. Subjective Evaluation Results

The enhanced results are shown in Figure 3. The SCI algorithm results in less noise and better color restoration, but its brightness enhancement is still somewhat lacking compared to normal light images. Compared to the enhancement results of the presented algorithm, the brightness of the SCI method is relatively dim. The Zero-DCE and LIME algorithms exhibit less color distortion, but their brightness enhancement is inadequate, leaving the dark areas of the image insufficiently illuminated. The Retinex-Net algorithm achieves positive brightness enhancement, but it suffers from a loss of image detail and texture, and the variation in brightness across different areas is not natural enough. The EnlightenGAN algorithm provides positive brightness enhancement, but the dark areas of the image show noticeable noise, and there is some color distortion present. The RUAS algorithm provides limited enhancement in extremely dark regions, while the brighter local areas are excessively enhanced, leading to overexposure. The SSIE algorithm clearly improves brightness, but the background color of the enhanced image shows a significant deviation.

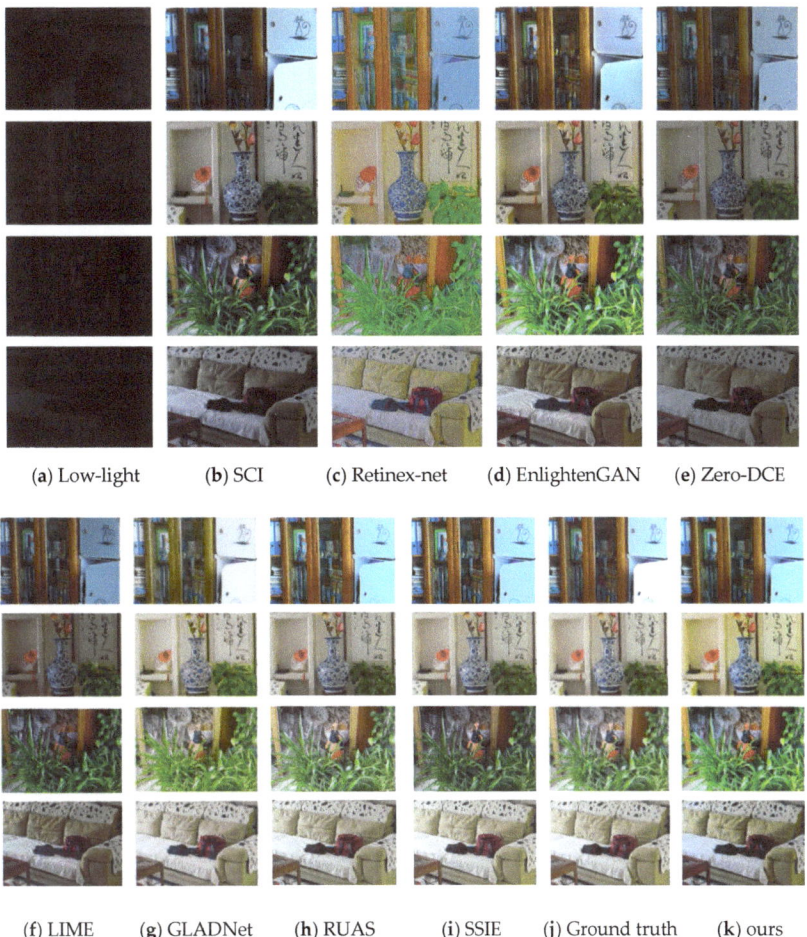

Figure 3. Comparison of different methods.

Figure 4 illustrates the enhancement effects of various algorithms when applied to a single image. Compared with SCI, the proposed model performs better in enhancing light-colored areas. The EnlightenGAN enhancement algorithm faces certain difficulties in distinguishing between the black areas of the image, failing to differentiate between inherent color and low-light conditions. The enhanced results of Retinex-net indicate significant color deviation. The GLADNet-enhanced image has less noise but exhibits low color saturation. The enhanced results of RUAS algorithm are not obvious in the dark. The SSIE algorithm faces image color distortion. It is noted that the proposed approach results in less color distortion compared to other methods.

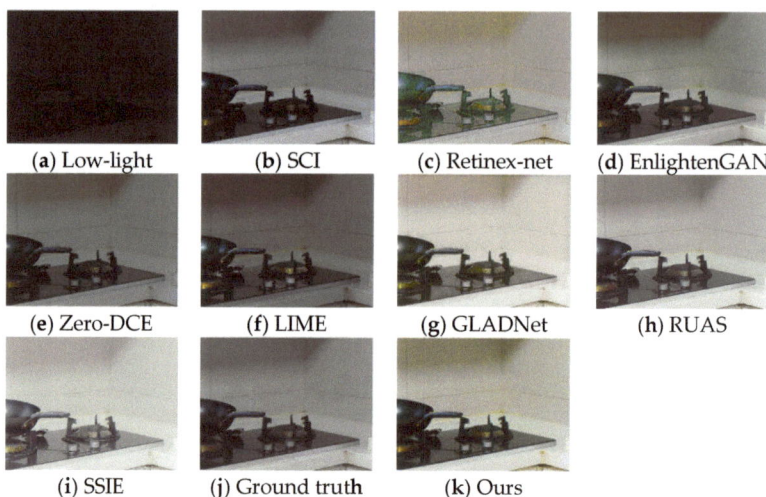

Figure 4. Comparison of details of different methods.

4.2.2. Objective Evaluation Results

The objective evaluation methods used include PSNR, SSIM [33], and NIQE [34]. In Table 1, an upward arrow (↑) indicates that the metric is positively correlated with image quality, while a downward arrow (↓) indicates a negative correlation.

Table 1. Objective evaluation indicators of different methods on the LOL dataset.

	SCI	EnlightenGAN	LIME	Zero-DCE	Retinex-Net	GLADNet	RUAS	SSIE	Ours
SSIM↑	0.635	0.752	0.590	0.664	0.502	0.778	0.441	0.723	0.826
PSNR↑	17.210	18.849	13.244	15.215	17.839	19.705	10.714	16.800	20.200
NIQE↓	8.878	7.174	8.640	8.497	11.250	7.084	7.833	3.882	5.05

The SCI, EnlightenGAN, and Zero-DCE algorithms exhibit poor NIQE and PSNR metrics due to insufficient illumination enhancement and noise in dark areas. The GALDNet algorithm performs well across these three metrics due to its effective brightness enhancement and reduced image noise. However, subjective observation reveals significant color distortion in the results of this algorithm. LIME and Retinex-Net show poor performance in objective evaluation metrics. Their enhancement results contain substantial noise, and the Retinex-Net algorithm suffers from severe detail loss. The RUAS algorithm underperforms when using the proposed approach on all three indicators, and its dark region enhancement is insufficient. The SSIE algorithm performs best on the NIQE indicator, but not as well as the proposed approach on SSIM and PSNR, and it also has color distortion problems in terms of subjective performance.

4.3. Ablation Experiment

To demonstrate the effectiveness of the CBAM attention mechanism and the color restoration term in the loss function of the proposed algorithm, ablation studies are conducted on each module.

4.3.1. CBAM Attention Mechanism

This section quantitatively assesses the impact of the CBAM module. Training and testing are performed on the same dataset, and various evaluation metrics are compared, as shown in Table 2. The addition of the attention mechanism module lowers the NIQE index, while both SSIM and PSNR show improvements, indicating that the module improves brightness. Notably, the performance is best when two attention mechanism modules are added, with the approach of applying channel attention first, followed by spatial attention (CBAM), yielding the most effective results.

Table 2. Index data with attention mechanisms.

Model	Attention Mechanism	SSIM	PSNR	NIQE
1	none	0.782	20.144	7.030
2	channel attention	0.797	20.169	5.924
3	spatial attention	0.804	20.166	5.600
4	spatial and channel attention	0.822	20.188	5.105
5 (Ours)	channel and spatial attention (CBAM)	0.826	20.200	5.057

4.3.2. Color Restoration Term

To validate the contribution of the color restoration term in boosting model performance, several ablation experiments are conducted, as shown in Table 3. In these experiments, the color restoration term is removed to observe changes in performance, providing a clearer understanding of its significance in enhancing overall model effectiveness. Initially, we modify a model that already uses our optimized loss function by removing the color restoration term. We then retrain the modified model using the same datasets and training parameters, documenting its performance. It is observed that the configuration using CBAM and our optimized loss function produces the highest performance. Even when CBAM is not used, the configuration using the loss function with the added color restoration loss item performs better than the configuration using the regular loss function. The color restoration loss term reduces the NIQE metric, making the enhanced images appear more natural by reducing color deviation.

Table 3. Index data with color restoration terms.

Model	CBAM	Color Restoration Term	SSIM	PSNR	NIQE
1	×	×	0.793	19.822	6.142
2	√	×	0.819	20.050	5.520
3	×	√	0.782	20.144	7.030
4 (Ours)	√	√	0.826	20.200	5.057

5. Conclusions

In this paper, a U-net network based on attention mechanisms is built, decomposing the illumination and reflectance components of low-light images based on Retinex theory. The local, adaptive enhancement function adjusts the enhancement level for different regions of the image, ensuring that both dark and bright areas are optimally enhanced for improved overall image quality. In addition, an unsupervised learning loss function is introduced. The proposed algorithm exhibits minimal dependence on the quality of the training dataset, low computational complexity, and rapid training speed. Experimental results show that the algorithm produces enhanced outcomes that closely mimic normal lighting conditions, featuring more natural lighting enhancement, improved color restoration, minimal color deviation, and preserved image details. It also shows good model generalization and robustness, with the peak signal-to-noise ratio and structural similarity index on real images outperforming other state-of-the-art methods. However, there are still some shortcomings in this study. The proposed model is suitable for unsupervised low-light image enhancement, and can only process still images, not videos. The local adaptive enhancement function adopts the equal division strategy when it divides the image into blocks as well. In the future, we plan to extend the proposed model to handle video data, enabling real-time, low-light video enhancement. Additionally, we will explore more sophisticated image division strategies, such as adaptive or content-aware partitioning, to further improve the local adaptive enhancement function for better performance and finer detail preservation.

Author Contributions: S.J.: conceptualization, methodology, supervision, writing—original draft preparation, and funding acquisition; Y.S.: methodology and writing—review and editing; Y.Z. (Yingchun Zhang): methodology and validation; Y.Z. (Yulin Zhang): conceptualization, data curation, formal analysis, and investigation. All authors have read and agreed to the published version of the manuscript.

Funding: This research was supported by the National Natural Science Foundation of China (52105167)

Data Availability Statement: The data presented in this study are available in Low Light paired dataset (LOL) at https://daooshee.github.io/BMVC2018website/ (accessed on 14 May 2024). These data were derived from the following resources available in the public domain: Wei, C., Wang, W., Yang, W. and Liu, J. (2018). Deep retinex decomposition for low-light enhancement. arXiv preprint arXiv:1808.04560 [27].

Conflicts of Interest: The authors declare no conflicts of interest.

References

1. Zhang, F.; Shao, Y.; Sun, Y.; Gao, C.; Sang, N. Self-supervised Low-Light Image Enhancement via Histogram Equalization Prior. In Proceedings of the Chinese Conference on Pattern Recognition and Computer Vision (PRCV), Xiamen, China, 13–15 October 2023; Springer Nature: Singapore, 2023; pp. 63–75.
2. Wu, W.; Weng, J.; Zhang, P.; Wang, X.; Yang, W.; Jiang, J. Uretinex-net: Retinex-based deep unfolding network for low-light image enhancement. In Proceedings of the IEEE/CVF Conference on Computer Vision and Pattern Recognition, New Orleans, LA, USA, 18–24 June 2022; pp. 5901–5910.
3. Yi, X.; Xu, H.; Zhang, H.; Tang, L.; Ma, J. Diff-retinex: Rethinking low-light image enhancement with a generative diffusion model. In Proceedings of the IEEE/CVF International Conference on Computer Vision, Paris, France, 1–6 October 2023; pp. 12302–12311.
4. Land, E.H. The retinex. In *Ciba Foundation Symposium-Colour Vision: Physiology and Experimental Psychology*; John Wiley & Sons, Ltd.: Chichester, UK, 1965; pp. 217–227.
5. Tao, L.; Zhu, C.; Xiang, G.; Li, Y.; Jia, H.; Xie, X. LLCNN: A convolutional neural network for low-light image enhancement. In Proceedings of the 2017 IEEE Visual Communications and Image Processing (VCIP), St. Petersburg, FL, USA, 10–13 December 2017; IEEE: Piscataway, NJ, USA, 2017; pp. 1–4.
6. Jiang, Q.; Mao, Y.; Cong, R.; Ren, W.; Huang, C.; Shao, F. Unsupervised decomposition and correction network for low-light image enhancement. *IEEE Trans. Intell. Transp. Syst.* **2022**, *23*, 19440–19455. [CrossRef]
7. Hu, J.; Guo, X.; Chen, J.; Liang, G.; Deng, F.; Lam, T.L. A two-stage unsupervised approach for low light image enhancement. *IEEE Robot. Autom. Lett.* **2021**, *6*, 8363–8370. [CrossRef]
8. Shi, Y.; Wang, B.; Wu, X.; Zhu, M. Unsupervised low-light image enhancement by extracting structural similarity and color consistency. *IEEE Signal Process. Lett.* **2022**, *29*, 997–1001. [CrossRef]
9. Ma, Y.; Xie, S.; Xu, W.; Chen, X.; Huang, X.; Sun, Y.; Liu, W. Region-Based Unsupervised Low-Light Image Enhancement in the Wild with Explicit Domain Supervision. *IEEE Trans. Instrum. Meas.* **2024**, *73*, 5024511. [CrossRef]
10. Guo, H.; Xu, W.; Qiu, S. Unsupervised low-light image enhancement with quality-task-perception loss. In Proceedings of the 2021 International Joint Conference on Neural Networks (IJCNN), Shenzhen, China, 18–22 July 2021; IEEE: Piscataway, NJ, USA, 2021; pp. 1–8.
11. Wang, R.; Jiang, B.; Yang, C.; Li, Q.; Zhang, B. MAGAN: Unsupervised low-light image enhancement guided by mixed-attention. *Big Data Min. Anal.* **2022**, *5*, 110–119. [CrossRef]
12. Fu, Y.; Hong, Y.; Chen, L.; You, S. LE-GAN: Unsupervised low-light image enhancement network using attention module and identity invariant loss. *Knowl.-Based Syst.* **2022**, *240*, 108010. [CrossRef]

13. Zhao, Z.; Xiong, B.; Wang, L.; Ou, Q.; Yu, L.; Kuang, F. RetinexDIP: A unified deep framework for low-light image enhancement. *IEEE Trans. Circuits Syst. Video Technol.* **2021**, *32*, 1076–1088. [CrossRef]
14. Jiang, Z.; Li, H.; Liu, L.; Men, A.; Wang, H. A switched view of Retinex: Deep self-regularized low-light image enhancement. *Neurocomputing* **2021**, *454*, 361–372. [CrossRef]
15. Liu, X.; Xie, Q.; Zhao, Q.; Wang, H.; Meng, D. Low-light image enhancement by retinex-based algorithm unrolling and adjustment. *IEEE Trans. Neural Netw. Learn. Syst.* **2023**, 1–14. [CrossRef] [PubMed]
16. Ma, Q.; Wang, Y.; Zeng, T. Retinex-based variational framework for low-light image enhancement and denoising. *IEEE Trans. Multimed.* **2022**, *25*, 5580–5588. [CrossRef]
17. Yang, J.; Wang, J.; Dong, L.; Chen, S.; Wu, H.; Zhong, Y. Optimization algorithm for low-light image enhancement based on Retinex theory. *IET Image Process.* **2023**, *17*, 505–517. [CrossRef]
18. Chen, X.; Li, J.; Hua, Z. Retinex low-light image enhancement network based on attention mechanism. *Multimed. Tools Appl.* **2023**, *82*, 4235–4255. [CrossRef]
19. Ai, S.; Kwon, J. Extreme low-light image enhancement for surveillance cameras using attention U-Net. *Sensors* **2020**, *20*, 495. [CrossRef] [PubMed]
20. Lv, F.; Li, Y.; Lu, F. Attention guided low-light image enhancement with a large scale low-light simulation dataset. *Int. J. Comput. Vis.* **2021**, *129*, 2175–2193. [CrossRef]
21. Atoum, Y.; Ye, M.; Ren, L.; Tai, Y.; Liu, X. Color-wise attention network for low-light image enhancement. In Proceedings of the IEEE/CVF Conference on Computer Vision and Pattern Recognition Workshops, Seattle, WA, USA, 14–19 June 2020; pp. 506–507.
22. Zhang, X.; Wang, X. Marn: Multi-scale attention retinex network for low-light image enhancement. *IEEE Access* **2021**, *9*, 50939–50948. [CrossRef]
23. Zhang, C.; Yan, Q.; Zhu, Y.; Li, X.; Sun, J.; Zhang, Y. Attention-based network for low-light image enhancement. In Proceedings of the 2020 IEEE International Conference on Multimedia and Expo (ICME), London, UK, 6–10 July 2020; IEEE: Piscataway, NJ, USA, 2020; pp. 1–6.
24. Woo, S.; Park, J.; Lee, J.Y.; Kweon, I.S. Cbam: Convolutional block attention module. In Proceedings of the European Conference on Computer Vision (ECCV), Munich, Germany, 8–14 September 2018; pp. 3–19.
25. Wei, C.; Wang, W.; Yang, W.; Liu, J. Deep retinex decomposition for low-light enhancement. *arXiv* **2018**, arXiv:1808.04560.
26. Guo, X.; Li, Y.; Ling, H. LIME: Low-light image enhancement via illumination map estimation. *IEEE Trans. Image Process.* **2016**, *26*, 982–993. [CrossRef] [PubMed]
27. Ma, L.; Ma, T.; Liu, R.; Fan, X.; Luo, Z. Toward fast, flexible, and robust low-light image enhancement. In Proceedings of the IEEE/CVF Conference on Computer Vision and Pattern Recognition, New Orleans, LA, USA, 18–24 June 2022; pp. 5637–5646.
28. Guo, C.; Li, C.; Guo, J.; Loy, C.C.; Hou, J.; Kwong, S.; Cong, R. Zero-reference deep curve estimation for low-light image enhancement. In Proceedings of the IEEE/CVF Conference on Computer Vision and Pattern Recognition, Seattle, WA, USA, 13–19 June 2020; pp. 1780–1789.
29. Jiang, Y.; Gong, X.; Liu, D.; Cheng, Y.; Fang, C.; Shen, X.; Yang, J.; Zhou, P.; Wang, Z. Enlightengan: Deep light enhancement without paired supervision. *IEEE Trans. Image Process.* **2021**, *30*, 2340–2349. [CrossRef] [PubMed]
30. Wang, W.; Wei, C.; Yang, W.; Liu, J. Gladnet: Low-light enhancement network with global awareness. In Proceedings of the 2018 13th IEEE International Conference on Automatic Face & Gesture Recognition (FG 2018), Xi'an, China, 15–19 May 2018; IEEE: Piscataway, NJ, USA, 2018; pp. 751–755.
31. Liu, R.; Ma, L.; Zhang, J.; Fan, X.; Luo, Z. Retinex-Inspired Unrolling With Cooperative Prior Architecture Search for Low-Light Image Enhancement. In Proceedings of the IEEE/CVF Conference on Computer Vision and Pattern Recognition, Nashville, TN, USA, 20–25 June 2021; IEEE: Piscataway, NJ, USA, 2021; pp. 10561–10570.
32. Zhang, Y.; Di, X.; Zhang, B.; Wang, C. Self-supervised Image Enhancement Network: Training with Low Light Images Only. *arXiv* **2020**, arXiv:2002.11300.
33. Hore, A.; Ziou, D. Image quality metrics: PSNR vs. SSIM. In Proceedings of the 2010 20th International Conference on Pattern Recognition, Istanbul, Turkey, 23–26 August 2010; IEEE: Piscataway, NJ, USA, 2010; pp. 2366–2369.
34. Mittal, A.; Soundararajan, R.; Bovik, A.C. Making a "completely blind" image quality analyzer. *IEEE Signal Process. Lett.* **2012**, *20*, 209–212. [CrossRef]

Disclaimer/Publisher's Note: The statements, opinions and data contained in all publications are solely those of the individual author(s) and contributor(s) and not of MDPI and/or the editor(s). MDPI and/or the editor(s) disclaim responsibility for any injury to people or property resulting from any ideas, methods, instructions or products referred to in the content.

Article

Multi-Agent Deep Reinforcement Learning for Blockchain-Based Energy Trading in Decentralized Electric Vehicle Charger-Sharing Networks

Yinjie Han [1,*], Jingyi Meng [2] and Zihang Luo [3]

1. International Business School, Xi'an Jiaotong-Liverpool University, Suzhou 215000, China
2. Gies College of Business, University of Illinois Urbana-Champaign, Urbana, IL 61802, USA; jingyimeng0211@163.com
3. School of Electrical and Electronic Engineering, Nanyang Technological University, Singapore 639798, Singapore; zihangluo123@163.com
* Correspondence: yinjiehan1218@gmail.com

Citation: Han, Y.; Meng, J.; Luo, Z. Multi-Agent Deep Reinforcement Learning for Blockchain-Based Energy Trading in Decentralized Electric Vehicle Charger-Sharing Networks. *Electronics* 2024, *13*, 4235. https://doi.org/10.3390/electronics13214235

Academic Editors: Tao Zhang, Xiangyun Tang, Jiacheng Wang and Jiqiang Liu

Received: 12 September 2024
Revised: 16 October 2024
Accepted: 17 October 2024
Published: 29 October 2024

Copyright: © 2024 by the authors. Licensee MDPI, Basel, Switzerland. This article is an open access article distributed under the terms and conditions of the Creative Commons Attribution (CC BY) license (https://creativecommons.org/licenses/by/4.0/).

Abstract: With The integration of renewable energy sources into smart grids and electric vehicle (EV) charger-sharing networks is essential for achieving the goal of environmental sustainability. However, the uneven distribution of distributed energy trading among EVs, fixed charging stations (FCSs), and mobile charging stations (MCSs) introduces challenges such as inadequate supply at FCSs and prolonged latencies at MCSs. In this paper, we propose a multi-agent deep reinforcement learning (MADRL)-based auction algorithm for energy trading that effectively balances charger supply with energy demand in distributed EV charging markets, while also reducing total charging latency. Specifically, this involves a MADRL-based hierarchical auction that dynamically adapts to real-time conditions, optimizing the balance of supply and demand. During energy trading, each EV, acting as a learning agent, can refine its bidding strategy to participate in various local energy trading markets, thus enhancing both individual utility and global social welfare. Furthermore, we design a cross-chain scheme to securely record and verify transaction results of energy trading in decentralized EV charger-sharing networks to ensure integrity and transparency. Finally, experimental results show that the proposed algorithm significantly outperforms both the second-price and double auctions in increasing global social welfare and reducing total charging latency.

Keywords: electric vehicles; mobile charging stations; charger sharing; blockchain; deep reinforcement learning

1. Introduction

Electric vehicles (EVs), by utilizing electricity as their primary energy source within smart grids, play a pivotal role in reducing reliance on finite fossil fuels and enhancing environmental sustainability [1–5]. By 2035, it is projected that over 60% of all vehicles will be electrified, necessitating a significant expansion in both the number and capacity of EV charging infrastructures [6]. To meet the escalating energy demands of EVs, the development of an efficient and scalable charging infrastructure is imperative. While existing fixed charging stations (FCSs) provide reliable and accessible charging points in urban and suburban areas, the surge in EV adoption has placed these facilities under considerable strain, often leading to congestion and extended waiting periods for charging services. To mitigate this pressure, mobile charging stations (MCSs) have been introduced as a versatile addition to the smart grid infrastructure, offering adaptable and on-demand services, particularly in areas of high demand and remote locations. The integration of FCSs and MCSs fosters a more resilient and efficient charging ecosystem, capable of dynamically accommodating the varied demands of EVs [7–9]. However, the implementation of peer-to-peer energy trading between EVs and MCSs is poised to further alleviate system strain and enhance the overall energy efficiency of EV charger-sharing networks [10].

Despite the many benefits of this hybrid EV charging infrastructure, distributed EV charging still faces significant challenges, particularly in terms of provisioning enough incentives for FCSs and MCSs and reducing the charging latency of EVs [11]. Without well-structured incentives, FCSs and MCSs may hesitate to share their energy with EVs. In the meanwhile, the absence of methods to reduce charging latency might lead to operational inefficiencies and potential conflicts among EVs. Therefore, it is essential to ensure that FCSs and MCSs can receive adequate incentives to not only foster participation but also reduce the charging latency of EVs in the distributed EV charger-sharing networks.

The application of auction theory to the allocation of incentives in EV charger-sharing networks presents a range of unique challenges [10,12,13]. Although second-price auctions are commonly utilized to balance supply and demand, their effectiveness is often compromised in the EV charging context due to significant variability in service values among users. This variability can lead to suboptimal outcomes that fail to effectively match supply with demand. On the other hand, double auctions [14], which allow both buyers and sellers to submit bids according to their valuations, aim to maximize the income of MCSs. Yet, these auctions frequently face challenges in practical applications due to their inherent complexity and often do not achieve an ideal balance between maximizing income and ensuring fair service provision [15,16]. Consequently, it becomes imperative to develop a novel auction mechanism that addresses these issues, thereby optimizing the distributed energy trading in EV charger-sharing networks for better social welfare and operational efficacy.

In this paper, we propose a multi-agent reinforcement learning (MADRL)-based auction algorithm for distributed energy trading in EV charger-sharing networks that integrates both fixed and mobile charging stations. Utilizing MADRL [16], the proposed auction mechanism not only achieves a more efficient balance of supply and demand compared to second-price auctions but also excels at maximizing revenue for MCSs compared to existing double auctions. Specifically, this algorithm employs a multi-agent system where each agent (EV or MCS) dynamically adjusts its bids based on real-time market conditions and historical data, employing predictive analytics and adaptive learning to enhance decision-making. By integrating dynamic pricing strategies and adaptive incentive structures, our framework ensures an efficient and equitable allocation of charging resources. The EV charger-sharing market employs a cross-chain scheme that coordinates local and global markets through side and main blockchains, respectively. The process begins with local market energy trading confirmation on the side blockchain, followed by the aggregation of results into the global market on the main blockchain, utilizing a Two-Phase Commit protocol to ensure synchronization and atomicity in cross-chain transactions [17]. We validate the effectiveness and scalability of the proposed algorithm through simulations on real-world datasets, where the experimental results demonstrate significant performance improvements in global social welfare and total charging latency.

Our main contributions can be summarized as follows.

1. We propose a MADRL-based distributed energy trading algorithm for EV charger-sharing networks, where EVs can request charging services from either FCSs or MCSs. Specifically, the distributed energy trading in EV charger-sharing networks can enhance the scalability and adaptability of the charging infrastructure by allowing EVs to flexibly select their charging mode, ensuring access to necessary services under a wide range of scenarios.

2. We introduce a distributed energy trading structure that enables EVs to choose from various submarkets based on their immediate energy demands within their local area. This adaptable market design promotes efficient resource allocation and adheres to principles of individual rationality and incentive compatibility. To enhance economic efficiency, we have developed a multi-agent deep reinforcement learning (MADRL) algorithm to aid EVs and MCSs in making decisions about market participation based on real-time data and local market conditions.

3. To enhance the security and reliability of energy trading transaction recording, we propose a cross-chain scheme that leverages a Two-Phase Commit protocol-based approach. Specifically, all transaction data of each local market are first accurately and securely confirmed at the side blockchain and then aggregated into the main blockchain of the global market.
4. Experimental results confirm significant improvements in the efficiency and effectiveness of the proposed charging and trading system. Through controlled simulations and real-world tests, we have demonstrated the robustness of our auction framework under varied operational conditions, showing marked reductions in charging latency and the improvement of global social welfare.

The rest of the paper is organized as follows. A literature review identifies gaps in existing approaches in Section 2. The system model is formulated in Section 3. The MADRL-based auction is introduced in Section 4. In Section 5, experimental validations are presented. The paper is concluded in Section 6.

2. Related Work

2.1. Energy Trading for EVs in Smart Grids

With the widespread adoption of EVs, the role of smart grids in managing and optimizing charging infrastructure has become increasingly important [18]. Smart grids can effectively manage power by integrating Distributed Energy Resources (DERs) and renewable energy sources, such as solar and wind, to meet the significant power demands posed by EVs. For instance, Danial et al. [1] conduct a techno-economic analysis that emphasizes cost considerations that are crucial for promoting the widespread adoption of EVs. They highlight the economic viability threshold for EV charging stations and propose governmental interventions like subsidies and tax strategies to support the installation of an estimated 646 to 3300 charging stations in Brunei by 2035. Building on the framework of energy optimization, Kim et al. [19] design a system that enables EV owners to engage in energy trading, facilitated by an aggregator. They propose a non-cooperative game model for energy trading decisions and a coordinated charging/discharging algorithm to optimize cost efficiency at the aggregator level and minimize energy expenses for EV owners. Their experimental simulations utilize a double auction mechanism to explore market dynamics and price uncertainty, thereby enhancing the adaptability of the model to real-world conditions.

Furthermore, Alvaro-Hermana et al. [20] explore peer-to-peer energy trading among EVs to alleviate grid strain during peak tariff periods. They propose a system model employing quadratic programming to optimize energy trading and minimize grid impact during business hours. The uniqueness of their proposed solutions is validated through experiments that demonstrate the potential of peer-to-peer trading to mitigate the effects of EV charging on the grid during peak periods. Additionally, Aggarwal et al. [11] tackle the challenges of energy trading for EVs in smart grids, emphasizing the integration of blockchain technology to enhance the security and efficiency of peer-to-peer transactions. Their approach not only addresses the balancing of energy demands during peak hours but also enhances transaction security against cyber threats like false data injections. Experiments validate the effectiveness of their distributed secure energy trading scheme, showcasing its capability to facilitate reliable and secure energy exchanges within smart grids. Houda et at. [21] proposes a blockchain-based system for vehicle-to-vehicle (V2V) electricity trading using a reverse auction mechanism. This approach aims to create a decentralized, secure, and transparent electricity market among electric vehicles (EVs) within a smart grid environment. By utilizing Ethereum's smart contracts, the system facilitates automated and fair trading without the need for third-party intermediaries, thus eliminating single points of failure associated with centralized models. These studies collectively underscore the progressive efforts to integrate advanced technological solutions, including blockchain, game theory, and economic incentives to optimize energy trading and management within smart grid environments tailored for EVs.

2.2. Economic Optimization of EV Charging in Smart Grids

In smart grids, economic optimization is pivotal for effective EV charging management [22]. FCSs, while reliable, lack the flexibility required to adapt to rapidly changing power demands and price fluctuations. Recent studies have explored dynamic pricing and auction mechanisms to enhance the economics of EV charging [23]. Wang et al. [24] focus on the interactions of storage units within smart grids, particularly plug-in hybrid EVs and batteries, aimed at intelligent decision-making to maximize utility. They introduce a non-cooperative game model allowing storage units to decide strategically on energy sales, integrating dynamic pricing and double auction models to optimize trading benefits against costs. Simulation results reveal up to a 130.2% improvement in the average utility per storage unit, underscoring the model's effectiveness in enhancing trading efficiency. Building on these insights, Hou et al. [12] address EV charging scheduling in a distributed context to boost social welfare, aligning with user preferences and considering the state of charge. Their iterative bidding framework enables efficient negotiation on charging times and prices, with experiments illustrating an 85% efficiency relative to optimal solutions and highlighting the impact of information disclosure on scheduling efficiency.

Further extending the discussion on optimizing smart grid-based EV charging stations, Wang et al. [25] introduce a novel operation mechanism named JoAP. This mechanism optimizes EV admission control, pricing, and charging schedules to maximize profitability. Using a tandem queueing network model, their study analytically characterizes the influence of admission control and pricing policies on profits, with simulations showing a 531% increase in profitability compared to conventional methods. Kikusato et al. [13] propose a management scheme to optimize the use of photovoltaic power in EV charging, aiming to reduce operation costs and curtailment in low-voltage distribution systems. Their auction mechanism ensures voluntary participation, maintaining fairness and autonomy among customers. Simulations demonstrate effective cost reductions and curtailment mitigation, even under forecasting errors and unexpected disconnections. Finally, Kim et al. [10] develop an auction-based incentive mechanism for energy trading between EVs and MCSs, focusing on efficiently utilizing MCS energy resources. Their distributed auction-based mechanism ensures truthfulness, individual rationality, and budget balance. Simulation studies confirm the mechanism's efficiency, enhancing system performance by more than twice as much as existing approaches. They highlight the potential of innovative auction mechanisms and dynamic pricing to adapt to and optimize energy trading within evolving market conditions, thereby facilitating more efficient and flexible smart grid operations.

2.3. Deep Reinforcement Learning in EV Charging

DRL has emerged as a potent machine learning method, demonstrating significant potential in addressing complex decision-making problems, particularly in EV charging optimization within smart grids [22,26,27]. By engaging continuously with the environment and refining policies, DRL adapts to uncertainties and dynamic demands effectively. For instance, Zou et al. [28] tackle the unique challenges of EV charging in urban prosumer communities, characterized by varied energy generation patterns and fluctuating prices. They introduce an innovative DRL strategy, employing the Asynchronous Advantage Actor–Critic with Long Short-Term Memory (A3C-LSTM) model, a facet of multi-agent deep reinforcement learning aimed at optimizing energy purchasing decisions for EVs. Experimental results highlight significant improvements in charging rates and social welfare, surpassing traditional methods.

Further exploring the optimization of EV charging, Wang et al. [29] utilize a reinforcement learning (RL) approach to refine charging scheduling and pricing strategies at EV charging stations. Motivated by the unpredictability of EV arrivals and departures, their model-free RL algorithm focuses on maximizing profit through strategic adjustments to charging schedules and pricing. Experiments with real-world data demonstrate that their approach yields a 138.5% increase in profit over benchmark algorithms, showcasing the efficacy of RL in real-time operational environments. Fan et al. [15] leverage MADRL to address supply and demand challenges in EV charging. They develop a distributed service allocation mechanism where Road-Side Units (RSUs) and Internet of Vehicles (IoV) [30] serve as markets for AI-generated content (AIGC). In this paper, we propose a MADRL-based distributed energy trading algorithm for EV charger-sharing networks that optimizes real-time EV charging decisions to improve global social welfare and reduce local charging latency.

3. System Model

3.1. Overview

As illustrated in Figure 1, the system aims to optimize EV charging management within smart grids by integrating three essential components: FCSs, MCSs, and EVs. Represented as $\mathcal{F} = \{1, \ldots, F\}$, the set of FCSs forms the backbone of the charging network, offering continuous and dependable charging services from their permanent locations. Each FCS f is equipped with substantial capacity to handle regular and predictable charging demands in the local market. Conversely, the set of MCSs under the coverage of FCS f is denoted as $\mathcal{M}^f = \{1, \ldots, M\}$. MCSs can relocate in response to real-time demand, effectively mitigating peak load pressures and extending services to remote areas that fixed stations cannot conveniently cover. This flexibility ensures that the system is responsive to varying charging requirements, providing timely support where necessary. EVs under the coverage of FCS f, represented by the set $\mathcal{E}^f = \{1, \ldots, E\}$, are the primary consumers within this ecosystem. Each EV requires strategic management to efficiently meet its charging demands while maximizing the utilization of both fixed and mobile charging resources. Our auction-based optimization framework orchestrates the interactions among f, $\mathcal{M}^f$, and $\mathcal{E}^f$, ensuring seamless coordination. Specifically, when an EV, denoted as e, acts as a buyer, it pays a price p_e^b that is equal to or lower than its valuation v_e, i.e., $p_e^b \leq v_e$. Conversely, when an MCS, denoted as m, acts as a seller, it receives a payment p_m^s that is equal to or higher than its cost c_m, i.e., $p_m^s \geq c_m$.

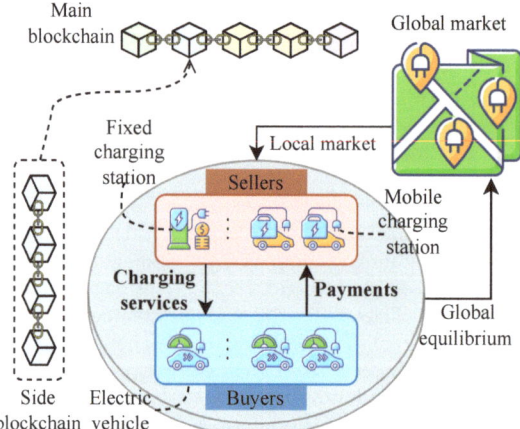

Figure 1. Blockchain-based energy trading in distributed EV charger-sharing networks, where each local market maintains its blockchain.

3.2. Charger Sharing Market

In this system, we consider a charger-sharing market with distributed energy trading where each FCS serves as an auctioneer for its local energy charging market. In each local market, MCSs act as sellers, and EVs act as buyers. In a local charger-sharing market, multiple bids from energy consumers (such as EVs) and providers (such as MCSs) are consolidated at the FCS for determining both pricing and allocation strategies.

Upon detecting an energy-sharing request from EVs, the system prompts MCSs in the local market, which may possess surplus charging capacity, to participate in energy trading. To engage in the market, both EVs and MCSs submit their bids to their FCSs. Before allocations and pricing can be determined, auctioneers at FCSs must compile detailed data from the local market to develop an exhaustive supply and demand matrix. The defined rules for allocation, termed as Π, include a supply matrix $X(t) \subseteq \{0,1\}^{|\mathcal{E}^f(t)| \times |\mathcal{M}^f(t)|} = \{x_1(t), \ldots, x_{|\mathcal{E}^f(t)|}(t)\}$ and a corresponding demand matrix $Y(t) \subseteq \{0,1\}^{|\mathcal{E}^f(t)| \times |\mathcal{M}^f(t)|} = \{y_1(t), \ldots, y_{|\mathcal{M}^f(t)|}(t)\}$. The supply vector of MCS m is depicted as $x_m \subseteq \{x_{m,1}(t), \ldots, x_{m,|\mathcal{E}^f(t)|}(t)\}$, and for EV e, the demand vector is shown as $y_e \subseteq \{y_{e,1}(t), \ldots, y_{e,|\mathcal{M}^f(t)|}(t)\}$. Then, each FCS calculates allocations and prices according to the auction protocol $M = (\Pi, \Psi)$ for its local charger-sharing market, where $\Pi = (X, Y)$ indicates the allocation rules and $\Psi = (p_b, p_s)$ describes the pricing rules. In this model, a trustworthy bid $b_{t,e}$ from buyer e represents their true valuation v_e, ensuring that its payment $p_e^b(t)$ remains within its budget, i.e., $p_e^b(t) \leq v_e$. Similarly, a seller m offers a selling bid $a_{t,m}$ reflecting its real cost c_m, ensuring its earning $p_m^s(t)$ meets or exceeds these costs, i.e., $p_m^s(t) \geq c_m$. These methods guarantee the pricing framework, defined by the vectors $p_b(t)$ and $p_s(t)$ for buyers and sellers, respectively.

3.3. Problem Formulation

Meanwhile, the mechanism needs to allocate and price energy to meet the demand and supply conditions and at the same time minimize the total charging time of both buyers and sellers under imperfect information conditions that any buyer or seller will act truthfully under individual rationality (IR). It is strategically rational for each participant, whether as a buyer or as a seller, to gain something out of the auction and therefore must prevent a utility that is not less than zero from engaging in the auction. Truthfulness in auctions can be referred to as a notion that reflects the fact that in an auction, buyers and sellers tender bids that are real regarding their appraisal or cost. This characteristic makes the auctions accurate and efficient, since all those interested can give an estimation of the value of the good or service that is being auctioned. In the marketplace, each buyer's bid $b_e(t)$ aligns precisely with their actual valuation v_e, ensuring $b_e(t) = v_e$. Consequently, the auction design ensures that the amount paid by buyers, $p_e^b(t)$, remains within their evaluated value, namely $p_e^b(t) \leq v_e$. Conversely, each seller's offer $a_m(t)$ mirrors the actual expenses incurred c_m, establishing $a_m(t) = c_m$. This arrangement ensures that the income received by sellers, $p_m^s(t)$, matches or exceeds their expenses, i.e., $p_m^s(t) \geq c_m$. In this bidirectional market, to preserve integrity, the buyer's valuation must match or exceed what they eventually pay, and similarly, the seller's listed prices reflect or exceed their perceived value of the goods.

Furthermore, the total societal benefit, labeled as $SW(t)$ at time t, is the aggregate of values accumulated from both sellers and buyers involved, which can be calculated as

$$SW(t) = \sum_{e \in \mathcal{E}^f(t)} \sum_{m \in \mathcal{M}^f(t)} y_{e,m}(t) v_e(t) + \sum_{e \in \mathcal{E}^f(t)} \sum_{m \in \mathcal{M}^f(t)} x_{m,e}(t) c_m(t). \tag{1}$$

Furthermore, the total charging latency at time slot t is denoted as $L(t)$, which can be computed as

$$L(t) = \sum_{e \in \mathcal{E}^f(t)} \left[\left(1 - \sum_{m \in \mathcal{M}^f(t)} y_{e,m}(t)\right) \left(T_e^{\text{charge}} + T_e^{\text{travel}}(t) + T_f^{\text{wait}}(t)\right) \right. \\ \left. + \sum_{m \in \mathcal{M}^f(t)} y_{e,m}(t) \left(T_e^{\text{charge}} + T_m^{\text{travel}}(t)\right) \right], \tag{2}$$

where T^{charge}_e is the charging time of EV e, T^{travel}_e is the traveling time of EV e, and T^{wait}_f is the waiting time at FCS f. This formula accounts for the total charging time, which includes the energy transfer time and the travel time to MCSs for winning EVs in the auction. For losing EVs, the charging time involves energy transfer, travel to FCSs, and additional waiting times at these stations, thus highlighting the impact of auction outcomes on charging efficiency.

4. Multi-Agent Deep-Reinforcement-Learning-Based Energy Trading Algorithm
4.1. Distributed Incentive Mechanism

In this subsection, we discuss the details of distributed energy trading in terms of the following points: Each MCS creates a local market in the region they cover; this includes all EVs within that region. As illustrated in Figure 2, there are two submarkets in each local market, i.e., the single-side urgent submarket and the double-side mundane submarket. In the urgent submarket, there is transacting immediately into clearing since bids for buying and selling are matched directly. On the other hand, in the mundane submarket, the transactions require procedures to be cleared at certain points to enable those with non-urgent energy requirements to participate in the market at certain times. At time t, EV e places a bid $b_e(t)$ to acquire energy, and MCS m offers a bid $a_m(t)$ catering to these energy requests.

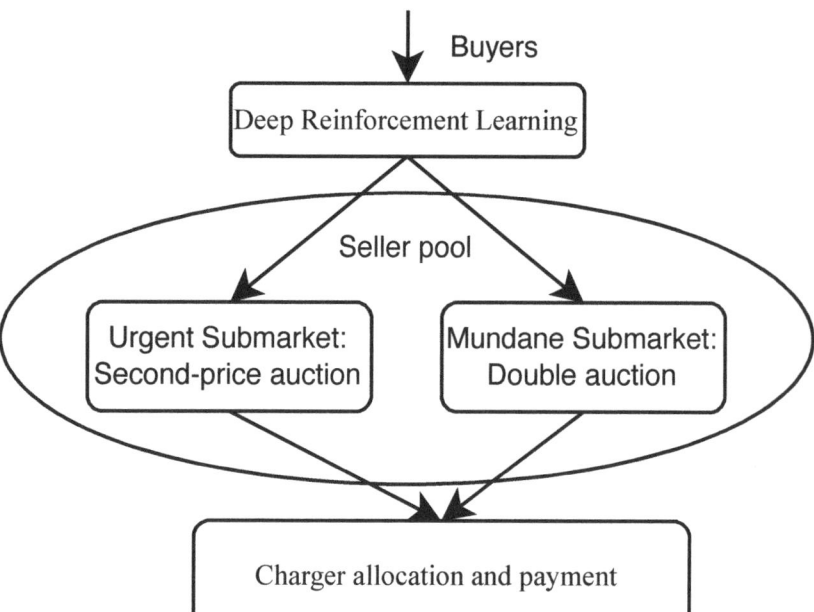

Figure 2. The workflow of the MADRL-based energy trading algorithm.

Within the coverage of FCS f, sellers are arranged into a local seller pool $\mathcal{P}^S_f(t) = \{m \mid \sum_{e \in \mathcal{E}^f(t)} x_{m,e}(t) = 0, m \in \mathcal{M}^f(t)\}$, where they react to incoming requests from buyers. The bids submitted by these sellers are accumulated in a designated value pool $\mathcal{A}^S_f(t) = \{a_m(t) \mid \sum_{e \in \mathcal{E}^f(t)} x_{m,e}(t) = 0, m \in \mathcal{M}^f(t)\}$ and are arranged to ensure $a_m(t) \leq a_{m+1}(t), \forall m, m+1 \in \mathcal{P}^S_f(t)$. Concurrently, EVs engaging in the routine submarket are sorted into a buyers' pool $\mathcal{P}^B_f(t)$, where their bids are organized in $\mathcal{O}^B_f(t)$, ranked such that $b_e(t) \geq b_{e+1}(t), \forall e, e+1 \in \mathcal{P}^B_f(t)$. For the urgent submarket on the buyers side, a second-price auction protocol is utilized, whereas the routine submarket adopts McAfee's method.

In the single-sided urgent submarket: The auctioneer evaluates the seller pool and adjusts the supply and demand dynamics along with the monetary stipulations of MCS m. The logic of the selection of the highest bid from the given number of qualified sellers for EV e is established by setting up

$$x_{m,e}(t) = y_{e,m}(t) = 1(a_m(t) > \max\{\mathcal{A}^S_{f,-m}(t)\}), \qquad (3)$$

where $1(\cdot)$ is the indicator function and $\mathcal{A}^S_{f,-m}(t)$ represents the highest bid in the seller pool excluding MCS m. A second-price sealed-bid auction determines the transaction price for buying EV e in the urgent market:

$$p^b_e(t) = \sum_{m \in \mathcal{P}^S_f(t)} x_{m,e}(t) \cdot \max\{\mathcal{A}^S_{f,-m}(t)\}, \qquad (4)$$

and the revenue for the selling MCS m is

$$p^s_m(t) = y_{e,m}(t) \cdot \max\{\mathcal{A}^S_f(t)\}. \qquad (5)$$

Double-side mundane submarket: This submarket comprises the buyer pool $\mathcal{P}^B_f(t)$ and untraded sellers in the seller pool $\mathcal{P}^S_f(t)$, which are cleared periodically. Using McAfee's mechanism, the auctioneer sorts buyers and sellers and determines the allocation and pricing rules by finding the breakeven index k in $\mathcal{A}^B_f(t)$ and $\mathcal{O}^B_f(t)$. The average price is calculated as

$$p^b_e(t) = p^s_m(t) = \frac{b_{k+1} + s_{k+1}}{2}, \qquad (6)$$

ensuring the first k buyers and sellers trade at this price, with adjustments made for trade reduction if necessary.

After all local markets have cleared, the local auctioneers of MCSs calculate the local budget cost $\beta_f(t)$ for their market, and the aggregate budget cost across the globally distributed market is computed as

$$\beta(t) = \sum_{f \in \mathcal{F}} \beta_f(t) = \sum_{f \in \mathcal{F}} \left[\sum_{e \in \mathcal{E}^f} |p^b_e(t) - \bar{p}(t)| + \sum_{m \in \mathcal{M}^f} |p^s_m(t) - \bar{p}(t)| \right], \qquad (7)$$

where the market clearning price is $\bar{p}(t) = \frac{\sum_{e \in \mathcal{E}^f(t)} p^b_e(t) + \sum_{m \in \mathcal{M}^f(t)} p^s_m(t)}{\sum_{m \in \mathcal{M}^f(t)} \sum_{e \in \mathcal{E}^f(t)} x_{m,e}(t) + \sum_{m \in \mathcal{M}^f(t)} \sum_{e \in \mathcal{E}^f(t)} y_{e,m}(t)}$.

To minimize the total budget cost while optimizing social welfare, the buying of EVs acts as a learning agent, adopting strategies that ensure equilibrium between supply and demand across the submarkets.

4.2. Partially Observable Markov Decision Process

Within this framework, every purchaser functions as a cognitive entity governed by a Partially Observable Markov Decision Process (POMDP), which comprises the components outlined below:

1. Observation: The observation of EV e at each time step t, denoted as $O_e(t)$, encompasses several key market dynamics. These include the number of buyers and sellers in each local market, represented as $|\mathcal{E}^f(t)|, \forall f \in \mathcal{F}$ and $|\mathcal{M}^f(t)|, \forall f \in \mathcal{F}$, respectively; the price of the last transaction denoted by $\bar{p}(t-1)$; and the charging latency, traveling time, and waiting time of EV e, represented by T^{charge}_e, $T^{\text{travel}}_e(t)$, $T^{\text{wait}}_n(t)$, respectively. The comprehensive observation set is formalized as

$$O_e(t) = \{|\mathcal{E}^1(t)|, \ldots, |\mathcal{E}^f(t)|, |\mathcal{M}^1(t)|, \ldots, |\mathcal{M}^f(t)|, \bar{p}(t-1), T^{\text{charge}}_e, T^{\text{travel}}_e(t), T^{\text{wait}}_f(t)\}. \qquad (8)$$

2. Action: The action $A_e(t)$ for EV e at time slot t is defined as the market selection strategy, where $A_e(t) = 0, 1$. Here, $A_e(t) = 0$ implies participation in the urgent submarket, while $A_e(t) = 1$ indicates entry into the mundane submarket within the buyer pool.
3. Reward: The reward function, $R_e(O_e(t), A_e(t))$, incorporates the social welfare, budget, and total charging time at the current time slot, calculated as

$$R_e(O_e(t), A_e(t)) = SW(t) - \alpha \beta(t)^2 - L(t), \tag{9}$$

where α is a coefficient that scales the budget cost. Social welfare, denoted by $SW(t)$, reflects the total utility of all buyers and sellers based on transaction prices; the budget, represented by $\beta(t)$, measures the net fiscal impact of transactions; and the total charging time, $L(t)$, accounts for delays due to energy transfer and travel times.
4. Value Function: The value function $V_{\pi_e}(O_e(t))$ for the policy π_e of EV e is the expected return starting from state S and following policy π_e, which is defined as

$$V_{\pi_e}(S) := E_\pi [\sum_{t=0}^{T} \gamma^k R_e(O_e(t), A_e(t)) | S_0 = S], \tag{10}$$

where $E_\pi(\cdot)$ represents the expected value under policy π, and $\gamma \in [0, 1]$ is the discount factor that progressively reduces the weight of future rewards.

4.3. Policy Iteration

The POMDP framework offers a comprehensive mathematical model to enhance decision-making for buyers. By evaluating system outcomes and executing suitable actions, agents can maximize their long-term expected rewards. This model facilitates the development of learning agents engaged in P2P energy trading, optimizing their utility while improving overall system welfare. To refine the valuation function, the Multi-agent Proximal Policy Optimization (MAPPO) [31], an algorithm based on reinforcement learning, facilitates the training of numerous agents within settings where rewards serve as feedback. Within the POMDP framework, each agent assesses the current state of the system and strategizes to enhance rewards over an extended period.

Define θ_e as the settings for the policy network specific to EV e and ϕ_e as those for the value network. Within MAPPO, every agent adheres to a policy $\pi_e(\theta_e)$, undergoing periodic adjustments via a centralized critic $V(s; \phi_e)$, which appraises the overarching state S. Both the critic and policy frameworks undergo simultaneous training with a clipped loss metric, expressed as $L_{\text{CLIP}}(\theta_e, \phi_e) = L_P(\theta_e) + L_V(\phi_e)$, integrating losses from both networks to reflect their collective efficacy in the global scenario. This methodology supports effective learning and adaptation within a multi-agent environment, ensuring that each agent's actions contribute optimally to the collective goals of the energy trading system. Algorithm 1 provides a summary of the proposed MADRL algorithm.

The complexity of the proposed MADRL-based energy trading algorithm increases with the number of agents, as each agent (EV or MCS) operates within a dynamic state-action space, which grows exponentially with the number of participants. This scaling challenge impacts the learning algorithm, as more agents require additional computational resources to update policies and value functions through deep learning iterations. Communication overheads also rise with the number of agents, particularly in decentralized systems where data exchange for coordination becomes necessary across both local and global markets. Auction mechanisms further introduce complexity, particularly in double auction scenarios where both buyer and seller bids need to be evaluated. Despite these challenges, the system is designed to maintain scalability through decentralized learning and localized markets, which effectively mitigate complexity, making the algorithm feasible for large-scale deployment. However, the careful management of computational resources and communication protocols will be critical to ensure efficiency as the number of agents increases.

Algorithm 1: Multi-agent deep reinforcement learning-based auction algorithm

1. Initialize policy networks $\pi_e(\theta_e)$ and value networks and $V(\phi_e)$ for each EV e;
2. **for** *episode in range(max_episodes)* **do**
3.   Initialize state $O_e(t)$;
4.   **for** *t in range(max_timesteps)* **do**
5.   **for** *each EV e in EV_set* **do**
6.   Observe the current state for $O_e(t)$;
7.   Select an action $A_e(t)$ based on its policy network $\pi_e(O_e(t); \theta_e)$;
8.   **end**
9.   Execute actions and observe the next state $O_e(t+1)$ and reward $R_e(t)$;
10.   **for** *each EV e in $\mathcal{E}^f$* **do**
11.   Store the experience tuple $(O_e(t), A_e(t), R_e(t), O_e(t+1))$ in replay buffer $\mathcal{B}$;
12.   Sample a mini-batch of experiences from replay buffers;
13.   Update the value network $V(\phi_e)$ using the sampled mini-batch;
14.   **for** *Each $(O_e(t), A_e(t), R_e(t), O_e(t+1))$ in minibatch* **do**
15.   Value_loss = $(V(O_e(t); \phi_e) - \text{target})^2$;
16.   Update ϕ_e using gradient descent on value_loss;
17.   **end**
18.   **end**
19.   Update the policy network $\pi_e(\theta_e)$ using the sampled mini-batch;
20.   **for** *each experience in minibatch* **do**
21. $(O_e(t), A_e(t), R_e(t), O_e(t+1))$ = experience;
22.   Advantage = $R_e(t) + \gamma \cdot V(O_e(t+1); \phi_e) - V(O_e(t); \phi_e)$;
23.   Policy_loss = $-\log(\pi_e(A_e(t); \theta_e)) \cdot$ advantage;
24.   Update θ_e using gradient descent on policy_loss;
25.   **end**
26.   **end**
27.   Update the centralized critic $V(s; \phi_e)$ using global state $O_e(t)$;
28.   **for** *each global state $O_e(t)$ in minibatch* **do**
29.   Global_target = $R(t) + \gamma \cdot V(O_e(t+1); \phi_e)$;
30.   Critic_loss = $(V(O_e(t); \phi_e) - \text{global\_target})^2$;
31.   Update ϕ_e using gradient descent on critic_loss;
32.   **end**
33. **end**
34. Store results and statistics for the episode.

4.4. Property Analysis

Utilizing the principles of second-price and McAfee's double auctions, we demonstrate that our innovative distributed hierarchical auction structure promotes both IR and truthfulness across a distributed market setting. It is essential initially to verify that this framework supports IR and truthfulness consistently in local markets.

Lemma 1. *With the established market entry strategies $A_e, \forall e \in \mathcal{E}^f(t)$, this system sustains IR and truthfulness locally.*

This principle is derived from the fundamental characteristics of second-price auctions and the dominant strategies used in double auctions. Expanding from this foundation, the local maintenance of IR and truthfulness is projected onto the broader, globally distributed market.

Theorem 1. *Across a diverse network of local markets that make up the global market, our framework reliably preserves individual rationality and truthfulness.*

Proof. Assessing individual rationality and truthfulness involves examining both urgent and routine submarkets, following the set market entry strategies. Specifically, an EV e with $A_e(t) = 0$ consistently opts for urgent submarkets, whereas one with $A_e(t) = 1$ chooses routine submarkets. □

We then demonstrate that our auction model guarantees IR for all participants. In urgent submarkets facilitated by a second-price auction, the top bidder pays only the second-highest bid, not exceeding their actual valuation. Consequently, the net benefit for winners remains positive, as shown by

$$\mu_e(t) = v_e(t) - p_e^b(t) \geq 0, \tag{11}$$

where $\sum_{m \in \mathcal{M}^f(t)} x_{m,e} = 1$. For those not winning, their utility remains zero as no payment is made:

$$\mu_e(t) = v_e(t) - p_e^b(t) = 0. \tag{12}$$

In the mundane submarkets, McAfee's mechanism ensures that winning buyers pay the average of the lowest winning bid and the highest losing bid, which is also less than or equal to their valuation. Hence, the utility for these buyers remains non-negative. For buyers not succeeding, and for sellers, both losing and winning, the mechanism ensures their utility is aligned with their actions, maintaining non-negative utility for winners and zero utility for non-participants.

Next, we establish that the mechanism is truthful for all involved. In the urgent submarket's second price auction, the optimal strategy for buyers is to bid their true valuation since the payment is the second-highest bid, not their own. In the mundane submarket, McAfee's mechanism incentivizes both buyers and sellers to bid truthfully, making truth-telling a dominant strategy. In conclusion, the proposed distributed hierarchical auction mechanism consistently upholds individual rationality and truthfulness across a globally distributed market comprising multiple local markets. This ensures efficient and equitable distributed energy sharing within EV charging networks, thereby benefiting all participants in their involvement.

5. Cross-Chain Scheme for Decentralized EV Charger Sharing

In EV charger-sharing networks, the cross-chain scheme for energy trading employs a structured workflow that coordinates local and global markets through side and main blockchains, respectively. This technical process can be broken down as follows.

5.1. Local Market Energy Trading Confirmation in Side Blockchain

The energy trading process begins at the local market, where each side blockchain, which manages local market transactions among charging stations and electric vehicles, ensuring decentralized verification of energy trades, is maintained by FCS, MCSs, and EVs.

1. Trading Request and Auction Mechanism: In the energy trading process of the local market, EVs submit charging requests based on their energy needs, while MCSs offer available energy for sale through the proposed MADRL-based auction mechanism. The FCS acts as the auctioneer, managing the auction and matching EVs' demands with MCSs' supplies to determine charger allocation and payment.
2. Recording in the Side Blockchain: After the auction concludes, energy trading results, including successful bids, prices, and energy quantities, are confirmed and recorded in the side blockchain. Therefore, the side blockchain manages local market transactions among FCSs, MCSs, and EVs, ensuring decentralized verification of energy trades and transparency and reliability in the trading process.

5.2. Aggregation into Global Market in Main Blockchain

The next phase aggregates results from local markets into the global market through the main blockchain, which aggregates confirmed energy trading results from side blockchains to maintain data integrity with FCSs serving as recording nodes, which can ensure consistency and universal coordination between local and global energy demands and supplies.

1. Cross-Chain Interaction: The cross-chain interaction between the side blockchains of local markets and the main blockchain of global market involves a two-step process. First, the side blockchain communicates with the main blockchain through cross-chain interaction protocols. Then, confirmed energy trading results from the side blockchain are aggregated and submitted to the main blockchain, with FCSs acting as gateways between the two blockchains. This process ensures the seamless integration of local market data into the global energy market while maintaining data integrity and security.
2. Main Blockchain Record Update: On the main blockchain, representing the global energy market, FCSs act as validators to record aggregated results from various local markets. These results update the global market's ledger, reflecting the total energy exchanged, pricing trends, and participation of MCSs and EVs across all local markets.
3. Final Confirmation: Validators on the main blockchain confirm the legitimacy of aggregated results. Once confirmed, the global ledger is updated, ensuring consolidation and accurate reflection of all energy trading data across multiple local markets.

5.3. Cross-Chain Scheme with Two-Phase Commit Protocol

The cross-chain interaction uses the Two-Phase Commit (2PC) protocol, which ensures synchronization in cross-chain transactions through a prepare phase for result collection and a commit phase for result aggregation, to ensure synchronization and atomicity in cross-chain transactions:

1. Phase 1 (Prepare): Collators in the side blockchain collect local market results (energy trading outcomes) and submit them to main blockchain validators. Validators check result validity through lightweight verification, using simplified payment verification to ensure legitimate and accurate transaction data.
2. Phase 2 (Commit): After verification, the main blockchain validators approve the transaction. The cross-chain event is recorded, and the results are aggregated into the main blockchain, completing the global energy market update.

This cross-chain process guarantees decentralized, tamper-resistant verification of energy trading, ensuring seamless collaboration between local and global markets without compromising blockchain data integrity or security.

6. Numerical Results

6.1. Experimental Settings

The experimental environment is set up with 50 rounds and includes four FCSs, each representing a submarket. The total number of vehicles ranges from 20 to 80, and each FCS has a coverage area of 500 m. In the experiment, we utilize the data proposed in [32], which consist of 3395 high-resolution charging sessions involving 85 EV drivers across 105 stations at 25 workplace locations, meticulously recorded to analyze the effects of pricing strategies and workplace norms on optimizing shared EV charging resources. As shown in Figure 3, the EV charging data statistics for the experiments are provided as follows: the total kWh required has a mean of 5.81, a standard deviation of 2.89, and a range from 0 to 23.68, with a median of 6.23 and a peak range between 6 and 7. The charge time has a mean of 2.84 h, a standard deviation of 1.51 h, and a range from 0.0125 to 55.24 h, with a median of 2.81 h and a peak range between 2 and 3.5 h. The distance traveled has a mean of 18.65 km, a standard deviation of 11.42 km, and a range from 0.86 to 43.06 km, with a median of 21.02 km. We implemented a prototype system of our cross-chain-empowered charger-sharing market using Hyperledger Fabric for both the side and the main blockchains, with Chaincode smart contracts in Go, DPoS consensus, and Hyperledger Cactus for cross-chain interactions.

The algorithm settings involve several parameters crucial for the MADRL approach. The replay buffer size is set to 10,000, with a learning rate of 1×10^{-4} and a discount factor (γ) of 0.95. The training is set to 1000 epochs, with each epoch consisting of 2000 steps. During each epoch, 16 episodes are collected, and each episode is repeated four times. The batch size for training is set to 64, and the hidden layers in the neural network have sizes of 256 and 256. The training involves eight parallel environments, while testing uses a single environment. Specific parameters for PPO include a value function coefficient of 0.5, an entropy coefficient of 0.05, an epsilon clip of 0.2, a maximum gradient norm of 0.5, and a Generalized Advantage Estimation (GAE) lambda of 0.95. Additionally, reward normalization is enabled, and several clipping and normalization parameters are set to ensure stable training. The environment settings include 20 users and 4 servers, simulating the interactions within the distributed markets.

The distribution of valuations for buyers and sellers is depicted in Figure 4. The left histogram shows the distribution of valuations for buyers, ranging from approximately 0.6 to 1.4. The distribution is centered around 1.2, indicating that the most frequent valuations are close to this value. The frequency peaks at around 1.2, with the highest frequency just above 140. The distribution appears to be approximately normal, with fewer buyers having valuations significantly lower or higher than 1.2. The right histogram shows the distribution of costs for sellers, ranging from 0 to 4. The distribution is centered around 2, indicating that the most frequent costs are close to this value. The frequency peaks at around 2, with the highest frequency just above 80. The distribution appears normal, with fewer sellers having costs significantly lower or higher than 2. Overall, both distributions exhibit a bell-shaped curve, suggesting a normal distribution with a central tendency around 1.2 for buyers' valuations and 2 for sellers' costs.

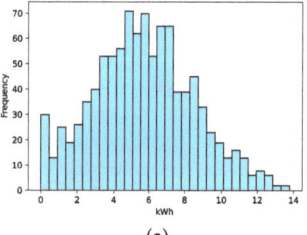
(a)

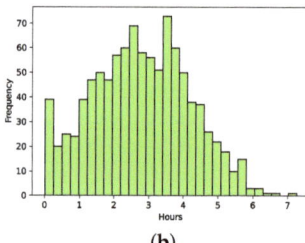
(b)

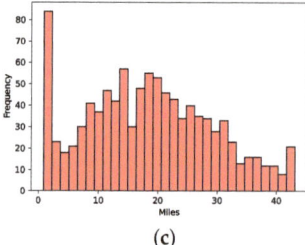
(c)

Figure 3. The data distribution of energy demands, charging time, and distance in the dataset. (**a**) Energy demands. (**b**) Charging time. (**c**) Distance.

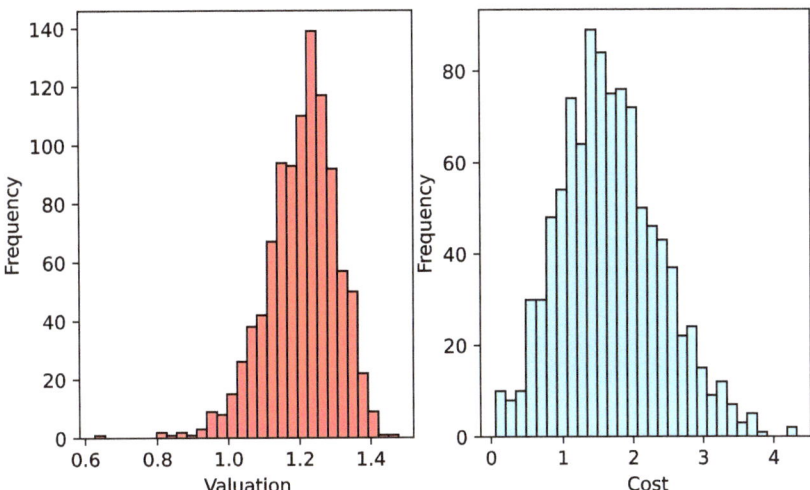

Figure 4. The distribution of valuation of buyers and sellers.

6.2. Convergence Analysis

The convergence performance of the proposed MADRL-based mechanism is analyzed under different market sizes: 20, 40, 60, and 80. Figure 5 illustrates four subplots comparing the performance of the DRL-based mechanism with Random, Single Price Auction (SPA), and Double Auction (DA) mechanisms across 5000 epochs. For a market size of 20, the DRL mechanism exhibits a steady increase in rewards, initiating at approximately −11 and converging to around −7. It significantly outperforms the Random, SPA, and DA mechanisms, which display relatively static reward trends at lower levels. The Random mechanism stabilizes around −11, SPA around −10, and DA around −12. In the scenario with a market size of 40, the DRL mechanism demonstrates consistent improvement, initiating at approximately −12 and converging to around −5. It markedly surpasses the other mechanisms. Random mechanism stabilizes around −11, SPA around −9, and DA around −12. With a market size of 60, the DRL mechanism begins with an initial dip followed by a steady increase, starting from around −12 and converging to approximately −4. The reward trajectory of the DRL mechanism surpasses those of the Random, SPA, and DA mechanisms. The Random mechanism stabilizes around −11, SPA around −9, and DA around −12. For the largest tested market size of 80, the DRL mechanism displays rapid initial improvement, beginning from around −12 and converging to approximately −4 within 2500 epochs. It consistently outshines the other mechanisms throughout the training process. The Random mechanism stabilizes around −11, SPA around −9, and DA around −12. In summary, across all market sizes, the DRL-based mechanism demonstrates superior convergence performance compared to the Random, SPA, and DA mechanisms. It consistently achieves higher rewards, indicating enhanced optimization and learning efficacy. The DRL mechanism exhibits a clear upward trend, steadily improving over time and converging to higher reward levels, while the other mechanisms maintain relatively constant and lower reward levels throughout the epochs. This underscores the effectiveness of the DRL-based approach in adapting to and optimizing the dynamics of EV charging market scenarios. MADRL shows a clear upward trend, steadily improving over time and converging to higher reward levels compared to SPA and DA. The consistent increase suggests that MADRL effectively learns over time, optimizing both the buyers' and sellers' utilities. The rewards for MADRL start relatively low, indicating a learning curve where the system first gathers data, adjusts bidding strategies, and progressively improves its decision-making. This is expected for reinforcement learning algorithms that require sufficient exploration of actions before optimizing for rewards. Meanwhile, the rapid initial improvements for market sizes of 40 and 80 suggest that the system's complexity and available data are more suited for larger market scenarios. This scalability is a crucial feature of MADRL, ensuring that the algorithm can perform effectively as the number of vehicles increases.

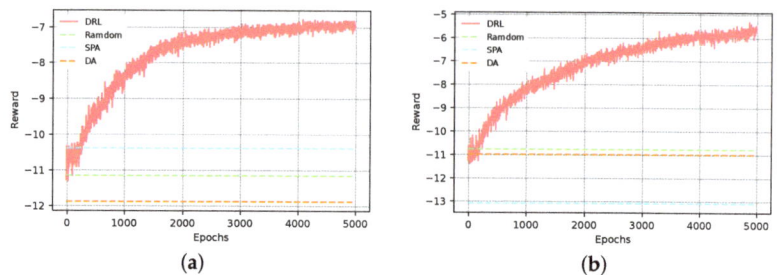

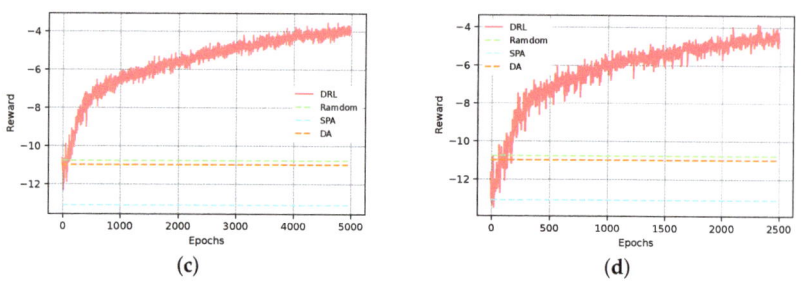

Figure 5. Convergence analysis of the proposed learning-based mechanism under different sizes of EV charging markets. (**a**) Market size = 20. (**b**) Market size = 40. (**c**) Market size = 60. (**d**) Market size = 80.

6.3. Performance Comparison

Figure 6 presents a performance comparison of the proposed DRL-based mechanism with the Random, SPA, and DA mechanisms across various sizes of EV charging markets (number of vehicles). The DRL mechanism consistently achieves the highest rewards across all market sizes, maintaining a stable reward close to −5 as the number of vehicles increases from 20 to 80. In contrast, the Random and SPA mechanisms exhibit relatively constant rewards around −10 and −11, respectively, while the DA mechanism shows a significant decrease in reward as the market size increases, dropping from around −10 to nearly −40. In terms of social welfare, the DRL, SPA, and DA mechanisms display a similar increasing trend as the number of vehicles increases. The DRL mechanism slightly outperforms the other mechanisms, particularly in larger market sizes, achieving social welfare close to 55 with 80 vehicles. The Random mechanism, however, lags, demonstrating lower social welfare across all market sizes. The DRL mechanism also maintains a relatively low and stable budget cost across all market sizes, approximately 10. The Random and SPA mechanisms show low budget costs that increase slightly with market size but remain below 20. Conversely, the DA mechanism experiences a substantial increase in budget cost as the number of vehicles increases, reaching nearly 50 with 80 vehicles. Finally, the charging latency performance of the DRL mechanism demonstrates competitiveness, increasing from about 20 to 55 as the number of vehicles grows. The SPA mechanism exhibits a similar trend but with slightly lower latency compared to DRL. The Random mechanism consistently displays higher latency than both DRL and SPA, while the DA mechanism shows the highest charging latency across all market sizes, peaking at 60 with 80 vehicles. Across all market sizes (20 to 80 vehicles), MADRL consistently achieves the highest rewards, maintaining stability near −5. The other mechanisms either stay at lower reward levels (e.g., around −10 for SPA) or decline significantly (e.g., DA's reward dropping to −40 as market size increases). This stability in rewards highlights MADRL's ability to maintain an optimal balance of supply and demand over time, even in larger markets. MADRL's ability to handle increasing market sizes while maintaining low latency, high social welfare, and low budget cost underscores its potential for scalability, making it a promising solution for the future of EV energy trading. Further analysis could focus on how MADRL adapts to even larger market sizes, different types of auction designs, or integration with renewable energy sources to improve overall system sustainability.

During the experimentation, the complexity of implementing a MADRL framework and cross-chain interactions using Hyperledger Fabric could imply potential computational challenges.

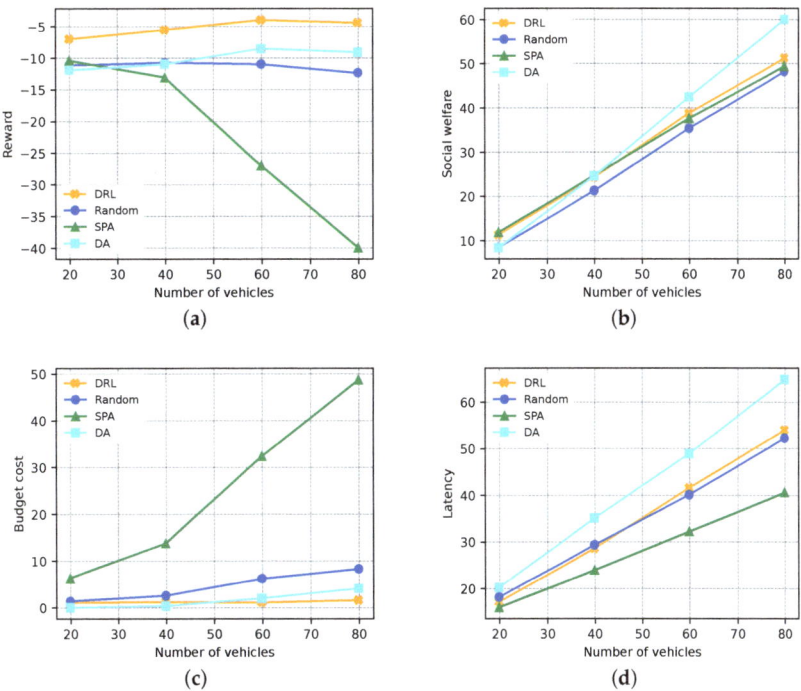

Figure 6. Performance comparison of the proposed learning-based mechanism under different sizes of EV charging markets. (**a**) Reward. (**b**) Social welfare. (**c**) Budget cost. (**d**) Charging latency.

7. Conclusions

In this paper, we introduce a MADRL-based auction algorithm for distributed energy trading in EV charger-sharing networks for achieving environmental sustainability. The proposed algorithm significantly enhances the scalability and efficiency of EV charging infrastructures by dynamically balancing supply and demand across various market sizes, demonstrating robust adaptability and superior performance in extensive simulations. By reducing charging latency and improving global social welfare, the proposed algorithm offers a sustainable solution that is adaptable to smart grid technologies globally. The proposed blockchain framework enables decentralized, secure, and scalable coordination for energy trading in EV charger-sharing markets through cross-chain collaboration, ensuring efficient resource management and transparent transactions between local and global markets. In future work, we will aim to benchmark our approach against a broader range of models, potentially including other machine learning techniques, to further validate its effectiveness and scalability. Moreover, we plan to perform real-world testing to validate the proposed algorithm in the future.

Author Contributions: Conceptualization, Y.H.; methodology, Y.H.; software, J.M.; validation, Y.H., J.M. and Z.L.; formal analysis, Y.H.; investigation, Y.H.; resources, Z.L.; data curation, Z.L.; writing—original draft preparation, Y.H.; writing—review and editing, Y.H.; visualization, J.M.; supervision, Y.H., J.M. and Z.L.; project administration, Y.H. All authors have read and agreed to the published version of the manuscript.

Funding: This research received no external funding.

Data Availability Statement: Data are contained within the article.

Conflicts of Interest: The authors declare no conflicts of interest.

References

1. Danial, M.; Azis, F.A.; Abas, P.E. Techno-economic analysis and feasibility studies of electric vehicle charging station. *World Electr. Veh. J.* **2021**, *12*, 264. [CrossRef]
2. Ma, J.; Zhang, Y.; Duan, Z.; Tang, L. PROLIFIC: Deep Reinforcement Learning for Efficient EV Fleet Scheduling and Charging. *Sustainability* **2023**, *15*, 13553. [CrossRef]
3. Shi, C.; Yu, M. Flexible solid-state lithium-sulfur batteries based on structural designs. *Energy Storage Mater.* **2023**, *57*, 429–459. [CrossRef]
4. Wang, J.; Du, H.; Niyato, D.; Zhou, M.; Kang, J.; Poor, H.V. Acceleration estimation of signal propagation path length changes for wireless sensing. *IEEE Trans. Wirel. Commun.* **2024**, *23*, 11476–11492. [CrossRef]
5. Wang, J.; Du, H.; Liu, Y.; Sun, G.; Niyato, D.; Mao, S.; Kim, D.I.; Shen, X. Generative AI based Secure Wireless Sensing for ISAC Networks. *arXiv* **2024**, arXiv:2408.11398.
6. Lai, P.; Fan, R.; Zhang, X.; Liu, F.; Zhou, J.T. Utility optimal thread assignment and resource allocation in multi-server systems. *IEEE/ACM Trans. Netw.* **2021**, *30*, 735–748. [CrossRef]
7. Wang, L.; Hou, L.; Liu, S.; Han, Z.; Wu, J. Reinforcement contract design for vehicular-edge computing scheduling and energy trading via deep Q-network with hybrid action space. *IEEE Trans. Mob. Comput.* **2023**, *23*, 6770–6784. [CrossRef]
8. Zhang, T.; Xu, C.; Lian, Y.; Tian, H.; Kang, J.; Kuang, X.; Niyato, D. When moving target defense meets attack prediction in digital twins: A convolutional and hierarchical reinforcement learning approach. *IEEE J. Sel. Areas Commun.* **2023**, *41*, 3293–3305. [CrossRef]
9. Zhang, T.; Xu, C.; Shen, J.; Kuang, X.; Grieco, L.A. How to disturb network reconnaissance: A moving target defense approach based on deep reinforcement learning. *IEEE Trans. Inf. Forensics Secur.* **2023**, *18*, 5735–5748. [CrossRef]
10. Kim, O.T.T.; Le, T.H.T.; Shin, M.J.; Nguyen, V.; Han, Z.; Hong, C.S. Distributed auction-based incentive mechanism for energy trading between electric vehicles and mobile charging stations. *IEEE Access* **2022**, *10*, 56331–56347. [CrossRef]
11. Aggarwal, S.; Kumar, N. Pets: P2p energy trading scheduling scheme for electric vehicles in smart grid systems. *IEEE Trans. Intell. Transp. Syst.* **2021**, *23*, 14361–14374. [CrossRef]
12. Hou, L.; Wang, C.; Yan, J. Bidding for preferred timing: An auction design for electric vehicle charging station scheduling. *IEEE Trans. Intell. Transp. Syst.* **2019**, *21*, 3332–3343. [CrossRef]
13. Kikusato, H.; Fujimoto, Y.; Hanada, S.I.; Isogawa, D.; Yoshizawa, S.; Ohashi, H.; Hayashi, Y. Electric vehicle charging management using auction mechanism for reducing PV curtailment in distribution systems. *IEEE Trans. Sustain. Energy* **2019**, *11*, 1394–1403. [CrossRef]
14. Gao, J.; Wong, T.; Wang, C.; Yu, J.Y. A price-based iterative double auction for charger sharing markets. *IEEE Trans. Intell. Transp. Syst.* **2021**, *23*, 5116–5127. [CrossRef]
15. Fan, J.; Xu, M.; Liu, Z.; Ye, H.; Gu, C.; Niyato, D.; Lam, K.Y. A Learning-based Incentive Mechanism for Mobile AIGC Service in Decentralized Internet of Vehicles. In Proceedings of the 2023 IEEE 98th Vehicular Technology Conference (VTC2023-Fall), Hong Kong, China, 10–13 October 2023; pp. 1–5.
16. Fan, J.; Xu, M.; Guo, J.; Shar, L.K.; Kang, J.; Niyato, D.; Lam, K.Y. Decentralized Multimedia Data Sharing in IoV: A Learning-based Equilibrium of Supply and Demand. *IEEE Trans. Veh. Technol.* **2023**, *73*, 4035–4050. [CrossRef]
17. Kang, J.; Li, X.; Nie, J.; Liu, Y.; Xu, M.; Xiong, Z.; Niyato, D.; Yan, Q. Communication-efficient and cross-chain empowered federated learning for artificial intelligence of things. *IEEE Trans. Netw. Sci. Eng.* **2022**, *9*, 2966–2977. [CrossRef]
18. Aggarwal, S.; Kumar, N.; Tanwar, S.; Alazab, M. A survey on energy trading in the smart grid: Taxonomy, research challenges and solutions. *IEEE Access* **2021**, *9*, 116231–116253. [CrossRef]

19. Kim, B.G.; Ren, S.; Van Der Schaar, M.; Lee, J.W. Bidirectional energy trading and residential load scheduling with electric vehicles in the smart grid. *IEEE J. Sel. Areas Commun.* **2013**, *31*, 1219–1234. [CrossRef]
20. Alvaro-Hermana, R.; Fraile-Ardanuy, J.; Zufiria, P.J.; Knapen, L.; Janssens, D. Peer to peer energy trading with electric vehicles. *IEEE Intell. Transp. Syst. Mag.* **2016**, *8*, 33–44. [CrossRef]
21. Abou El Houda, Z.; Hafid, A.S.; Khoukhi, L. Blockchain-based reverse auction for v2v charging in smart grid environment. In Proceedings of the ICC 2021-IEEE International Conference on Communications, Montreal, QC, Canada, 14–23 June 2021; pp. 1–6.
22. Osaba, E.; Villar-Rodriguez, E.; Del Ser, J.; Nebro, A.J.; Molina, D.; LaTorre, A.; Suganthan, P.N.; Coello, C.A.C.; Herrera, F. A tutorial on the design, experimentation and application of metaheuristic algorithms to real-world optimization problems. *Swarm Evol. Comput.* **2021**, *64*, 100888. [CrossRef]
23. Wang, K.; Zhang, X.; Duan, L.; Tie, J. Multi-UAV cooperative trajectory for servicing dynamic demands and charging battery. *IEEE Trans. Mob. Comput.* **2021**, *22*, 1599–1614. [CrossRef]
24. Wang, Y.; Saad, W.; Han, Z.; Poor, H.V.; Başar, T. A game-theoretic approach to energy trading in the smart grid. *IEEE Trans. Smart Grid* **2014**, *5*, 1439–1450. [CrossRef]
25. Wang, S.; Bi, S.; Zhang, Y.J.A.; Huang, J. Electrical vehicle charging station profit maximization: Admission, pricing, and online scheduling. *IEEE Trans. Sustain. Energy* **2018**, *9*, 1722–1731. [CrossRef]
26. Zhou, Y.; Yang, Z.; Zhang, X.; Wang, Y. A hybrid attention-based deep neural network for simultaneous multi-sensor pruning and human activity recognition. *IEEE Internet Things J.* **2022**, *9*, 25363–25372. [CrossRef]
27. Xie, Y.; Chan, T.T.; Zhang, X.; Lai, P.; Pan, H. Reflection-Optimized Covert Communication for Jammer-Aided Ambient Backscatter Systems. In Proceedings of the GLOBECOM 2023-2023 IEEE Global Communications Conference, Kuala Lumpur, Malaysia, 4–8 December 2023; pp. 4277–4282.
28. Zou, L.; Munir, M.S.; Tun, Y.K.; Kang, S.; Hong, C.S. Intelligent EV charging for urban prosumer communities: An auction and multi-agent deep reinforcement learning approach. *IEEE Trans. Netw. Serv. Manag.* **2022**, *19*, 4384–4407. [CrossRef]
29. Wang, S.; Bi, S.; Zhang, Y.A. Reinforcement learning for real-time pricing and scheduling control in EV charging stations. *IEEE Trans. Ind. Inform.* **2019**, *17*, 849–859. [CrossRef]
30. Zhang, T.; Xu, C.; Zou, P.; Tian, H.; Kuang, X.; Yang, S.; Zhong, L.; Niyato, D. How to mitigate DDoS intelligently in SD-IoV: A moving target defense approach. *IEEE Trans. Ind. Inform.* **2022**, *19*, 1097–1106. [CrossRef]
31. Zhang, T.; Xu, C.; Zhang, B.; Li, X.; Kuang, X.; Grieco, L.A. Towards attack-resistant service function chain migration: A model-based adaptive proximal policy optimization approach. *IEEE Trans. Dependable Secur. Comput.* **2023**, *20*, 4913–4927. [CrossRef]
32. Asensio, O.I.; Apablaza, C.Z.; Lawson, M.C.; Walsh, S.E. A field experiment on workplace norms and electric vehicle charging etiquette. *J. Ind. Ecol.* **2022**, *26*, 183–196. [CrossRef]

Disclaimer/Publisher's Note: The statements, opinions and data contained in all publications are solely those of the individual author(s) and contributor(s) and not of MDPI and/or the editor(s). MDPI and/or the editor(s) disclaim responsibility for any injury to people or property resulting from any ideas, methods, instructions or products referred to in the content.

Article

Blockchain-Assisted Secure Energy Trading in Electricity Markets: A Tiny Deep Reinforcement Learning-Based Stackelberg Game Approach

Yong Xiao [1,2], Xiaoming Lin [1,2,*], Yiyong Lei [3], Yanzhang Gu [3], Jianlin Tang [1,2], Fan Zhang [1,2] and Bin Qian [1,2]

1. Electric Power Research Institute of CSG, Guangzhou 510663, China; xiaoyong@csg.cn (Y.X.); tangjl2@csg.cn (J.T.); zhangfan4@csg.cn (F.Z.); qianbin@csg.cn (B.Q.)
2. Guangdong Provincial Key Laboratory of Intelligent Measurement and Advanced Metering of Power Grid, Guangzhou 510663, China
3. China Southern Power Grid Co., Ltd., Guangzhou 510663, China; leiyy@csg.cn (Y.L.); guyz@csg.cn (Y.G.)
* Correspondence: linxm@csg.cn

Citation: Xiao, Y.; Lin, X.; Lei, Y.; Gu, Y.; Tang, J.; Zhang, F.; Qian, B. Blockchain-Assisted Secure Energy Trading in Electricity Markets: A Tiny Deep Reinforcement Learning-Based Stackelberg Game Approach. *Electronics* **2024**, *13*, 3647. https://doi.org/10.3390/electronics13183647

Academic Editors: Fabio Grandi and Andreas Mauthe

Received: 20 August 2024
Revised: 6 September 2024
Accepted: 10 September 2024
Published: 13 September 2024

Copyright: © 2024 by the authors. Licensee MDPI, Basel, Switzerland. This article is an open access article distributed under the terms and conditions of the Creative Commons Attribution (CC BY) license (https://creativecommons.org/licenses/by/4.0/).

Abstract: Electricity markets are intricate systems that facilitate efficient energy exchange within interconnected grids. With the rise of low-carbon transportation driven by environmental policies and tech advancements, energy trading has become crucial. This trend towards Electric Vehicles (EVs) is bolstered by the pivotal role played by EV charging operators in providing essential charging infrastructure and services for widespread EV adoption. This paper introduces a blockchain-assisted secure electricity trading framework between EV charging operators and the electricity market with renewable energy sources. We propose a single-leader, multi-follower Stackelberg game between the electricity market and EV charging operators. In the two-stage Stackelberg game, the electricity market acts as the leader, deciding the price of electric energy. The EV charging aggregator leverages blockchain technology to record and verify energy trading transactions securely. The EV charging operators, acting as followers, then decide their demand for electric energy based on the set price. To find the Stackelberg equilibrium, we employ a Deep Reinforcement Learning (DRL) algorithm that tackles non-stationary challenges through policy, action space, and reward function formulation. To optimize efficiency, we propose the integration of pruning techniques into DRL, referred to as Tiny DRL. Numerical results demonstrate that our proposed schemes outperform traditional approaches.

Keywords: electricity market operators; secure energy trading; Stackelberg game; deep reinforcement learning; pruning techniques

1. Introduction

The electricity market is a structured marketplace where electricity is traded, aiming to ensure the efficient allocation and use of electrical resources to maintain a balance between supply and demand. Key participants in this market include generators, transmission companies, distribution companies, Load-Serving Entities (LSEs), and end users [1]. Price signals within the electricity market are essential, as they incentivize the optimal use and dispatch of electricity resources. The market operates through various segments, notably the day-ahead market, where electricity is traded a day in advance based on forecasts, and the real-time market, which addresses immediate imbalances in electricity demand and supply [2]. Moreover, intraday markets offer additional flexibility by allowing market participants to electricity closer to the time of delivery, further enhancing the market's ability to respond to unforeseen changes in demand or supply [3]. These mechanisms collectively contribute to the reliable and cost-effective delivery of electricity to consumers, facilitating the integration of renewable energy sources and supporting the overall stability of the power grid.

Electricity trading is a key strategy for achieving low-carbon transportation and offers additional benefits such as improving urban air quality and reducing environmental pressures [4]. This dual benefit motivates both national and local governments to take more decisive actions. In recent years, stronger environmental protection policies and significant reductions in technology costs have solidified commitments from governments and automakers toward the development of Electric Vehicles (EVs). These developments indicate that EVs are poised to become the mainstream choice for future transportation [5]. EV charging operators play a crucial role in the growing EV ecosystem, offering charging facilities and services that are vital for widespread EV adoption. As EV usage increases, these operators become key players in the electricity market. Beyond providing charging services, they actively participate in energy trading, mainly electricity trading, through the use of smart grid technologies [6]. EVs can function as mobile energy storage units, charging during periods of low electricity demand and prices and discharging back to the grid when demand and prices are high. This bidirectional energy flow helps optimize electricity distribution, enhance grid stability, and maximize economic benefits. The integration of vehicle-to-grid technology further enhances this capability by enabling more efficient energy management and supporting the overall stability and efficiency of smart grids [7].

Currently, power trading faces several key challenges that hinder its efficiency and reliability. First, there are inadequate incentive mechanisms in environments with incomplete information. Without proper incentives, market participants may be reluctant to provide reliable and accurate electricity resources, leading to inefficiencies. This issue is compounded by the lack of transparency and trust between stakeholders, which can further discourage active and honest participation in the market [8]. Secondly, the dynamic nature of the trading environment presents significant difficulties. Traditional methods often fail to achieve optimal trading strategies in real time due to rapid price fluctuations and the complex requirements of demand response. These methods are generally not equipped to handle the high volatility and the swift changes in supply and demand, which are characteristic of modern electricity markets. As a result, there is a pressing need for the development of more flexible and efficient technological solutions. Advanced approaches such as machine learning and Deep Reinforcement Learning (DRL), have shown promise in this regard. These technologies can adapt to changing market conditions and optimize trading strategies in real time, thereby ensuring more effective market operations [9,10].

The electricity market is essential for the optimal allocation of electrical resources, ensuring a balance between supply and demand. EV charging operators enhance this process by integrating smart grid technologies and actively participating in the electricity market, thereby promoting efficient electricity utilization. To overcome the challenges posed by incomplete information and dynamic trading environments, it is crucial to continuously innovate and improve market mechanisms and technological solutions [11]. These advancements are vital for maintaining the efficient operation of the electricity market and supporting the green transition of energy systems. In the context of emerging technologies and market dynamics, continuous innovation and the development of advanced market mechanisms are crucial. For instance, integrating Demand Response (DR) strategies and employing advanced algorithms, such as those based on game theory and DRL, can significantly enhance market efficiency and reliability. By leveraging these technologies, the market can better accommodate the variability of renewable energy sources and ensure a more resilient and adaptive power system.

Therefore, to address the challenge of ensuring that electricity markets provide real and reliable resources, we propose a Stackelberg game. This game-theoretic approach effectively structures interactions between market participants, promoting optimal decision making and efficient resource allocation. Furthermore, we integrate DRL with pruning techniques to solve the model efficiently. This combination enables dynamic adaptation to changing market conditions, significantly enhancing the security and efficiency of electricity resource provision. The main contributions of this paper are summarized as follows:

- We introduce a blockchain-assisted secure electricity trading framework that facilitates transactions between EV charging operators and the electricity market. Central to this framework is an aggregator that leverages blockchain technology to securely record

- To address the pricing challenges within the electricity market, we propose a single-leader, multi-follower Stackelberg model involving the electricity market and EV charging operators. Here, the electricity market assumes the role of the leader, establishing the selling price of electric energy units. EV charging operators, as followers, adjust their resource demand strategies based on the pricing set by the market leader. This model aims to optimize resource allocation and pricing decisions within the system.
- Recognizing the computational complexity associated with training traditional DRL models, we present a Tiny DRL algorithm that integrates pruning techniques with DRL methodologies. This novel approach enhances computational efficiency while aiming to achieve Stackelberg equilibrium. By combining pruning techniques with DRL, our algorithm efficiently navigates complex and dynamic environments, ultimately improving performance in reaching the desired equilibrium state.

The rest of this paper is organized as follows: Section 2 reviews the related work and introduces the combination of DRL with pruning techniques. In Section 3, we introduce the system model considering electricity trading between EV charging operators and the electricity market. In Section 4, we introduce the single-leader, multi-follower Stackelberg game model between EV charging operators and the electricity market in detail. In Section 5, we propose a Tiny DRL algorithm to find the Stackelberg equilibrium. The numerical results of the proposed scheme are shown in Section 6. Section 7 concludes the paper.

2. Related Work

In this section, we review several related works, with a focus on reliable energy trading in electricity markets. Ensuring reliable energy trading is crucial for maintaining grid stability and optimizing resource allocation. Therefore, compared to traditional schemes, blockchain technology is employed to enhance the security of transactions in this paper, safeguarding the integrity and transparency of the process. Furthermore, advanced DRL methods incorporating pruning techniques are utilized to optimize strategic bidding, energy trading, and load management. By removing less significant neurons or parameters from the network, these techniques enable more efficient decision making, leading to faster convergence and more robust learning outcomes.

2.1. Reliable Energy Trading in Electricity Markets

EVs possess dual attributes as both electrical loads and power sources. They play a crucial role in creating a safe, economical, and environmentally friendly intelligent power system. EVs significantly contribute to the solving of transportation, energy, and environmental challenges by reducing greenhouse gas emissions, enhancing energy efficiency, and supporting grid stability through the use of smart charging and vehicle-to-grid technologies [12]. Integrating EVs into smart grids and urban infrastructure not only mitigates pollution but also fosters the development of sustainable and resilient energy systems. Therefore, numerous scholars have undertaken extensive and in-depth research on the integration of EVs into the electricity market [13–16]. The authors of [13] proposed a joint demand response and energy trading model for electric vehicles in off-grid microgrid systems, optimizing transaction prices through a broker-led Stackelberg game approach. The results demonstrated that this model achieves up to 25.8% lower transaction prices compared to existing markets while maintaining high power reliability, showcasing its suitability for isolated microgrid environments. The authors of [14] presented a Peer-to-Peer (P2P) local electricity market model that integrates both energy and uncertainty trading to enhance the reliability of energy trading in electricity markets, particularly with the incorporation of EVs. The model significantly improves the local balancing of photovoltaic forecast errors by matching forecast power with time-flexible demand and uncertain power with power-flexible demand. The authors of [17] presented a data-driven probabilistic evaluation method for determining the hosting capacity of hydrogen fuel cell vehicles, incorporating a directional mapping approach, a probabilistic model considering high-dimensional uncertainties, and a cross-term decoupled polynomial chaos expansion for efficient computation. The authors of [15] introduced a decentralized Quality of Service (QoS)-based system for P2P energy trading among EVs, leveraging smart contracts to ensure reliable and resilient transactions without a third party. By employing QoS attributes and a fuzzy-based approach, the system effectively matches energy providers and consumers while implementing penalties to maintain contract integrity, thereby enhancing reliability in electricity markets. The authors of [18] presented a comprehensive analysis of the application and evolution of cooperative, non-cooperative, and evolutionary game theory within the electricity market. They examined the effects of these game theory models on the power generation, power sale, and power consumption sectors, with a particular focus on energy trading. Additionally, the study assessed the current status and scale of electricity markets, both domestically and internationally, providing insights and prospects for future research and the application of game theory in this domain.

2.2. Blockchain-Based Energy Trading in the Electricity Market

With the exponential increase in data volume and the inherent value of these data, transactions within the electricity market are encountering a critical demand for enhanced security measures [19–21]. For example, the authors of [22] presented FedPT-V2G, a federated transformer learning approach for real-time vehicle-to-grid dispatch that addresses non-IID data issues and data privacy concerns through the use of proximal algorithms and transformer models, achieving performance comparable to that of centralized learning in both balanced and imbalanced datasets. The adoption of blockchain technology also represents a viable solution for the establishment of trustworthiness and ensuring the continuity of secure transactions within the electricity market. By leveraging blockchain for secure storage and management, a decentralized system can be established that guarantees data integrity through encryption protocols, ensuring transparency and robust security throughout the entire process [23]. The authors of [19] reviewed the role of blockchain technology, combined with smart contracts, in facilitating peer-to-peer energy trading among prosumers, highlighting its potential to reshape the energy sector, the challenges it faces, emerging start-ups, and its application in EV charging. The authors of [20] proposed a novel blockchain-based distributed community energy trading mechanism designed to optimize energy trading efficiency and security in the context of shifting from consumers to producers. The authors of [21] pointed out that the security characteristics of blockchain technology can improve the efficiency of energy transactions and establish the basic stability and robustness of the energy market, e.g., the electricity market, and also reviewed the basic characteristics of blockchain and energy markets. In conclusion, the pivotal role of blockchain technology in energy trading, particularly electricity trading, is increasingly recognized by scholars, as evidenced by the growing body of research in this area. Therefore, in this paper, blockchain technology is utilized to enhance the security of the transaction process, underscoring its significance in ensuring the integrity and trustworthiness of energy transactions compared to current electricity trading methods.

2.3. Deep Reinforcement Learning with Pruning Techniques

DRL combines the advantages of deep learning and reinforcement learning, enabling the creation of algorithms that dynamically interact with and adapt to their environment. By employing privacy-preserving techniques, DRL algorithms iteratively learn and optimize decision making while safeguarding sensitive information. In the context of Stackelberg games, which involve leader–follower dynamics and strategic decision making, participants might be hesitant to disclose too much information due to competition or security concerns. DRL is essential for effectively reaching equilibrium solutions in such settings, as it allows agents to learn optimal strategies through interaction without requiring full disclosure of private information [24]. This capability is particularly beneficial in applications like security games, energy trading, and multi-agent systems, where balancing strategic advantage and information privacy is crucial [25].

However, training DRL models is resource-intensive in terms of computing power and storage. To address the need for more efficient DRL models in specific scenarios, researchers have increasingly adopted pruning techniques to optimize and enhance DRL performance [24,26–29]. For example, the authors of [29] introduced a novel multi-agent deep reinforcement learning method for urban distribution network reconfiguration, incorporating a "switch contribution" concept to reduce the action space, an improved QMIX algorithm for policy enhancement, and a two-stage learning structure with reward sharing to improve learning efficiency, which was validated through numerical results on a 297-node system. Pruning techniques are mainly divided into structured pruning and unstructured pruning [30]. Structured pruning involves the removal of entire components of a neural network, e.g., layers, neurons, or channels [24]. With the pruning of these larger structures, the shape of the model changes, leading to a more streamlined and often faster-to-execute network. Unstructured pruning, also known as magnitude pruning, targets individual parameters or weights within the neural network [30]. It removes weights that have the smallest magnitude, resulting in a sparse network. Pruning techniques have emerged as a promising approach to compress DRL models and improve algorithm efficiency, with an increasing amount of research focused on integrating pruning techniques with DRL. The authors of [26] proposed a novel model compression framework for DRL models using a sparse regularized pruning method and policy-shrinking technology, achieving a balance between high sparsity and compression rate. The authors of [27] proposed a compact DRL algorithm that leverages adaptive pruning and knowledge distillation to achieve high long-term transaction efficiency and lightweight routing for payment channel networks in resource-limited Internet of Things (IoT) devices. Simulation results show that the algorithm significantly outperforms baseline methods. The authors of [24] proposed a Tiny Multi-Agent DRL (Tiny MADRL) algorithm to facilitate the efficient migration of Unmanned Aerial Vehicle Twins (UTs) in Unmanned Aerial Vehicle (UAV) metaverses. By using pruning techniques, the algorithm reduces the network parameters and computational demands, optimizing Roadside Unit (RSU) selection and bandwidth allocation for seamless UT migration.

3. System Model

Decarbonizing transportation is crucial for climate change mitigation. With the increasing supply of renewable energy, governments are actively promoting the electrification of vehicle fleets [31]. Figure 1 shows the proposed blockchain-assisted secure electricity trading between EV charging operators and the electricity market with renewable energy sources. We provide more details of the system model as follows:

- **EV Charging Operator:** EV charging operators are responsible for managing and operating charging stations where EV owners can recharge their vehicles [32]. They ensure the availability, functionality, and efficiency of charging infrastructure. These charging operators purchase electricity from different kinds of electricity markets to supply their charging stations, maintaining a reliable energy source for EVs.
- **Aggregator:** Traditionally, the aggregator purchases time-varying electricity from the power grid and sells it to traditional users [33]. In this paper, we consider the aggregator responsible for managing electric energy trading between the EV charging operator and electricity markets. Specifically, the aggregator utilizes blockchain technology to securely record and verify energy trading transactions [34], which ensures the transparency, traceability, and efficiency of electric energy trading between the EV charging operator and electricity markets [34]. Note that the Practical Byzantine Fault Tolerance (PBFT) consensus algorithm is used in the blockchain system to achieve lightweight consensus. The incorporation of blockchain technology into energy trading enhances security, transparency, and traceability, surpassing the capabilities of traditional electricity market trading mechanisms [21]. This advancement empowers

EV charging operators to make well-informed and optimized operational decisions, thereby ensuring the efficiency and reliability of electric energy trading processes.
- **Electricity Markets:** Electricity market operators facilitate the buying and selling of electrical energy, with EV charging operators participating by purchasing the electricity needed to supply their stations. These markets—especially those incorporating renewable energy resources—regulate prices by continuously adjusting them based on the supply-and-demand dynamics of EV charging operators.

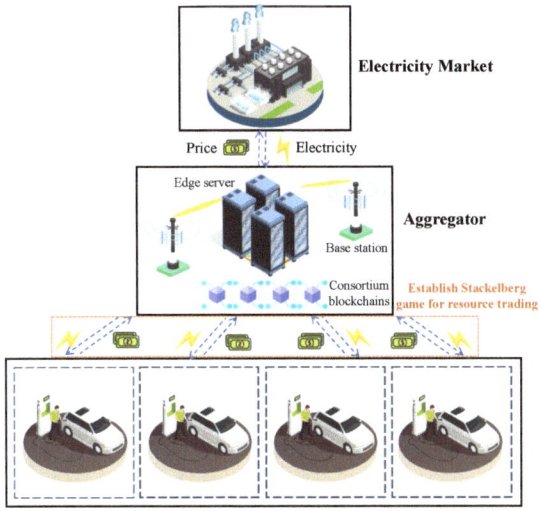

Figure 1. A blockchain-assisted secure electricity trading framework between EV charging operators and the electricity market.

4. Stackelberg Model for Electric Energy Trading

In this section, we consider that one electricity market and a set ($\mathcal{M} = \{1, \ldots, m, \ldots, M\}$) of M EV charging operators participate in electric energy trading.

During electric energy trading, the electricity market is the sole electricity resource, and EV charging operators rely on electricity resources provided by the electricity market to supply energy for EVs. Since electric energy trading between the electricity market and EV charging operators is an incomplete process [35], a monopoly market is formed [36]. Specifically, the electricity market operates as a monopoly with the authority to regulate electricity, while market supply and demand drive price adjustments. Electric vehicle charging operators must decide how much electricity to purchase based on the prevailing prices. If prices are low, EV charging operators may buy more energy to ensure a reliable supply for EVs. Conversely, high prices may discourage purchases. Therefore, balancing energy trading is crucial to maximizing the utility of the electricity market while maintaining its monopoly power.

The Stackelberg game, acting as an effective game-theoretical model, has been widely used to strategically regulate the price of oligopolies, which can be described as an oligopoly model [23,36]. The Stackelberg game has two stages, where the leader sets its strategy first, followed by the followers, who respond accordingly. We model this as a single-leader, multi-follower Stackelberg game between the electricity market and EV charging operators. In the first stage, the electricity market, as the leader, sets the selling price to maximize its utility. In the second stage, each EV charging operator, as a follower, determines its energy demand to maximize its utility. The Stackelberg game model is described in detail as follows.

4.1. Electric Energy Demands of EV Charging Operators in Stage II

We formulate the utility function of EV charging operators, which is the difference between the profit corresponding to the purchased electric energy and the cost of purchasing electric energy. Specifically, for EV charging operator m, we define E_m as the electric energy provided by the electricity market. The more electric energy obtained from the electricity market, the more profits that EV charging operators can obtain. Thus, motivated by [36], the profit of EV charging operator m can be defined as

$$\mathcal{G}_m(E_m) = \alpha_m \log(1 + E_m), \tag{1}$$

where α_m is the unit profit for the purchased electric energy of EV charging operator m. Thus, the utility function of EV charging operator m is given by

$$U_m(E_m) = \mathcal{G}_m(E_m) - P \cdot E_m, \tag{2}$$

where $P > 0$ is the unit selling price of electric energy. In Stage II, each EV charging operator (m) aims to maximize its utility $U_m(E_m)$ by deciding the optimal electric energy demand to purchase. Therefore, the optimization problem that maximizes the utility of EV charging operator m is formulated as

$$\begin{aligned}\textbf{P1:} \max_{E_m}\ & U_m(E_m) \\ \text{s.t.}\ & E_m > 0.\end{aligned} \tag{3}$$

4.2. Selling Price of the Electricity Market in Stage I

The electricity market, as the energy provider, ensures that its energy allocation meets the demands of EV charging operators while maximizing its utility [23]. To achieve this, it formulates a dynamic pricing strategy, adjusting based on the energy demands of the EV charging operators. The utility of the electricity market is the difference between the total charges paid by EV charging operators and the cost of energy harvesting and transmission. Thus, the utility of the electricity market is expressed as

$$U_e(p) = \sum_{m=1}^{M} (P \cdot E_m - C \cdot E_m), \tag{4}$$

where $C > 0$ is the unit cost of supplying electric energy to EV charging operators. From (4), we know that the electricity market can obtain profits by providing electric energy to EV charging operators but needs to pay the costs of supplying electric energy. Considering that the renewable energy harvested by the electricity market is not unlimited, the energy sold by the electricity market has an upper limit of E_{max}, and the energy price also has an upper limit of P_{max}. The electricity market aims to maximize its utility by deciding a selling price under the constraints that the total electric energy sales do not exceed E_{max} and the energy price does not exceed P_{max}. Hence, the optimization problem of maximizing the utility of the electricity market is given by

$$\begin{aligned}\textbf{P2:} \max_{P}\ & U_e(p) = \sum_{m=1}^{M} (P \cdot E_m - C \cdot E_m) \\ \text{s.t.}\ & 0 < \sum_{m=1}^{M} E_m \leq E_{max}, \\ & E_m > 0,\ \forall m \in \{1,\ldots,M\}, \\ & 0 < C \leq P \leq p_{max}.\end{aligned} \tag{5}$$

Note that no EV charging operator would buy electric energy from the electricity market if the selling price of unit electric energy were to exceed P_{max}. Finally, we formulate the Stackelberg game based on (3) and (5).

4.3. Stackelberg Equilibrium Analysis

In this part, we seek the Stackelberg equilibrium to find the optimal solution for the game. This equilibrium ensures that the electricity market maximizes its utility, while EV charging operators can design energy request policies based on their best response. Both parties maximize their utility by adjusting strategies until they reach equilibrium [23]. The Stackelberg equilibrium is defined as follows:

Definition 1 (Stackelberg Equilibrium). *We denote $E^* = \{E_m^*\}$, $m \in \mathcal{M}$ and P^* as the optimal electric energy demands of EV charging operators and the optimal energy pricing of the electricity market, respectively. The strategy (E^*, P^*) can be the Stackelberg equilibrium if and only if the following set of inequalities is strictly satisfied [23,36]:*

$$\begin{cases} U_e(P^*, E^*) \geq U_e(P, E^*), \\ U_m(E_m^*, E_{-m}^*, P^*) \geq U_m(E_m, E_{-m}^*, P^*), \forall m \in \mathcal{M}. \end{cases} \quad (6)$$

In the following, we utilize the backward induction method to analyze the Stackelberg equilibrium [23,36].

4.3.1. EV Charging Operators' Optimal Strategies as Equilibrium in Stage II

In the Stackelberg game, EV charging operators act as followers, which determine the optimal strategies of electric energy demands based on the selling price of a unit of electric energy (P), thereby maximizing their profits.

Theorem 1. *The perfect equilibrium in the EV charging operators' subgame is unique.*

Proof. We derive the first-order derivative and the second-order derivative of $U_m(E_m)$ with respect to E_m as follows:

$$\begin{aligned} \frac{\partial U_m(E_m)}{\partial E_m} &= \frac{\alpha_m}{1 + E_m} - P, \\ \frac{\partial^2 U_n(b_n)}{\partial b_n^2} &= -\frac{\alpha_m}{(1 + E_m)^2} < 0. \end{aligned} \quad (7)$$

Since the first-order derivative of $U_m(E_m)$ has a unique zero point and the second-order derivative of $U_m(E_m)$ is negative, the utility function ($U_m(E_m)$) of EV charging operators is strictly concave with respect to the electric energy demand strategy (E_m) of EV charging operators. Based on the first-order optimality condition, i.e., $\frac{\partial U_m(E_m)}{\partial E_m} = 0$, we can obtain the best response function (E_m^*) of EV charging operator m, which is given by

$$E_m^* = \frac{\alpha_m}{P} - 1. \quad (8)$$

Therefore, perfect equilibrium in the subgame of EV charging operators is unique. □

4.3.2. The Electricity Market's Optimal Strategy as Equilibrium in Stage I

In this part, we focus on studying the concavity of the utility function of the electricity market, proving the existence and uniqueness of the Stackelberg equilibrium. In Stage I, the electricity market acts as the leader in maximizing its utility by predicting the strategies of EV charging operators.

Theorem 2. *The uniqueness of the Stackelberg equilibrium (E^*, P^*) can be guaranteed in the formulated Stackelberg game.*

Proof. According to Theorem 1, there exists a unique Nash equilibrium among EV charging operators under any given value of P. Thus, the electricity market can maximize its utility by choosing the optimal value of P. Based on the optimal electric energy demand strategies of EV charging operators, the utility function of the electricity is given by

$$U_e(P) = \sum_{m=1}^{M} (P - C)\left(\frac{\alpha_m}{P} - 1\right). \tag{9}$$

By taking the first-order derivative and the second-order derivative of $U_e(P)$ with respect to P, we can obtain

$$\frac{\partial U_e(P)}{\partial P} = \sum_{m=1}^{M} \left(\frac{\alpha_m C}{P^2} - 1\right),$$
$$\frac{\partial^2 U_e(P)}{\partial^2 P} = \sum_{m=1}^{M} -\frac{2\alpha_m C}{P^3} < 0. \tag{10}$$

Since the first-order derivative of $U_e(P)$ has a unique zero point, we can obtain $P^* = \sqrt{\frac{C\sum_{m=1}^{M}\alpha_m}{M}}$, and the second-order derivative of $U_e(P)$ is negative, so $U_e(P)$ is also strictly concave, which indicates that the electricity market has a unique optimal solution to the formulated game [36]. Based on the optimal strategy of the electricity market, the optimal strategies of EV charging operators can be obtained [37]. Therefore, the uniqueness of the Stackelberg game's equilibrium is proven. □

Due to the dynamic nature of the environment of energy trading between the electricity market and EV charging operators [38], traditional methods may be difficult to adapt to the dynamics of energy trading and not be able to efficiently find the Stackelberg equilibrium. Since DRL agents can learn to adapt their behavior based on environmental dynamics [39], we utilize a DRL algorithm to find the Stackelberg equilibrium. Furthermore, we innovatively add dynamic structured pruning techniques to the DRL algorithm for efficient implementation in energy trading.

5. Tiny Deep Reinforcement Learning for an Optimal Pricing Strategy

In intricate decision-making contexts, sophisticated AI methodologies such as DRL [40,41] represent promising approaches for the development of incentive mechanisms while addressing privacy concerns [42,43]. In this section, we model the formulated Stackelberg game between the electricity market and EV charging operators as a Partially Observable Markov Decision Process (POMDP) [36,44]. To address the challenge posed by incomplete information and enhance the efficiency of finding the Stackelberg equilibrium, we propose a Tiny DRL algorithm. The Tiny DRL algorithm is designed to find the Stackelberg equilibrium by identifying the optimal solutions of the Stackelberg game, enabling the electricity market to quickly converge to near-optimal decisions. Unlike traditional DRL approaches that focus on estimating fixed policies or single-step models, the proposed method leverages Markov properties to effectively decompose the problem.

5.1. POMDP for the Stackelberg Game between the Electricity Market and EV Charging Operators

Because of the effect of the competition between the electricity market and EV charging operators, each EV charging operator has local incomplete information in the Stackelberg game and determines electric energy strategies in a completely non-cooperative manner. The energy trading environment following a POMDP is needed to train the DRL agent, which is formulated by conceptualizing the dynamic relationship between the electricity market and EV charging operators as a Stackelberg game. Let $\mathcal{F} = \{\mathcal{S}, \mathcal{O}, \mathcal{A}, \mathcal{R}, \gamma\}$ represent a POMDP [45], where $\mathcal{S}$, $\mathcal{O}$, $\mathcal{A}$, $\mathcal{R}$, and γ represent the state space, partially observable policy, action space, reward function, and discounted factor for the electricity market, respectively [36,45].

In each time step (t, where $t \in \mathcal{T} = \{0, \ldots, t, \ldots, T\}$), the electricity market interacts with the environment to determine its current state, which is denoted as $S(t)$. During the training process, the electricity market, acting as the DRL agent, engages in interactions with the environment. At each time step, when the electricity market executes an action ($P(t)$) according to the current state ($S(t)$), the environment provides an immediate reward

($R(t)$) [46]. In the realm of electric energy trading, the electricity market functions as a game leader, responsible for selecting the action, i.e., the pricing policy ($P(t)$). After that, EV charging operators, acting as followers, identify an optimal strategic decision based on (8). Following this, the environment provides a reward ($R(t)$) to the electricity market by considering the strategies decided by all EV charging operators. The system contains a finite relay buffer, denoted as $\mathcal{D}$, which can store historical operation data, and the capacity of the finite relay buffer is defined as D. Relevant data of the electricity market can be extracted from the relay buffer to create new states, triggering the subsequent time step [24].

5.1.1. State Space

In each time step ($t \in \mathcal{T} = \{0, \ldots, t, \ldots, T\}$), the state space is defined as a union of the current pricing strategy of the electricity market and the electric energy demand strategies of EV charging operators, which is denoted as

$$S(t) \triangleq \{P(t), E(t)\}, \tag{11}$$

where $P(t)$ and $E(t)$ are the price of the electricity market and the electric energy demand vector of EV charging operators at time step t, respectively.

5.1.2. Partially Observable Policy

We formulate the partially observable space for energy trading between the electricity market and EV charging operators, tackling the non-stationary problem in the DRL system. Throughout the POMDP, the electricity market agent can solely base decisions on local environmental observations. We define the observation space of the electricity market in at time step t as $O(t)$, which is a union of its historical pricing strategies and the electric energy demand strategies of EV charging operators for the previous L games involving the electricity market and all EV charging operators. Consequently, the observation space ($O(t)$) of the electricity market at time step t is represented as

$$O(t) \triangleq \{P(t-L), E(t-L), P(t-L+1), E(t-L+1), \ldots, P(t-1), E(t-1)\}, \tag{12}$$

where $P(t-L)$ and $E(t-L)$ can be generated randomly during the initial stage when $t < L$. By considering historical information, the electricity market agent can learn how changes in its strategy impact the game result in the current time slot [36]. When receiving an observation ($O(t)$) from the environment, the electricity market agent needs to design the selling price ($P(t)$) of electric energy to maximize its utility.

5.1.3. Action Space

$\mathcal{A} \triangleq \{P\}$ denotes the action space of the electricity market. Given the lower-bound cost (C) and the upper-bound price (P_{max}) for the pricing action, the electricity market decides its action ($P(t)$) at each time step (t), where $P(t) \in [C, P_{max}]$. This decision-making process relies on the information encapsulated in the observation space ($O(t)$).

5.1.4. Reward Function

$\mathcal{R} \triangleq \{R\}$ denotes the reward function of the electricity market. Following the state transition, the electricity market can acquire an immediate reward based on the current state ($S(t)$) and the corresponding action ($P(t)$) [36]. The reward function is defined as the utility function of the electricity market that we construct in the Stackelberg game. At time step t, the reward function for the electricity market is represented as $R(t) = U_e(t)$.

In the actor–critic network framework, the system consists of two crucial elements, i.e., the actor network and the critic network [24]. Proximal Policy Optimization (PPO) is a DRL algorithm based on policy gradients [47]. By employing proximal optimization techniques on the policy, the stability and convergence of agent learning can be enhanced, ensuring more reliable and efficient learning processes. In the proposed tiny DRL framework, we denote the actor–critic network as (θ, ω). Note that the actor and critic networks are all neural networks. The actor network essentially functions as a policy function ($\pi_\theta(P|S)$) with parameters (θ), which helps to generate the action of the electricity market, namely the pricing strategy (P), and facilitate interactions with the environment. Conversely, the critic network, characterized by the value function ($V_\omega(S)$) parameterized by ω, evaluates the performance of the electricity market agent and guides the actions of the agent in subsequent phases, which is defined as

$$V_\omega(S) \triangleq \hat{\mathbb{E}}_{\pi_\theta}\left[\sum_{t=0}^{T} \gamma^t R(S(t), P(t)) \mid S_0 = S\right], \tag{13}$$

where $\hat{\mathbb{E}}_{\pi_\theta}(\cdot)$ is the expected value of a random variable, given that the electricity market agent follows the policy (π_θ).

The primary objective of the critic network is to minimize the Temporal Difference (TD) error, which is expressed as

$$d = R(t) + \gamma V_\omega(S(t+1)) - V_\omega(S(t)), \tag{14}$$

where $V_\omega(S(t))$ and $V_\omega(S(t+1))$ represent the value functions associated with the current state ($S(t)$) and the subsequent state ($S(t+1)$), respectively. Therefore, the loss function of the critic network is derived by minimizing the expected value of the squared temporal difference (TD) value, which is given by [27]

$$\min_{\omega} L_c(\omega) = \min_{\omega} \mathbb{E}\big[(R(t) + \gamma V_\omega(S(t+1)) \\ - V_\omega(S(t)))^2\big]. \tag{15}$$

Furthermore, the objective of the actor network is specifically defined as

$$\max_{\theta} J_a(\theta) = \max_{\theta} \mathbb{E}\big[\min\big(\zeta(\theta)\hat{A}_{\pi_\theta}(S, P), \\ I(\iota, \zeta(\theta))\hat{A}_{\pi_\theta}(S, P)\big)\big], \tag{16}$$

where $\zeta(\theta) = \frac{\pi_\theta(P|S)}{\pi_{\hat{\theta}}(P|S)}$ represents the important ratio between the old policy and the new policy, $\hat{\theta}$ represents the parameters of the strategy used for sampling (P), and $\pi_{\hat{\theta}}(P|S)$ denotes the policy employed for importance sampling [48]. $I(\iota, \zeta(\theta))$ is a piece-wise function with intervals, which is given by [48]

$$I(\iota, \zeta(\theta)) = \begin{cases} 1 + \iota, & \zeta(\theta) > 1 + \iota, \\ \zeta(\theta), & 1 - \iota \leq \zeta(\theta) \leq 1 + \iota, \\ 1 - \iota, & \zeta(\theta) < 1 - \iota, \end{cases} \tag{17}$$

where ι represents an adjustable hyper-parameter. $\hat{A}_{\pi_\theta}(S, P)$ denotes the estimator for the advantage function that utilizes $V_\omega(S)$, which is expressed as

$$\hat{A}_{\pi_\theta}(S(t), P(t)) = \gamma^{T-t} V_\omega(S(T)) - V_\omega(S(t)) \\ + \sum_{x=t}^{T-1} \gamma^{x-t} R(S(x), P(x)), \tag{18}$$

5.2. Dynamic Structured Pruning

In the DRL algorithm, the actor and critic networks are essentially deep neural networks [49], which typically consist of an input layer, multiple hidden layers, and an output layer [24]. These layers have numerous parameters, like neurons and weights. Without loss of generality, we consider an actor network with K layers and denote the weights in the

k-th fully connected layer as $\theta^{(k)}$, where $k \in \{1,\ldots,K\}$. By inputting the state ($S(t)$) at time step t into the first layer, the output of the first layer is calculated as

$$h^{(1)} = \sigma^{(1)}\big(\theta^{(1)}S(t) + b^{(1)}\big), \tag{19}$$

where $\sigma^{j(1)}$ represents the nonlinear response of the first layer, which is typically set to the ReLU function, and $b^{(1)}$ is the deviation at the h-th layer. The output of each layer in the network is fed to the subsequent laye ras the input. Therefore, the output of the k-th layer is expressed as

$$h^{(k)} = \sigma^{(k)}\big(\theta^{(k)}h^{(k-1)} + b^{(k)}\big). \tag{20}$$

Finally, at time step t, the actor network outputs the action, i.e., the price strategy ($P(t)$), which is expressed as

$$P(t) = \sigma^{(K)}\big(\theta^{(K)}h^{(K-1)}\big). \tag{21}$$

To achieve the Tiny DRL algorithm, we incorporate dynamic structured pruning techniques into the actor network. This helps eliminate neurons and weights that do not significantly contribute to the performance of the actor network [49]. Unlike unstructured pruning techniques for the acceleration of DRL training, which often results in irregular network structures [24], structured pruning is a technique used to reduce model complexity by strategically eliminating redundant neurons or connections [50].

To indicate the pruning status of neurons, a binary mask ($m^{(k)}$) is employed. Specifically, we denote $m_i^{(k)} = 1$ as a non-pruning neuron ($o_i^{(k)}$) and $m_i^{(k)} = 0$ as a pruning neuron ($o_i^{(k)}$)[24]. Thus, the action output from the actor network is expressed as

$$P(t) = \sigma^{(H)}\big(\theta^{(H)}h^{(H-1)} \odot m^{(H)}\big), \tag{22}$$

where $\odot$ denotes the element-wise multiplication of two matrices. Based on the above analysis, the loss function of the actor network is rewritten as [24,50]

$$J_a(\theta,m) = \mathbb{E}\big[\min\big(\zeta(\theta,m)\hat{A}_{\pi_\theta}(S,P), \\ I(\iota,\zeta(\theta,m))\hat{A}_{\pi_\theta}(S,P)\big)\big]. \tag{23}$$

As D records accumulate in the replay buffer, the actor and critic networks are updated. Specifically, the electricity market updates the parameters of the actor network by using the gradient ascent method, which is given by

$$\theta^{(k)\prime} = \theta^{(k)} - \varepsilon \frac{\partial J_a(\theta,m)}{\partial\big(h^{(k)} \odot m^{(k)}\big)} \cdot \frac{\partial\big(h^{(k)} \odot m^{(k)}\big)}{\partial \theta^{(k)}}, \tag{24}$$

where ε represents the learning rate employed in the training process of the actor network and $\theta^{(k)\prime}$ represents the updated parameters of the actor network. The parameters of the critic network are updated through the gradient descent method as follows [24,50]:

$$\omega^{(k)\prime} = \omega^{(k)} - \epsilon \frac{\partial L_c(\omega)}{\partial \omega^{(k)}}, \tag{25}$$

where ϵ represents the learning rate employed in the training process of the critic network and $\omega^{(h)\prime}$ represents the updated parameters of the critic network.

The dynamic structured pruning of non-essential neurons consists of two key steps, namely, determining the pruning threshold and updating the binary mask used for pruning [24,50]. The pruning threshold plays a crucial role in identifying and eliminating unnecessary parameters or connections during the pruning process. Motivated by [24,50], we formulate a dynamic pruning threshold, which is given by

$$\chi(t) = \sum_{n=1}^{N} \sum_{k=1}^{K} \rho_n^{(k)} \cdot \tau(t), \qquad (26)$$

$$\tau(t) = \check{\tau} + (\hat{\tau} - \check{\tau})\left(1 - \frac{t}{Y \triangle t}\right)^3, \qquad (27)$$

where $\rho_n^{(k)}$ and K represent the neuronal importance of the n-th neuron of layer k and the total number of pruning steps, respectively. $\triangle$ represents the pruning frequency. $\tau(t)$, $\hat{\tau}$, and $\check{\tau}$ represent the current sparsity in epoch t, the initial sparsity, and the target sparsity, respectively. This dynamic pruning method can adaptively enhance the sparsity of the model as the iteration goes on, providing a more refined and effective method for structured pruning. Neurons are ranked according to their importance, from least to most important. Neurons whose ranks are below a set threshold are then pruned to improve the overall sparsity of the model. The mask of the n-th neuron of layer k is updated as

$$m_n^{(k)} = \begin{cases} 1, & \text{if abs}\left[m_n^{(k)}, \theta_n^{(k)}\right] \geq \psi, \\ 0, & \text{otherwise.} \end{cases} \qquad (28)$$

The above process of dynamic structured pruning is shown in Algorithm 1. In the Tiny DRL model, we adopt a fully connected deep neural network architecture for the actor network, which consists of K layers. Algorithm 1 consists of a two-step process, namely, initially training the DRL model, then using a dynamic pruning threshold to remove unimportant neurons. Note that the complexity of Algorithm 1 over T episodes is $\mathcal{O}(T|S|) + \mathcal{O}\left(T \sum_{k=1}^{K-1} u^{(h)}\right)$, where $u^{(h)}$ is the number of neurons in each hidden layer (k) up to the penultimate layer [24,50].

Algorithm 1: Tiny DRL algorithm with dynamic structured pruning for Stackelberg equilibrium.

Input: State S.
Output: The optimal strategy (E^*, P^*).
1 Initialize tiny DRL model, training episodes T, reward R, batch size B, binary mask m, and replay buffer $\mathcal{D}$.
2 **for** time step $t = 1$ to T **do**
3   ## *Interacting with environment*
4   the electricity market observes a state $S(t)$ and updates its observation $O(t-1)$ into $O(t)$.
5   Input $O(t)$ into the actor policy π_θ and determine the current price strategy $P(t)$.
6   EV charging operators make bandwidth demand decisions based on (8).
7   Update $S(t)$ into $S(t+1)$.
8   Calculate reward $R(t)$ for the electricity market.
9   Update $U_{best}(t)$ when a higher reward is obtained.
10   Store transition $(O(t), P(t), R(t), O(t+1))$ into $\mathcal{D}$.
11   **if** $t\%|B| == 0$ **then**
12   **for** $x \in 1, \ldots, X$ **do**
13   Sample a random mini-batch of data with a size $|B|$ from $\mathcal{D}$.
14   **end**
15   **end**
16   ## *Dynamic structured pruning*
17   Compute neuron importance $\rho_n^{(k)}$.
18   Update actor network parameters $\theta^{(k)}$ and critic network parameters $\omega^{(k)}$ by (24) and (25), respectively.
19   Compute dynamic pruning threshold $\chi^{(k)}$ by (26).
20   Update binary mask $m^{(k)}$ by (28).
21   **if** $\rho_n^{(k)} < \chi(t)$ **then**
22   Remove n-th neuron in k-layer and associated parameters θ from the actor network.
23   **end**
24 **end**
25 Reconstruct the compact tiny DRL model $(\theta, \omega)^{(K)}$.
26 **return** (E^*, P^*).

6. Numerical Results

In this section, we present numerical results to demonstrate the effectiveness of the proposed tiny DRL algorithm and analyze the proposed Stackelberg game model.

Figure 2 presents a performance comparison between the proposed Tiny PPO algorithm and the PPO algorithm. We set the pruning rate, the learning rate of the actor and critic networks, the discount factor, the training epoch, and the batch size as 0.05, 1×10^{-4}, 0.95, 400, and 512, respectively. From Figure 2, we can observe that the proposed Tiny PPO algorithm is more stable than the PPO algorithm and can obtain more test rewards. The Tiny PPO algorithm can also promote higher utility of the electricity market and sum utilities of all EV charging operators, demonstrating the superior performance of the proposed Tiny PPO algorithm.

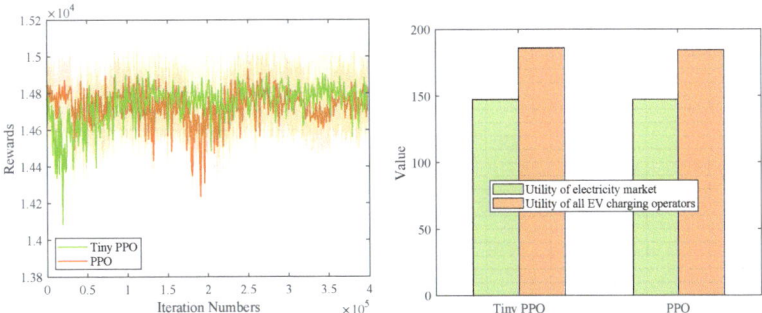

Figure 2. Performance comparison between the proposed Tiny PPO algorithm and the PPO algorithm.

Figure 3 shows the utilities and optimal strategies of the electricity market and EV charging operators under different costs (C), with $M = 5$ corresponding to the number of EV charging operators and a unit profit of $\alpha = 50$. From Figure 3, we can observe that as the unit cost (C) increases, the selling price of a unit of electric energy (P) set by the electricity market also rises. Concurrently, the electric energy demands (E_m) determined by the EV charging operators decrease. The underlying reason for this trend is that an increase in the unit cost (C) compels the electricity market to raise prices to maintain stable and increasing profits. Then, this price hike discourages EV charging operators from purchasing large amounts of electricity, leading to a reduction in electric energy demands. Moreover, the utilities of the electricity market and EV charging operators decrease as the unit cost (C) increases. That is because the electric energy demands of EV charging operators decrease, while the selling price of a unit of electric energy (P) increases. Specifically, the reduction in electric energy demand has a more substantial negative impact on the utility of the electricity market than the positive impact of the increased selling price, resulting in a net decrease in the utility of the electricity market. Similarly, for EV charging operators, the adverse effect of a higher selling price per unit of electric energy outweighs the effect of reduced electric energy demands, leading to a decrease in their utility as well.

Figure 4 illustrates the utilities and strategies of the electricity market and EV charging operators under different numbers of EV charging operators, with a unit cost of $C = 5$ and unit profit of $\alpha = 50$. From Figure 4, it is evident that the electric energy demands increase as the number of EV charging operators (M) rises, while the selling price of a unit of electric energy (P) remains stable, regardless of changes in the number of EV charging operators. According to the the equation $P^* = \sqrt{\frac{C\sum_{m=1}^{M} \alpha_m}{M}}$, since C and α are constant, P does not change. Specifically, the stability of the selling price (P) amidst increasing demand can be attributed to the constancy of the unit cost (C) and unit profit (α), ensuring that the price equilibrium is maintained. Additionally, we can observe that the utilities of both the electricity market and the EV charging operators increase as the number of EV charging operators grows. This is because the increased energy demands of EV charging operators positively impact the utilities of both the electricity market and the EV charging operators.

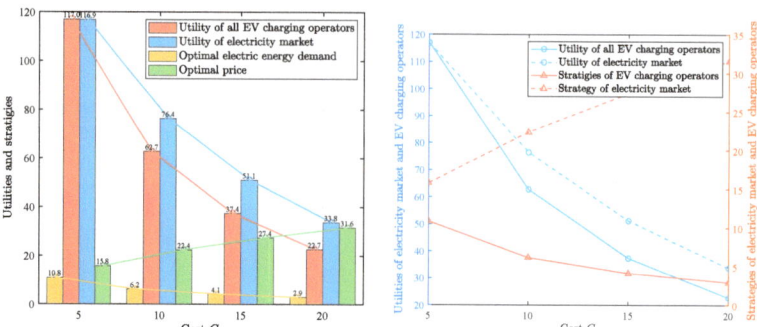

Figure 3. Utilities and strategies of the electricity market and EVs under different costs, with $M = 5$ corresponding to the number of EV charging operators and a unit profit of $\alpha = 50$.

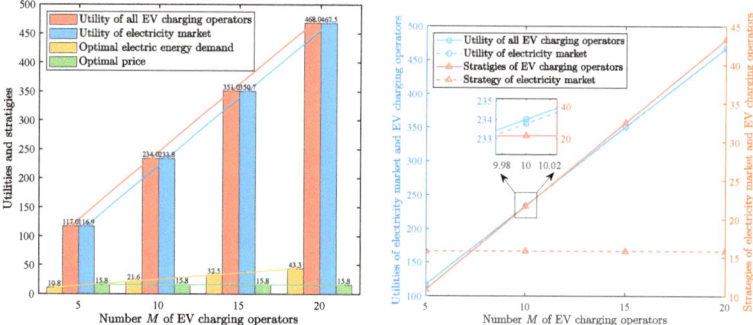

Figure 4. Utilities and strategies of the electricity market and EV charging operators under different numbers of EV charging operators with cost of $C = 5$ and unit profit of $\alpha = 50$.

Figure 5 shows the utilities and strategies of the electricity market and EV charging operators under different unit profits (α), with $M = 5$ corresponding to the number of EV charging operators and a cost of $C = 5$. It is observed that as the unit profit (α) increases, both the electric energy demands and the selling price per unit of electric energy rise. This is because a higher unit profit (α) incentivizes EV charging operators to purchase more electricity resources. The increased demand for electric energy enables the electricity market to set higher prices to maximize its profit. Furthermore, we can observe that the utilities of the electricity market and EV charging operators increase as the unit profit (α) increases. It is obvious that the simultaneous growth in selling price and electric energy demands boosts the utility of the electricity market. For EV charging operators, the increase in utility may be attributed to the fact that the positive impact of higher electric energy demands outweighs the negative impact of rising selling prices.

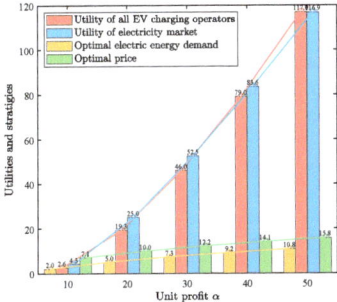
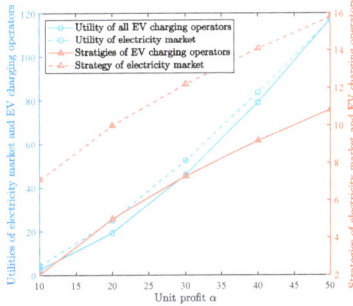

Figure 5. Utilities and strategies of the electricity market and EV charging operators under different unit profits (α), with $M = 5$ corresponding to the number of EV charging operators and cost of $C = 5$.

Figure 6 shows the security performance of the PBFT consensus algorithm in the proposed blockchain system for electricity trading. From Figure 6, we can see that regardless of the probability of a delegate being malicious, p_m exists, and the security probability increases as the number of miners increases. The PBFT algorithm relies on a majority consensus, requiring more than half of the nodes to agree. Therefore, as the number of miners increases, the proportion of honest nodes involved in the consensus process also grows, which enhances the overall robustness of the system, making it increasingly difficult for malicious attackers to compromise its integrity [51]. Therefore, the proposed blockchain system utilizing the PBFT consensus algorithm ensures reliable and secure electricity trading by guaranteeing trustworthy block verification.

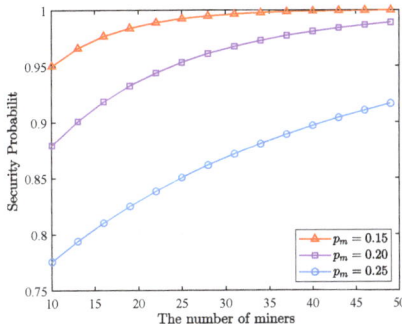

Figure 6. Security probability under different numbers of miners.

7. Conclusions

In this paper, we proposed a blockchain-assisted secure energy trading framework. Specifically, we utilized blockchain technology to securely manage energy trading between the electricity market and EV charging operators. Then, we proposed a single-leader, multi-follower Stackelberg game model to address the electricity trading problem between the electricity market and EV charging operators. In this model, the electricity market acts as the leader, setting the price of a unit of electric energy. The EV charging operators, as followers, determine their electricity demand based on the price set by the electricity market. During the trading process, blockchain technology is utilized by EV charging aggregators to securely record and verify energy transactions. To find the Stackelberg equilibrium, we employed a DRL algorithm. Given the resource-intensive nature of training DRL models, we introduced pruning techniques into the DRL framework, referred to as Tiny DRL, to enhance the efficiency of the algorithm in terms of computing power and storage requirements. In future work, we will consider formulating a multi-leader, multi-follower Stackelberg game between electricity markets and EV charging operators. Our focus will be on enhancing the verification of our model through rigorous testing and validation procedures. Furthermore, we will aim to enhance consensus mechanisms, optimize smart contract functionalities, and explore interoperability with other blockchain networks to improve security, scalability, and efficiency within the energy trading ecosystem.

Author Contributions: Conceptualization, Y.X.; Methodology, Y.L.; Software, F.Z.; Validation, X.L.; Formal analysis, J.T.; Investigation, B.Q.; Resources, F.Z.; Data curation, X.L.; Writing—original draft preparation, X.L.; Writing—review and editing, X.L.; Visualization, F.Z.; Supervision, Y.G.; Project administration, Y.X.; Funding acquisition, Y.L. All authors have read and agreed to the published version of the manuscript.

Funding: This work was financially supported by the Major Science and Technology Project of China Southern Power Grid Co., Ltd. (ZBKJXM20232456).

Data Availability Statement: All data underlying the results are available as part of the article and no additional source data are required.

Conflicts of Interest: Author Yiyong Lei and Yanzhang Gu were employed by the company China Southern Power Grid Co., Ltd. The remaining authors declare that the research was conducted in the absence of any commercial or financial relationships that could be construed as a potential conflict of interest.

References

1. Liu, P.; Ding, T.; Zou, Z.; Yang, Y. Integrated demand response for a load serving entity in multi-energy market considering network constraints. *Appl. Energy* **2019**, *250*, 512–529. [CrossRef]
2. Krishnamurthy, D.; Uckun, C.; Zhou, Z.; Thimmapuram, P.R.; Botterud, A. Energy storage arbitrage under day-ahead and real-time price uncertainty. *IEEE Trans. Power Syst.* **2017**, *33*, 84–93. [CrossRef]
3. Shah, D.; Chatterjee, S. A comprehensive review on day-ahead electricity market and important features of world's major electric power exchanges. *Int. Trans. Electr. Energy Syst.* **2020**, *30*, e12360. [CrossRef]
4. Xie, D.; Gou, Z.; Gui, X. How electric vehicles benefit urban air quality improvement: A study in Wuhan. *Sci. Total Environ.* **2024**, *906*, 167584. [CrossRef] [PubMed]
5. LaMonaca, S.; Ryan, L. The state of play in electric vehicle charging services–A review of infrastructure provision, players, and policies. *Renew. Sustain. Energy Rev.* **2022**, *154*, 111733. [CrossRef]
6. Sultan, V.; Aryal, A.; Chang, H.; Kral, J. Integration of EVs into the smart grid: A systematic literature review. *Energy Inform.* **2022**, *5*, 65. [CrossRef]
7. Sovacool, B.K.; Kester, J.; Noel, L.; de Rubens, G.Z. Actors, business models, and innovation activity systems for vehicle-to-grid (V2G) technology: A comprehensive review. *Renew. Sustain. Energy Rev.* **2020**, *131*, 109963. [CrossRef]
8. Silva, C.; Faria, P.; Vale, Z.; Corchado, J. Demand response performance and uncertainty: A systematic literature review. *Energy Strategy Rev.* **2022**, *41*, 100857. [CrossRef]
9. Motalleb, M.; Annaswamy, A.; Ghorbani, R. A real-time demand response market through a repeated incomplete-information game. *Energy* **2018**, *143*, 424–438. [CrossRef]
10. Wen, J.; Nie, J.; Kang, J.; Niyato, D.; Du, H.; Zhang, Y.; Guizani, M. From generative ai to generative internet of things: Fundamentals, framework, and outlooks. *IEEE Internet Things Mag.* **2024**, *7*, 30–37. [CrossRef]
11. Parker, G.G.; Tan, B.; Kazan, O. Electric power industry: Operational and public policy challenges and opportunities. *Prod. Oper. Manag.* **2019**, *28*, 2738–2777. [CrossRef]
12. Rauf, M.; Kumar, L.; Zulkifli, S.A.; Jamil, A. Aspects of artificial intelligence in future electric vehicle technology for sustainable environmental impact. *Environ. Chall.* **2024**, *14*, 100854. [CrossRef]
13. Kim, J.; Lee, J.; Choi, J.K. Joint demand response and energy trading for electric vehicles in off-grid system. *IEEE Access* **2020**, *8*, 130576–130587. [CrossRef]
14. Zhang, Z.; Li, R.; Li, F. A novel peer-to-peer local electricity market for joint trading of energy and uncertainty. *IEEE Trans. Smart Grid* **2019**, *11*, 1205–1215. [CrossRef]
15. Al-Obaidi, A.A.; Farag, H.E. Decentralized quality of service based system for energy trading among electric vehicles. *IEEE Trans. Intell. Transp. Syst.* **2021**, *23*, 6586–6595. [CrossRef]
16. Salmani, H.; Rezazadeh, A.; Sedighizadeh, M. Robust stochastic blockchain model for peer-to-peer energy trading among charging stations of electric vehicles. *J. Oper. Autom. Power Eng.* **2024**, *12*, 54–68.
17. Xia, W.; Ren, Z.; Li, H.; Pan, Z. A data-driven probabilistic evaluation method of hydrogen fuel cell vehicles hosting capacity for integrated hydrogen-electricity network. *Appl. Energy* **2024**, *376*, 123895. [CrossRef]

18. Huang, W.; Li, H. Game theory applications in the electricity market and renewable energy trading: A critical survey. *Front. Energy Res.* **2022**, *10*, 1009217. [CrossRef]
19. Thukral, M.K. Emergence of blockchain-technology application in peer-to-peer electrical-energy trading: A review. *Clean Energy* **2021**, *5*, 104–123. [CrossRef]
20. Wang, B.; Xu, J.; Ke, J.; Chen, C.P.; Wang, J.; Wang, N.; Li, X.; Zhang, F.; Li, L. CE-SDT: A new blockchain-based distributed community energy trading mechanism. *Front. Energy Res.* **2023**, *10*, 1091350. [CrossRef]
21. Jiang, T.; Luo, H.; Yang, K.; Sun, G.; Yu, H.; Huang, Q.; Vasilakos, A.V. Blockchain for Energy Market: A Comprehensive Survey. *arXiv* **2024**, arXiv:2403.20045.
22. Shang, Y.; Li, S. FedPT-V2G: Security enhanced federated transformer learning for real-time V2G dispatch with non-IID data. *Appl. Energy* **2024**, *358*, 122626. [CrossRef]
23. Zhong, Y.; Wen, J.; Zhang, J.; Kang, J.; Jiang, Y.; Zhang, Y.; Cheng, Y.; Tong, Y. Blockchain-assisted twin migration for vehicular metaverses: A game theory approach. *Trans. Emerg. Telecommun. Technol.* **2023**, *34*, e4856. [CrossRef]
24. Kang, J.; Zhong, Y.; Xu, M.; Nie, J.; Wen, J.; Du, H.; Ye, D.; Huang, X.; Niyato, D.; Xie, S. Tiny Multi-Agent DRL for Twins Migration in UAV Metaverses: A Multi-Leader Multi-Follower Stackelberg Game Approach. *IEEE Internet Things J.* **2024**, *11*, 21021–21036. [CrossRef]
25. Zulfiqar, M.; Kamran, M.; Rasheed, M. A blockchain-enabled trust aware energy trading framework using games theory and multi-agent system in smat grid. *Energy* **2022**, *255*, 124450. [CrossRef]
26. Su, W.; Li, Z.; Yang, Z.; Lu, J. Deep reinforcement learning with sparse regularized pruning and compressing. In Proceedings of the 2021 China Automation Congress (CAC), Beijing, China, 22–24 October 2021; IEEE: New York, NY, USA 2021; pp. 8041–8046.
27. Li, Z.; Su, W.; Xu, M.; Yu, R.; Niyato, D.; Xie, S. Compact learning model for dynamic off-chain routing in blockchain-based IoT. *IEEE J. Sel. Areas Commun.* **2022**, *40*, 3615–3630. [CrossRef]
28. Livne, D.; Cohen, K. Pops: Policy pruning and shrinking for deep reinforcement learning. *IEEE J. Sel. Top. Signal Process.* **2020**, *14*, 789–801. [CrossRef]
29. Gao, H.; Jiang, S.; Li, Z.; Wang, R.; Liu, Y.; Liu, J. A Two-stage Multi-agent Deep Reinforcement Learning Method for Urban Distribution Network Reconfiguration Considering Switch Contribution. *IEEE Trans. Power Syst.* **2024**, 1–12. [CrossRef]
30. He, Y.; Xiao, L. Structured pruning for deep convolutional neural networks: A survey. *IEEE Trans. Pattern Anal. Mach. Intell.* **2023**, *46*, 2900–2919. [CrossRef]
31. Camilleri, S.F.; Montgomery, A.; Visa, M.A.; Schnell, J.L.; Adelman, Z.E.; Janssen, M.; Grubert, E.A.; Anenberg, S.C.; Horton, D.E. Air quality, health and equity implications of electrifying heavy-duty vehicles. *Nat. Sustain.* **2023**, *6*, 1643–1653. [CrossRef]
32. Jin, C.; Tang, J.; Ghosh, P. Optimizing electric vehicle charging with energy storage in the electricity market. *IEEE Trans. Smart Grid* **2013**, *4*, 311–320. [CrossRef]
33. Amin, U.; Hossain, M.J.; Tushar, W.; Mahmud, K. Energy trading in local electricity market with renewables—A contract theoretic approach. *IEEE Trans. Ind. Inform.* **2020**, *17*, 3717–3730. [CrossRef]
34. Kang, J.; Wen, J.; Ye, D.; Lai, B.; Wu, T.; Xiong, Z.; Nie, J.; Niyato, D.; Zhang, Y.; Xie, S. Blockchain-empowered federated learning for healthcare Metaverses: User-centric incentive mechanism with optimal data freshness. *IEEE Trans. Cogn. Commun. Netw.* **2023**, *10*, 348–362. [CrossRef]
35. Liu, Z.; Huang, B.; Li, Y.; Sun, Q.; Pedersen, T.B.; Gao, D.W. Pricing Game and Blockchain for Electricity Data Trading in Low-Carbon Smart Energy Systems. *IEEE Trans. Ind. Inform.* **2024**, *20*, 6446–6456. [CrossRef]
36. Zhang, J.; Nie, J.; Wen, J.; Kang, J.; Xu, M.; Luo, X.; Niyato, D. Learning-based incentive mechanism for task freshness-aware vehicular twin migration. In Proceedings of the 2023 IEEE 43rd International Conference on Distributed Computing Systems Workshops (ICDCSW), Hong Kong, China, 18–21 July 2023; IEEE: New York, NY, USA, 2023; pp. 103–108.
37. Jiang, Y.; Kang, J.; Niyato, D.; Ge, X.; Xiong, Z.; Miao, C.; Shen, X. Reliable distributed computing for metaverse: A hierarchical game-theoretic approach. *IEEE Trans. Veh. Technol.* **2022**, *72*, 1084–1100. [CrossRef]
38. Kiran, P.; Vijaya Chandrakala, K.; Balamurugan, S.; Nambiar, T.; Rahmani-Andebili, M. A new agent-based machine learning strategic electricity market modelling approach towards efficient smart grid operation. In *Applications of Artificial Intelligence in Planning and Operation of Smart Grids*; Springer: Berlin/Heidelberg, Germany, 2022; pp. 1–29.
39. Zhang, T.; Xu, C.; Shen, J.; Kuang, X.; Grieco, L.A. How to Disturb Network Reconnaissance: A Moving Target Defense Approach Based on Deep Reinforcement Learning. *IEEE Trans. Inf. Forensics Secur.* **2023**, *18*, 5735–5748. [CrossRef]
40. Zhang, T.; Xu, C.; Lian, Y.; Tian, H.; Kang, J.; Kuang, X.; Niyato, D. When Moving Target Defense Meets Attack Prediction in Digital Twins: A Convolutional and Hierarchical Reinforcement Learning Approach. *IEEE J. Sel. Areas Commun.* **2023**, *41*, 3293–3305. [CrossRef]
41. Wen, J.; Nie, J.; Zhong, Y.; Yi, C.; Li, X.; Jin, J.; Zhang, Y.; Niyato, D. Diffusion Model-based Incentive Mechanism with Prospect Theory for Edge AIGC Services in 6G IoT. *IEEE Internet Things J.* **2024**, 1. [CrossRef]
42. Huang, X.; Li, P.; Yu, R.; Wu, Y.; Xie, K.; Xie, S. FedParking: A federated learning based parking space estimation with parked vehicle assisted edge computing. *IEEE Trans. Veh. Technol.* **2021**, *70*, 9355–9368. [CrossRef]
43. Ning, Z.; Sun, S.; Wang, X.; Guo, L.; Guo, S.; Hu, X.; Hu, B.; Kwok, R.Y. Blockchain-enabled intelligent transportation systems: A distributed crowdsensing framework. *IEEE Trans. Mob. Comput.* **2021**, *21*, 4201–4217. [CrossRef]

44. Zhang, T.; Xu, C.; Zhang, B.; Li, X.; Kuang, X.; Grieco, L.A. Towards Attack-Resistant Service Function Chain Migration: A Model-Based Adaptive Proximal Policy Optimization Approach. *IEEE Trans. Dependable Secur. Comput.* **2023**, *20*, 4913–4927. [CrossRef]
45. Liang, H.; Zhang, W. Stochastic Stackelberg Game Based Edge Service Selection for Massive IoT Networks. *IEEE Internet Things J.* **2023**, *10*, 22080–22095. [CrossRef]
46. Dewa, C.K.; Miura, J. A framework for DRL navigation with state transition checking and velocity increment scheduling. *IEEE Access* **2020**, *8*, 191826–191838. [CrossRef]
47. Wen, J.; Zhang, Y.; Chen, Y.; Zhong, W.; Huang, X.; Liu, L.; Niyato, D. Learning-based Big Data Sharing Incentive in Mobile AIGC Networks. *arXiv* **2024**, arXiv:2407.10980.
48. Zhang, R.; Xiong, K.; Lu, Y.; Fan, P.; Ng, D.W.K.; Letaief, K.B. Energy efficiency maximization in RIS-assisted SWIPT networks with RSMA: A PPO-based approach. *IEEE J. Sel. Areas Commun.* **2023**, *41*, 1413–1430. [CrossRef]
49. Wen, J.; Kang, J.; Niyato, D.; Zhang, Y.; Mao, S. Sustainable Diffusion-based Incentive Mechanism for Generative AI-driven Digital Twins in Industrial Cyber-Physical Systems. *arXiv* **2024**, arXiv:2408.01173.
50. Su, W.; Li, Z.; Xu, M.; Kang, J.; Niyato, D.; Xie, S. Compressing Deep Reinforcement Learning Networks with a Dynamic Structured Pruning Method for Autonomous Driving. *arXiv* **2024**, arXiv:2402.05146.
51. Sameera, K.; Nicolazzo, S.; Arazzi, M.; Nocera, A.; KA, R.R.; Vinod, P.; Conti, M. Privacy-preserving in Blockchain-based Federated Learning systems. *Comput. Commun.* **2024**, *222*, 38–67.

Disclaimer/Publisher's Note: The statements, opinions and data contained in all publications are solely those of the individual author(s) and contributor(s) and not of MDPI and/or the editor(s). MDPI and/or the editor(s) disclaim responsibility for any injury to people or property resulting from any ideas, methods, instructions or products referred to in the content.

Article

Integrated Extraction of Entities and Relations via Attentive Graph Convolutional Networks

Chuhan Gao [1], Guixian Xu [2,*] and Yueting Meng [2]

1 School of Electrical Engineering, Southeast University, Nanjing 210018, China
2 College of Information Engineering, Minzu University of China, Beijing 100081, China
* Correspondence: guixian_xu@muc.edu.cn

Abstract: For information security, entity and relation extraction can be applied in sensitive information protection, data leakage detection, and other aspects. The current approaches to entity relation extraction not only ignore the relevance and dependency between name entity recognition and relation extraction but also may result in the cumulative propagation of errors. To solve this problem, it is proposed that an end-to-end joint entity and relation extraction model based on the Attention mechanism and Graph Convolutional Network (GCN) to simultaneously extract named entities and their relationships. The model includes three parts: the detection of entity span, the construction of an entity relation weighted graph, and the inference of entity relation type. Firstly, the detection of entity spans is viewed as a sequence labeling problem, and a multi-feature fusion approach for word embedding representation is designed to calculate all entity spans in a sentence to form an entity span matrix. Secondly, the entity span matrix is employed in the Multi-Head Attention mechanism for constructing the weighted adjacency matrix of the entity relation graph. Finally, for the inference of entity relation type, considering the interaction between entities and relations, the entity span matrix and relation connection matrix are simultaneously fed into the GCN for integrated extraction of entities and relations. Our model is evaluated on the public NYT dataset, attaining a precision of 66.4%, a recall of 63.1%, and an F1 score of 64.7% for joint entity and relation extraction, significantly outperforming other approaches. Experiments demonstrate that the proposed model is helpful for inferring entities and relations, considering the interaction between entities and relations through the Attention mechanism and GCN.

Keywords: Graph Convolutional Network; attention mechanism; entity relation extraction

Citation: Gao, C.; Xu, G.; Meng, Y. Integrated Extraction of Entities and Relations via Attentive Graph Convolutional Networks. *Electronics* **2024**, *13*, 4373. https://doi.org/10.3390/electronics13224373

Academic Editor: Aryya Gangopadhyay

Received: 22 August 2024
Revised: 13 October 2024
Accepted: 24 October 2024
Published: 8 November 2024

Copyright: © 2024 by the authors. Licensee MDPI, Basel, Switzerland. This article is an open access article distributed under the terms and conditions of the Creative Commons Attribution (CC BY) license (https://creativecommons.org/licenses/by/4.0/).

1. Introduction

In information security situational awareness systems, entity relation extraction can help construct entity relationship networks in cyberspace, enabling real-time monitoring and analysis of security incidents and abnormal behaviors within the network [1]. Through in-depth mining and analysis of entity relationships, potential security threats and attack paths can be discovered. How to extract effective information from text quickly and efficiently has become an important issue.

The end-to-end method maps the input sentence into meaningful vectors and then produces the tag sequence. This method is widely used in sequence tagging tasks [2] as well as in entity and relation extraction [3]. As the core task of information extraction, the main task of entity relation extraction is to simultaneously detect entities and their relations from unstructured texts. Entities are words in the given sentence. Relation words are extracted from a predefined relational set, which may not be explicitly present in the given sentence. For instance, in the phrase "Qingdao is in the territory of Shandong Province", "Qingdao" is an entity, "Shandong" is an entity, and the relation of the two entities is classified as "located in" in the predefined relational set. Entity recognition and relation extraction are pivotal stages in constructing knowledge bases and are instrumental in diverse natural language processing applications, such as semantic analysis and question answering systems, occupying a vital role in enhancing the understanding and utilization of text data.

To solve the problems of entity relation extraction, many methods have been proposed. According to the order of name entity recognition and relation extraction, these methods can be divided into two classes: pipeline learning and joint extraction learning. In the pipeline models, named entity recognition and relation extraction are regarded as independent subtasks. Firstly, named entity extraction is used to extract entities, and then the relation is extracted based on named entity recognition. The separated framework is conducive to the modularization of different stages of language understanding, making tasks easier to handle and each component more flexible. However, each subtask is treated as an independent model, which ignores the correlation between the two subtasks. The results of named entity recognition may potentially affect the results of relation extraction. Seriously, it will lead to error propagation, producing unsatisfactory performance.

In contrast to pipeline methods, joint extraction approaches concurrently identify entities and their relations within a unified model. These methods can utilize the mutual information between entities and relations, achieving superior results in the field of entity relation extraction. However, the majority of current joint extraction techniques rely heavily on feature engineering [4], which involves constructing feature vectors by extracting semantic features from sentences. Subsequently, algorithms such as Conditional Random Field (CRF) and Support Vector Machine (SVM) are employed to extract relations. These methods require intricate feature engineering and a large workload. They also rely heavily on Natural Language Processing (NLP) toolkits, which may lead to error propagation. In order to reduce the workload of feature engineering, an end-to-end entity relation extraction based on neural networks has been successfully applied to the task. In recent years, the research of Graph Neural Networks (GNN) has received more and more attention, and GNN has been successfully applied to many NLP tasks, such as Machine Translation [5], Text Classification [6], Semantic Role Labeling [7], and Relation Extraction [8].

However, the intricate interactions between entities are ignored in the above models. In this paper, an end-to-end relation extraction model is proposed that utilizes GCNs and an attention mechanism to jointly learn entities and their relations. The proposed joint extraction model is divided into three parts: entity span detection, construction of an entity–relation weighted graph, and inference of entity relation types. Firstly, entity span detection is treated as a sequence labeling problem. A multi-feature fusion word vector representation approach is devised to identify all entity spans within sentences, thereby constructing an entity span matrix. Then, for the construction of the entity relation weighted graph, based on the attention mechanism, the entity span matrix is input into the Multi-Head attention model. The entity relation weights are calculated to form the relation adjacency matrix. Finally, for the inference of entity relation types, considering the interaction between entities and relations, a joint model based on GCN is proposed. Based on the entity span matrix and relation adjacency matrix obtained in the previous stages, the entities and relations are jointly inferred to get the final entity relations.

2. Related Work

The task of joint extraction of entities and relations is to simultaneously extract entities and relations between two entities. There has been a lot of research on entity and relation extraction. The problem we focused on is related to GCN, attention mechanisms, and extraction of entities and relations.

2.1. GCN

GCN is a network structure that performs semi-supervised learning on graph structure data in a scalable method and is an effective variant of neural network. In GCN, the convolution is performed directly, and the convolution architecture is improved by the first-order approximate localization of the spectral graph convolution.

Several studies have demonstrated the powerful capabilities of GCNs. Gilmer et al. [9] explored the effectiveness of message passing in quantum chemistry by applying GNNs to predict molecular properties. Garcia & Bruna [10] demonstrated the capability of GNNs to learn classifiers on image datasets in a few-shot learning paradigm. Dhingra et al. [11] applied message passing on graphs constructed from common reference links to answer relational questions. Kipf & Welling (2016) [12] introduced GCNs and applied them to citation networks and knowledge graph datasets, marking a significant milestone. Marcheggiani & Titov [6] further extended GCNs to sequence labeling for semantic role labeling, while Liu et al. (2018) [13] utilized GCNs to encode long documents for text matching tasks. Schlichtkrull et al. [14] applied GNNs to knowledge base completion and Zhang et al. [15] encoded dependency trees with GNNs for relation extraction. Lastly, Cao et al. [16] demonstrated the effectiveness of GNNs in multi-hop question answering by encoding co-occurrence and coreference relations.

GCNs offer several advantages in text mining by providing a powerful and flexible framework for modeling and analyzing textual data as graphs. Their ability to capture complex relationships, incorporate contextual information, and propagate relevant information efficiently makes them a valuable tool for tackling a wide range of text mining tasks.

2.2. Attention Mechanism

The attention mechanism dynamically assigns varying weight parameters to each input element, thereby emphasizing relevant aspects while suppressing irrelevant information. Its main advantage lies in its capability to concurrently consider both global and local connections, facilitating parallel computing.

As the attention mechanism has been widely applied to image processing tasks, some researchers have tried to use the attention mechanism to enhance neural networks and apply them to NLP. The Google team [17] propelled attention to the forefront of research by proposing the Self-Attention mechanism for machine translation, revolutionizing text representation learning. Zheng Y. et al. [18] devised a deep learning architecture that seamlessly fused BiLSTM (Bidirectional Long Short-Term Memory) with an attention mechanism, emphatically demonstrating the important role of the attention mechanism in enhancing the model's performance for text classification tasks. The integration emphasized the significance of guiding the model's focus on the most informative parts of the text, thereby improving classification accuracy and efficiency. Furthermore, Y. Liu et al. [19] introduced an innovative approach that harnesses both the attention mechanism and an embedding perturbed encoder, significantly bolstering the style transfer quality of text sentiment.

Attention mechanisms help capture context-specific details that might otherwise be overlooked by traditional models. This targeted focus results in a more precise understanding and representation of the text's content, leading to better performance in tasks such as sentiment analysis, topic classification, and question answering.

2.3. Extraction of Entities and Relations

Joint extraction of entities and relations is a crucial step in constructing knowledge bases, which can significantly benefit numerous NLP applications. At present, two main frameworks have been widely used to solve the problem of entity relation extraction. One is the pipeline method, and the other is the joint learning method.

Pipeline methods, employed in earlier works [20], treat the task as two discrete tasks. Initially, entities within sentences are identified and extracted. Subsequently, the relations among these recognized entities are obtained. Ultimately, these entity–relation triples are output as the predicted outcomes. However, the inherent error propagation in pipeline methods has promoted the emergence of joint extraction of entities and relations. Based on the principle of parameter sharing strategy, Miwa and Bansal [21] first used neural networks to jointly extract entities and relations. The approach incorporated sentence-level Recurrent Neural Networks (RNNs) for entity extraction and dependency tree-based

RNNs for relation prediction. Furthermore, Katiyar and Cardie [22] first used the attention mechanism and BiLSTM to jointly extract entities and relations. The model can extend the defined relation types and is the first joint extraction model of a neural network in the true sense.

The aforementioned joint methods, while achieving joint learning through parameter sharing, often lack explicit interaction during type inference. Zheng et al. [3] proposed an entity relation extraction method based on a novel labeling strategy. Then the original joint model, which contained two subtasks of named entity recognition and relation extraction, had completely become a sequence labeling problem. Sequence labeling was used in the model to identify entities and relations at the same time, which avoided complex feature engineering. The entity relation triplets were directly obtained through an end-to-end neural network model, which solved the problem of entity redundancy. Zeng et al. [23] proposed to use a BiLSTM encoder and multiple LSTM (Long Short-Term Memory) decoders to get the relation triplets dynamically. A transition-based method was proposed to generate directed graphs that convert the joint task into a directed graph, which can model both entity–relationship and relationship–relationship dependencies [24]. Hidden layer vectors obtained from a pre-trained named entity recognition model were utilized as entity features, and there was no need to manually design entity features [25]. COTYPE was introduced, a domain-independent framework that learned embeddings from both text corpora and knowledge bases [26]. Utilizing heuristic data from knowledge bases, COTYPE extracted type entities and relations concurrently, demonstrating remarkable versatility and adaptability [27]. A prediction framework was designed that double-headed entities and relations based BERT are extracted. Relation Attention-Guided Graph Neural Networks were designed to extract joint entities in Chinese electronic medical records [28].

Owing to the excellent expressive capabilities of graphs, the research of GNN has received more and more attention. Initially, GNN was proposed by Gori et al. in an attempt to extend the neural network to handle arbitrary graphs. Sun et al. [29] proposed to use GCN to construct a graph structure to extract entity relations in sentences. A tagging scheme and designed Character Graph Convolutional Network was proposed to obtain character vectors in the text [4]. The Multi-Head Self-Attention Mechanism was seamlessly integrated within the BiLSTM encoding architecture, while the Dense Connected Convolutional Network was elegantly embedded in the decoding framework, facilitating a unified and efficient method for joint extraction of entities and relations from textual data. GCN was used to capture feature representations of the document-level dependency graph, where the dependency graph was used to capture dependency syntactic information across sentences [30]. The Multi-Head attention mechanism was used to learn relatively important contextual features from different semantic subspaces. Chen, Y. [31], on the other hand, presented a causality–extraction approach that integrated an entity-location-aware graph attention (GAT) mechanism. This innovative strategy effectively mitigated redundant content within graph-dependency trees and strengthened the connections between long-span entities, thereby enhancing the overall extraction capability.

Different from the above methods, an end-to-end relation extraction model is proposed in this paper. First, a multi-feature fusion word vector representation method is proposed to calculate all entity spans in sentences to form an entity span matrix. Then, based on the attention mechanism, the entity span matrix is input into the Multi-Head Attention model. The entity relation weights are calculated to form the relation adjacency matrix. Finally, a joint model based on GCN is put forward, the entities and relations are jointly inferred to get the final entity relations based on the entity span matrix and relation adjacency matrix obtained in the previous stages.

3. Research Methods

Firstly, the integrated extraction task of entities and relations is defined. Assuming s is a sentence, $s = x_1, x_2, \ldots, x_n$, where x_i represents a word and n denotes the sentence length. The task objective is to extract a group of entity span E and relation R from a given context s. The relation R is formulated as a triplet (e_1, e_2, l), where e_1 and e_2 represent the two distinct entity spans, and l signifies the specific type of relationship that interconnects these two entities.

The frame figure of the whole process is shown in Figure 1.

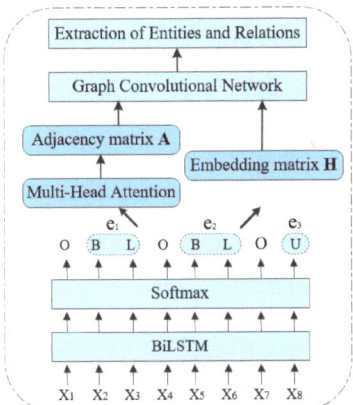

Figure 1. The integrated extraction frame of entities and relations.

3.1. Entity Span Detection

For entity span detection, a tagging scheme is used to switch the task to a labeling question. Figure 2 is an example of how to mark the result of entity span.

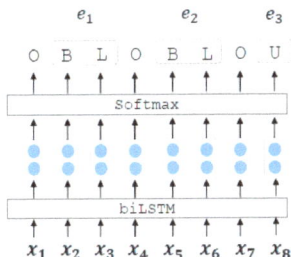

Figure 2. Diagram of entity span detection.

The method of multi-feature fusion is used to train word embedding. In addition to using distributed word vector features, part-of-speech tagging and dependency parsing will also be used. Then the three parts of embedding are stitched together to form word embedding.

In the model of conventional neural networks, the issue of vanishing gradients appeared during training. The threshold mechanism introduced by LSTM effectively mitigates the vanishing gradient problem inherent in RNNs to a considerable degree. Nevertheless, information can only be propagated from front to back in LSTM, implying that the information at time t is solely reliant on the preceding information up to time t. To capture contextual features comprehensively at every temporal point, BiLSTM is employed to learn sentence representations. Forward and backward LSTMs are included in BiLSTM, enabling it to comprehend the semantic content of vocabulary to the fullest extent possible.

Ultimately, the softmax function is employed to forecast the label $\hat{y}$ of x_i, as shown in Figure 2. "BIESO" (Begin, Inside, End, Single, Other) is adopted to designate the positional status of words within an entity and to mark the entity span in a sentence. "B" and "E" express the "Begin" and "End" positions in the entity, respectively. "I" stands for the set of positions other than "Begin" and "End" in the entity, and "S" stands for the entity consisting of a single word. The label "O" stands for the "other" label, which represents that the word is not an entity in the sentence.

3.2. Calculation of Relation Weight

Next, edges are constructed between entity span nodes to indicate the strength of the correlation between entity span pairs. The input sentence is a sequence, and the relation extraction models based on the sequence only work on the word sequence, ignoring the non-local syntactic relation between words. Dependency-based relation extraction models use a syntactic dependency graph to construct tree-structure sentences, ignoring the relation information between entities. In view of the defects of the existing models, the attention mechanism is adopted to learn the connection relation between entity spans, construct an entity relation weighted graph, and finally form an adjacency matrix A of the entity spans. The attention mechanism is utilized to capture the interaction between two words in arbitrary positions of a sequence. The key idea is to use attention to deduce the relations between nodes, especially for those nodes that are indirectly connected by multi-hop paths. Multi-Head Attention [17] is adopted in this paper to compute the relation weight between entities. The structure of Multi-Head Attention is shown in Figure 3.

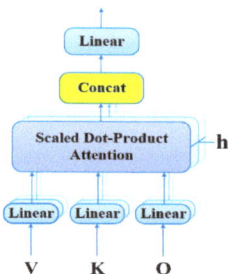

Figure 3. Structure of the Multi-Head Attention.

The calculation formula of Multi-Head Attention is:

$$head_i = Attention\left(QW_i^Q, KW_i^K, VW_i^V\right) \tag{1}$$

$$MultiHead(Q, K, V) = Concat(head_1, \ldots, head_h)W^O \tag{2}$$

$head_i$ represents the i-th attention head, Q is a d_q-dimensional query vector, K is a d_k-dimensional key vector, and V is a d_v-dimensional value vector. d_q, d_k, d_v express the dimensionality of query, key, and value vectors. Initially, Q, K, and V are the input word embeddings. W_i^Q, W_i^K, W_i^V, and W^O are the corresponding learnable parameters.

The most important part of Multi-Head Attention is Scaled Dot-Product Attention, whose framework is shown in Figure 4.

The calculation formula of Scaled Dot-Product Attention is:

$$Attention(Q, K, V) = softmax\left(\frac{QK^T}{\sqrt{d_k}}\right)V \tag{3}$$

In order to use the Scaled Dot-Product Attention, Q and K must have the same dimension. So in the model, Q and K are mapped into d dimension, and V is mapped into d_v dimension respectively by $h = 8$ different linear transformations. Then the above matrix is substituted into the attention mechanism to produce a total of $h \times d_v$-dimensional output. Then the encoded information from h subspaces is fused and the final output is obtained by a linear transformation.

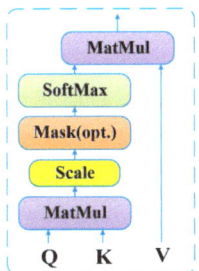

Figure 4. Structure of the Scaled Dot-Product Attention.

The superiority of Multi-Head Attention is that it can acquire the global connection in one step and addresses the challenge of long-distance dependencies. Since parallel computing is performed directly in the matrix, it significantly reduces computational overhead and enhances overall efficiency.

To fully consider the relation information between two connected entities, Multi-Head Attention is used in this paper to construct a fully connected edge-weighted graph. The process is shown in Figure 5.

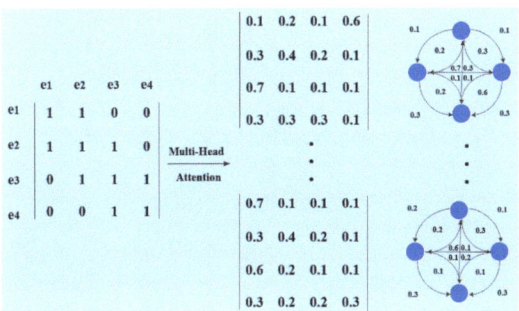

Figure 5. Construction of relation weight graph.

3.3. Joint Type Inference

Considering the interactions between entities and relations, we devised a joint model based on GCN. The entity span matrix and relationship adjacency matrix obtained in the previous stages are used as inputs, and the entities and relations are jointly inferred to obtain the final entity relations. The architecture of GCN is displayed in Figure 6.

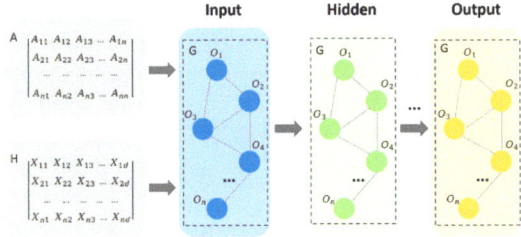

Figure 6. The architecture of the GCN.

Given a graph G with n nodes, the nodes in the graph are denoted as O_1 to O_n. The input part is the input node embedding matrix $H \in n \times d$ and adjacency matrix $A \in n \times n$. n represents the number of nodes and d represents the embedding dimension of input nodes.

Each row of H represents the feature vector of the node, and A denotes the connection relation between the nodes. $A_{ij} = 1$ means two nodes are connected. In an L-layer GCN, each layer is expressed as a nonlinear function:

$$H^{l+1} = \sigma\left(AH^{(l)}W^{(l)} + b^{(l)}\right) \tag{4}$$

Among them, $H^{(0)} = H$, $W^{(l)}$ is the weight matrix of the L-th layer neural network, $b^{(l)}$ is a bias vector of the L-th layer, and σ is the nonlinear activation function of the network in the layer, such as ReLU, sigmoid.

By stacking multiple GCN layers, GCN can extract the local features of each node. Considering the different degrees and aggregation of different relations, two layers of GCN are used in this paper. First, matrix $\hat{A}$ is obtained through preprocessing with A. Then ReLU is utilized as the first layer activation function, and Softmax is adopted as the second layer activation function. Then the entire GCN is expressed as:

$$H = f(H, \hat{A}) = softmax\left(\hat{A}\ ReLU\left(\hat{A}HW^{(0)}\right)W^{(1)}\right) \tag{5}$$

$$ReLU(x) = \max(0, x) \tag{6}$$

$$softmax(x_i) = \frac{\exp(x_i)}{\sum_i \exp(x_i)} \tag{7}$$

The traditional GCN only considered undirected graphs when designing. In order to consider the dependency between entities and relations, as well as the features of both incoming and outgoing, bi-GCN is used in this paper.

$$H^{l+1} = \overrightarrow{H^{l+1}} \oplus \overleftarrow{H^{l+1}} \tag{8}$$

Specifically, based on the entity span extraction of the first part, the entity span matrix is obtained. Based on the relation weight calculation in the second part, the relation adjacency matrix is obtained. Then bi-GCN is applied to each graph to integrate entity relation information.

During the process of training, cross-entropy is adopted as the classification loss function. To comprehensively account for the interaction between the entities and the relations, the total loss function L is defined as the sum of the entity loss L_{entity} and the relation loss $L_{relation}$:

$$L = L_{entity} + L_{relation} \tag{9}$$

$$L_{entity} = -\frac{1}{n}\sum_{i=1}^{n} \log P(\hat{y} = y|e_i, s) \tag{10}$$

$$L_{relation} = -\sum_{e_i, e_j} \log P(r|e_i, e_j, s) \tag{11}$$

In Formula (10), n means the number of entities in the sentence s. $\hat{y}$ means the predicted label of the entity e_i. y means the true label of the entity. $P(\hat{y} = y|e_i, s)$ means the probability that the model predicts the entity label as y given entity e_i and s.

In Formula (11), e_i, e_j is a pair of entities within s. r means the relation label between entities e_i and e_j. $P(r|e_i, e_j, s)$ means the probability that the model predicts the relation between e_i and e_j as given s.

4. Experiments

4.1. Dataset and Setting

To validate the performance of the devised methodology, the public dataset NYT (https://github.com/shanzhenren/CoType (accessed on 26 May 2020)) generated by the distant supervision method [26] is used. NYT includes training data 353 k triplets, test set 3880 triplets, and the size of the relation set is 24. To guarantee the accuracy of the experimental results, the average values of five randomly initialized experiments are utilized as the evaluation results.

The results are evaluated with Precision (P), Recall (R), and F1 scores. Specifically, if the output entity spans correctly encompass both $e1$ and $e2$, and the relation l is accurately identified, then the final result is deemed correct.

The pre-trained word vector Glove [32], which is 300-dimensional, is utilized as word embedding in this paper. Stanford CoreNLP is used to get part-of-speech tagging and dependency parsing of all data sets. The dimensionality of the distributed word vectors is 300, while that of the Part-of-Speech (POS) tagging and dependency parsing is 50, respectively. Other parameter settings are presented in Table 1.

Table 1. The experiment parameter setting.

Hyper-Parameter	Value
Batch size	50
Learning rate	0.001
Optimization function	Mini-Batch Gradient Descent
Loss function	Cross-Entropy Loss Function
Dropout rate	0.5
Hidden state size	256
Non-linear activation	Softmax

4.2. Experiment

4.2.1. Comparison with Existing Models

Firstly, to demonstrate the efficacy of the entity relation extraction model proposed in this paper, a comparative analysis is conducted between the proposed method and several existing models, utilizing a common corpus as the benchmark for evaluation. The compared approaches are as follows:

Pipeline models:

DS-logistic [33] is a sophisticated method that leverages both distant supervision and feature-based approaches, integrating supervised and unsupervised information for enhanced performance.

LINE [34] is a network embedding method capable of any type of information network.

FCM [35] is a combined model of linguistic vocabulary and word vector representation.

Joint models:

MultiR [36] is a distant supervision method based on a multi-instance learning algorithm, used to combat noisy training data.

CopyR [23] is an end-to-end model that employs a replication mechanism, proficiently addressing the issue of overlapping in a seamless manner.

Novel Tagging [3] introduces an innovative labeling scheme that transforms the complex joint extraction task into a more manageable sequence labeling problem.

The comparative experimental results of the various methods, including the proposed approach, are presented in Table 2. The best-performing results on each dataset are highlighted in bold for clarity.

According to the data in Table 2, a comparison of various entity relation extraction experiments is illustrated in Figures 7–9.

Table 2. The results of extraction of entity relation.

Type	Model	P	R	F1
Pipeline models	DS + logistic	25.8	39.3	31.1
	LINE	33.5	32.9	33.2
	FCM	55.3	15.4	24.0
Joint models	MutiR	33.8	32.7	33.3
	CopyR	48.6	38.6	43.0
	Novel Tagging	61.5	41.4	49.5
Proposed model	ATGCN	**66.4**	**63.1**	**64.7**

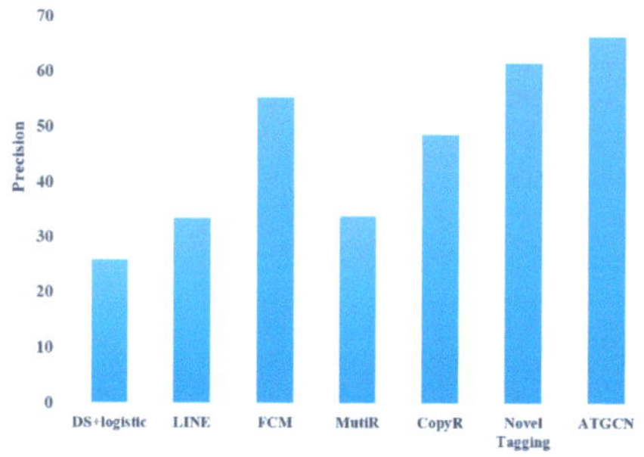

Figure 7. Precision of different entity relation extraction models.

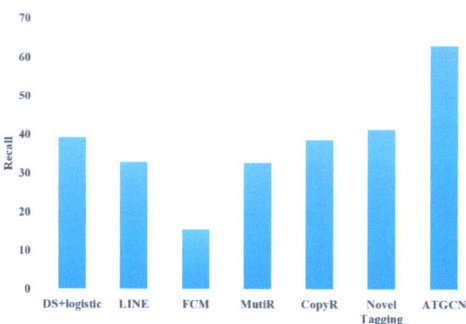

Figure 8. Recall of various entity relation extraction models.

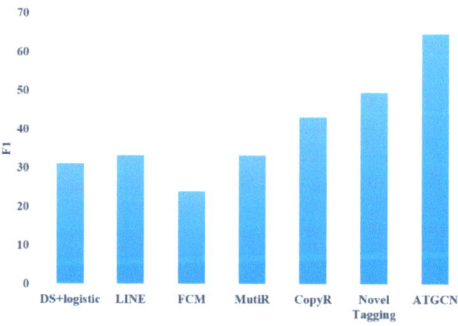

Figure 9. F1 of different entity relation extraction models.

As evident from the above figures, the model introduced in this paper outperforms all baseline models in terms of precision, recall, and F1, reaching 66.4%, 63.1%, and 64.7%, respectively. This illustrates that the proposed method can effectively deal with the task of entity relation extraction. Compared with the pipeline methods, the model proposed in this paper improves the F1 value by 33.6%, 31.5%, and 40.7%, respectively, with an average increase of 35.3%. The reason may be that such methods ignore the relation between the two subtasks. At the same time, errors may occur in two independent subtasks, resulting in cumulative propagation, which ultimately affects the performance of the models. Compared with the joint extraction models, the model proposed in this paper improves the F1 value by 31.4%, 21.7%, and 15.2%, respectively, with an average increase of 22.8%. The reason may be that most of the joint extraction methods are feature-based models, which leads to unsatisfactory experimental results.

At the same time, it can be found from Figure 10 and Table 3 that the average precision, recall, and F1 values of the pipeline methods reach 38.2%, 29.2%, and 29.4% while the average precision, recall, and F1 values of the joint extraction methods are 48.0%, 37.6% and 41.9%. In contrast, the results of the proposed model are obviously better than these two methods, which is also as expected. Firstly, we used word vectors with different features to empower the learning capabilities of the model. Secondly, Multi-Head Attention is adapted to achieve the entity–relation connection graph to better measure the interaction between entities and relations. Finally, the entity information and relation information are trained by GCN, which can fully learn the entity relation information.

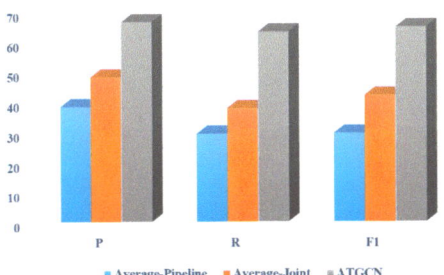

Figure 10. Comparison of different entity relation extraction models.

Table 3. Comparison of various entity relation extraction models.

	P	R	F1
Average of Pipeline	38.2	29.2	29.4
Average of Joint	48.0	37.6	41.9
Proposed model	66.4	63.1	64.7

4.2.2. Verification of Effectiveness

To validate the impact of each individual component within the proposed model, comparative experiments are performed with different settings to verify the contribution of each part.

① Influence of word vector

The deep learning method can effectively consider the syntactic structure information of sentences, so it is widely utilized in entity relation extraction tasks. However, the lexical features and semantic information of the two entities in the sentence cannot be well considered simultaneously in the method. Therefore, the part-of-speech features and dependency parsing features are placed into word embedding in this paper. The experimental outcomes are displayed in Table 4 and Figure 11.

Table 4. Comparison of various word embedding.

Word Embedding	P	R	F1
word2vec	65.3	61.6	63.3
word2vec + part of speech	66.2	62.7	64.4
word2vec + part of speech + dependency syntax analysis	66.4	63.1	64.7

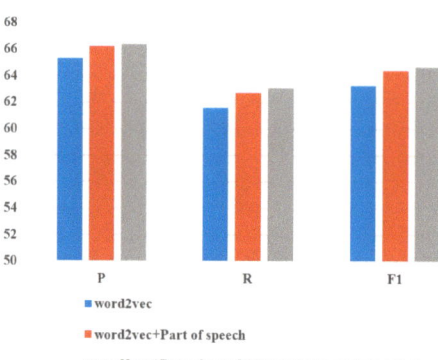

Figure 11. Comparison of various word embedding.

The experimental outcomes demonstrate that compared with the word vector trained only with Word2vec, the multi-feature fusion word vector representation method proposed in this paper has obtained good results, increasing the precision, recall, and F1 values by 1.1%, 1.5%, and 1.4%, respectively. It can be seen from the experimental results that each feature has improved the performance, but the improvement contribution is not the same. Relatively speaking, the addition of part-of-speech features improved the experimental results significantly. Compared with the baseline experiment, precision, recall, and F1 values of "word2+ part of speech" method were improved by 0.9%, 1.1%, and 1.1%, respectively. The addition of dependency syntax analysis has limited improvement in recognition effects. Compared with "word2+ part of speech" experiment, precision, recall, and F1 values of muti-feature fusion method were improved by 0.2%, 0.4%, and 0.3%, respectively. In summary, the various features introduced in the word vector representation have been proven effective in this paper. The part-of-speech and the dependency syntax analysis of words in sentences significantly contribute to entity relation extraction.

② Influence of attention

Traditionally, sequence-based and dependency tree-based methods are usually used in entity relation extraction. Sun et al. [29] proposed to use the structure of entity relation bipartite graph in entity relation extraction. Considering the interaction between entities and relations, the original dependency tree is replaced with Self-Attention in this paper to generate a fully connected entity connection weighted graph. The experimental results of different methods are shown in Table 5 and Figure 12.

Table 5. Comparison of different extraction models.

	P	R	F1
Dependency trees	63.9	60.0	61.9
Bipartite graph	68.1	52.3	59.1
Multi-Head Attention	66.4	63.1	64.7

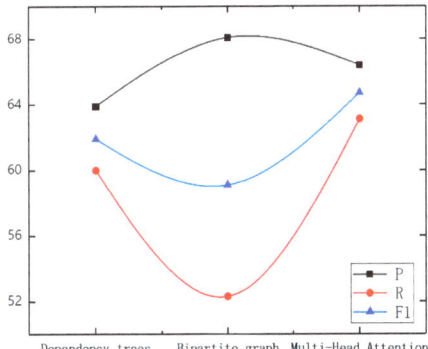

Figure 12. Comparison of different extraction models.

It is evident from the experimental outcomes that compared with the method based on the dependency tree, the Self-Attention method proposed in this paper achieved better results, increasing the precision, recall, and F1 values by 2.5%, 3.1%, and 2.8%, respectively. The Self-Attention mechanism employed in the paper could attain the sequential information and non-local dependent words simultaneously.

Then GCN is used to consider the dependency between entities and relations, which can extract more abundant features to improve the performance of the relation extraction task. At the same time, it shows that the performance of entity relation extraction could be improved without any external syntactic tools, which saves unnecessary generation and propagation of some errors. Compared with the model based on the bipartite graph structure, the proposed Multi-Head Attention method in this paper improves recall and F1 by 10.8% and 5.6%, respectively, which are significant improvements. However, it has a poor performance in precision. The reason may be that the bipartite graph-based method can better represent the relation between two entities by using binary classification. On the whole, our model can obtain a higher F1 score, which is superior to the other two methods in overall performance.

③ Influence of GCN layer

The number of layers in GCN represents the reasoning ability of the model. Shallow GCN may not capture non-local interactions in the graph, while deep GCN can capture more information. However, according to experience, the two-layer GCN exhibits optimal experimental performance. To substantiate the impact of varying layer counts, comparative experiments are carried out with the different numbers of layers.

From Table 6 and Figure 13, we can see that when GCN has two layers, the experimental results reach the best. When the number of layers increases from one to two, the result is improved, which illustrates that the deeper GCN model can obtain abundant information and bring better performance. However, when the number of layers increases from two to three, the result of the experiment decreases. This may be due to the overfitting of the model. It also shows that a deeper GCN layer may not necessarily bring better experimental results.

Table 6. Comparison of various GCN layers.

GCN Layer	P	R	F1
Layer = 1	65.6	54.8	59.7
Layer = 2	66.4	63.1	64.7
Layer = 3	64.9	53.4	58.5

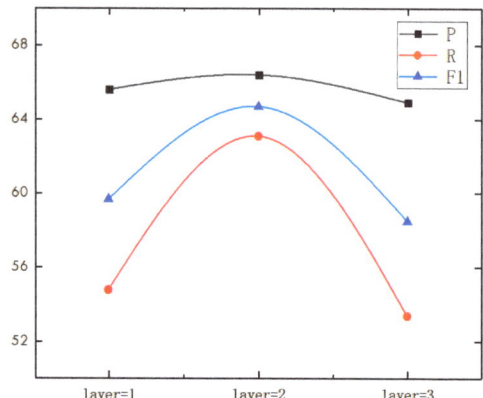

Figure 13. Comparison of various GCN layers.

5. Conclusions

An end-to-end relation extraction model is presented that innovatively integrates GCN with an attention mechanism to facilitate the concurrent learning of entities and their relations. We introduce a novel multi-feature fusion technique for word vector representation, alongside a Multi-Head Attention model, which meticulously computes entity spans and relation weights across sentences. These computations culminate in the construction of an entity span matrix and a relation adjacency matrix, respectively. Subsequently, a joint model based on GCN is proposed, where entities and relations are seamlessly inferred based on these two matrices, ultimately yielding the definitive entity relations. The empirical evaluation of the NYT dataset demonstrates the model's superiority in extracting entity relations, attributed to its nuanced consideration of the interaction between entities and relations, facilitated by the attention mechanism and GCN. Specifically, in the domain of information security, entity relation extraction plays a pivotal role in identifying potential threats, vulnerabilities, and actors involved in cyber attacks. Notably, while this work represents a significant step forward, it does not delve into the challenge of overlapping relation extraction. In future research, it is imperative to focus on analyzing and addressing this complex aspect, which holds immense potential for promoting the model's applicability, particularly in the context of information security.

Author Contributions: Conceptualization, C.G. and Y.M.; methodology, Y.M., G.X. and C.G.; software, Y.M.; validation, Y.M. and G.X.; writing—original draft preparation, Y.M. and G.X.; writing—review and editing, C.G. and G.X. All authors have read and agreed to the published version of the manuscript.

Funding: This research was supported by the Beijing Social Science Foundation Project, grant number 20YYB011.

Data Availability Statement: The data presented in this study are available in the article.

Conflicts of Interest: The authors declare no conflicts of interest.

References

1. Tang, X.; Shen, M.; Li, Q.; Zhu, L.; Xue, T.; Qu, Q. Pile: Robust privacy-preserving federated learning via verifiable perturbations. *IEEE Trans. Dependable Secur. Comput.* **2023**, *20*, 5005–5023. [CrossRef]
2. Lample, G.; Ballesteros, M.; Subramanian, S.; Kawakami, K.; Dyer, C. Neural architectures for named entity recognition. *arXiv* **2016**, arXiv:1603.01360.
3. Zheng, S.; Wang, F.; Bao, H.; Hao, Y.; Zhou, P.; Xu, B. Joint Extraction of Entities and Relations Based on a Novel Tagging Scheme. In Proceedings of the 55th Annual Meeting of the Association for Computational Linguistics, Vancouver, BC, Canada, 30 July–4 August 2017; Volume 1, pp. 1227–1236.

4. Meng, Z.; Tian, S.; Yu, L.; Lv, Y. Joint extraction of entities and relations based on character graph convolutional network and multi-head self-attention mechanism. *J. Exp. Theor. Artif. Intell.* **2021**, *33*, 349–362. [CrossRef]
5. Bastings, J.; Titov, I.; Aziz, W.; Marcheggiani, D.; Sima'An, K. Graph convolutional encoders for syntax-aware neural machine translation. In Proceedings of the 2017 Conference on Empirical Methods in Natural Language Processing, Copenhagen, Denmark, 9–11 September 2017; pp. 1957–1967.
6. Yao, L.; Mao, C.; Luo, Y. Graph convolutional networks for text classification. In Proceedings of the 33rd AAAI Conference on Artificial Intelligence, Honolulu, HI, USA, 27 January–1 February 2019.
7. Marcheggiani, D.; Titov, I. Encoding Sentences with Graph Convolutional Networks for Semantic Role Labeling. In Proceedings of the 2017 Conference on Empirical Methods in Natural Language Processing, Copenhagen, Denmark, 9–11 September 2017; pp. 1506–1515.
8. Fu, T.J.; Ma, W.Y. GraphRel: Modeling Text as Relational Graphs for Joint Entity and Relation Extraction. In Proceedings of the 57th Annual Meeting of the Association for Computational Linguistics, Florence, Italy, 28 July–2 August 2019; pp. 1409–1418.
9. Gilmer, J.; Schoenholz, S.; Riley, P.; Vinyals, O.; Dahl, G. Neural message passing for quantum chemistry. In Proceedings of the 34th International Conference on Machine Learning, Sydney, Australia, 6–11 August 2017.
10. Garcia, V.; Bruna, J. Few-shot learning with graph neural networks. In Proceedings of the 5th International Conference on Learning Representations, Toulon, France, 24–26 April 2017.
11. Dhingra, B.; Yang, Z.; Cohen, W.; Salakhutdinov, R. Linguistic knowledge as memory for recurrent neural networks. *arXiv* **2017**, arXiv:1703.02620.
12. Kipf, T.N.; Welling, M. Semi-supervised classification with graph convolutional networks. In Proceedings of the International Conference on Learning Representations, San Juan, Puerto Rico, 2–4 May 2016.
13. Liu, B.; Zhang, T.; Niu, D.; Lin, J.; Lai, K.; Xu, Y. Matching long text documents via graph convolutional networks. *arXiv* **2018**, arXiv:1802.07459.
14. Schlichtkrull, M.; Kipf, T.N.; Bloem, P.; Berg, R.V.; Welling, M. Modeling Relational Data with Graph Convolutional Networks. In Proceedings of the Semantic Web: 15th International Conference, Extended Semantic Web Conference (ESWC) 2018, Heraklion, Crete, Greece, 3–7 June 2018.
15. Zhang, Y.; Qi, P.; Manning, C. Graph convolution over pruned dependency trees improves relation extraction. In Proceedings of the 2018 Conference on Empirical Methods in Natural Language Processing, Brussels, Belgium, 31 October–4 November 2018.
16. De Cao, N.; Aziz, W.; Titov, I. Question answering by reasoning across documents with graph convolutional networks. *arXiv* **2018**, arXiv:1808.09920.
17. Vaswani, A.; Shazeer, N.; Parmar, N.; Uszkoreit, J.; Jones, L.; Gomez, A.; Kaiser, L.; Polosukhin, I. Attention is all you need. *Adv. Neural Inf. Process. Syst.* **2017**, *30*, 5998–6008.
18. Zheng, Y.; Gao, Z.; Shen, J.; Zhai, X. Optimizing Automatic Text Classification Approach in Adaptive Online Collaborative Discussion–A Perspective of Attention Mechanism-Based Bi-LSTM. *IEEE Trans. Learn. Technol.* **2023**, *16*, 591–602. [CrossRef]
19. Liu, Y.; He, M.; Yang, Q.; Jeon, G. An Unsupervised Framework With Attention Mechanism and Embedding Perturbed Encoder for Non-Parallel Text Sentiment Style Transfer. *IEEE/ACM Trans. Audio Speech Lang. Process.* **2023**, *31*, 2134–2144. [CrossRef]
20. Rink, B.; Harabagiu, S. Utd: Classifying semantic relations by combining lexical and semantic resources. In Proceedings of the 5th International Workshop on Semantic Evaluation, Uppsala, Sweden, 15–16 July 2010; pp. 256–259.
21. Miwa, M.; Bansal, M. End-to-end relation extraction using LSTMs on sequences and tree structures. In Proceedings of the 54rd Annual Meeting of the Association for Computational Linguistics, Berlin, Germany, 7–12 August 2016.
22. Katiyar, A.; Cardie, C. Going out on a limb: Joint Extraction of Entity Mentions and Relations without Dependency Trees. In Proceedings of the 55th Annual Meeting of the Association for Computational Linguistics, Vancouver, BC, Canada, 30 July–4 August 2017; Volume 1, pp. 917–928.
23. Zeng, X.; Zeng, D.; He, S.; Liu, K.; Zhao, J. Extracting relational facts by an End-to-End neural model with copy mechanism. In Proceedings of the 56th Annual Meeting of the Association for Computational Linguistics, Melbourne, Australia, 15–20 July 2018; Volume 1, pp. 506–514.
24. Wang, S.; Zhang, Y.; Che, W.; Liu, T. Joint extraction of entities and relations based on a novel graph scheme. In Proceedings of the 27th International Joint Conference on Artificial Intelligence, Stockholm, Sweden, 13–19 July 2018; pp. 4461–4467.
25. Zhou, Y.; Huang, L.; Guo, T.; Hu, S.; Han, J. An attention-based model for joint extraction of entities and relations with implicit entity features. In *Proceedings of the Companion Proceedings of The 2019 World Wide Web Conference, San Francisco, CA, USA, 13–17 May 2019*; pp. 729–737.
26. Ren, X.; Wu, Z.; He, W.; Qu, M.; Voss, C.R.; Ji, H.; Abdelzaher, T.F.; Han, J. Cotype: Joint extraction of typed entities and relations with knowledge bases. In Proceedings of the 26th International Conference on World Wide Web, Perth, Australia, 3–7 April 2017; pp. 1015–1024.
27. Xiao, Y.; Chen, G.; Du, C.; Li, L.; Yuan, Y.; Zou, J.; Liu, J. A Study on Double-Headed Entities and Relations Prediction Framework for Joint Triple Extraction. *Mathematics* **2023**, *11*, 4583. [CrossRef]
28. Pang, Y.; Qin, X.; Zhang, Z. Specific Relation Attention-Guided Graph Neural Networks for Joint Entity and Relation Extraction in Chinese EMR. *Appl. Sci.* **2022**, *12*, 8493. [CrossRef]

29. Sun, C.; Gong, Y.; Wu, Y.; Gong, M.; Duan, N. Joint Type Inference on Entities and Relations via Graph Convolutional Networks. In Proceedings of the 57th Annual Meeting of the Association for Computational Linguistics, Florence, Italy, 28 July–2 August 2019; pp. 1361–1370.
30. Wang, J.; Chen, X.; Zhang, Y.; Zhang, Y.; Wen, J.; Lin, H.; Yang, Z.; Wang, X. Document-level biomedical relation extraction using graph convolutional network and multihead attention: Algorithm development and validation. *JMIR Med. Inform.* **2020**, *8*, e17638. [CrossRef] [PubMed]
31. Chen, Y.; Wan, W.; Hu, J.; Wang, Y.; Huang, B. Complex Causal Extraction of Fusion of Entity Location Sensing and Graph Attention Networks. *Information* **2022**, *13*, 364. [CrossRef]
32. Pennington, J.; Socher, R.; Manning, C.D. GloVe: Global vectors for word representation. In Proceedings of the Conference on Empirical Methods in Natural Language Processing, Doha, Qatar, 25–29 October 2014.
33. Mintz, M.; Bills, S.; Snow, R.; Jurafsky, D. Distant supervision for relation extraction without labeled data. In Proceedings of the 47th Annual Meeting of the Association for Computational Linguistics, Singapore, 2–7 August 2009; pp. 1003–1011.
34. Tang, J.; Qu, M.; Wang, M.; Zhang, M.; Yan, J.; Mei, Q. Line: Large-scale information network embedding. In Proceedings of the 24th International Conference on World Wide Web, Florence, Italy, 18–22 May 2015; pp. 1067–1077.
35. Gormley, M.; Yu, M.; Dredze, M. Improved relation extraction with feature-rich compositional embedding models. In Proceedings of the Conference on Empirical Methods in Natural Language Processing, Lisbon, Portugal, 17–22 September 2015.
36. Hoffmann, R.; Zhang, C.; Ling, X.; Zettlemoyer, L.; Weld, D. Knowledge based weak supervision for information extraction of overlapping relations. In Proceedings of the 49th Annual Meeting of the Association for Computational Linguistics, Portland, OR, USA, 19–24 June 2011; pp. 541–550.

Disclaimer/Publisher's Note: The statements, opinions and data contained in all publications are solely those of the individual author(s) and contributor(s) and not of MDPI and/or the editor(s). MDPI and/or the editor(s) disclaim responsibility for any injury to people or property resulting from any ideas, methods, instructions or products referred to in the content.

Article

Graph Neural Network-Based Modeling with Subcategory Exploration for Drug Repositioning

Rong Lu [1,2,*], Yong Liang [1,3], Jiatai Lin [4] and Yuqiang Chen [2]

1. Faculty of Innovation Engineering, Macau University of Science and Technology, Macau 999078, China; liangy02@pcl.ac.cn
2. School of Artificial Intellgence, Dongguan Polytechnic, Dongguan 523808, China; chenyq@dgpt.edu.cn
3. Peng Cheng Laboratory, Shenzhen 518118, China
4. School of Computer Science and Engineering, South China University of Technology, Guangzhou 510641, China; 202010107324@mail.scut.edu.cn
* Correspondence: 2009853gia30004@student.must.edu.mo

Abstract: Drug repositioning is a cost-effective approach to identifying new indications for existing drugs by predicting their associations with new diseases or symptoms. Recently, deep learning-based models have become the mainstream for drug repositioning. Existing methods typically regard the drug-repositioning task as a binary classification problem to find the new drug–disease associations. However, drug–disease associations may encompass some potential subcategories that can be used to enhance the classification performance. In this paper, we propose a prototype-based subcategory exploration (PSCE) model to guide the model learned with the information of a potential subcategory for drug repositioning. To achieve this, we first propose a prototype-based feature-enhancement mechanism (PFEM) that uses clustering centroids as the attention to enhance the drug–disease features by introducing subcategory information to improve the association prediction. Second, we introduce the drug–disease dual-task classification head (D3TC) of the model, which consists of a traditional binary classification head and a subcategory-classification head to learn with subcategory exploration. It leverages finer-grained pseudo-labels of subcategories to introduce additional knowledge for precise drug–disease association classification. In this study, we conducted experiments on four public datasets to compare the proposed PSCE with existing state-of-the-art approaches and our PSCE achieved a better performance than the existing ones. Finally, the effectiveness of the PFEM and D3TC was demonstrated using ablation studies.

Keywords: drug repositioning; prototype; subcategory exploration; graph neural network

Citation: Lu, R.; Liang, Y.; Lin, J.; Chen, Y. Graph Neural Network-Based Modeling with Subcategory Exploration for Drug Repositioning. *Electronics* **2024**, *13*, 3835. https://doi.org/10.3390/electronics13193835

Academic Editor: Stefanos Kollias

Received: 14 September 2024
Revised: 23 September 2024
Accepted: 25 September 2024
Published: 28 September 2024

Copyright: © 2024 by the authors. Licensee MDPI, Basel, Switzerland. This article is an open access article distributed under the terms and conditions of the Creative Commons Attribution (CC BY) license (https://creativecommons.org/licenses/by/4.0/).

1. Introduction

Drug development is crucial for the treatment of diseases [1,2]. Traditional drug development is divided into three stages: the discovery stage, preclinical stage, and clinical stage. Developing a new drug typically requires 10–20 years and costs billions of dollars, which poses considerable challenges. To address these issues, drug repositioning offers an alternative approach by identifying new therapeutic uses for existing approved drugs. This strategy significantly reduces the drug development time and lowers the costs [3–5]. Consequently, drug repositioning is widely applied by research-based pharmaceutical companies in their drug-discovery efforts.

Drug-repositioning algorithms can be typically categorized into feature-based, matrix-factorization-based, and network-based methods to predict the associations between drugs and diseases [6,7]. (1) Feature-based methods involve analyzing the chemical and biological properties of drugs, as well as the phenotypic characteristics of diseases, using data-driven machine learning models to predict potential connections between drugs and diseases [8]. (2) Matrix-factorization-based methods decompose the interaction matrix between drugs and diseases into feature vectors through mathematical techniques to compute their similarity, thereby predicting new indications for drugs. This approach can handle large-scale datasets, flexibly integrate more prior information, identify potential connections between drugs and diseases, and aid in the rapid discovery of new therapeutic approaches [9,10]. (3) Network-based drug-repositioning methods aim to use the internal association matrix (e.g., drug–drug or disease–disease matrix) to predict the external associations between drugs and diseases, which can be regarded as a binary classification task for each drug–disease association [11].

With the development of neural networks, network-based algorithms have gradually become the mainstream for drug-repositioning tasks. As a typical approach, Xuan et al. developed a drug-repositioning approach based on convolutional neural networks (CNNs) and bidirectional long short-term memory (BiLSTM) networks, with the BiLSTM module using an attention mechanism to learn path representations of drug–disease pairs by balancing contributions from different paths [12]. Graph convolutional networks (GCNs) are also widely used in this task because the connection nature of association matrices can be transformed into graphs to capture the features of drug–drug or disease–disease associations. For example, Wang et al. utilized bipartite graph convolution operations to model macroscopic and microscopic information exchange between drugs and diseases through protein nodes, thus effectively leveraging interaction relationships to predict potential diseases that drugs may treat [13]. Yu et al. further introduced a hierarchical-attention-based graph convolutional network for drug repositioning by utilizing relationships at different graph convolution layers to enhance the predictive accuracy [14].

Since the drug-repositioning model learns from a small-scale internal association matrix, it struggles to acquire sufficient knowledge for effective drug repositioning [15]. However, the aforementioned network-based methods hardly rely on the introduced information for model training. Meanwhile, we observe that there might be diversity in the associations between each drug and disease, and it is possible to further explore subcategories of these associations to introduce more information for model learning. Therefore, the main challenge of this work is how to uncover this potential diversity or subcategory knowledge to improve the classification performance for drug repositioning.

In this paper, we propose a **p**rototype-based **s**ubcategory **e**xploration (PSCE) model to introduce the potential knowledge of subcategories for model training for drug repositioning. First, we propose a prototype-based feature-enhancement mechanism (PFEM) that employs the K-means method [16,17] to obtain the clustering subcategories for each sample, and the clustering centroids are regarded as the class-relevant prototypes [18–20]. In the proposed PFEM, prototypes are used to attach attention to original graph features to obtain the enhanced features. Second, we introduce a drug–disease dual-task classification head (D3TC) of the model, which consists of a traditional binary classification head and a subcategory-classification head to learn with subcategory exploration. It leverages finer-grained pseudo-labels of subcategories to introduce additional knowledge for precise drug–disease association classification. We conducted experiments on four public datasets to compare with several existing drug-repositioning methods. In the experiment, the PSCE achieved a state-of-the-art performance. Finally, we conducted ablation studies to demonstrate the effectiveness of the proposed PFEM and D3TC. The contributions of this paper are summarized as follows:

- This paper presents a prototype-based feature-enhancement mechanism (PFEM) by making full use of the potential knowledge of subcategories for model training, based on which the classification performance in the drug-repositioning task can be significantly improved.
- For the proposed PFEM, we propose a drug–disease dual-task classification head (D3TC) of the model for subcategory exploration to learn the potential feature representation of subcategories by building additional constraints to improve the performance of the drug–disease association predictions.
- Experimental comparisons showed that the PSCE could achieve state-of-the-art performance with respect to the best existing drug-repositioning methods on four datasets.

2. Materials and Methods

As shown in Figure 1, in this section, we systematically introduce the PSCE method proposed for the drug-repositioning task. We first introduce the datasets we used, and then we show the overall framework of our model and provide detailed introductions to the two main modules of our model: the PFEM and D3TC modules. Finally, we present the implementation details of our approach.

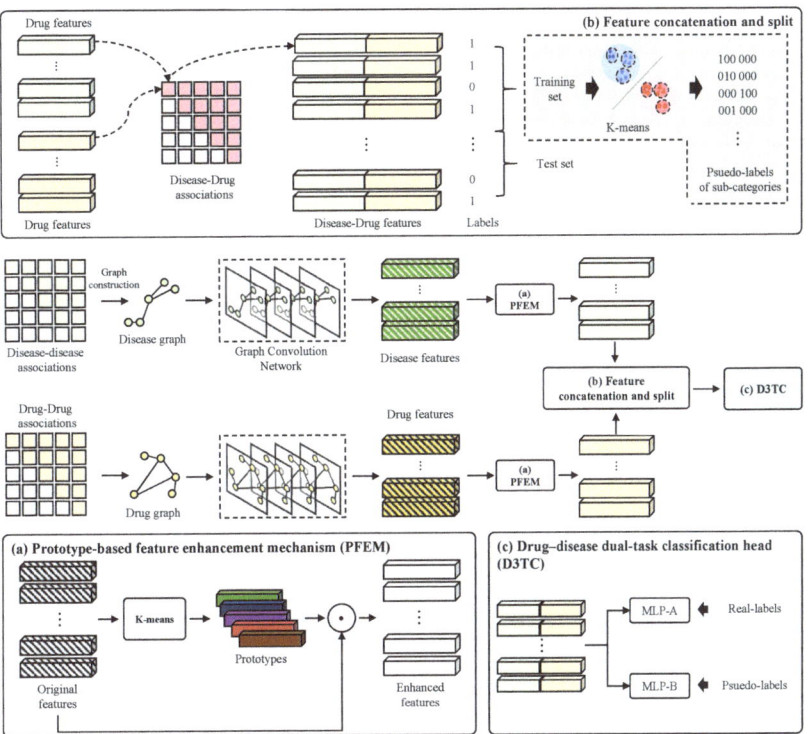

Figure 1. Illustration of the proposed PSCE pipeline. The middle part of this diagram shows the main process of the entire pipeline. (**a**) The proposed prototype-based feature enhancement mechanism (PFEM), (**b**) the feature concatenation and split steps, and (**c**) the proposed drug–disease dual-task classification head (D3TC).

2.1. Datasets

We used four datasets to demonstrate the effectiveness and evaluate the performance of our method: Gdataset [21], Cdataset [22], Ldataset [14], and LRSSL [23]. These datasets are widely used in the drug-repositioning task. Among them, the Gdataset includes 1933 confirmed drug–disease associations, including 593 drugs from the DrugBank database and 313 diseases from the OMIM database. The Cdataset contains 663 drugs, 409 diseases, and 2352 drug–disease interaction pairs. The Ldataset was compiled from the CTD dataset, which includes 18,416 associations between 269 drugs and 598 diseases. The last dataset, namely, LRSSL, contains 3051 validated drug–disease associations involving 763 drugs and 681 diseases. The specific statistical information of these datasets is shown in Table 1.

In our method, by observing the relationship between the disease and drug features in the feature space, we propose a novel feature that combines clustering features to calculate the similarity between drugs and diseases. To better interpret the features, we also propose a method that divides the binary classification task into more subtasks through unsupervised clustering so that the model can better distinguish hard samples.

Table 1. Comparison of the proposed PSCE with six respective algorithms for drug repositioning under 10-fold cross-validation on Gdataset, Cdataset, the LRSSL dataset, and the Ldataset. The red and blue markers indicate the best and second-best performances, respectively.

Methods	Metrics	Performance on Datasets (Mean ± Sd)				
		Gdataset	Cdataset	LRSSL	Ldataset	Avg
MBiRW [22]	AUROC	0.896 ± 0.014	0.920 ± 0.008	0.893 ± 0.015	0.765 ± 0.007	0.868
	AUPRC	0.106 ± 0.019	0.161 ± 0.019	0.030 ± 0.004	0.032 ± 0.003	0.082
BNNR [24]	AUROC	0.937 ± 0.010	0.952 ± 0.010	0.922 ± 0.012	0.866 ± 0.004	0.919
	AUPRC	0.328 ± 0.029	0.431 ± 0.020	0.226 ± 0.021	0.142 ± 0.007	0.282
iDrug [25]	AUROC	0.905 ± 0.019	0.926 ± 0.010	0.900 ± 0.008	0.838 ± 0.005	0.892
	AUPRC	0.167 ± 0.027	0.250 ± 0.027	0.070 ± 0.009	0.086 ± 0.004	0.143
NIMCGCN [26]	AUROC	0.821 ± 0.011	0.827 ± 0.017	0.777 ± 0.012	0.843 ± 0.001	0.817
	AUPRC	0.123 ± 0.028	0.174 ± 0.071	0.087 ± 0.010	0.117 ± 0.002	0.125
DRHGCN [27]	AUROC	0.948 ± 0.011	0.964 ± 0.005	0.961 ± 0.006	0.851 ± 0.007	0.931
	AUPRC	0.490 ± 0.041	0.580 ± 0.035	0.384 ± 0.022	0.498 ± 0.012	0.488
DRWBNCF [28]	AUROC	0.923 ± 0.013	0.941 ± 0.011	0.935 ± 0.011	0.824 ± 0.005	0.906
	AUPRC	0.484 ± 0.027	0.559 ± 0.021	0.349 ± 0.034	0.419 ± 0.006	0.453
PSCE (ours)	AUROC	0.953 ± 0.014	0.964 ± 0.011	0.952 ± 0.016	0.877 ± 0.004	0.936
	AUPRC	0.535 ± 0.036	0.582 ± 0.028	0.443 ± 0.032	0.568 ± 0.008	0.532

2.2. Overview

We used the drug–disease association matrix, drug–drug similarity matrix, and disease–disease similarity matrix to construct a graph network structure and obtain potential drug–disease relationships. The drug–disease association matrix X represents the known associations between drugs and diseases and is a binary $p * q$ matrix, where p and q represent the numbers of drug and disease types, respectively. Each element X_{ij} in X indicates the association between drug R_i and disease D_j, where if there is an association, $X_{ij} = 1$, and otherwise, $X_{ij} = 0$:

$$X_{ij} = \begin{cases} 1 & \text{If } R_i \text{ is associated with } D_j \\ 0 & \text{otherwise} \end{cases} \quad (1)$$

The drug–drug similarity matrix R represents the similarity between drugs and is a $p * p$ matrix, where p is the number of drug types. Each element R_{ij} in R represents the degree of similarity between the i-th drug and the j-th drug, which is specifically defined as

$$R_{ij} = \begin{cases} k & \text{If } R_i \text{ is associated with } R_j, 0<k<1 \\ 0 & \text{otherwise} \end{cases} \quad (2)$$

Similarly, the disease–disease similarity matrix D represents the similarity between diseases and is defined as

$$D_{ij} = \begin{cases} k & \text{If } D_i \text{ is associated with } D_j, 0<k<1 \\ 0 & \text{otherwise} \end{cases} \quad (3)$$

The purpose of the drug-repositioning task is to predict unknown potential associations between drugs and diseases by studying the similarity between drugs, the similarity between diseases, and the known associations between drugs and diseases.

2.3. Model Architecture

Existing methods have already shown the effectiveness of a GNN in constructing associations between drugs and diseases. Our method takes the drug similarity matrix

R and the disease similarity matrix D as the input of the network to construct the corresponding graph structures G_R and G_D, respectively, according to the element adjacency relationship. The obtained graph structures are then fed into the graph neural network for preliminary feature extraction, which results in drug features $F_R = G(R, G_R)$ and disease features $F_D = G(D, G_D)$. To better represent the features of similar drugs/diseases, we used a clustering feature-enhancement method (PFEM) to strengthen the expression ability of the features, thus obtaining the enhanced drug features $\widehat{F_R} = f(F_R)$ and disease features $\widehat{F_D} = f(F_D)$. We obtained the drug–disease similarity features by unfolding the obtained drug and disease features in the form of a tensor product, which was then used for the predictions:

$$F_{R\_D} = \begin{bmatrix} \widehat{F_R^1} \oplus \widehat{F_D^1}, & \widehat{F_R^1} \oplus \widehat{F_D^2}, & \cdots, & \widehat{F_R^1} \oplus \widehat{F_D^q} \\ \widehat{F_R^2} \oplus \widehat{F_D^1}, & \widehat{F_R^2} \oplus \widehat{F_D^2}, & \cdots, & \widehat{F_R^2} \oplus \widehat{F_D^q} \\ \cdots & \cdots & \cdots & \cdots \\ \widehat{F_R^p} \oplus \widehat{F_D^1}, & \widehat{F_R^p} \oplus \widehat{F_D^2}, & \cdots, & \widehat{F_R^p} \oplus \widehat{F_D^q} \end{bmatrix} \quad (4)$$

where p is the number of drug types, q is the number of disease types, and $\oplus$ represents the concatenation operation.

We then used the drug–disease association matrix M_{R_D} as the label to supervise the learning of these features. In previous methods, a simple decoder was used to parse the features to achieve classification, but we believe that simple binary classification cannot distinguish some difficult samples, and thus, we propose a new classification head (D3TC) to improve the classification performance and obtain the final prediction probability matrix $Y = D(\widehat{F_R}, \widehat{F_D})$.

2.4. Prototype-Based Feature-Enhancement Mechanism

In order to obtain the underlying associations between drugs and between diseases, previous methods often relied on the k-nearest neighbor graph of the similarity matrix to construct stronger similarity. However, in this paper, we believe that features with closer clustering in the feature space have stronger similarity. To enhance this similarity, and thus, obtain more subtle associations between diseases and drugs, we propose a prototype-based feature-enhancement method (PFEM).

We used the features extracted by the graph neural network as the initial features for enhancement. For the drug features $F_R \in R^{p*s}$, where p is the number of drug types and s is the feature dimension, we performed k-means clustering on the features to group the p drugs into k clusters and obtained the feature of each cluster center $\overline{F}_R^i (0 < i < k)$. We then fused each drug's own feature $F_R^j (0 < j < p)$ with the feature of the cluster center $\overline{F}_R^i$ it belonged to to obtain the enhanced features $\widehat{F_R} = \delta(F_R, \overline{F}_R^i)$. Specifically, we used an attention mechanism to acquire more representative features. Similarly, for the disease features $F_D \in R^{q*s}$, we adopted the same method to obtain the enhanced disease features $\widehat{F_D} = \delta(F_D, \overline{F}_D^i)$.

2.5. Drug–Disease Dual-Task Classification Head

Although we obtained representative features, predicting the potential similarity probability between drugs and diseases is still a challenging task, as there are still some difficult samples. The traditional decoder treats this prediction task as a binary classification problem that results in classification results with high inter-class similarity, which hinders the formation of diverse features. To obtain a better prediction performance, we propose a drug–disease dual-task classification head (D3TC).

In addition to the binary classification task of predicting whether there is an association between a drug and a disease, we further extended each class into T sub-classes that represent different degrees of relevance and irrelevance (e.g., extremely irrelevant, possibly irrelevant, possibly relevant, extremely relevant). This encourages the model to not only focus on the differences in binary classification but also on the differences in different degrees, thus ultimately obtaining a more subtle feature representation:

$$Y_p \to Y_c = \begin{cases} (0,...,0,Y_c^{T+1},...,Y_c^{2T}), & Y_p = 1 \\ (Y_c^1,...,Y_c^T,0,...,0), & Y_p = 0 \end{cases} \quad (5)$$

where $Y_p \in \{0,1\}$ is the binary classification label, $Y_c \in \{0,1\}^{2T}$ is the one-hot pseudo-label for the molecular sub-classes, and $\to$ represents the process of using the original labels to generate a subcategory label.

First, we trained the binary classification model until it converged. Then, we extracted deep features for each sample and obtained the pseudo-labels for the sub-classes through unsupervised clustering. Finally, we jointly trained the network using both the binary classification labels and the sub-class pseudo-labels. To better train the network, we used a weighted binary cross-entropy loss to supervise the binary classification task:

$$\mathcal{L}_{wbce} = -\sum_j w_j \sum_i y_{ji} log(\hat{y}_{ji}) + (1 - y_{ji}) log(1 - \hat{y}_{ji}) \quad (6)$$

At the same time, we introduced focal loss and center loss to learn the knowledge of the pseudo-labels. This allowed us to bring the samples of the same class closer in the feature space and push the samples of different classes farther apart. By introducing focal loss, we reduced the weight of the easy samples and focused more on the difficult samples, which helped to push the different classes apart in the feature space:

$$\mathcal{L}_{Focal} = -\sum_i [(1 - \hat{y}_i)^\gamma y_i log \hat{y}_i + (\hat{y}_i)^\gamma (1 - y_i) log(1 - \hat{y}_i)] \quad (7)$$

Center loss was used to minimize the intra-class variability by encouraging the feature vectors of the same class to be close to their corresponding class centers. The center loss was defined as

$$\mathcal{L}_{Center} = \frac{1}{2} \sum_{i=1}^N \|x_i - c_{y_i}\|_2^2 \quad (8)$$

By combining the loss of the binary classification and the sub-class pseudo-labels, we optimized the classification model:

$$\mathcal{L}_{total} = \mathcal{L}_{wbce} + \lambda(\mathcal{L}_{Focal} + \mathcal{L}_{Center}) \quad (9)$$

3. Results

In this section, we first give the implementation details of the proposed PSCE in Section 3.1 and describe the evaluation metrics in Section 3.2. Then, we give the results of the local leave-one-out 10-time 10-fold cross-validation in Section 3.3 and ablation study in Section 3.4.

3.1. Implementation Details

During the training process, we divided the training samples and validation samples based on the drug–disease association matrix. For each element in the matrix, we could treat it as a sample. We randomly split these samples into a training set and a validation set at a ratio of 9:1, and adopted a 5-fold cross-validation experiment to obtain the model's performance.

Our model used the Adam optimizer for optimization, with a learning rate of 0.01. The mini-batch size for the model training was set to 2000, and a 5-fold cross-validation was adopted. Our experiments were conducted on PyTorch 1.13.1 and a workstation equipped with a 24 GB NVIDIA RTX3090 GPU. In the PFEM, the number of clustering centers was set to half the number of samples, and in the D3TC, the number of sub-classes T was set to five. In the loss function, the weights in L_{wbce} were set according to the ratio of the number of positive samples to negative samples in the training set. The value of λ was set to 0.005.

3.2. Evaluation Metrics

We used two metrics, namely, the area under the receiver operating characteristic (AUROC) [29] and the area under the precision–recall curve (AUPRC) [30], to evaluate the performance of our model. These two metrics are widely used for evaluating the performance of binary classification models. The AUROC measures the trade-off between the true positive rate (TPR) and the false positive rate (FPR) across different classification thresholds. It represents the probability that a randomly selected positive sample will be ranked higher than a randomly selected negative sample by the classifier. In contrast, the AUPRC evaluates the trade-off between the precision and recall across different classification thresholds. It provides a more comprehensive assessment of the classifier's performance, especially when dealing with imbalanced datasets where the positive and negative classes are significantly unequal.

3.3. Comparison with Existing Methods

In this section, we present the results of the local leave-one-out 10-time 10-fold cross-validation to compare the proposed PSCE method with six representative methods to examine the robustness and effectiveness of our PSCE for discovering novel drug candidates for new diseases without any treatment information on four datasets, which are mentioned in Section 2.1. The six representative methods were MBiRW [22], BNNR [24], iDrug [25], NIMCGCN [26], DRHGCN [27], and DRWBNCF [28]. In this experiment, we used the AUROC and AUPRC metrics to evaluate the performances of methods.

Table 1 presents the quantization results of our PSCE method compared with six existing methods. In this table, we highlighted the best and second-best performances in red and blue, respectively. The results demonstrate that our method consistently achieved the best performance across the Gdataset, Cdataset, and Ldataset. In the LRSSL dataset experiment, although our method attained the second-best performance for the AUROC metric, it still achieved the best performance for the AUPRC metric. The last column of the table displays the mean performances across the four datasets, where it shows that our method performed well on all datasets and achieved comprehensive optimality.

In Figure 2, we visualized the mean performance of this experiment on four datasets using a bar chart. This figure demonstrates that our PSCE method outperformed the others and achieved a state-of-the-art performance. To intuitively demonstrate the robustness and effectiveness, we visualized the performance of the 10-time 10-fold cross-validation for each time in Figure 3. We can observe that our method, like other methods, demonstrated consistent results across repeated experiments, where the outcomes remained within a certain range and exhibited no significant random fluctuations. This indicates that the quantification results of our method are robust. The performance stability of our PSCE method was evident, where it consistently maintained a high performance. This visual confirmation aligned with the quantitative results presented in our table, which further verified the effectiveness of our method. Additionally, this stability across various datasets underscored the reliability of our approach in different experimental conditions. The robustness of our method ensures that it can be confidently applied in practical scenarios since it maintains accuracy and efficiency. Overall, these observations highlight the strength and dependability of our PSCE method in achieving superior quantification results. Compared with the existing methods, especially NIMCGCN and DRHGCN, which are also GCN-based methods, the proposed PSCE learned additional potential knowledge with subcategory pseudo-labels, and the experimental results demonstrated that our method could indeed achieve better and more robust performance than the existing ones.

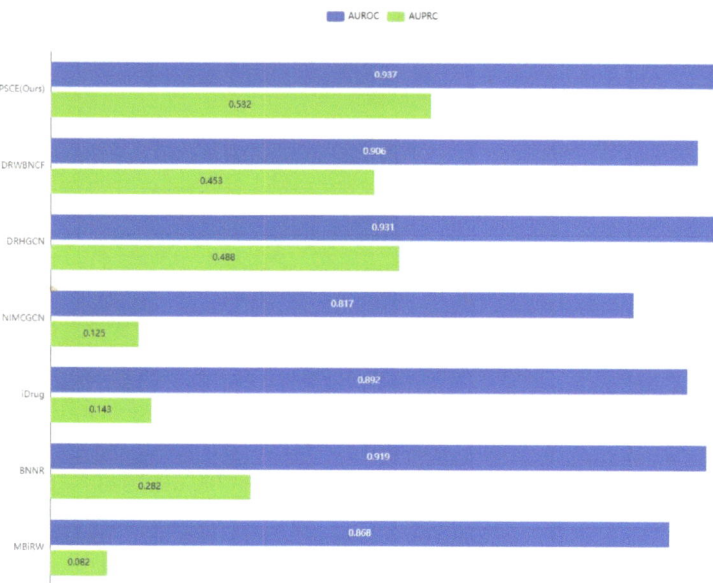

Figure 2. Bar chart of performance that compares our PSCE and six existing methods. The blue and green bars represent the performances according to the AUROC and AUPRC metrics, respectively.

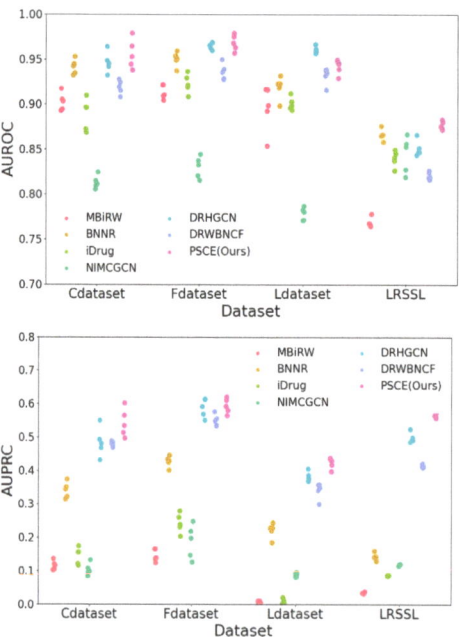

Figure 3. Visualization of performance generated by our PSCE and existing methods. Top and bottom represent the scatter plot of performances according to AUROC and AUPRC metrics, respectively.

3.4. Ablation Study on the Proposed PFEM and D3TC

This work presents a novel drug-repositioning model (PSCE) that incorporates two modules: PFEM and D3TC, which were designed for subcategory exploration. To investigate the effectiveness of these two modules, we conducted the ablation study detailed in this section. In these experiments, we compared the impacts of different combinations of the two modules, with the quantification results reported in Table 2.

In Tables 2 and 3, we see that when using each module individually, only a comparable performance could be achieved. However, combining both modules yielded the best performance; this even led to significant improvements, such as an increase of about 0.1–0.2 on the Cdataset. This not only indicates that both modules are effective but also that they are complementary. By integrating the two modules, they can leverage each other's strengths, thus resulting in superior performance. Figure 4 visually illustrates the quantization results described above with a line chart. We can observe that combining the two modules achieved significant and stable improvements over using them individually. This visual representation further validated the effectiveness of our method.

Table 2. Ablation study using the AUROC metric on the PFEM module and D3TC module. The **bold** marker indicates the best performance.

Setting		Performance with AUROC Metric on Datasets (Mean ± Sd)				
PFEM	D3TC	Gdataset	Cdataset	LRSSL	Ldataset	Avg
√		0.922 ± 0.015	0.945 ± 0.009	0.932 ± 0.014	0.850 ± 0.008	0.912
	√	0.924 ± 0.008	0.946 ± 0.014	0.940 ± 0.011	0.866 ± 0.005	0.919
√	√	**0.953 ± 0.014**	**0.964 ± 0.011**	**0.952 ± 0.016**	**0.877 ± 0.004**	**0.936**

Table 3. Ablation study using the AUPRC metric on the PFEM module and D3TC module. The **bold** marker indicates the best performance.

Setting		Performance with AUPRC Metric on Datasets (Mean ± Sd)				
PFEM	D3TC	Gdataset	Cdataset	LRSSL	Ldataset	Avg
√		0.396 ± 0.027	0.458 ± 0.016	0.382 ± 0.018	0.513 ± 0.011	0.437
	√	0.453 ± 0.044	0.488 ± 0.033	0.401 ± 0.025	0.541 ± 0.009	0.470
√	√	**0.535 ± 0.036**	**0.582 ± 0.028**	**0.443 ± 0.032**	**0.568 ± 0.008**	**0.532**

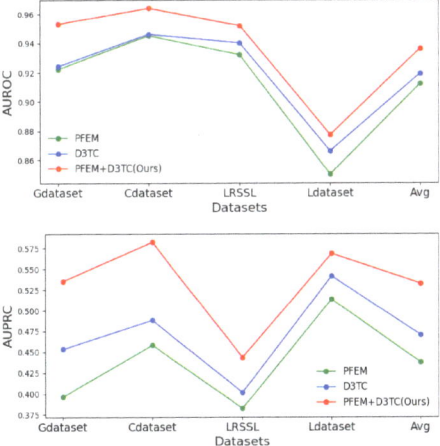

Figure 4. The effects of different combinations of the proposed PFEM and D3TC on four datasets. The top and bottom represent the line charts of performances with AUROC and AUPRC metrics, respectively.

4. Conclusions

In conclusion, our proposed PSCE model represents a significant advancement in the field of drug repositioning by effectively incorporating subcategory information into the prediction process. Through the innovative use of a prototype-based feature-enhancement mechanism (PFEM) and a dual-task classification head (D3TC), we demonstrated that it is possible to achieve more precise and reliable drug–disease association predictions. The PFEM's clustering centroids and the D3TC's subcategory exploration enable our model to leverage finer-grained pseudo-labels, thus providing a richer source of information compared with traditional binary classification methods. Experimental results on four public datasets confirmed that our PSCE model outperformed the current state-of-the-art approaches, which underscored the potential of our method to improve the accuracy and efficiency of drug-repositioning tasks. The effectiveness of both PFEM and D3TC was further validated through comprehensive ablation studies, which highlighted the robustness and applicability of our approach.

Author Contributions: Conceptualization, R.L. and Y.L.; methodology, R.L.; software, J.L.; validation, R.L. and J.L.; formal analysis, R.L.; investigation, R.L.; resources, Y.L.; data curation, R.L.; writing—original draft preparation, R.L.; writing—review and editing, J.L.; visualization, J.L.; supervision, Y.L.; project administration, R.L. and Y.C.; funding acquisition, Y.L. All authors read and agreed to the published version of this manuscript.

Funding: This work was supported by the Artificial Intelligence Technology Application Research and Service Center of Dongguan Polytechnic School-Level Fund Project of Dongguan Polytechnic (no. 2023c27), and was also supported by SSL Sci-tech Commissioner Program Project (no. 20234400-01KCJ-G).

Data Availability Statement: The data underlying this article are available in our provided github repository at https://github.com/lu-rong/PSCE_DR/ (accessed on 13 September 2024).

Conflicts of Interest: The authors declare no conflicts of interest.

References

1. Morgan, S.; Grootendorst, P.; Lexchin, J.; Cunningham, C.; Greyson, D. The cost of drug development: A systematic review. *Health Policy* **2011**, *100*, 4–17. [CrossRef]
2. Ingber, D.E. Human organs-on-chips for disease modelling, drug development and personalized medicine. *Nat. Rev. Genet.* **2022**, *23*, 467–491. [CrossRef]
3. Jourdan, J.P.; Bureau, R.; Rochais, C.; Dallemagne, P. Drug repositioning: A brief overview. *J. Pharm. Pharmacol.* **2020**, *72*, 1145–1151. [CrossRef]
4. Jarada, T.N.; Rokne, J.G.; Alhajj, R. A review of computational drug repositioning: Strategies, approaches, opportunities, challenges, and directions. *J. Cheminformatics* **2020**, *12*, 1–23. [CrossRef] [PubMed]
5. Hua, Y.; Dai, X.; Xu, Y.; Xing, G.; Liu, H.; Lu, T.; Chen, Y.; Zhang, Y. Drug repositioning: Progress and challenges in drug discovery for various diseases. *Eur. J. Med. Chem.* **2022**, *234*, 114239. [CrossRef] [PubMed]
6. Yu, J.L.; Dai, Q.Q.; Li, G.B. Deep learning in target prediction and drug repositioning: Recent advances and challenges. *Drug Discov. Today* **2022**, *27*, 1796–1814. [CrossRef] [PubMed]
7. Dang, Q.; Liang, Y.; Ouyang, D.; Miao, R.; Ling, C.; Liu, X.; Xie, S. Improved Computational Drug-Repositioning by Self-Paced Non-Negative Matrix Tri-Factorization. *IEEE/ACM Trans. Comput. Biol. Bioinform.* **2022**, *20*, 1953–1962. [CrossRef]
8. Hou, L.; Samaras, D.; Kurc, T.M.; Gao, Y.; Davis, J.E.; Saltz, J.H. Patch-based convolutional neural network for whole slide tissue image classification. In Proceedings of the IEEE Conference on Computer Vision and Pattern Recognition, Las Vegas, NV, USA, 27–30 June 2016; pp. 2424–2433.
9. Peska, L.; Buza, K.; Koller, J. Drug-target interaction prediction: A Bayesian ranking approach. *Comput. Methods Programs Biomed.* **2017**, *152*, 15–21. [CrossRef]
10. Ceddia, G.; Pinoli, P.; Ceri, S.; Masseroli, M. Matrix factorization-based technique for drug repurposing predictions. *IEEE J. Biomed. Health Inform.* **2020**, *24*, 3162–3172. [CrossRef]
11. Zeng, X.; Zhu, S.; Liu, X.; Zhou, Y.; Nussinov, R.; Cheng, F. deepDR: A network-based deep learning approach to in silico drug repositioning. *Bioinformatics* **2019**, *35*, 5191–5198. [CrossRef]
12. Xuan, P.; Ye, Y.; Zhang, T.; Zhao, L.; Sun, C. Convolutional neural network and bidirectional long short-term memory-based method for predicting drug–disease associations. *Cells* **2019**, *8*, 705. [CrossRef]
13. Wang, Z.; Zhou, M.; Arnold, C. Toward heterogeneous information fusion: Bipartite graph convolutional networks for in silico drug repurposing. *Bioinformatics* **2020**, *36*, i525–i533. [CrossRef] [PubMed]

14. Yu, Z.; Huang, F.; Zhao, X.; Xiao, W.; Zhang, W. Predicting drug–disease associations through layer attention graph convolutional network. *Briefings Bioinform.* **2021**, *22*, bbaa243. [CrossRef] [PubMed]
15. Chen, H.G.; Zhou, X.H. MNBDR: A Module Network Based Method for Drug Repositioning. *Genes* **2021**, *12*, 25. [CrossRef] [PubMed]
16. Ahmed, M.; Seraj, R.; Islam, S.M.S. The k-means algorithm: A comprehensive survey and performance evaluation. *Electronics* **2020**, *9*, 1295. [CrossRef]
17. Ikotun, A.M.; Ezugwu, A.E.; Abualigah, L.; Abuhaija, B.; Heming, J. K-means clustering algorithms: A comprehensive review, variants analysis, and advances in the era of big data. *Inf. Sci.* **2023**, *622*, 178–210. [CrossRef]
18. Zhou, T.; Wang, W.; Konukoglu, E.; Van Gool, L. Rethinking semantic segmentation: A prototype view. In Proceedings of the IEEE/CVF Conference on Computer Vision and Pattern Recognition, New Orleans, LA, USA, 18–24 June 2022; pp. 2582–2593.
19. Zhu, X.; Toisoul, A.; Perez-Rua, J.M.; Zhang, L.; Martinez, B.; Xiang, T. Few-shot action recognition with prototype-centered attentive learning. *arXiv* **2021**, arXiv:2101.08085.
20. Rymarczyk, D.; Struski, Ł.; Górszczak, M.; Lewandowska, K.; Tabor, J.; Zieliński, B. Interpretable image classification with differentiable prototypes assignment. In Proceedings of the European Conference on Computer Vision, Tel Aviv, Israel, 23–27 October 2022; pp. 351–368.
21. Gottlieb, A.; Stein, G.Y.; Ruppin, E.; Sharan, R. PREDICT: A method for inferring novel drug indications with application to personalized medicine. *Mol. Syst. Biol.* **2011**, *7*, 496. [CrossRef]
22. Luo, H.; Wang, J.; Li, M.; Luo, J.; Peng, X.; Wu, F.X.; Pan, Y. Drug repositioning based on comprehensive similarity measures and Bi-Random walk algorithm. *Bioinformatics* **2016**, *32*, 2664–2671. [CrossRef]
23. Liang, X.; Zhang, P.; Yan, L.; Fu, Y.; Peng, F.; Qu, L.; Shao, M.; Chen, Y.; Chen, Z. LRSSL: Predict and interpret drug–disease associations based on data integration using sparse subspace learning. *Bioinformatics* **2017**, *33*, 1187–1196. [CrossRef]
24. Yang, M.; Luo, H.; Li, Y.; Wang, J. Drug repositioning based on bounded nuclear norm regularization. *Bioinformatics* **2019**, *35*, i455–i463. [CrossRef] [PubMed]
25. Chen, H.; Cheng, F.; Li, J. iDrug: Integration of drug repositioning and drug-target prediction via cross-network embedding. *PLOS Comput. Biol.* **2020**, *16*, 1–20. [CrossRef] [PubMed]
26. Li, J.; Zhang, S.; Liu, T.; Ning, C.; Zhang, Z.; Zhou, W. Neural inductive matrix completion with graph convolutional networks for miRNA-disease association prediction. *Bioinformatics* **2020**, *36*, 2538–2546. [CrossRef] [PubMed]
27. Cai, L.; Lu, C.; Xu, J.; Meng, Y.; Wang, P.; Fu, X.; Zeng, X.; Su, Y. Drug repositioning based on the heterogeneous information fusion graph convolutional network. *Briefings Bioinform.* **2021**, *22*, bbab319. [CrossRef]
28. Meng, Y.; Lu, C.; Jin, M.; Xu, J.; Zeng, X.; Yang, J. A weighted bilinear neural collaborative filtering approach for drug repositioning. *Briefings Bioinform.* **2022**, *23*, bbab581. [CrossRef]
29. Nahm, F.S. Receiver operating characteristic curve: Overview and practical use for clinicians. *Korean J. Anesthesiol.* **2022**, *75*, 25–36. [CrossRef]
30. Miao, J.; Zhu, W. Precision–recall curve (PRC) classification trees. *Evol. Intell.* **2022**, *15*, 1545–1569. [CrossRef]

Disclaimer/Publisher's Note: The statements, opinions and data contained in all publications are solely those of the individual author(s) and contributor(s) and not of MDPI and/or the editor(s). MDPI and/or the editor(s) disclaim responsibility for any injury to people or property resulting from any ideas, methods, instructions or products referred to in the content.

Article

Byzantine-Robust Multimodal Federated Learning Framework for Intelligent Connected Vehicle

Ning Wu [1], Xiaoming Lin [2,3,*], Jianbin Lu [1], Fan Zhang [2,3], Weidong Chen [1], Jianlin Tang [2,3] and Jing Xiao [1]

[1] Guangxi Power Grid Co., Ltd., Nanning 530013, China; wu_n.sy@gx.csg.cn (N.W.); lu_jb.sy@gx.csg.cn (J.L.); chen_wd.sy@gx.csg.cn (W.C.); xiao_j.sy@gx.csg.cn (J.X.)
[2] Electric Power Research Institute of CSG, Guangzhou 510663, China; zhangfan4@csg.cn (F.Z.); tangjl2@csg.cn (J.T.)
[3] Guangdong Provincial Key Laboratory of Intelligent Measurement and Advanced Metering of Power Grid, Guangzhou 510663, China
* Correspondence: linxm4@csg.cn

Abstract: In the rapidly advancing domain of Intelligent Connected Vehicles (ICVs), multimodal Federated Learning (FL) presents a powerful methodology to harness diverse data sources, such as sensors, cameras, and Vehicle-to-Everything (V2X) communications, without compromising data privacy. Despite its potential, the presence of Byzantine adversaries–malicious participants who contribute incorrect or misleading updates–poses a significant challenge to the robustness and reliability of the FL process. This paper proposes a Byzantine-robust multimodal FL framework specifically designed for ICVs. Our framework integrates a robust aggregation mechanism to mitigate the influence of adversarial updates, a multimodal fusion strategy to effectively manage and combine heterogeneous input data, and a global optimization objective that accommodates the presence of Byzantine clients. The theoretical foundation of the framework is established through formal definitions and equations, demonstrating its ability to maintain reliable and accurate learning outcomes despite adversarial disruptions. Extensive experiments highlight the framework's efficacy in preserving model performance and resilience in real-world ICV environments.

Keywords: federated learning; multimodal learning; intelligent connected vehicle; Byzantine-robust federated learning

Citation: Wu, N.; Lin, X.; Lu, J.; Zhang, F.; Chen, W.; Tang, J.; Xiao, J. Byzantine-Robust Multimodal Federated Learning Framework for Intelligent Connected Vehicle. *Electronics* **2024**, *13*, 3635. https://doi.org/10.3390/electronics13183635

Academic Editor: Felipe Jiménez

Received: 12 July 2024
Revised: 23 August 2024
Accepted: 26 August 2024
Published: 12 September 2024

Copyright: © 2024 by the authors. Licensee MDPI, Basel, Switzerland. This article is an open access article distributed under the terms and conditions of the Creative Commons Attribution (CC BY) license (https://creativecommons.org/licenses/by/4.0/).

1. Introduction

The advent of Intelligent Connected Vehicles (ICVs) marks a transformative shift in transportation technology [1], promising to revolutionize road safety [2], traffic efficiency [3], and the overall driving experience [4]. ICVs leverage an intricate network of sensors, including high-resolution cameras, Light Detection and Ranging (LiDAR) systems [5], millimeter-wave radars [6], and Global Positioning System (GPS) receivers, to create a comprehensive understanding of their environment [7]. This sensor fusion, combined with advanced communication technologies such as Vehicle-to-Everything (V2X) protocols [8], enables ICVs to make informed decisions [9], navigate complex traffic scenarios [10], and interact seamlessly with other vehicles and infrastructure [11].

However, the proliferation of ICVs introduces unprecedented challenges in data management and processing [12]. The sheer volume of data generated by a single vehicle–estimated to be up to 25 gigabytes per hour–multiplied across millions of vehicles, creates a data deluge that traditional centralized computing paradigms struggle to handle efficiently [13–15]. Moreover, these data often contain sensitive information about vehicle locations, driving patterns, and potentially even biometric data of drivers, raising significant privacy concerns [16].

Federated Learning (FL) [17] has emerged as a promising solution to address these challenges. FL enables collaborative machine learning without the need for centralized data storage or processing [18]. In the context of ICVs, this means that vehicles can collectively train sophisticated models for tasks such as object detection [19], traffic prediction [14], and autonomous navigation [20,21], while keeping their raw sensor data securely on-board. This decentralized approach not only preserves privacy but also significantly reduces the bandwidth required for model training, as only model updates, rather than raw data, are transmitted [22].

Despite its potential, the application of FL in ICV scenarios faces several critical challenges that demand innovative solutions:

- **Multimodal Data Integration.** ICVs generate a diverse array of data types from various sensors [23,24]. Each sensor modality provides unique and complementary information. For example, cameras provide rich visual data that are critical for object recognition and scene understanding, while LiDAR provides precise depth information and 3D point clouds for accurate distance measurement and object localization [19]. These different modality types of data are extremely important for the proper operation of ICVs. Effectively fusing these heterogeneous data sources while maintaining their privacy-preserving nature in a FL setup is a complex challenge [25]. Traditional centralized fusion techniques are not directly applicable, necessitating novel approaches that can operate on distributed, privacy-sensitive data.
- **Byzantine Attacks.** In a distributed learning environment like FL, the system is vulnerable to Byzantine attacks, where malicious participants or compromised vehicles may inject false or manipulated data or model updates [26–28]. These attacks can take many forms, such as data poisoning [26,28], where the adversary injects crafted malicious samples into local training data, or model poisoning [29–31], where the adversary sends malicious model updates to corrupt the global model. The consequences of such attacks in an ICV context could be severe, potentially leading to erroneous object detection or navigation decisions that compromise road safety [32,33]. Developing robust defense mechanisms that can detect and mitigate these attacks without compromising the efficiency of the federated learning process is crucial.
- **Communication Constraints.** The mobility of vehicles presents unique challenges to the FL process, such as vehicles may experience periods of disconnection or weak signal strength, especially in rural or underground areas [7,9,34]. In addition, the network capacity available to vehicles may fluctuate widely depending on location, and network congestion and frequent high-bandwidth communications can put stress on the vehicle's power system, especially in electric vehicles [5]. Designing a communication-efficient federated learning protocol that can adapt to these dynamic conditions while ensuring timely and effective model updates is essential.

To address these challenges, we propose a Byzantine-robust multimodal federated learning framework specifically designed for intelligent connected vehicles. Specifically, we first design a novel multimodal fusion architecture that can effectively integrate various sensor data while preserving privacy. The architecture adopts a hierarchical approach to first locally fuse data within each modality and then use a privacy-preserving cross-modal attention mechanism to integrate information across modalities. In addition, we design a Byzantine-robust aggregation algorithm based on gradient compression that can detect and mitigate the impact of malicious participants in the FL process while maintaining high communication efficiency. Our approach combines a statistical analysis of model updates with a reputation system that tracks the historical reliability of participants. Our framework not only addresses the immediate challenges facing intelligent connected vehicles, but also lays the foundation for building a scalable, secure, and efficient federated learning ecosystem in the broader context of intelligent transportation systems.

The contributions of this paper are listed as follows:

(1) We develop a novel Byzantine-robust aggregation technique based on gradient compression, enhancing the resilience of federated learning against adversarial nodes.

(2) We introduce an advanced cross-node multimodal alignment and fusion technique that efficiently combines data from diverse sensors to improve model performance in ICVs.
(3) We implement top-k gradient compression to improve communication efficiency. This reduces the communication overhead between nodes and the central server, making the framework suitable for large-scale deployment.
(4) We conducted extensive experiments on three public datasets for the proposed framework and evaluated prior work to demonstrate the advantages of the proposed framework. Our framework can achieve a better cost–utility trade-off.

The remainder of this paper is organized as follows: Section 2 provides a comprehensive review of related work in federated learning, multimodal fusion techniques, Byzantine-robust algorithms, and their applications in intelligent transportation systems. Section 3 presents our problem definition in detail, elaborating on the challenges and constraints. Section 4 presents our proposed framework in detail, including the cross-node multimodal alignment and fusion method, gradient compression-based Byzantine aggregation algorithm, and time complexity analysis. Section 5 discusses the results of our experiments, providing a comparative analysis with existing methods and an ablation study to quantify the impact of each component of our framework. Finally, Section 6 concludes the paper by summarizing our contributions, discussing the limitations of our approach, and outlining promising directions for future research in this rapidly evolving field.

2. Related Work

This section provides an overview of the existing literature relevant to our proposed Byzantine-robust multimodal FL framework for ICVs. We organize the related work into four key areas: federated learning in vehicular networks, multimodal learning for ICVs, Byzantine-robust federated learning, and communication-efficient federated learning.

2.1. Federated Learning in Vehicular Networks

FL has gained significant attention in the context of vehicular networks due to its ability to leverage distributed data while preserving privacy [35,36]. McMahan et al. [17] introduced the seminal FedAvg algorithm, which forms the basis for many federated learning approaches. In the vehicular domain, Du et al. [25] proposed a blockchain-based FL framework for securing data sharing in the Internet of Vehicles (IoVs). Their approach addresses trust issues in data sharing but does not consider multimodal data or Byzantine attacks. Samarakoon et al. [35] developed a FL approach for joint power control and resource allocation in vehicular networks. While their work demonstrates the potential of FL in optimizing network performance, it focuses on network-level optimization rather than perception and decision-making tasks. Lu et al. [37] introduced a FL framework for cooperative sensing in connected and autonomous vehicles. Their approach shows promise in improving sensing accuracy, but it does not address the challenges of multimodal data fusion or Byzantine robustness.

2.2. Multimodal Learning for ICVs

Multimodal learning is crucial for ICVs to effectively integrate data from various sensors [38]. Feng et al. [39] proposed a deep multimodal fusion framework for object detection in autonomous driving, combining data from cameras and LiDAR. However, their approach assumes centralized data processing, which is not suitable for privacy-preserving federated learning scenarios. Caesar et al. [23] developed a multimodal attention network for sensor fusion in autonomous vehicles. While their work demonstrates improved perception accuracy, it does not consider the distributed nature of data in federated learning settings. In the context of FL, Liu et al. [40] proposed a multimodal federated learning framework for medical image analysis. Although their work addresses privacy concerns in multimodal learning, it is not tailored to the specific challenges of vehicular networks and does not consider Byzantine attacks.

2.3. Byzantine-Robust Federated Learning

Byzantine robustness is critical for ensuring the reliability of FL systems, especially in safety-critical applications like ICVs [28,31,41]. Yin et al. [42] introduced the Byzantine-robust distributed learning algorithm, which can tolerate up to a certain fraction of Byzantine workers. However, their approach assumes a centralized parameter server, which may not be suitable for fully decentralized vehicular networks. Blanchard et al. [43] proposed the Krum algorithm for Byzantine-robust aggregation in FL [43]. While Krum provides theoretical guarantees against Byzantine attacks, it may not be computationally efficient for the large-scale and time-sensitive nature of ICV applications. More recently, Fung et al. [26] developed FoolsGold, a Byzantine-robust federated learning system that can defend against Sybil attacks [28,33]. Their approach shows promise in identifying and mitigating the impact of malicious clients, but it does not consider the multimodal nature of ICV data.

2.4. Communication-Efficient Federated Learning

Communication efficiency is paramount in vehicular networks due to bandwidth limitations and the mobile nature of vehicles [44]. Konečný et al. [34] proposed structured updates and sketched updates to reduce the communication cost in FL. While their methods show significant bandwidth savings, they do not address the specific challenges of vehicular networks. Sattler et al. [35] introduced Sparse Ternary Compression (STC) for communication-efficient federated learning. STC achieves high compression rates while maintaining model accuracy, but it does not consider the dynamic nature of vehicular network conditions. In the context of vehicular networks, Ye et al. [45] proposed an efficient federated learning scheme with adaptive model aggregation. Their approach considers vehicle mobility and network conditions but does not address multimodal data fusion or Byzantine robustness.

While the existing literature has made significant strides in various aspects of federated learning for vehicular networks, there remains a critical gap in addressing the combined challenges of multimodal data integration, Byzantine robustness, and communication efficiency in a unified framework for ICVs. By addressing these challenges simultaneously, our framework aims to provide a comprehensive solution for secure, efficient, and reliable federated learning in Intelligent Connected Vehicle systems.

3. Problem Definition

In this section, we formally define the problem of Byzantine-robust multimodal federated learning for ICVs. We outline the system model, the objectives of our framework, and the specific challenges we aim to address.

3.1. System Model

Consider a network of K ICVs, denoted as $V = \{v_1, v_2, \ldots, v_k\}$. Each vehicle v_k is equipped with a set of M sensors $S = \{s_1, s_2, \ldots, s_m\}$, where each sensor captures a different modality of data (e.g., camera images, LiDAR point clouds, radar signals, GPS coordinates). Each vehicle v_k maintains its local dataset $\mathcal{D}_k = \{(\mathbf{x}_i, y_i)\}_{i=1}^{n_k}$, where $\mathbf{x}_i$ represents the multimodal input data and y_i the corresponding labels. As shown in Figure 1, the goal is to collaboratively train a global model $\mathbf{w}$ that can accurately perform a given task (e.g., object detection, traffic prediction) by aggregating local updates $\Delta \mathbf{w}_i$ from each vehicle without sharing raw data. The federated learning process can be formalized as follows:

$$\mathbf{w}_{t+1} = \mathbf{w}_t + \eta \sum_{i=1}^{K} \alpha_i \Delta \mathbf{w}_i^t, \qquad (1)$$

where $\mathbf{w}_t$ is the global model at iteration t, η is the learning rate, α_i is the weight assigned to the i-th vehicle, and $\Delta \mathbf{w}_i^t$ is the local model update from vehicle i at iteration t.

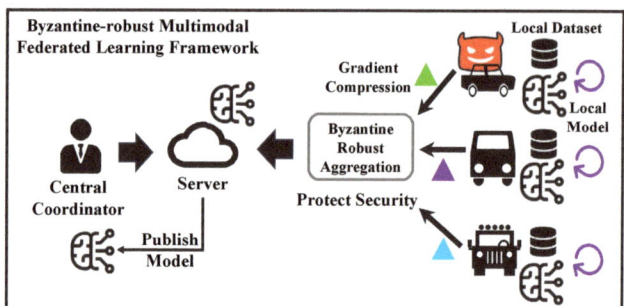

Figure 1. Workflow overview of Byzantine-robust multimodal federated learning framework.

Multimodal Fusion. Each vehicle processes multimodal data, necessitating an effective fusion strategy to handle different types of input data. Let $\mathbf{x}_i$ denote the multimodal input data from vehicle v_k, comprising m modalities $\mathbf{x}_i = \{\mathbf{x}_i^1, \mathbf{x}_i^2, \ldots, \mathbf{x}_i^m\}$. The local model $f_i(\mathbf{x}_i; \mathbf{w}_i)$ integrates these modalities to produce predictions $\hat{y}_i = f_i(\mathbf{x}_i; \mathbf{w}_i)$. The multimodal fusion within each vehicle can be formulated as follows:

$$\mathbf{h}_i = \mathcal{F}(\mathbf{x}_i^1, \mathbf{x}_i^2, \ldots, \mathbf{x}_i^m) \tag{2}$$

where $\mathcal{F}$ denotes the fusion function that combines the features from different modalities into a unified representation $\mathbf{h}_i$.

Byzantine Adversaries. In this setup, a subset of vehicles may act as Byzantine adversaries, sending arbitrary or malicious updates $\Delta \mathbf{w}_i^{t,\text{adv}}$. These adversarial updates can significantly deteriorate the performance of the global model. Let $\mathcal{B} \subseteq \{1, 2, \ldots, N\}$ denote the set of Byzantine vehicles, with $|\mathcal{B}| = b$. To mitigate the influence of Byzantine adversaries, we introduce a Byzantine-robust aggregation mechanism. The objective is to aggregate the local updates in a way that minimizes the impact of adversarial updates. Formally, the robust aggregation function $\mathcal{A}$ is defined as follows:

$$\mathbf{w}_{t+1} = \mathbf{w}_t + \eta \mathcal{A}(\{\Delta \mathbf{w}_i^t\}_{i=1}^N). \tag{3}$$

The aggregation function $\mathcal{A}$ should satisfy the following properties: (1) Resilience: It should be resilient to at most b Byzantine adversaries. (2) Accuracy: It should ensure that the aggregated update is close to the mean of the non-adversarial updates.

Objective Function. The overall objective is to minimize the global loss function $\mathcal{L}(\mathbf{w})$ over all vehicles, accounting for the presence of Byzantine adversaries:

$$\min_{\mathbf{w}} \mathcal{L}(\mathbf{w}) = \sum_{i \notin \mathcal{B}} \alpha_i \mathcal{L}_i(\mathbf{w}), \tag{4}$$

where $\mathcal{L}_i(\mathbf{w})$ is the local loss function for vehicle i. Thus, the proposed Byzantine-robust multimodal federated learning framework aims to ensure robust and efficient collaborative learning among ICVs, leveraging diverse data modalities while safeguarding against adversarial disruptions.

3.2. Challenges and Constraints

Implementing the above robust framework for ICVs poses several challenges and limitations that must be addressed to ensure the effectiveness and reliability of the system.

- **Byzantine Robustness.** Ensuring robustness against Byzantine adversaries is a significant challenge. Malicious nodes can send faulty updates that can severely degrade the performance of the global model. Designing efficient and effective robust aggregation methods to mitigate these attacks while maintaining high model performance is complex.

- **Communication Overhead.** FL inherently involves substantial communication between nodes and the central server. The gradient compression technique helps reduce this overhead, but finding the optimal balance between compression rate and model accuracy is crucial. Excessive compression can lead to the loss of important information, while insufficient compression can cause excessive communication delays.
- **Heterogeneous Data.** Multimodal datasets from different vehicles may vary in quality, resolution, and format. Ensuring effective data fusion across these heterogeneous sources without losing critical information is a key constraint.

Addressing these challenges and constraints requires continuous innovation and rigorous testing to ensure the framework's reliability, efficiency, and security in real-world ICV applications.

4. Our Approach

This section presents the Byzantine-robust multimodal federated learning framework for ICVs. The framework includes a Byzantine aggregation algorithm based on gradient compression, a modality alignment fusion method across nodes, and an objective function designed to enhance learning performance despite adversarial interference, as shown in Figure 1.

4.1. Cross-Node Multimodal Alignment and Fusion

The cross-node multimodal alignment and fusion technique is designed to handle the diverse data modalities from different ICVs and align them into a consistent latent space for effective fusion. This technique ensures that the multimodal features from different nodes are comparable and can be effectively aggregated for federated learning.

Local Feature Extraction. Each vehicle v_i extracts features from its local multimodal data using dedicated subnetworks. Let $\mathbf{x}_i = \{\mathbf{x}_i^1, \mathbf{x}_i^2, \ldots, \mathbf{x}_i^m\}$ represent the input data from m modalities. For each modality j, a feature extraction subnetwork ϕ_j is used to obtain the local features:

$$\mathbf{h}_i^j = \phi_j(\mathbf{x}_i^j) \tag{5}$$

where $\mathbf{h}_i^j$ denotes the extracted feature vector for modality j from vehicle v_i.

Discussion. To effectively manage high-dimensional multimodal data in the proposed framework for ICVs, a combination of dimensionality reduction techniques, feature extraction, and multimodal fusion strategies is employed. Methods like the above Local Feature Extraction reduce the dimensionality of data from various sensors and cameras while preserving essential features. Sparse representations and low-rank approximations further minimize the complexity of high-dimensional inputs. Additionally, adaptive fusion strategies integrate the reduced representations of different modalities, allowing for efficient information aggregation across diverse data sources. This ensures that the framework can handle the high-dimensionality of multimodal data without overwhelming computational resources while maintaining robustness against adversarial attacks.

Global Modality Alignment. To ensure that the features from different nodes are aligned into a common latent space, we employ a modality alignment network $\mathcal{A}_j$ for each modality. This network aligns the local features $\mathbf{h}_i^j$ to a global latent space:

$$\tilde{\mathbf{h}}_i^j = \mathcal{A}_j(\mathbf{h}_i^j), \tag{6}$$

where $\tilde{\mathbf{h}}_i^j$ is the globally aligned feature for modality j from vehicle i.

Alignment Network. The alignment network $\mathcal{A}_j$ can be implemented as a neural network trained to minimize the distance between features of the same class across different nodes. The loss function for training $\mathcal{A}_j$ could be a contrastive loss or a triplet loss:

$$\mathcal{L}_{\text{align}} = \sum_{i,k} \left[\|\mathcal{A}_j(\mathbf{h}_i^j) - \mathcal{A}_j(\mathbf{h}_k^j)\|^2 - \|\mathcal{A}_j(\mathbf{h}_i^j) - \mathcal{A}_j(\mathbf{h}_{\text{neg}}^j)\|^2 + \alpha \right]_+, \tag{7}$$

where $\mathbf{h}_k^j$ is a feature from another vehicle with the same label as $\mathbf{h}_i^j$, $\mathbf{h}_{neg}^j$ is a feature from a different class, and α is a margin parameter.

Feature Fusion. After aligning the features from all modalities, the next step is to fuse them into a single representation. This unified representation combines information from all modalities and serves as the input for the local prediction model. The fused representation $\mathbf{h}_i$ for vehicle i is obtained by concatenating the aligned features:

$$\mathbf{h}_i = \text{Concat}(\tilde{\mathbf{h}}_i^1, \tilde{\mathbf{h}}_i^2, \ldots, \tilde{\mathbf{h}}_i^m), \tag{8}$$

where Concat denotes the concatenation operation across all m modalities.

Concatenation and Fusion Network. The concatenated feature vector $\mathbf{h}_i$ is then passed through a fusion network $\mathcal{F}$ to integrate the information from different modalities:

$$\mathbf{z}_i = \mathcal{F}(\mathbf{h}_i), \tag{9}$$

where $\mathbf{z}_i$ is the final fused feature vector used for prediction. The fused feature vector $\mathbf{z}_i$ is used by the local model f_i to make predictions:

$$\hat{y}_i = f_i(\mathbf{z}_i; \mathbf{w}_i), \tag{10}$$

where $\mathbf{w}_i$ are the local model parameters.

Training and Optimization. The local models are trained to minimize the empirical risk over their local datasets. The local loss function for vehicle i is defined as follows:

$$\mathcal{L}_i(\mathbf{w}) = \frac{1}{n_i} \sum_{j=1}^{n_i} \ell(f_i(\mathbf{z}_{i,j}; \mathbf{w}_i), y_{i,j}), \tag{11}$$

where $\ell(\cdot, \cdot)$ is the loss function (e.g., cross-entropy loss for classification tasks). The overall objective is to minimize the global loss function across all vehicles, accounting for the presence of Byzantine adversaries (see the following section):

$$\min_{\mathbf{w}} \mathcal{L}(\mathbf{w}) = \sum_{i \notin B} \alpha_i \mathcal{L}_i(\mathbf{w}). \tag{12}$$

4.2. Gradient Compression-Based Byzantine Aggregation

This section provides a detailed description of the Byzantine aggregation technique based on top-k gradient compression.

Local Gradient Calculation. Each vehicle v_k computes the local gradient $\Delta \mathbf{w}_k$ based on its local dataset $\mathcal{D}_k$:

$$\Delta \mathbf{w}_k = \nabla \mathcal{L}_k(\mathbf{w}_k) \tag{13}$$

where $\mathcal{L}_k(\mathbf{w}_k)$ is the local loss function for vehicle v_k, and $\mathbf{w}_k$ are the local model parameters. Then we use top-k gradient compression to improve the communication efficiency, where top-k gradient compression involves retaining only the most significant elements of the gradient vector to reduce communication overhead. Given a gradient vector $\Delta \mathbf{w}_k$ from vehicle v_k, we can compute the magnitudes of all elements in $\Delta \mathbf{w}_k$:

$$\text{magnitude}_k = |\Delta \mathbf{w}_k|. \tag{14}$$

Top-k Selection. Here, we identify the indices of the top-k largest magnitudes by using the following equation:

$$\text{topk\_indices} = \text{argsort}(\mathbf{magnitude}_i)[-k:]. \tag{15}$$

Then, we create a binary mask $\mathbf{m}_i$ where the positions corresponding to the top-k indices are set to 1, and the rest are set to 0:

$$\mathbf{m}_i[j] = \begin{cases} 1 & \text{if } j \in \text{topk\_indices} \\ 0 & \text{otherwise} \end{cases} \tag{16}$$

Gradient Compression. We apply the binary mask to the gradient vector:

$$\mathcal{C}(\Delta \mathbf{w}_k) = \Delta \mathbf{w}_k \odot \mathbf{m}_k \tag{17}$$

In this context, the compressed gradient $\mathcal{C}(\Delta \mathbf{w}_i)$ contains only the top-k elements of $\Delta \mathbf{w}_i$, reducing the communication load.

Robust Aggregation. To mitigate the influence of Byzantine adversaries, a robust aggregation method like trimmed mean aggregation is used at the central server. Given compressed gradients $\{\mathcal{C}(\Delta \mathbf{w}_k)\}_{k=1}^{K}$ from K vehicles:

- **Dimension-wise Sorting and Trimming.** For each dimension d of the gradient vector, we collect the k-th elements of the compressed gradients from all vehicles, i.e., $\{\mathcal{C}(\Delta \mathbf{w}_k)_d\}_{k=1}^{K}$. Then, we sort the collected values, i.e., $\mathcal{C}(\Delta \mathbf{w}_{(1)})_d \leq \mathcal{C}(\Delta \mathbf{w}_{(2)})_d \leq \cdots \leq \mathcal{C}(\Delta \mathbf{w}_{(K)})_d$. After that, we trim the largest and smallest b values, where b is the estimated number of Byzantine adversaries.
- **Mean Calculation.** First, we compute the mean of the remaining values after trimming:

$$\mathcal{A}_d(\{\mathcal{C}(\Delta \mathbf{w}_k^t)\}_{k=1}^{K}) = \frac{1}{K-2b} \sum_{i=b+1}^{K-b} \mathcal{C}(\Delta \mathbf{w}_k^t)_d. \tag{18}$$

Then, we construct the aggregated gradient $\mathcal{A}(\{\mathcal{C}(\Delta \mathbf{w}_k^t)\}_{k=1}^{K})$ by applying $\mathcal{A}_d$ to each dimension d:

$$\mathcal{A}(\{\mathcal{C}(\Delta \mathbf{w}_i^t)\}_{i=1}^{N}) = \left(\mathcal{A}_1(\{\mathcal{C}(\Delta \mathbf{w}_i^t)\}_{i=1}^{N}), \ldots, \mathcal{A}_d(\{\mathcal{C}(\Delta \mathbf{w}_i^t)\}_{i=1}^{N})\right), \tag{19}$$

where d is the dimensionality of the gradient vector.
- **Global Model Update.** The server updates the global model using the robustly aggregated gradient:

$$\mathbf{w}_{t+1} = \mathbf{w}_t + \eta \mathcal{A}(\{\mathcal{C}(\Delta \mathbf{w}_k^t)\}_{k=1}^{K}), \tag{20}$$

where η is the learning rate.

The Byzantine aggregation technique based on top-k gradient compression involves compressing local gradients by retaining only the top-k elements and using a robust trimmed mean aggregation method at the server. This approach effectively reduces communication overhead and mitigates the impact of Byzantine adversaries, ensuring resilient and accurate global model updates in the federated learning framework for ICVs. The detailed implementation steps (see Algorithm 1) and formulas provided establish the theoretical and practical foundations of the technique, ensuring it can be effectively applied in real-world scenarios.

4.3. Time Complexity Analysis

Analyzing the time complexity of the Byzantine-robust aggregation technique based on top-k gradient compression involves examining the computational cost of each step in the process. Here, we break down the time complexity for the key steps: local gradient calculation, gradient compression, transmission, robust aggregation at the server, and the global model update.

- **Local Gradient Calculation.** Each vehicle computes the local gradient $\Delta \mathbf{w}_i$ based on its local dataset. Assume the dataset has m samples and the model has d parameters. The time complexity for gradient computation is $\mathcal{O}(m \cdot d)$. This is because each parameter gradient is typically calculated as a sum over the dataset, involving m operations per parameter.

- **Top-k Gradient Compression.** After computing the gradient, each vehicle compresses it by retaining the top-k elements, i.e., $\mathcal{O}(d)$ for magnitude calculation, $\mathcal{O}(d \log k)$ for top-k selection, and $\mathcal{O}(d)$ for binary mask creation and gradient compression. The overall time complexity for top-k gradient compression: $\mathcal{O}(d + d \log k + d) = \mathcal{O}(d \log k)$.
- **Transmission.** The transmission time depends on the communication bandwidth and is not typically considered in time complexity analysis. However, since only k elements are transmitted, the communication cost is $\mathcal{O}(k)$.
- **Robust Aggregation at Server.** The server aggregates the compressed gradients using the trimmed mean method, i.e., $\mathcal{O}(N \cdot d)$ for dimension-wise collection, $\mathcal{O}(d \cdot N \log N)$ for sorting, and $\mathcal{O}(d \cdot (N - 2b)) = \mathcal{O}(d \cdot N)$ for trimming and mean calculation. Overall time complexity for robust aggregation: $\mathcal{O}(d \cdot N \log N + d \cdot N) = \mathcal{O}(d \cdot N \log N)$.
- **Global Model Update.** The server updates the global model using the aggregated gradient. The time complexity for this step is $\mathcal{O}(d)$.

Combining all the steps, the total time complexity of the Byzantine-robust aggregation technique based on top-k gradient compression is dominated by the robust aggregation at the server, which involves sorting and averaging operations. The overall time complexity is

$$\mathcal{O}(m \cdot d) + \mathcal{O}(d \log k) + \mathcal{O}(k) + \mathcal{O}(d \cdot N \log N) + \mathcal{O}(d) \tag{21}$$

Since $\mathcal{O}(d \cdot N \log N)$ is the dominant term, the overall time complexity is

$$\mathcal{O}(d \cdot N \log N)$$

This complexity ensures that the framework can efficiently handle large-scale federated learning with numerous participants, provided the number of parameters d and the number of vehicles K remain manageable.

Algorithm 1: Byzantine-robust Multimodal Federated Learning Algorithm.

Input: Local model ω_k and local multimodal dataset $\mathcal{D}_k$.
Output: Global model ω
The server initializes the generator and global model and sends them to each vehicle;
while *local training* **do**
> Use the local model ω_k to perform feature extraction on the complete modality;
> Each vehicle v_k computes its local gradient $\Delta \mathbf{w}_k$ based on its local dataset;
> Calculate the magnitudes of the elements in $\Delta \mathbf{w}_k$;
> Identify the top-k largest magnitudes;
> Create a binary mask $\mathbf{m}_i$;
> Apply the binary mask to the gradient;

Transmit the compressed gradient $\mathcal{C}(\Delta \mathbf{w}_k)$ to the central server;
do
> Collect the compressed gradients from all participating vehicles;
> Sort the k-th elements of the received gradients;
> Trim the largest and smallest b values;
> Compute the mean of the remaining values;
> Construct the aggregated gradient;
> Update the global model using the aggregated gradient;
>
> $$\mathbf{w}_{t+1} = \mathbf{w}_t + \eta \mathcal{A}(\{\mathcal{C}(\Delta \mathbf{w}_i^t)\}_{i=1}^N)$$

while *execute the above aggregation*;

5. Experiments

5.1. Experiment Setup

To evaluate the performance of our framework, we conducted extensive experiments on four benchmarking datasets. All experiments were implemented using Python 3.9 and PyTorch 1.12 and evaluated on a server with an NVIDIA A100 GPU.

Datasets. Our proposed framework was evaluated using three comprehensive multimodal datasets: KITTI [46], nuScenes [23], and KAIST Multispectral Pedestrian Detection Dataset [47]. KITTI provides RGB images, LiDAR point clouds, and GPS/IMU data for 2D and 3D object detection in urban and highway scenes. nuScenes offers a larger-scale dataset with additional RADAR data, covering diverse driving scenarios in multiple cities. The KAIST dataset focuses on pedestrian detection using RGB and thermal infrared images, challenging the framework with day/night variations. These datasets are adapted for federated learning by partitioning data among simulated ICVs, ensuring non-IID distributions, implementing privacy-preserving data handling, introducing Byzantine nodes, and simulating varying communication conditions. Together, they provide a robust testbed for evaluating our framework's performance in multimodal fusion, Byzantine resilience, and adaptation to diverse ICV environments and object detection tasks.

Models. Our framework employs a diverse set of state-of-the-art models adapted for FL scenarios. These include PointPillars [48], which efficiently processes LiDAR point clouds and can be extended to incorporate RGB data; MVX-Net [49], designed for the multimodal fusion of LiDAR and image data; AVOD [50], a 3D object detection model that fuses LiDAR and RGB inputs; a custom KAIST Multispectral Pedestrian Detection Network for handling RGB and thermal infrared data; and YOLOv4-Multispectral, an extension of YOLOv4 [51] adapted for fast, multispectral object detection.

Parameters. In the proposed framework, key parameters include the number of participating nodes ($K = 100$ vehicles), gradient compression rate ($r = 100$ elements), and learning rate $\eta = 0.001$. The framework is designed to handle $b = \{10, 15, 20, 25\}$ Byzantine nodes. The model typically involves $d = 10^6$ parameters, with each node processing local datasets of $m = 10,000$ samples. The datasets used include RGB images with resolutions of 1242×375 (KITTI), 1600×900 (nuScenes), and 1920×1280 pixels (Waymo). LiDAR point clouds have densities of around 100,000 (KITTI), 300,000 (nuScenes), and 200,000 points per frame (Waymo). Radar data are captured at approximately 13 Hz, and GPS accuracy is within 1–2 m. These parameters ensure the framework's efficiency, robustness, and effectiveness in real-world ICV scenarios.

Baselines. The proposed framework was evaluated using the following baselines:

- **FedAvg [17].** FedAvg aggregates local models from all vehicles by averaging their parameters but does not account for Byzantine robustness.
- **Krum [43] and Multi-Krum [52].** They are robust aggregation techniques designed to resist Byzantine attacks by selecting gradients that deviate the least from the majority.
- **Trimmed Mean [53] and Median [28].** These aggregation methods enhance robustness by trimming extreme values and using median values to mitigate the influence of adversarial updates.
- **Byzantine-resilient SGD (BrSGD) [54].** This approach focuses on detecting and excluding malicious updates during training.
- **FLTrust [55].** This approach focuses on computing trust scores to select high-quality clients.

These baselines provide a comprehensive evaluation framework, allowing for a robust comparison of the proposed framework's effectiveness in handling adversarial scenarios, maintaining accuracy, and ensuring efficient multimodal data fusion in ICV tasks.

Evaluation Metrics. Evaluating the proposed framework requires a comprehensive set of metrics to assess its performance across various dimensions. Key evaluation metrics include accuracy, which measures the proportion of correctly detected objects in multimodal datasets such as KITTI, nuScenes, and Waymo. Robustness metrics, i.e., the percentage of successful attacks detected and mitigated, are essential for evaluating the framework's resilience against Byzantine adversaries. We use the communication overhead to assess the efficiency of the gradient compression and transmission processes, while convergence time measures how quickly the model reaches a satisfactory performance level. Together, these metrics ensure a thorough evaluation of the framework's accuracy, robustness, efficiency, and overall effectiveness in real-world ICV scenarios.

5.2. Numerical Analysis

System Performance. This experiment aimed to study the system performance of the proposed framework. Specifically, we adopted local label-flipping attacks and Gaussian attacks as Byzantine attacks. We explored the performance of the proposed framework and baselines on different benchmark datasets under local label-flipping attacks. The experimental results are shown in Table 1, which shows that the proposed framework outperforms the baselines on different datasets, indicating that the proposed scheme can filter poisonous data well and maintain model performance. The experimental results show that the framework outperforms other baselines in terms of system performance and anti-poisoning attacks due to the efficient Byzantine defense mechanism and multimodal fusion design.

Table 1. Accuracy of the proposed framework and benchmarks on different datasets.

Method	KITTI	nuScenes	KAIST
FedAvg	65.4 ± 0.3	58.7 ± 0.2	67.8 ± 0.2
Krum	67.7 ± 0.1	62.4 ± 0.2	71.2 ± 0.1
Multi-Krum	68.9 ± 0.1	65.7 ± 0.3	74.1 ± 0.2
Trimmed Mean	66.8 ± 0.2	64.1 ± 0.2	72.6 ± 0.2
Mean	65.8 ± 0.1	59.7 ± 0.4	70.1 ± 0.2
BrSGD	71.2 ± 0.2	68.3 ± 0.3	75.4 ± 0.2
Ours	**73.2 ± 0.2**	**72.5 ± 0.2**	**77.9 ± 0.2**

Secondly, we explored the impact of different numbers of Byzantine clients on the performance of the proposed framework and baselines under the above two attacks. Specifically, we set $b = \{10, 15, 20, 25\}$. The experimental results are summarized in Tables 2 and 3. The experimental results show that the proposed framework is still more robust than other baselines under different numbers of attackers, which indicates that the proposed Byzantine defense based on gradient compression is very effective against these Byzantine attacks.

Table 2. Accuracy of the proposed framework and benchmarks under different numbers of compromised clients.

Method	$b = 10$	$b = 15$	$b = 20$	$b = 25$
FedAvg	65.4 ± 0.1	63.8 ± 0.2	58.8 ± 0.3	52.4 ± 0.2
Krum	67.7 ± 0.1	65.6 ± 0.1	60.1 ± 0.2	54.8 ± 0.3
Multi-Krum	68.9 ± 0.2	67.1 ± 0.3	62.5 ± 0.2	58.7 ± 0.1
Trimmed Mean	66.8 ± 0.2	65.6 ± 0.4	63.7 ± 0.3	59.8 ± 0.1
Mean	65.8 ± 0.2	62.7 ± 0.1	58.9 ± 0.2	55.6 ± 0.1
BrSGD	71.2 ± 0.3	68.7 ± 0.2	66.5 ± 0.2	62.7 ± 0.1
FLTrust	72.2 ± 0.1	71.4 ± 0.2	68.7 ± 0.3	65.6 ± 0.1
Ours	**73.2 ± 0.1**	**71.9 ± 0.2**	**69.7 ± 0.1**	**68.4 ± 0.2**

Communication Efficiency. Table 4 records the communication overhead results of the proposed framework and the baselines under different numbers of clients. The experimental results show that the proposed framework has a higher communication efficiency due to the use of a gradient compression scheme, which requires a small gradient size. In addition, cross-node multimodal alignment and fusion provide high-quality model update aggregation, thereby accelerating the convergence of the model.

Table 3. Accuracy of the proposed framework and benchmarks under different numbers of compromised clients for Gaussian attack.

Method	$b = 10$	$b = 15$	$b = 20$	$b = 25$
FedAvg	58.6 ± 0.2	54.2 ± 0.3	48.6 ± 0.3	42.7 ± 0.2
Krum	65.2 ± 0.2	63.2 ± 0.2	61.8 ± 0.3	56.7 ± 0.2
Multi-Krum	67.7 ± 0.2	65.4 ± 0.2	61.6 ± 0.2	56.5 ± 0.1
Trimmed Mean	64.6 ± 0.2	62.4 ± 0.3	58.7 ± 0.2	54.4 ± 0.1
Mean	62.7 ± 0.2	57.7 ± 0.1	55.4 ± 0.2	53.1 ± 0.1
BrSGD	68.7 ± 0.2	67.1 ± 0.2	64.8 ± 0.2	60.7 ± 0.1
FLTrust	71.7 ± 0.1	66.7 ± 0.2	65.4 ± 0.2	61.8 ± 0.1
Ours	**74.2 ± 0.1**	**73.1 ± 0.2**	**70.8 ± 0.1**	**69.3 ± 0.2**

Table 4. Communication overhead of the proposed framework and baselines with different numbers of clients.

Method	$K = 100$	$K = 120$	$K = 140$	$K = 150$
FedAvg	4896 MB	5432 MB	5831 MB	6123 MB
Krum	4984 MB	5641 MB	6023 MB	6457 MB
Multi-Krum	5014 MB	5425 MB	5987 MB	6398 MB
Trimmed Mean	5021 MB	5531 MB	6015 MB	6157 MB
Mean	4974 MB	5324 MB	6074 MB	6248 MB
BrSGD	3697 MB	4125 MB	4897 MB	5324 MB
Ours	**49.64 MB**	**53.24 MB**	**57.41 MB**	**60.23 MB**

Parameter Sensitivity. Here, we aim to explore the impact of the gradient compression rate parameter on the communication overhead of the proposed framework. Table 5 shows the communication overhead results under different gradient compression rates, where the results show that the proposed framework can achieve a better communication efficiency.

Table 5. Communication overhead of the proposed framework and baselines under compression rates.

Method	$r = 100$	$r = 110$	$r = 120$	$r = 150$
FedAvg	4896 MB	5432 MB	5831 MB	6123 MB
Krum	4984 MB	5641 MB	6023 MB	6457 MB
Multi-Krum	5014 MB	5425 MB	5987 MB	6398 MB
Trimmed Mean	5021 MB	5531 MB	6015 MB	6157 MB
Mean	4974 MB	5324 MB	6074 MB	6248 MB
BrSGD	3697 MB	4125 MB	4897 MB	5324 MB
Ours	**49.64 MB**	**48.23 MB**	**46.65 MB**	**41.25 MB**

Ablation Studies. Finally, we conducted ablation experiments to study the performance impact of different components within the proposed framework. Specifically, we explored the impact of the multimodal fusion mechanism and the Byzantine aggregation mechanism based on gradient compression on the framework, respectively. Table 6 summarizes the experimental results. We observed that the performance of the proposed framework with and without the multimodal fusion mechanism was relatively close, indicating a good privacy–performance trade-off. In addition, we observed that the Byzantine aggregation mechanism based on gradient compression significantly improved the model's robustness and performance.

Discussion. The proposed Byzantine-robust multimodal FL framework for ICVs can effectively scale to larger networks by leveraging adaptive robust aggregation mechanisms, hierarchical structures, and resource-aware optimization techniques. The dynamic network topology of ICVs is managed through asynchronous aggregation and buffer mechanisms, ensuring stability even with fluctuating connectivity. The framework's multimodal fusion strategy accommodates varying data rates and heterogeneous sensor inputs by employing dynamic fusion weights and adaptive sampling. To handle increasing adversarial presence, hierarchical Byzantine-resilient aggregation, combined with reinforcement learning-based optimization, ensures that the system remains robust. Resource constraints are mitigated through bandwidth-aware compression and gradient sparsification, allowing for the framework to maintain efficiency even under communication limitations. Overall, these strategies enable the framework to scale effectively while preserving robustness, resilience, and performance in real-world ICV environments.

Table 6. Ablation study results.

Method	$K = 100$	$K = 120$	$K = 140$	$K = 150$
w/o Fusion	68.9	67.7	66.8	65.7
w/o Aggregation	66.1	65.4	64.6	62.8
Ours	73.2	72.5	71.1	70.9

6. Conclusions

In this paper, we introduce a Byzantine-robust multimodal federated learning framework designed for ICVs. This framework addresses critical challenges in federated learning, particularly those related to data privacy, security, and robustness against adversarial attacks. By leveraging advanced techniques such as gradient compression and robust aggregation methods, the framework ensures efficient and secure training across multiple nodes, even in the presence of Byzantine adversaries. We highlighted the importance of multimodal data fusion by integrating diverse sensor data, including RGB images, LiDAR point clouds, radar data, and GPS/IMU measurements, to enhance the accuracy and reliability of object detection in autonomous driving. Through the use of benchmark datasets like KITTI, nuScenes, and Waymo Open Dataset, we demonstrated the framework's capability to maintain high performance and robustness. Our evaluation metrics, including accuracy, precision, recall, robustness, communication overhead, and computational cost, provide a comprehensive assessment of the framework's effectiveness. The proposed approach not only advances the state of federated learning in autonomous driving but also sets a foundation for future research on secure and resilient distributed machine learning systems.

Author Contributions: Methodology, J.T.; Software, J.L.; Formal analysis, W.C.; Data curation, F.Z.; Writing—original draft, N.W.; Writing—review & editing, J.X.; Supervision, X.L. All authors have read and agreed to the published version of the manuscript.

Funding: This work was financially supported by the Science and Technology Project of Guangxi Power Grid Co., Ltd. (GXKJXM20222206).

Data Availability Statement: Data available in a publicly accessible repository.

Conflicts of Interest: Author Ning Wu, Jianbin Lu, Weidong Chen and Jing Xiao were employed by the company Guangxi Power Grid Co., Ltd.; Xiaoming Lin, Fan Zhang and Jianlin Tang were employed by the company Electric Power Research Institute of CSG. The remaining authors declare that the research was conducted in the absence of any commercial or financial relationships that could be construed as a potential conflict of interest. And the authors declare that this study received funding from Science and Technology Project of Guangxi Power Grid Co., Ltd. The funder was not involved in the study design, collection, analysis, interpretation of data, the writing of this article or the decision to submit it for publication.

References

1. Liu, J.; Liu, J. Intelligent and connected vehicles: Current situation, future directions, and challenges. *IEEE Commun. Stand. Mag.* **2018**, *2*, 59–65. [CrossRef]
2. Han, M.; Wan, A.; Zhang, F.; Ma, S. An attribute-isolated secure communication architecture for intelligent connected vehicles. *IEEE Trans. Intell. Veh.* **2020**, *5*, 545–555. [CrossRef]
3. Uhlemann, E. Introducing connected vehicles [connected vehicles]. *IEEE Veh. Technol. Mag.* **2015**, *10*, 23–31. [CrossRef]
4. Lu, N.; Cheng, N.; Zhang, N.; Shen, X.; Mark, J.W. Connected vehicles: Solutions and challenges. *IEEE Internet Things J.* **2014**, *1*, 289–299. [CrossRef]

5. Kim, I.; Martins, R.J.; Jang, J.; Badloe, T.; Khadir, S.; Jung, H.-Y.; Kim, H.; Kim, J.; Genevet, P.; Rho, J. Nanophotonics for light detection and ranging technology. *Nat. Nanotechnol.* **2021**, *16*, 508–524. [CrossRef]
6. Mead, J.B.; Pazmany, A.L.; Sekelsky, S.M.; McIntosh, R.E. Millimeter-wave radars for remotely sensing clouds and precipitation. *Proc. IEEE* **1994**, *82*, 1891–1906. [CrossRef]
7. Duan, W.; Gu, J.; Wen, M.; Zhang, G.; Ji, Y.; Mumtaz, S. Emerging technologies for 5 g-iov networks: Applications, trends and opportunities. *IEEE Netw.* **2020**, *34*, 283–289. [CrossRef]
8. Noor-A-Rahim, M.; Liu, Z.; Lee, H.; Khyam, M.O.; He, J.; Pesch, D.; Moessner, K.; Saad, W.; Poor, H.V. 6 g for vehicle-to-everything (v2x) communications: Enabling technologies, challenges, and opportunities. *Proc. IEEE* **2022**, *110*, 712–734. [CrossRef]
9. Chen, S.; Hu, J.; Shi, Y.; Peng, Y.; Fang, J.; Zhao, R.; Zhao, L. Vehicle-to-everything (v2x) services supported by lte-based systems and 5 g. *IEEE Commun. Stand. Mag.* **2017**, *1*, 70–76. [CrossRef]
10. Lu, R.; Zhang, L.; Ni, J.; Fang, Y. 5 g vehicle-to-everything services: Gearing up for security and privacy. *Proc. IEEE* **2019**, *108*, 373–389. [CrossRef]
11. Campolo, C.; Molinaro, A.; Iera, A.; Menichella, F. 5 g network slicing for vehicle-to-everything services. *IEEE Wirel. Commun.* **2017**, *24*, 38–45. [CrossRef]
12. Zavvos, E.; Gerding, E.H.; Yazdanpanah, V.; Maple, C.; Stein, S.; Schraefel, M.C . Privacy and trust in the internet of vehicles. *IEEE Trans. Intell. Transp. Syst.* **2021**, *23*, 10126–10141. [CrossRef]
13. Liu, Y.; Wang, Y.; Chang, G. Efficient privacy-preserving dual authentication and key agreement scheme for secure v2v communications in an iov paradigm. *IEEE Trans. Intell. Transp.* **2017**, *18*, 2740–2749. [CrossRef]
14. Liu, Y.; James, J.; Kang, J.; Niyato, D.; Zhang, S. Privacy-preserving traffic flow prediction: A federated learning approach. *IEEE Internet Things J.* **2020**, *7*, 7751–7763. [CrossRef]
15. Mei, Q.; Xiong, H.; Chen, J.; Yang, M.; Kumari, S.; Khan, M.K. Efficient certificateless aggregate signature with conditional privacy preservation in iov. *IEEE Syst. J.* **2020**, *15*, 245–256. [CrossRef]
16. Bao, Y.; Qiu, W.; Cheng, X.; Sun, J. Fine-grained data sharing with enhanced privacy protection and dynamic users group service for the iov. *IEEE Trans. Intell. Transp. Syst.* **2022**, *24*, 13035–13049. [CrossRef]
17. McMahan, B.; Moore, E.; Ramage, D.; Hampson, S.; Arcas, B.A.Y. Communication-efficient learning of deep networks from decentralized data. In Proceedings of the 20th International Conference on Artificial Intelligence and Statistics (PMLR), Lauderdale, FL, USA, 20–22 April 2017 ; pp. 1273–1282.
18. Liu, Y.; Garg, S.; Nie, J.; Zhang, Y.; Xiong, Z.; Kang, J.; Hossain, M.S. Deep anomaly detection for time-series data in industrial iot: A communication-efficient on-device federated learning approach. *IEEE Internet Things J.* **2020**, *8*, 6348–6358. [CrossRef]
19. Liu, Y.; Huang, A.; Luo, Y.; Huang, H.; Liu, Y.; Chen, Y.; Feng, L.; Chen, T.; Yu, H.; Yang, A.Q. Fedvision: An online visual object detection platform powered by federated learning. In Proceedings of the AAAI Conference on Artificial Intelligence, New York, NY, USA, 7–12 February 2020; Volume 34, pp. 13172–13179.
20. Li, Y.; Tao, X.; Zhang, X.; Liu, J.; Xu, J. Privacy-preserved federated learning for autonomous driving. *IEEE Trans. Intell. Transp. Syst.* **2021**, *23*, 8423–8434. [CrossRef]
21. Liu, B.; Wang, L.; Liu, M. Lifelong federated reinforcement learning: A learning architecture for navigation in cloud robotic systems. *IEEE Robot. Autom. Lett.* **2019**, *4*, 4555–4562. [CrossRef]
22. Liu, Y.; Yuan, X.; Xiong, Z.; Kang, J.; Wang, X.; Niyato, D. Federated learning for 6g communications: Challenges, methods, and future directions. *China Commun.* **2020**, *17*, 105–118. [CrossRef]
23. Caesar, H.; Bankiti, V.; Lang, A.H.; Vora, S.; Liong, V.E.; Xu, Q.; Krishnan, A.; Pan, Y.; Baldan, G.; Beijbom, O. Nuscenes: A multimodal dataset for autonomous driving. In Proceedings of the IEEE/CVF Conference on Computer Vision and Pattern Recognition, Seattle, WA, USA, 13–19 June 2020; pp. 11621–11631.
24. Zhu, Y.; Ye, Y.; Liu, Y.; James, J. Cross-area travel time uncertainty estimation from trajectory data: A federated learning approach. *IEEE Trans. Intell. Transp. Syst.* **2022**, *23*, 24966–24978. [CrossRef]
25. Du, Z.; Wu, C.; Yoshinaga, T.; Yau, K.-L.A.; Ji, Y.; Li, J. Federated learning for vehicular internet of things: Recent advances and open issues. *IEEE Open J. Comput. Soc.* **2020**, *1*, 45–61. [CrossRef] [PubMed]
26. Fung, C.; Yoon, C.J.; Beschastnikh, I. The limitations of federated learning in sybil settings. In Proceedings of the 23rd International Symposium on Research in Attacks, Intrusions and Defenses (RAID 2020), San Sebastian, Spain, 14–15 October 2020; pp. 301–316.
27. Tolpegin, V.; Truex, S.; Gursoy, M.E.; Liu, L. Data poisoning attacks against federated learning systems. In Proceedings of the Computer Security—ESORICs 2020: 25th European Symposium on Research in Computer Security, Proceedings, Part i 25 , Guildford, UK, 14–18 September 2020; Springer: Berlin/Heidelberg, Germany, 2020; pp. 480–501.
28. Liu, Y.; Wang, C.; Yuan, X. BadSampler: Harnessing the Power of Catastrophic Forgetting to Poison Byzantine-robust Federated Learning. In Proceedings of the 30th ACM SIGKDD Conference on Knowledge Discovery and Data Mining (KDD'24), Barcelona, Spain, 25–29 August 2024.
29. Ma, Z.; Ma, J.; Miao, Y.; Li, Y.; Deng, R.H. Shieldfl: Mitigating model poisoning attacks in privacy-preserving federated learning. *IEEE Trans. Inf. Forensics Secur.* **2022**, *17*, 1639–1654. [CrossRef]
30. Taheri, R.; Shojafar, M.; Alazab, M.; Tafazolli, R. FED-IIoT: A robust federated malware detection architecture in industrial IoT. *IEEE Trans. Ind. Inform.* **2020**, *17*, 8442–8452. [CrossRef]

31. Nabavirazavi, S.; Taheri, R.; Shojafar, M.; Iyengar, S.S. Impact of aggregation function randomization against model poisoning in federated learning. In Proceedings of the 22nd IEEE International Conference on Trust, Security and Privacy in Computing and Communications, TrustCom 2023, Exeter, UK, 1–3 November 2023; pp. 165–172.
32. Cui, Y.; Liang, Y.; Luo, Q.; Shu, Z.; Huang, T. Resilient Consensus Control of Heterogeneous Multi-UAV Systems with Leader of Unknown Input Against Byzantine Attacks. *IEEE Trans. Autom. Sci. Eng.* **2024**, 1–12. 10.1109/TASE.2024.3420697. [CrossRef]
33. Cui, Y.; Jia, Y.; Li, Y.; Shen, J.; Huang, T.; Gong, X. Byzantine resilient joint localization and target tracking of multi-vehicle systems. in *IEEE Trans. Intell. Veh.* **2023**, *8*, 2899–2913. [CrossRef]
34. Konečný, J.; McMahan, H.B.; Ramage, D.; Richtárik, P. Federated optimization: Distributed machine learning for on-device intelligence. *arXiv* **2016**, arXiv:1610.02527.
35. Samarakoon, S.; Bennis, M.; Saad, W.; Debbah, M. Distributed federated learning for ultra-reliable low-latency vehicular communications. *IEEE Trans. Commun.* **2019**, *68*, 1146–1159. [CrossRef]
36. Posner, J.; Tseng, L.; Aloqaily, M.; Jararweh, Y. Federated learning in vehicular networks: Opportunities and solutions. *IEEE Netw.* **2021**, *35*, 152–159. [CrossRef]
37. Lu, Y.; Huang, X.; Zhang, K.; Maharjan, S.; Zhang, Y. Blockchain empowered asynchronous federated learning for secure data sharing in internet of vehicles. *IEEE Trans. Veh. Technol.* **2020**, *69*, 4298–4311. [CrossRef]
38. Salehi, B.; Reus-Muns, G.; Roy, D.; Wang, Z.; Jian, T.; Dy, J.; Ioannidis, S.; Chowdhury, K. Deep learning on multimodal sensor data at the wireless edge for vehicular network. *IEEE Trans. Veh. Technol.* **2022**, *71*, 7639–7655. [CrossRef]
39. Feng, D.; Haase-Schütz, C.; Rosenbaum, L.; Hertlein, H.; Glaeser, C.; Timm, F.; Wiesbeck, W.; Dietmayer, K. Deep multi-modal object detection and semantic segmentation for autonomous driving: Datasets, methods, and challenges. *IEEE Trans. Intell. Transp. Syst.* **2020**, *22*, 1341–1360. [CrossRef]
40. Liu, X.; Gao, K.; Liu, B.; Pan, C.; Liang, K.; Yan, L.; Ma, J.; He, F.; Zhang, S.; Pan, S.; et al. Advances in deep learning-based medical image analysis. *Health Data Sci.* **2021**, *2021*, 8786793. [CrossRef] [PubMed]
41. Rabe, M.; Milz, S.; Mader, P. Development methodologies for safety critical machine learning applications in the automotive domain: A survey. In Proceedings of the IEEE/CVF Conference on Computer Vision and Pattern Recognition, Nashville, TN, USA, 19–25 June 2021; pp. 129–141.
42. Yin, D.; Chen, Y.; Kannan, R.; Bartlett, P. Byzantine-robust distributed learning: Towards optimal statistical rates. In Proceedings of the International Conference on Machine Learning (PMLR), Stockholm, Sweden, 10–15 July 2018; pp. 5650–5659.
43. Blanchard, P.; Mhamdi, E.M.E.; Guerraoui, R.; Stainer, J. Machine learning with adversaries: Byzantine tolerant gradient descent. *Adv. Neural Inf. Process. Syst.* **2017**, *30*, 118–128.
44. Hayat, S.; Yanmaz, E.; Muzaffar, R. Survey on unmanned aerial vehicle networks for civil applications: A communications viewpoint. *IEEE Commun. Surv. Tutorials* **2016**, *18*, 2624–2661. [CrossRef]
45. Ye, D.; Yu, R.; Pan, M.; Han, Z. Federated learning in vehicular edge computing: A selective model aggregation approach. *IEEE Access* **2020**, *8*, 23920–23935. [CrossRef]
46. Geiger, A.; Lenz, P.; Urtasun, R. Are we ready for autonomous driving? The kitti vision benchmark suite. In Proceedings of the 2012 IEEE Conference on Computer Vision and Pattern Recognition, Providence, RI, USA, 16–21 June 2012; pp. 3354–3361.
47. Hwang, S.; Park, J.; Kim, N.; Choi, Y.; Kweon, I.S. Multispectral pedestrian detection: Benchmark dataset and baseline. In Proceedings of the IEEE Conference on Computer Vision and Pattern Recognition, Boston, MA, USA, 7–12 June 2015; pp. 1037–1045.
48. Lang, A.H.; Vora, S.; Caesar, H.; Zhou, L.; Yang, J.; Beijbom, O. Pointpillars: Fast encoders for object detection from point clouds. In Proceedings of the IEEE/CVF Conference on Computer Vision and Pattern Recognition, Long Beach, CA, USA, 16–17 June 2019; pp. 12697–12705.
49. Sindagi, V.A.; Zhou, Y.; Tuzel, O. Mvx-net: Multimodal voxelnet for 3D object detection. In Proceedings of the 2019 International Conference on Robotics and Automation (ICRA), Montreal, QC, Canada, 20–24 May 2019; pp. 7276–7282.
50. Ku, J.; Mozifian, M.; Lee, J.; Harakeh, A.; Waslander, S.L. Joint 3D proposal generation and object detection from view aggregation. In Proceedings of the 2018 IEEE/RSJ International Conference on Intelligent Robots and Systems (IROS), Madrid, Spain, 1–5 October 2018; pp. 1–8.
51. Bochkovskiy, A.; Wang, C.-Y.; Liao, H.-Y.M. Yolov4: Optimal speed and accuracy of object detection. *arXiv* **2020**, arXiv:2004.10934.
52. Colosimo, F.; Rango, F.D. Median-krum: A joint distance-statistical based byzantine-robust algorithm in federated learning. In Proceedings of the Int'l ACM Symposium on Mobility Management and Wireless Access, Montreal, QC, Canada, 30 October–3 November 2023; pp. 61–68.
53. Wang, T.; Zheng, Z.; Lin, F. Federated Learning Framew Ork Based on Trimmed Mean Aggregation Rules. 2022. Available online: https://www.ssrn.com/abstract=4181353 (accessed on 28 January 2022).
54. Data, D.; Diggavi, S. Byzantine-resilient sgd in high dimensions on heterogeneous data. In Proceedings of the 2021 IEEE International Symposium on Information Theory (ISIT), Melbourne, Australia, 12–20 July 2021; pp. 2310–2315.
55. Cao, X.; Fang, M.; Liu, J.; Gong, N.Z. FLTrust: Byzantine-robust Federated Learning via Trust Bootstrapping. In Proceedings of the ISOC Network and Distributed System Security Symposium (NDSS), Online, 21–25 February 2021.

Disclaimer/Publisher's Note: The statements, opinions and data contained in all publications are solely those of the individual author(s) and contributor(s) and not of MDPI and/or the editor(s). MDPI and/or the editor(s) disclaim responsibility for any injury to people or property resulting from any ideas, methods, instructions or products referred to in the content.

Article

P2P Federated Learning Based on Node Segmentation with Privacy Protection for IoV

Jia Zhao [1,2], Yating Guo [1,2,*], Bokai Yang [1,2] and Yanchun Wang [1,2]

1. Beijing Key Laboratory of Security and Privacy in Intelligent Transportation, Beijing Jiaotong University, Beijing 100044, China; zhaojia@bjtu.edu.cn (J.Z.)
2. School of Computer and Information Technology, Beijing Jiaotong University, Beijing 100044, China
* Correspondence: 21120471@bjtu.edu.cn

Abstract: The current usage of federated learning in applications relies on the existence of servers. To address the inability to conduct federated learning for IoV (Internet of Vehicles) applications in serverless areas, a P2P (peer-to-peer) architecture for federated learning is proposed in this paper. Following node segmentation based on limited subgraph diameters, an edge aggregation mode is employed to propagate models inwardly, and a mode for propagating the model inward to the C-node (center node) while aggregating is proposed. Simultaneously, a personalized differential privacy scheme was designed under this architecture. Through experimentation and verification, the approach proposed in this paper demonstrates the combination of both security and usability.

Keywords: federated learning; IoV; differential privacy; P2P

Citation: Zhao, J.; Guo, Y.; Yang, B.; Wang, Y. P2P Federated Learning Based on Node Segmentation with Privacy Protection for IoV. *Electronics* **2024**, *13*, 2276. https://doi.org/10.3390/electronics13122276

Academic Editor: Felipe Jiménez

Received: 29 March 2024
Revised: 20 May 2024
Accepted: 27 May 2024
Published: 10 June 2024

Copyright: © 2024 by the authors. Licensee MDPI, Basel, Switzerland. This article is an open access article distributed under the terms and conditions of the Creative Commons Attribution (CC BY) license (https://creativecommons.org/licenses/by/4.0/).

1. Introduction

IoV (Internet of Vehicles) applications often require the utilization of big data for model training, which inevitably raises concerns about user privacy [1]. Therefore, employing a privacy-preserving algorithm becomes imperative. Federated learning [2,3] emerged as a privacy-preserving paradigm commonly utilized in machine learning. However, the prevalent C-S (client-server) architecture presents certain limitations, notably, the requirement for server involvement. This limitation restricts the application of federated learning in regions where servers are unavailable or not readily deployable, hindering its adoption for IoT applications in such areas. An alternative federated learning architecture, P2P (peer-to-peer), offers a solution to this challenge. However, P2P architectures are more complex, and most of the research on federated learning for P2P architectures is based on a complete node distribution network. The implementation of federated learning for P2P architectures in the context of vehicular networking must also consider the issue of the distance between vehicles, which need to be sufficiently close to each other to communicate and exchange model parameters. Therefore, it can be beneficial to group the vehicle nodes in proximity based on distance before federated learning, ensuring that vehicle nodes at each position in the node distribution network graph can form a P2P architecture with nearby vehicle nodes. Additionally, the system should be designed to be straightforward and efficient to implement, facilitating convenient application in real-world scenarios.

Federated learning, despite its privacy-preserving benefits, has certain security risks, such as inference attacks and poisoning attacks. Common privacy computation methods used to enhance the security of federated learning include encrypting the model or using differential privacy by adding noise. In the context of IoV, model parameters are interchanged between vehicle nodes in a P2P architecture, which introduces the possibility of inferring certain privacy information from the received model parameters if a malicious node is present. The use of differential privacy reduces this risk. However, the addition of noise affects the quality of the model. Malicious nodes often choose nearby nodes for inference attacks, and the risk of privacy information leakage decreases as the distance between nodes increases. Therefore, the degree of differential privacy can be adjusted according to the geographic distance between nodes. When the distance between nodes is short, the risk of inference attacks is higher, necessitating the addition of more noise to the model parameters for protection. Conversely, when the distance between nodes is greater, the risk is reduced, allowing for less noise addition and a greater focus on maintaining model quality.

Therefore, to extend the provision of federated learning services to a broader customer base, employing federated learning with a P2P architecture can address the serverless scenario. However, the realization of P2P architecture federated learning on a complete node distribution graph is not suitable for IoV. We can consider grouping nodes in proximity based on distance, which can be used to partition the complete graph into subgraphs as the basis for grouping before federated learning. The data security of IoV applications is very important. To prevent vehicles participating in federated learning from inferring private data from the received model parameters, each vehicle should add noise to the propagation model to realize the differential privacy mechanism. Furthermore, the degree of differential privacy can be adjusted based on distance: when the distance between nodes is greater, the risk of data leakage is smaller, allowing more focus on the quality of the model. Conversely, when nodes are closer together, the risk of data leakage increases, necessitating the addition of more noise to the model parameters to enhance privacy protection.

This paper introduces a federated learning scheme specifically designed for the IoV within a peer-to-peer architecture. In utilizing the minimum spanning tree algorithm and centrality algorithm, the node distribution graph is segmented to control the diameter of the subgraph. This segmentation serves as the foundation for node grouping before federated learning, and the propagation process of federated learning was designed to align with the topology within the subgraph. To enhance the privacy protection capabilities of federated learning, a personalized differential privacy scheme is introduced based on distance adjustment. This scheme enables nodes to dynamically adapt the degree of differential privacy according to their environmental context.

The primary contributions include the following:

- An F-Prim algorithm, derived from Prim's algorithm and centrality algorithm, was devised to group nodes based on proximity while constraining the diameters of the subgraphs, thereby forming a P2P architecture.
- The propagation path of models within the P2P architecture is designed according to the node hierarchy, wherein nodes propagate from the periphery to the core of the subgraph for aggregation, facilitating the completion of the model aggregation process at the C-node (central node).
- A personalized differential privacy scheme was formulated, enabling each node to adjust the amount of noise added to the model parameters based on its distance from other nodes. This scheme aims to strike a balance between security and model quality.

The remainder of this article is structured as follows. In Section 2, existing studies that deployed P2P-based federated learning in vehicle networks are reviewed. Section 3 introduces the application scenarios of the scheme and the P2P architecture formed after node segmentation. In Section 4, the federated learning process and its privacy preserving scheme under P2P architecture are elaborated on. In Section 5, some experiments based on the scheme are designed to verify the proposed architecture. Section 6 show relevant proofs of some of the programs. Finally, Section 7 concludes this article.

A summary of the main notations is provided in Table 1.

Table 1. Main symbols.

Symbol	Meaning
$\hat{N}$	The maximum number of nodes in a single subgraph
$|\cdot|$	The cardinality of a set
v_i	The i-th node
D_i	The database held by the owner v_i
e_{ij}	The edge between v_i and v_j
d_{ij}	The distance between v_i and v_j
$d_{\max}$	The maximum of distance in G
$\hat{d}_i$	The maximum of the distance between v_i and v_i's neighbor node
l_{ij}	The minimum length between v_i and v_j
center	The ID of the C-node
$C_h(i)$	The value of the harmonic centrality of v_i
L_1	The set of one-layer node IDs
L_2	The set of two-layer node IDs
t	The index of the t-th aggregation
T	The number of aggregation times
ω	The vector of model parameters
ω^0	Initial parameters
ω_i^t	The local training parameters of the i-th node at the t-th aggregation
$\tilde{\omega}_i^t$	Local training parameters ω_i^t with noise n_i
$\omega_{v_i}^t$	Aggregated parameters on v_i
$n(\epsilon, \sigma, \triangle f)$	Gaussian noise function
n_i	The noise added by v_i
$\triangle f_i$	The sensitivity of v_i
σ	Sigma
C	Clipping threshold

2. Related Work

Federated learning research has been widely applied in the field of IoV. As a privacy paradigm for machine learning, federated learning helps to address the privacy issues of sensitive information such as of path and location in IoV applications without affecting the model training on IoV data. Samarakoon et al. [4] investigated the joint power and resource allocation problem for ultra-reliable and low-latency communication in vehicular networks and used Lyapunov optimization to derive a joint power and resource allocation strategy with ultra-reliable and low-latency communication in a distributed approach as well. Kong et al. [5] proposed a federated learning-based cooperative vehicle localization system, which takes full advantage of the Internet of Things and the potential of collaborative edge computing to ensure user privacy while providing highly accurate localization corrections.

Architectures for federated learning contain both C-S and P2P, and most of the research has focused on the C-S architecture. In IoV, V2V(Vehicle-to-Vehicle) communication is also possible, which allows P2P-based federated learning to be considered in IoV scenarios. Yuan et al. [6] introduced a novel framework named FedPC aimed at tackling driver privacy concerns stemming from in-cabin cameras in NDAR. FedPC employs a peer-to-peer federated learning approach coupled with continual learning to ensure privacy, enhance learning efficiency, and reduce communication, computational, and storage overheads. Barbieri et al. [7] investigated decentralized federated learning methods to enhance road user/object classification based on LiDAR data in smart connected vehicles. They proposed a consensus-driven FLapproach facilitating the collaborative training of deep ML models among vehicles by sharing model parameters via V2X links, eliminating the need for a central parameter server.

Privacy and security in IoV applications have been a major concern. In the domain of privacy-preserving federated learning within P2P networks under IoV, several noteworthy methodologies have emerged to address challenges in security, privacy preservation, and robustness. Lu et al. [8] proposed an asynchronous federated learning scheme for resource sharing in vehicular IoT. They used a local differential privacy technique to protect the privacy of local updates. An asynchronous approach was employed with FL to enable distributed peer-to-peer model updates between vehicles, which is more suitable for a decentralized vehicular network. Chen et al. [9] proposed a novel decentralized federated learning method called BDFL (Byzantine Fault-Tolerance Decentralized Federated Learning), which combines Byzantine fault-tolerance mechanisms and privacy-preserving techniques to address security and privacy challenges. This method utilizes a P2P FL architecture and the HydRand protocol to establish a robust and fault-tolerant FL environment and adopts a PVSS (publicly verifiable secret-sharing) scheme to protect the privacy of autonomous vehicle models.

It is evident that federated learning with a P2P architecture is well suited for the connected car environment. However, the complexity of the P2P architecture poses challenges compared to the C-S architecture. Moreover, most existing studies on federated learning in IoV with a P2P architecture are based on a complete node distribution network. In real-world environments, the changing distances between nodes may lead to connection distances that are too far to facilitate the federated learning process effectively. Therefore, in this paper, a novel approach is proposed. A method is designed to partition the node distribution network graph and group nearby nodes into the same subgraph as the basis for federated learning. Subsequently, the federated learning process is deployed, and its associated privacy protection scheme is used in this framework to address the challenges posed by real-world IoV environments.

3. System Model

In this section, the operation of a P2P-based IoV scenario is described. And the F-Prim (Finite-length Prim) algorithm designed in this study is proposed for partitioning the node distribution graph to realize the P2P federated learning architecture.

3.1. P2P-Based IoV Scenarios

In the study, an IoV scenario was established to offer federated learning services within a server-less urban environment, as illustrated in Figure 1. In areas devoid of servers, solely vehicle terminals are observable, forming the entirety of the vehicle network. Each terminal is endowed with computational and storage capacities and is adept at communicating with other terminals.

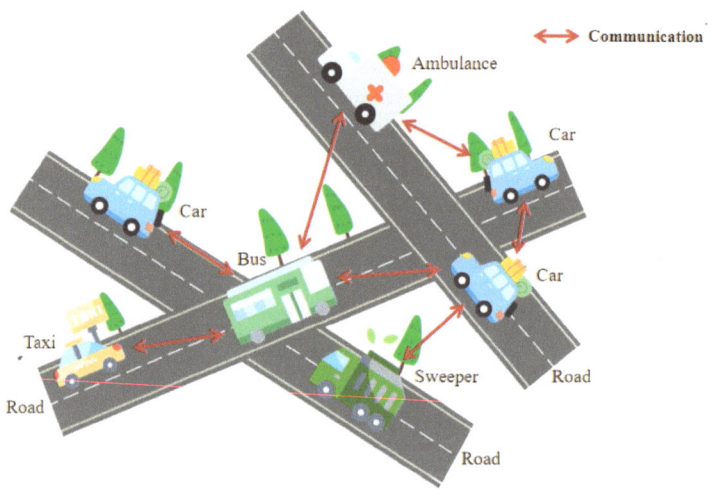

Figure 1. IoV scenario.

To represent the distribution of vehicle terminals, a terminal node network graph was constructed: $G = \{v, e, d \mid v \in V, e \in E, |V| = N\}$, as illustrated in Figure 2. In this graph G, $V = \{v_1, v_2, \ldots, v_N\}$ denotes the set of vehicle terminal nodes. Each terminal v_i is associated with a local dataset D_i. If terminals v_i and v_j can communicate with each other, there exists an edge $e_{ij} \in E$ between the corresponding nodes, and the weight d_{ij} of edge e_{ij} represents the geographic distance between the two nodes. However, connections may become unstable if the distance between two terminals is too large. Therefore, consideration is given to two terminals capable of communication if the distance between them is less than $d_{\max}$. In summary, the weights of edges e_{ij} on the node distribution network graph are represented as $|d_{ij}| \in (0, d_{\max}]$.

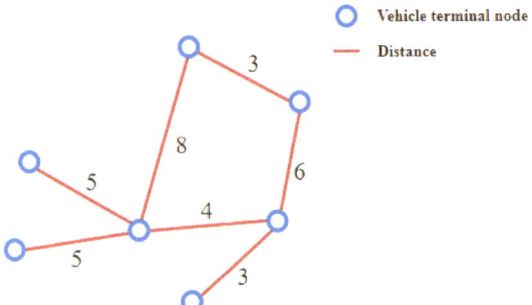

Figure 2. Node mapping network graph.

3.2. Node Segmentation to Build P2P-Based Federated Learning Architecture

In federated learning with a C-S architecture, clients typically prefer selecting nearby servers to serve themselves [10]. However, in serverless P2P architectures, which exhibit more complex topologies, special algorithms are required to determine the grouping method of nodes that are distributed in close proximity to each other. Additionally, in the context of IoV where vehicle locations are dynamic, grouping methods with too many conditions may become obsolete as node distributions change rapidly. Therefore, there is a need for a grouping algorithm with fewer conditions and reduced computational complexity to facilitate P2P node grouping in IoV scenarios.

In the architecture of IoV, the node distribution graph consists of nodes, edges, and weights. The algorithm designed for proximity grouping aims to minimize edge weights mapped to geographic location distributions. Thus, an algorithm from graph theory that minimizes the sum of edge weights while finding nodes with the shortest distances is desirable. The Prim algorithm, a classical algorithm for finding a minimum spanning tree in weighted connected graphs, serves this purpose. This algorithm retrieves the generated tree that minimizes the sum of edge weights, thereby facilitating the efficient proximity grouping of nodes in IoV scenarios.

Remark 1. *In IoV applications, the primary goal is to group individual nodes rather than connections. Prim's algorithm and Kruskal's algorithm are both classic approaches for generating minimum spanning trees. However, Prim's algorithm, which selects nodes based on the shortest distances from the current spanning tree, aligns more closely with the objective of node grouping in IoV scenarios. Therefore, it is more suitable as a basis for improvement in this context.*

The core of the Prim algorithm lies in finding the shortest pathways among all nodes. When directly applied to grouping, it tends to include all nodes in a single group. To ensure effective grouping, a threshold value $\hat{N}$ for the number of nodes in each group is necessary. If the group size surpasses $\hat{N}$, the group becomes saturated, signaling the end of grouping, and a new grouping process starts from another node.

The Prim algorithm, although effective at grouping nodes, does not inherently limit the diameters of subgraphs. In the context of federated learning in P2P architectures, excessively long subgraph diameters can lead to extended propagation chains between nodes, resulting in prolonged propagation times unsuitable for vehicular networking. To address this, the Prim algorithm requires modifications to restrict the diameters of subgraphs.

To this end, this paper introduces the F-Prim algorithm, an adaptation of the Prim algorithm. In the C-S architecture, servers are designated as centers, and a C-node is established within each subgroup formed by grouping. This facilitates controlling the distances between remaining nodes and the C-node to limit the diameters of subgraphs. Ultimately, the number of nodes within each subgraph does not exceed $\hat{N}$.

Graph centrality serves as a vital metric in complex network analysis, quantifying the importance or influence of nodes in a graph. Various centrality algorithms exist, but for selecting a C-node to restrict the subgraph diameter, centrality algorithms related to shortest distances, such as harmonic centrality and betweenness centrality, are relevant. Their definitions are as follows.

Definition 1 (Harmonic Centrality). *Harmonic centrality [11] is a metric used in network analysis to assess the importance of a node within a network. A higher harmonic centrality indicates that the node has shorter average distances than other nodes, implying greater influence within the network.*

$$C_h(i) = \sum_{j=1}^{N} \frac{1}{l(i,j)}, \tag{1}$$

Definition 2 (Betweenness centrality). *Betweenness centrality [12,13] quantifies a node's importance by measuring how often it lies on the shortest paths between pairs of other nodes. It reflects a node's potential control over information or resource flow in the network.*

$$C_b(i) = \sum_{s \neq i \neq t} \frac{\beta_{st}(i)}{\beta_{st}} \tag{2}$$

where β_{st} represents the total number of shortest paths from node s to node t, and $\beta_{st}(i)$ denotes the number of those paths that pass through node i.

Given the constraints of IoV applications, harmonic centrality emerges as the more suitable choice for centrality computation due to its independence from knowledge of the entire graph. Unlike betweenness centrality, which requires information about all shortest paths between nodes, harmonic centrality only necessitates knowledge of distances from a node to others within its vicinity. This makes it compatible with P2P architectures where nodes have limited access to information beyond their local neighborhood.

Therefore, the F-Prim algorithm adopts harmonic centrality to identify the C-node of the subgraph. The algorithm aims to limit the subgraph diameter, thereby constraining the maximum propagation distance between nodes during model dissemination. By focusing on propagation length rather than physical distance between nodes, it better aligns with the dynamic nature of IoV applications. Using propagation length simplifies node segmentation, as nodes only need to assess connections with neighboring nodes without requiring stable distance information, which is impractical for vehicles whose positions change frequently.

To select the C-node accurately, the algorithm computes the harmonic centrality ($C_h(i)$) for each node within the subgraph as new nodes are added. According to the definition of harmonic centrality, the node with the highest centrality becomes the new C-node. With a predetermined upper limit of subgraph diameter set to 4, the algorithm ensures that the minimum propagation length from each newly added node to the C-node remains within two hops or less.

The complete procedure of the algorithm is delineated in Algorithm 1.

Algorithm 1: F-Prim Algorithm(G, V, d)

Input: A graph G, the set of nodes V in G, a matrix d representing the distances between nodes

```
1  sgNum ← 0;
2  while |V| ≠ 0 do
3      for i ← 1 to |V| do
4          disSG[i] ← ∞;
5      end
6      select v_r as root node;
7      disSG[r] ← 0;
8      center ← r;
9      while True do
10         minDis ← ∞;
11         for v_i ∈ V do
12             if dis[i] < minDis & l(center, i) ≤ 2 then
13                 minDis ← dis[i];
14                 rec ← i;
15             end
16         end
17         for v_u ∈ G.Adj[v_rec] do
18             if w(rec, u) < dis[u] then
19                 dis[u] ← w(rec, u);
20             end
21         end
22         SG[sgNum].add(v_rec);
23         V = V − {v_rec};
24         center ← SG[sgNum].harmCenter;
25         if |SG[sgNum]| ≥ K̂ then
26             break
27         end
28     end
29     sgNum ← sgNum + 1;
30 end
```

4. P2P-Based Federated Learning Process with Its Privacy Protection

In this study, the federal learning process and its privacy computation scheme were designed based on the P2P architecture proposed above.

4.1. P2P-Based Federated Learning Process

After partitioning the node graph, each subgraph is limited to a diameter of 4, and the distance from any node to the C-node is at most 2. Nodes are then organized into layers based on their distance from the C-node. Nodes at a distance of two hops from the C-node are labeled as two-layer nodes (set L_2), while those at a distance of one hop are labeled as one-layer nodes (set L_1). The C-node constitutes a separate layer. This layering facilitates efficient communication within the subgraph during federated learning.

4.1.1. Path Selection

In graph theory, directly connected edges do not always represent the shortest distance paths. In the hierarchical division discussed here, a two-layer node must pass through a one-layer node to propagate the model to the C-node for aggregation. However, a one-layer node connected to the center may also be connected to other one-layer nodes. Choosing the shortest distance path needs to consider the actual IoV application environment.

As illustrated in Figure 3, where the C is the central node, A and B are one-layer nodes, and a, b, and c represent geographical distances from B to the C-node, A to B, and A to the C-node, respectively. According to the triangle inequality theorem, $a + b > c$, in the actual geographic distance, the path from each node to the C-node via the minimum number of hops, i.e., the minimum length, must also be the path of the shortest distance. This means that the path from A to the C-node via the C-node directly represents the shortest distance path (Path ②) rather than the path via B first (Path ①).

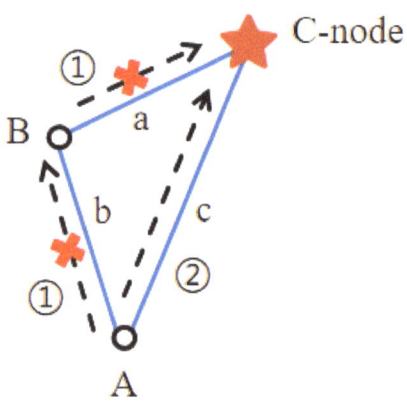

Figure 3. Path selection.

4.1.2. Aggregated Simultaneous Transmission

The federated learning subgraph topology of the P2P model forms a complex, multi-layered structure, requiring the careful consideration of propagation and aggregation operations within this topology.

In the general P2P model of federated learning, there are two potential approaches for propagating aggregation. The first involves each node exchanging locally trained models with neighboring nodes, resulting in potentially different global models on each node. The second approach entails finding a path in the topology where each node along the path can aggregate all models to obtain a global model on a specific node. In this study, with a C-node present in the subgraph itself, propagation and aggregation were designed based on the second method.

Following the hierarchical structure of the federated learning subgraph in the P2P model, propagation occurs from the inside out, starting from two-layer nodes, then moving inward through one-layer nodes, and finally reaching the C-node for aggregation.

In this propagation mode, all nodes initially train their local models. Once training is complete, two-layer nodes transmit their local models to all connected one-layer nodes. If network failure prevents global model aggregation at the C-node, models aggregated at one-layer nodes can temporarily replace global models to serve surrounding nodes. Therefore, one-layer nodes propagate to two-layer nodes while passing their local models to connected one-layer nodes, enhancing model availability.

Increased aggregations expedite model convergence. Consequently, after receiving all models from connected two-layer and one-layer nodes, a one-layer node aggregates them to lighten the C-node's workload and reduce the propagation time within the subgraph. After all one-layer nodes perform aggregation, they transmit models to the C-node. The C-node conducts a final aggregation by combining models from all one-layer nodes with locally trained models, resulting in the global model within the P2P federated learning subgraph. This transmission approach is termed AST (Aggregated Simultaneous Transmission).

4.1.3. Model Weight Adjustment

In the FedAvg algorithm, the weights are determined based on the data volume in the model, and the client c_i passes its local data volume $|D_i|$ to the server to compute its model weight. As shown in Equation (3), where p_i represents the weight of v_i's model ω_i in the global model ω,

$$p_i = \frac{|D_i|}{\sum_{k=1}^{K}|D_k|} \qquad (3)$$

However, in this propagation mode, adjustments for the information on the amount of data transmitted are necessary to maintain fairness in the final model, as discussed in Section 6.1.

After calculations, the nodes pass the models while transmitting the amount of dataset $|D_i|_\alpha$ to calculate the model weights:

$$|D_i|_\alpha = \frac{|D_i|}{\alpha_i} \qquad (4)$$

where α_i is the following value:

$$\begin{cases} \alpha_i = \left|\sum_{e_{ij}\in E} e_{ij}\right| & i \in L_2 \\ \alpha_i = \left|\sum_{e_{ij}\in E} e_{ij}\right|, j \notin L_2 & i \in L_1 \\ \alpha_i = 1 & i = \text{center} \end{cases} \qquad (5)$$

4.2. Personalized Differential Privacy

In the proposed scheme, differential privacy is employed to ensure privacy protection during the propagation of federated learning model parameters.

Definition 3 (Differential privacy [14]). *For a function $f : D \to \mathbb{R}^d$, the mechanism M satisfies (ε, δ)-differential privacy if for all adjacent datasets D and D' that differ in at most one element and for all measurable sets S in the output space,*

$$\Pr[M(f(D)) \in S] \leq e^\varepsilon \Pr[M(f(D')) \in S] + \delta, \qquad (6)$$

Gaussian noise is a type of noise characterized by a probability density function equivalent to a normal distribution, also known as a Gaussian distribution. In essence, it manifests as values distributed according to this specific distribution pattern.

According to the definition of differential privacy, when equations

$$\sigma \geq \frac{c\Delta f}{\varepsilon} \qquad (7)$$

$$c^2 > 2\ln\frac{1.25}{\delta} \qquad (8)$$

are satisfied, the algorithm $M(f(D)) = f(D) + N(0, \delta^2)$ satisfies (ε, δ)-differential privacy, where $N(0, \delta^2)$ is a random vector sampled from the Gaussian distribution.

If choosing to add noise after local training to streamline privacy calculations, the training process of the vehicle terminal node v_i on the local dataset D_i during the t-th round of federal learning can be represented as

$$f_i \triangleq f(D_i) = \omega_i^t = \frac{1}{|D_i|}\sum_{j=1}^{|D_i|} \arg\min F_i(\omega_i^{t-1}, D_{i,j}) \qquad (9)$$

The sensitivity of the vehicle terminal node v_i is calculated based on this training process function. To streamline privacy calculations, Gaussian noise was chosen to be added after local training. In this case, the sensitivity of v_i [15] can be expressed as

$$\triangle f_i = \max_{D_i, D'_i} \|f(D_i) - f(D'_i)\|$$

$$= \max_{D_i, D'_i} \left\| \frac{1}{|D_i|} \sum_{j=1}^{|D_i|} \arg\min F_i(\omega_i^{t-1}, D_{i,j}) - \frac{1}{|D'_i|} \sum_{j=1}^{|D'_i|} \arg\min F_i(\omega_i^{t-1}, D'_{i,j}) \right\| \quad (10)$$

$$= \frac{2C}{|D_i|}$$

So, when σ_i satisfies

$$\sigma_i \geq \frac{c\triangle f}{\varepsilon} \geq \frac{2C\sqrt{2\ln\left(\frac{1.25}{\delta}\right)}}{\varepsilon |D_i|} \quad (11)$$

the algorithm complies with the (ε, δ)-differential privacy mechanism.

Differential privacy was selected as the model protection algorithm primarily to address the risk of curious nodes inferring the dataset from received models. Compared to encryption or other algorithms requiring extensive privacy calculations, it offers a more suitable solution for environments requiring rapid responses in IoV.

During federated learning, noise added to the model is determined based on inter-node distance before the propagation of local models. This approach aims to add more noise when vehicle nodes are close, thereby reducing the risk of data leakage from nearby nodes. Conversely, less noise is added when nodes are farther apart, balancing privacy protection with model quality considerations.

However, each node is generally connected to multiple nodes, and the distances between these nodes are not equal. If the added noise is computed multiple times, it will necessitate additional privacy computations. Hence, the minimum distance $\hat{d}_i$ of the node's neighbors is selected, calculated using Equation (12), as the parameter to compute the value of ε. This ensures that the node only needs to compute the noise once, and irrespective of the node to which it is passed, it is guaranteed to satisfy (ε, δ)-differential privacy.

$$\hat{d}_i = \min\{d_{ij}|v_j \in SG[h]\}, i \neq center \quad (12)$$

The function $f(x) = \ln(x+1)$ is utilized to compute the ε value, where the function monotonically increases in the range $(0, \varepsilon_{max}]$. Therefore, $0 < x \leq e^{\varepsilon_{max}} - 1$ in this function. In this design, the range of values for the distance between two nodes is $(0, d_{max}]$, and the privacy budget on node v_i is given by

$$\varepsilon_i = \ln\left(\frac{\hat{d}_i}{\frac{d_{max}}{e^{\varepsilon_{max}}-1}} + 1\right) = \ln\left(\frac{(e^{\varepsilon_{max}} - 1)\hat{d}_i}{d_{max}} + 1\right) \quad (13)$$

In this way, the noise added by node v_i after local training is

$$n_i = n(\varepsilon_i, \delta, \triangle f_i) = n(\ln\left(\frac{(e^{\varepsilon_{max}} - 1)\hat{d}_i}{d_{max}} + 1\right), \delta, \frac{2C}{|D_i|}) \sim N(0, \sigma_i^2) \quad (14)$$

In accordance with Equations (8), (10), and (7), σ_i needs to satisfy

$$\sigma_i \geq \frac{2C\sqrt{2\ln\left(\frac{1.25}{\delta}\right)}}{\ln\left(\frac{(e^{\varepsilon_{max}}-1)\hat{d}_i}{d_{max}} + 1\right)|D_i|} \quad (15)$$

Based on Equations (14) and (15), it can be observed that the amount of added noise decreases as the distance between nodes increases.

The entire federated learning process with differential privacy is presented in Algorithm 2.

Algorithm 2: Federated learning process

---

1 **for** $t \leftarrow 1$ **to** T **do**
2   **for** $i \leftarrow 1$ **to** N **do**
3   **if** $t = 1$ **then**
4   get ω^0
5   **end**
6      $\omega_i^t \leftarrow \text{Train}(\omega^{t-1}, D_i)$
7   **if** $i \neq center$ **then**
8        $\omega_i^t \leftarrow \dfrac{\omega_i^t}{\max\left(1, \frac{\omega_i^t}{C}\right)}$
9        $\tilde{\omega}_i^t \leftarrow \omega_i^t + n_i$
10   **end**
11   **end**
12   **for** $i \in L_2$ **do**
13   **for** $j \in L_1$ **do**
14   **if** $e_{ij} \in E$ **then**
15          $v_i \to v_j : \tilde{\omega}_i^t$
16   **end**
17   **end**
18   **end**
19   **for** $i \in L_1$ **do**
20   **for** $j \in L_1$ **do**
21   **if** $e_{ij} \in E$ **then**
22          $v_i \to v_j : \tilde{\omega}_i^t$
23   **end**
24   **end**
25      $\omega_{v_i}^t \leftarrow \text{Agg}\left(\tilde{\omega}_i^t, \sum \tilde{\omega}_{L_1}^t, \sum \tilde{\omega}_{L_2}^t\right)$
26      $v_i \to v_{center} : \omega_{v_i}^t$
27   **end**
28    $v_{center} : \omega^t \leftarrow \text{Agg}\left(\omega_{center}^t, \sum \omega_{v_{L_1}}^t\right)$
29   **for** $i \leftarrow 1$ **to** N **do**
30      $v_{center} \to v_i : \omega^t$
31   **end**
32 **end**

---

5. Experimentation and Analysis

In this study, the scheme presented in this paper was experimented with and analyzed.

Remark 2. *In the experiments conducted, it was observed that some subgraphs contain too few nodes. To better show the impact of node segmentation, subgraphs with insufficient nodes were split. The internal nodes of these split subgraphs were redistributed to the subgraphs closest to them, while any isolated nodes still remaining after the splitting process were discarded.*

Remark 3. *Because node partitioning generates multiple subgraphs, the results in the experiment were obtained by averaging the results of multiple subgraphs.*

5.1. Node Segmentation

The distribution of vehicle nodes at a given moment was simulated in two ways. The first method was implemented using the networkx package, while the second method utilized OpenStreetMap.

In the first approach, generating nodes with random horizontal and random vertical coordinates in a 100 × 100 square area, called an RC (randomized coordinate). In the second approach, nodes are randomly selected on the actual road map provided by OpenStreetMap, called MVN (moving vehicle nodes).

The sum of the shortest distances $cnodeDis$ from the C-node to the remaining nodes $V - \{v_{center}\}$ within the subgraph is computed according to Equation (16) as a measure.

$$cnodeDis = \sum_{j=1, i=center}^{N} \min(\{d_{im} + d_{mj}, d_{ij}\}) \tag{16}$$

Under the two node simulation schemes, the total number of nodes $N = 160$ and the upper limit of the number of nodes within each subgraph $\hat{K} = 20$ were set to compute $cnodeDis$, for comparing the betweenness centrality and the F-Prim algorithm designed in this study.

As shown in Figure 4, the dots in it represent the data for each subplot, the line in the middle of the box represents the data mean, and the top and bottom edges represent the maximum and minimum values of the data. Because of the uneven distribution of nodes, the data distribution is more discrete between subgraphs, but most nodes are distributed around the mean. The difference between the values of the two centrality algorithms is not really significant, as nodes that are at more intersections of shortest paths within a better connected subgraph are also more likely to be nodes closer to the rest of the nodes within that subgraph, i.e., when a node's harmonic centrality is high, its harmonic centrality is likely to be relatively high as well. However, it is still possible to see from the mean median that F-Prim yields smaller $cnodeDis$ values, i.e., the C-node computed under this algorithm is closer to the rest of the nodes. Moreover, compared to the RC simulation, the effect of F-Prim is a little more obvious under the MVN simulation, which may indicate that the algorithm is more effective on the actual vehicle distribution along the road, while it is weaker on the simulation with only a random distribution, implying that the algorithm is more suitable for practical IoV applications.

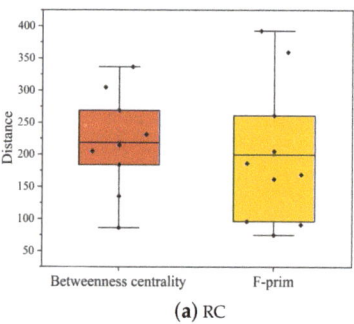
(a) RC

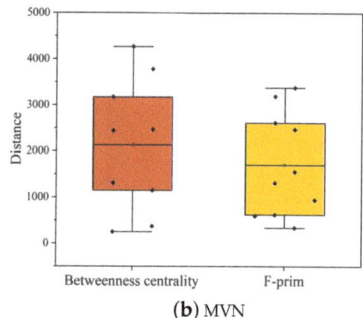
(b) MVN

Figure 4. Comparison of centrality algorithms.

We fixed the upper limit of the number of nodes within each subgraph $\hat{K} = 20$, adjusted the value of the total number of nodes N to 120, 140, 160, 180, and 200, and compared the resulting $cnodeDis$ values.

As indicated in Figure 5, the $cnodeDis$ values of both algorithms exhibit an overall upward trend as the total number of nodes increases. However, this trend is not strictly linear and fluctuates, reflecting the randomness and unpredictability of node distribution.

Overall, the betweenness centrality utilized by the F-Prim algorithm yields better results in subgraph segmentation by positioning the C-node closer to other nodes. While the betweenness centrality algorithm may occasionally outperform other methods, its computation typically requires access to information about all nodes in the graph, rendering it unsuitable for P2P mode.

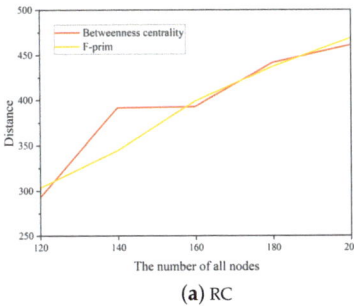 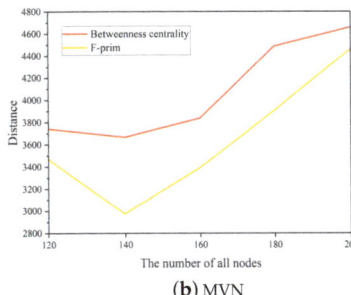

(a) RC   (b) MVN

Figure 5. cnodeDis.

5.2. Aggregated Simultaneous Transmission

To demonstrate the accelerated intra-subgraph propagation process facilitated by AST in the IoV environment, a comparison is drawn with propagation patterns in the PPT algorithm [16] and the CFL algorithm [17]. Both algorithms are grounded in P2P-mode federated learning and employ a single-line propagation mode of depth-first traversal. In the PPT algorithm, depth-first traversal occurs within all nodes participating in federated learning. Each propagation involves a single aggregation, followed by a backtrack to identify unaggregated nodes after surrounding nodes have been aggregated. The CFL algorithm builds upon the PPT algorithm by implementing subclustering. It conducts depth-first traversal within a single cluster, resulting in more localized aggregation operations.

5.2.1. Communication Time

In the PPT and CFL algorithms, only the target node participates in federated learning, and in order to facilitate a comparison among the three propagation modes, all nodes were designated as target nodes to partake in the federated learning process in P2P mode.

Given that the model propagated in the three modes remains unchanged, the model parameters are set to propagate at an identical rate across all modes. Consequently, the total communication time for model propagation between subgraph nodes is primarily determined using the distance of the paths traversed by the model during propagation.

As illustrated in Figure 6, with the same propagation speed, the communication time of the cluster-medium propagation model is notably shorter compared to the propagation models of the PPT and CFL algorithms. The cluster-based propagation approach prioritizes efficiency by distributing nodes in layers based on clustering within the CFL algorithm. This enables subgraph propagation and interlayer model propagation to occur in parallel, minimizing serial transmission between nodes and reducing the overall communication time. In contrast, the propagation modes employed in the PPT and CFL algorithms are more suited for scenarios with fewer nodes and simpler topologies. They are less effective in environments with a large number of nodes and complex distribution and connectivity patterns. Overall, the cluster-medium propagation model demonstrates superior capability in obtaining the global model and promptly responding to application requirements by efficiently propagating under the distribution of vehicle networking nodes.

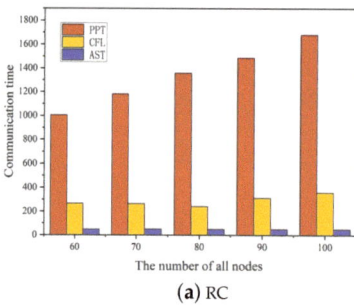
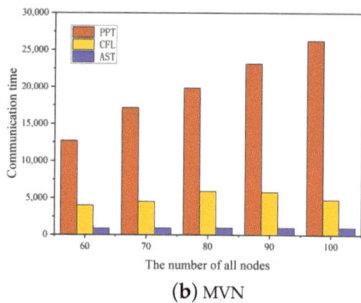

Figure 6. Communication time.

5.2.2. Number of Aggregations

We adjusted the number of vehicle terminal nodes N and compared the number of aggregations.

Figure 7 also presents the number of aggregations under all three methods. As the total number of nodes increases, the number of aggregations rises for all propagation modes. However, the cluster-in-propagation mode consistently requires fewer aggregations compared to the other two methods. Despite augmenting the number of aggregations on layer-1 nodes to expedite global model aggregation within the subgraph, the cluster-in-propagation mode maintains the number of aggregations within a reasonable range. This number does not exceed the one-step-at-a-time aggregation mode of the PPT and CFL algorithms. Additionally, aggregation operations on layer-1 nodes can be performed in parallel. In contrast, aggregation operations in the PPT and CFL propagation modes must be executed serially alongside model propagation between nodes. Consequently, even with the same number of aggregations, the cluster-in-propagation mode is expected to require less time than the PPT and CFL propagation modes.

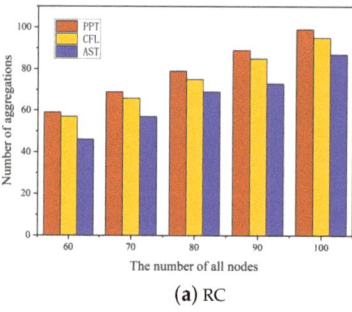
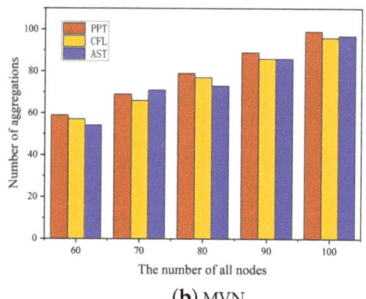

Figure 7. Number of aggregations.

5.3. *Personalized Differential Privacy*

This section will show the impact of personalized differential privacy on the algorithm.

Three datasets were utilized to simulate federated learning in this study, including the Mnist dataset, Cifar10 dataset, and a specialized vehicle image dataset, Car. This specific vehicle image dataset is categorized into six classes: garbage trucks, buses, trucks, cars, pickups, and dump trucks. The training set encompasses approximately 5500 images, while the test set comprises approximately 750 images. For example, images of the cars are shown in Figure 8.

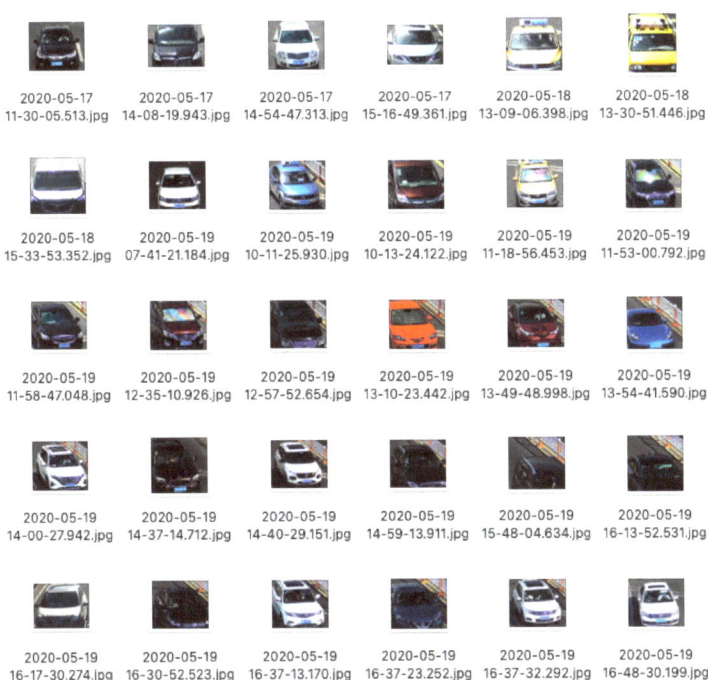

Figure 8. Special vehicle image dataset.

Three datasets were experimented with using specific CNN models and used for the same federated learning experiment. The results of the accuracy rate are shown in Figure 9, and loss is shown in Figure 10.

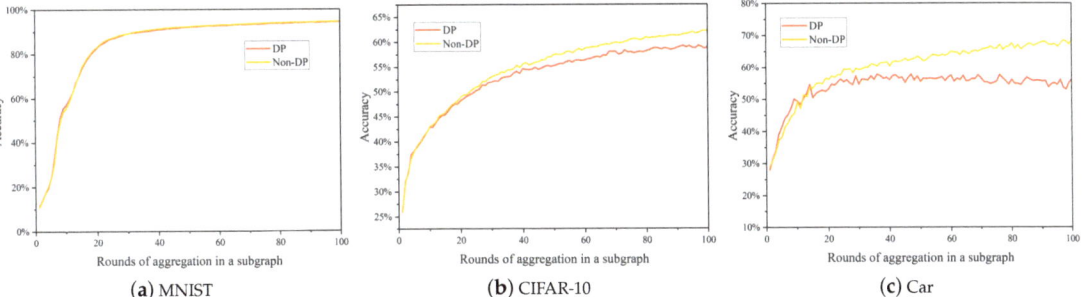

(**a**) MNIST   (**b**) CIFAR-10   (**c**) Car

Figure 9. Accuracy.

The impact of personalized differential privacy on the generation of the global model is evident due to the addition of noise, resulting in decreased accuracy when tested across three types of data. However, the extent of this impact may vary slightly under the same node distribution and privacy strategy in federated learning due to differences in datasets. The MNIST dataset experiences the least impact on model accuracy owing to its simple image color and abundant data. Conversely, the CIFAR-10 dataset, with its more complex RGB images and larger dataset for local training, is more sensitive to noise. Moreover, the Car dataset is the most susceptible to noise due to its intricate image hierarchies and smaller data volume. When no noise is added, the test accuracy of the Car dataset steadily increases with the number of aggregations. However, upon introducing noise, the test accuracy remains relatively consistent with minor fluctuations, and the upward trend in accuracy is not consistently maintained with an increase in the number of aggregations.

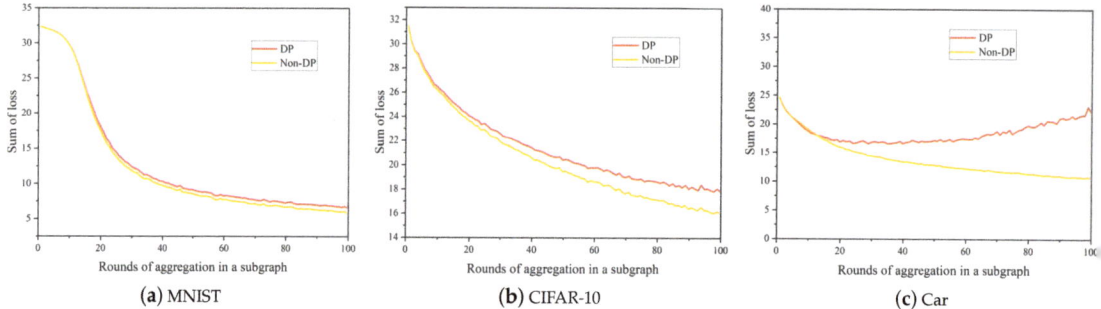

Figure 10. Sum of loss.

The impact of the personalized differential privacy scheme on the total loss value of federated learning follows the descending order of the Car, CIFAR-10, and MNIST datasets. The smaller number of instances in the self-constructed Car dataset results in significant fluctuations and challenges in convergence after introducing Gaussian noise to the model. Conversely, experiments conducted on larger datasets like MNIST and CIFAR-10 exhibit a smaller influence on the total loss value, allowing the trend of a decreasing total loss value with the number of aggregations to remain unaffected. This ensures the convergence of the model under the personalized differential privacy strategy, thereby safeguarding user security while maintaining the usability of federated learning in the foggy environment of connected cars.

6. Algorithm-Related Proofs

This section provides some proofs relevant to the scheme of this study.

6.1. Proof of P2P Architecture

To demonstrate that the segmentation performed by the F-Prim algorithm ensures a subgraph diameter of no more than 4, consider the hypothetical scenario illustrated in Figure 11. Suppose that there exists a subgraph with a diameter of 4, implying that at least two nodes within the subgraph are separated by a distance that requires four hops to traverse between them. Let us denote this path as A-B-C-D-E for the purpose of the proof.

Figure 11. Assumptions in node segmentation.

Indeed, if adding a node F such that the diameter of the subgraph exceeds 4, it implies that the C-node for this subgraph must be positioned at either D or B to maintain the condition that the distance from F to the C-node is at most 2. However, this contradicts the F-Prim algorithm's methodology.

According to the F-Prim algorithm, after the previous round of node additions, a C-node is selected through a harmonic centrality computation. Given that the computation involves nodes A, B, C, D, and E, C is determined to be closer to the center, resulting in a higher centrality value for C compared to D. Thus, the C-node should logically be located at node C rather than node D, which contradicts the assumptions.

Therefore, it can be concluded that the F-Prim algorithm effectively limits the diameter of the subgraph to 4.

6.2. Aggregation Weight Proof

Above, in FedAvg, it is noted that the weights of node v_i's local training model, denoted as ω_i, in the global model ω can be represented by Equation (3). Consequently, the global model yields

$$\omega_{FedAvg} = \sum_{i=1}^{K} p_i \omega_i = \sum_{i=1}^{K} \left(\frac{|D_i|}{\sum_{k=1}^{K} |D_k|} \cdot \omega_i \right) = \frac{\sum_{i=1}^{K} |D_i| \omega_i}{\sum_{k=1}^{K} |D_k|} \quad (17)$$

However, under the architecture, if not adjusted accordingly, there may be an imbalance in model weights. Within this architecture, the adjustment of model weights is delved into, simulating both a simple node network, as in Figure 12a, and a more complex node network, as in Figure 12b, and the global model ω was calculated without differential privacy.

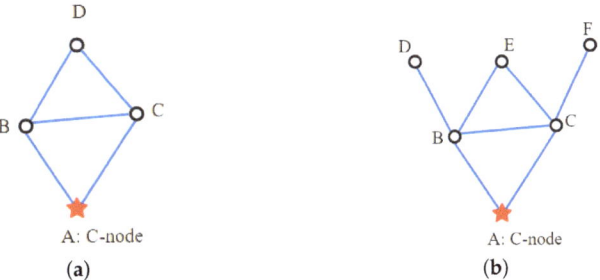

Figure 12. Node network graph, (**a**) simple node network and (**b**) complex node network.

6.2.1. Calculation of Weight

It is assumed that the amount of data collected on each node is different. So right now, in Figure 12a, $|D_A| \neq |D_B| \neq |D_C| \neq |D_D|$, and in Figure 12b, $|D_A| \neq |D_B| \neq |D_C| \neq |D_D| \neq |D_E| \neq |D_F|$.

In Figure 12a, after the one-layer nodes, that is, node v_B and node v_C, receive the model from the two-layer nodes and one-layer nodes, aggregation is completed on v_B and v_C. The result on node B and node C is

$$\omega_{v_B} = \omega_{v_C} = \frac{\omega_B |D_B| + \omega_C |D_C| + \omega_D |D_D|}{|D_B| + |D_C| + |D_D|}$$

At present, the amount of the dataset used for the aggregation in ω_{v_B} and ω_{v_C} is

$$|D_{v_B}| = |D_{v_C}| = |D_B| + |D_C| + |D_D|$$

Thus, after aggregating ω_{v_B}, ω_{v_C}, and v_A's model ω_A, the global model ω on v_A is

$$\omega = \frac{\omega_{v_B} \cdot |D_{v_B}| + \omega_{v_C} \cdot |D_{v_C}| + \omega_A \cdot |D_A|}{|D_{v_B}| + |D_{v_C}| + |D_A|}$$
$$= \frac{\omega_A |D_A| + 2\omega_B |D_B| + 2\omega_C |D_C| + 2\omega_D |D_D|}{|D_A| + 2|D_B| + 2|D_C| + 2|D_D|}$$

Also calculated in the same manner, in Figure 12b, the global model ω on v_A is

$$\omega = \frac{\omega_A |D_A| + 2\omega_B |D_B| + 2\omega_C |D_C| + \omega_D |D_D| + 2\omega_E |D_E| + \omega_F |D_F|}{|D_A| + 2|D_B| + 2|D_C| + |D_D| + 2|D_E| + |D_F|}$$

6.2.2. Analysis and Solutions

Through the above calculations, under the designed architecture, it can be summarized that without tuning, the global model, w, obtained with FedAvg as the aggregation algorithm is

$$w = \frac{\sum_{i=1}^{N} \alpha_i w_i |D_i|}{\sum_{n=1}^{N} \alpha_n |D_n|} = \sum_{i=1}^{N} \left(\frac{\alpha_i |D_i|}{\sum_{n=1}^{N} \alpha_n |D_n|} \cdot w_i \right) = \sum_{i=1}^{N} \acute{p}_i w_i \tag{18}$$

where the value of α_i is determined using Equation (5).

So, it becomes evident that there is a discernible pattern in the contribution of a node to the global model w:

$$\acute{p}_i = \frac{\sum_{i=1}^{N} \alpha_i |D_i|}{\sum_{n=1}^{N} \alpha_n |D_n|} \tag{19}$$

This will cause an imbalance in node v_i's contribution to the global model w, and the weight p_i is intended to be determined solely through the amount of the dataset D_i. Therefore, in order to ensure consistent contributions, a node v_i transmits its model w_i with the amount of dataset as in Equation (4).

After the adjustment, the weight share $\tilde{p}_i$ of v_i's model w_i is

$$\tilde{p}_i = \frac{\alpha_i |D_i|_\alpha}{\sum_{n=1}^{N} \alpha_n |D_i|_\alpha} = \frac{\alpha_i \frac{|D_i|}{\alpha_i}}{\sum_{n=1}^{N} \alpha_n \frac{|D_i|}{\alpha_n}} = \frac{|D_i|}{\sum_{n=1}^{N} |D_n|} = p_i \tag{20}$$

which is the same in FedAvg.

6.3. Convergence Proof for Global Model

When Gaussian noise is added by the nodes except the C-node, the global model's results in this study were

$$w = \sum_{i=1}^{N} \tilde{p}_i \tilde{w}_i (i \neq center) + \tilde{p}_{center} w_{center}$$

$$= \sum_{i=1}^{N} p_i (w_i + n_i)(i \neq center) + p_{center} w_{center} \tag{21}$$

$$= \sum_{i=1}^{N} p_i n_i (i \neq center) + \sum_{i=1}^{N} p_i w_i$$

The sum of the Gaussian noise added to the global model is

$$\sum_{i=1}^{N} n_i \sim N(0, \sum_{i=1}^{N} \sigma_i^2), i \neq center \tag{22}$$

where the value of σ_i needs to satisfy Equation (7).

According to Equation (22), $\sum_{i=1}^{N} n_i$ satisfies the mean value of 0. So, Equation (23) can be obtained as follows:

$$E[F(w)] = E[F(w_{FedAvg})] \tag{23}$$

Since the FedAvg converges [18], the global model w discussed in this paper also converges.

7. Conclusions

In summary, a P2P federated learning scheme was implemented for IoV applications, integrating personalized differential privacy and a special way of communication after partitioning nodes into multiple subgraphs. Through experiments and analyses, it was demonstrated that the design of the scheme prepares a good grouping of nodes for federated learning in P2P architectures, the inward aggregation propagation to C-nodes speeds up the process of federated learning within the grouping, and the introduction of personalized differential privacy provides privacy preservation without affecting the effect of federated learning too much.

This study can also be improved by thinking about the following aspects:

- The current design will limit the diameter of each subgraph; there is a better solution through implementing geolocation-based grouping.
- How other privacy-preserving algorithms should be implemented in this specific architecture.

Author Contributions: Conceptualization, J.Z. and Y.G.; methodology, J.Z. and Y.G.; validation, Y.G. and B.Y.; formal analysis, Y.G.; investigation, Y.W.; resources, J.Z.; writing—original draft preparation, Y.G.; writing—review and editing, J.Z.; supervision, J.Z. All authors have read and agreed to the published version of the manuscript.

Funding: This research was funded by systematic major projects of China State Railway Group Co., Ltd. (No. P2023W001).

Data Availability Statement: Data are contained within the article.

Conflicts of Interest: The authors declare no conflict of interest. The funders had no role in the design of the study.

Abbreviations

The following abbreviations are used in this manuscript:

IoV	Internet of Vehicles
C-S	Client–server
P2P	Peer-to-peer
C-node	Center node

References

1. Feng, Y.; Mao, G.; Chen, B.; Li, C.; Hui, Y.; Xu, Z.; Chen, J. MagMonitor: Vehicle speed estimation and vehicle classification through a magnetic sensor. *IEEE Trans. Intell. Transp. Syst.* **2020**, *23*, 1311–1322. [CrossRef]
2. McMahan, B.; Moore, E.; Ramage, D.; Hampson, S.; Arcas, B.A. Communication-efficient learning of deep networks from decentralized data. In Proceedings of the Artificial Intelligence and Statistics, PMLR, Fort Lauderdale, FL, USA, 20–22 April 2017; pp. 1273–1282.
3. Yang, Q.; Liu, Y.; Chen, T.; Tong, Y. Federated machine learning: Concept and applications. *ACM Trans. Intell. Syst. Technol. (TIST)* **2019**, *10*, 1–19. [CrossRef]
4. Samarakoon, S.; Bennis, M.; Saad, W.; Debbah, M. Distributed federated learning for ultra-reliable low-latency vehicular communications. *IEEE Trans. Commun.* **2019**, *68*, 1146–1159. [CrossRef]
5. Kong, X.; Gao, H.; Shen, G.; Duan, G.; Das, S.K. Fedvcp: A federated-learning-based cooperative positioning scheme for social internet of vehicles. *IEEE Trans. Comput. Soc. Syst.* **2021**, *9*, 197–206. [CrossRef]
6. Yuan, L.; Ma, Y.; Su, L.; Wang, Z. Peer-to-peer federated continual learning for naturalistic driving action recognition. In Proceedings of the IEEE/CVF Conference on Computer Vision and Pattern Recognition, Vancouver, BC, Canada, 17–24 June 2023; pp. 5249–5258.
7. Barbieri, L.; Savazzi, S.; Brambilla, M.; Nicoli, M. Decentralized federated learning for extended sensing in 6G connected vehicles. *Veh. Commun.* **2022**, *33*, 100396. [CrossRef]
8. Lu, Y.; Huang, X.; Dai, Y.; Maharjan, S.; Zhang, Y. Differentially private asynchronous federated learning for mobile edge computing in urban informatics. *IEEE Trans. Ind. Inform.* **2019**, *16*, 2134–2143. [CrossRef]
9. Chen, J.H.; Chen, M.R.; Zeng, G.Q.; Weng, J.S. BDFL: A byzantine-fault-tolerance decentralized federated learning method for autonomous vehicle. *IEEE Trans. Veh. Technol.* **2021**, *70*, 8639–8652. [CrossRef]
10. Niu, M.; Cheng, B.; Feng, Y.; Chen, J. GMTA: A geo-aware multi-agent task allocation approach for scientific workflows in container-based cloud. *IEEE Trans. Netw. Serv. Manag.* **2020**, *17*, 1568–1581. [CrossRef]
11. Dekker, A. Conceptual distance in social network analysis. *J. Soc. Struct.* **2005**, *6*, 31.
12. Freeman, L.C. Centrality in social networks: Conceptual clarification. *Soc. Netw.* **2002**, *1*, 238–263. [CrossRef]
13. Freeman, L.C. A set of measures of centrality based on betweenness. *Sociometry* **1977**, *40*, 35–41. [CrossRef]
14. Dwork, C. Differential privacy. In Proceedings of the International Colloquium on Automata, Languages, and Programming, Venice, Italy, 10–14 July 2006; Springer: Berlin/Heidelberg, Germany, 2006; pp. 1–12.
15. Wei, K.; Li, J.; Ding, M.; Ma, C.; Yang, H.H.; Farokhi, F.; Jin, S.; Quek, T.Q.; Poor, H.V. Federated learning with differential privacy: Algorithms and performance analysis. *IEEE Trans. Inf. Forensics Secur.* **2020**, *15*, 3454–3469. [CrossRef]

16. Chen, Q.; Wang, Z.; Zhang, W.; Lin, X. PPT: A privacy-preserving global model training protocol for federated learning in P2P networks. *Comput. Secur.* **2023**, *124*, 102966. [CrossRef]
17. Chen, Q.; Wang, Z.; Zhou, Y.; Chen, J.; Xiao, D.; Lin, X. CFL: Cluster federated learning in large-scale peer-to-peer networks. In Proceedings of the International Conference on Information Security, Taipei, Taiwan, 23–25 November 2022; Springer: Berlin/Heidelberg, Germany, 2022; pp. 464–472.
18. Li, X.; Huang, K.; Yang, W.; Wang, S.; Zhang, Z. On the convergence of fedavg on non-iid data. *arXiv* **2019**, arXiv:1907.02189.

Disclaimer/Publisher's Note: The statements, opinions and data contained in all publications are solely those of the individual author(s) and contributor(s) and not of MDPI and/or the editor(s). MDPI and/or the editor(s) disclaim responsibility for any injury to people or property resulting from any ideas, methods, instructions or products referred to in the content.

Article

Security-Aware Task Offloading Using Deep Reinforcement Learning in Mobile Edge Computing Systems

Haodong Lu [1], Xiaoming He [2] and Dengyin Zhang [2,*]

[1] College of Telecommunications and Information Engineering, Nanjing University of Posts and Telecommunications, Nanjing 210003, China; ihaodonglu@gmail.com
[2] School of Internet of Things, Nanjing University of Posts and Telecommunications, Nanjing 210003, China; hexiaoming@njupt.edu.cn
* Correspondence: zhangdy@njupt.edu.cn

Abstract: With the proliferation of intelligent applications, mobile devices are increasingly handling computation-intensive tasks but often struggle with limited computing power and energy resources. Mobile Edge Computing (MEC) offers a solution by enabling these devices to offload computation-intensive tasks to resource-rich edge servers, thus reducing processing latency and energy consumption. However, existing task-offloading strategies often neglect critical security concerns. In this paper, we propose a security-aware task-offloading framework that utilizes Deep Reinforcement Learning (DRL) to solve these challenges. Our framework is designed to minimize the latency of task accomplishment and energy consumption while ensuring data security. We model system utility as a Markov Decision Process (MDP) and design a Proximal Policy Optimization (PPO)-based algorithm to derive optimal offloading strategies. Experimental results demonstrate that the proposed algorithm outperforms traditional methods regarding task execution latency and energy consumption.

Keywords: task offloading; deep reinforcement learning; mobile edge computing

Citation: Lu, H.; He, X.; Zhang, D. Security-Aware Task Offloading Using Deep Reinforcement Learning in Mobile Edge Computing Systems. *Electronics* **2024**, *13*, 2933. https://doi.org/10.3390/electronics13152933

Academic Editor: José D. Martín-Guerrero

Received: 21 June 2024
Revised: 18 July 2024
Accepted: 22 July 2024
Published: 25 July 2024

Copyright: © 2024 by the authors. Licensee MDPI, Basel, Switzerland. This article is an open access article distributed under the terms and conditions of the Creative Commons Attribution (CC BY) license (https://creativecommons.org/licenses/by/4.0/).

1. Introduction

The rapid advancement of Artificial Intelligence (AI) has facilitated the widespread proliferation of intelligent applications, including personalized recommendations [1], face recognition [2], and keyboard Emoji prediction [3]. These applications, primarily based on Deep Learning (DL), require substantial computational resources. Although mobile devices have become more powerful, they still lack sufficient capacity to execute complex DL models locally. To address these challenges, Mobile Edge Computing (MEC), also known as multi-access edge computing, has become a promising solution [4,5]. MEC allows mobile devices to offload computing tasks to nearby edge servers, significantly reducing task processing latency and energy consumption [6].

In MEC, two critical issues related to task offloading need to be resolved. The first issue is determining whether each mobile device should offload its tasks to an edge server. Once the decision to offload is made, the next step is selecting the appropriate edge server. Various algorithms have been proposed to optimize these decisions. Xu et al. [7] introduced an algorithm to optimize task offloading in MEC by balancing latency and risk management. Ding et al. [8] explored a Non-Orthogonal Multiple Access (NOMA)-assisted MEC scenario, jointly optimizing power and time allocation to reduce energy consumption. Additionally, Bi et al. [9] proposed a strategy for a wireless-powered MEC scenario that optimizes offloading decisions and power transfer.

Despite these advancements, the security aspects of task offloading have not been sufficiently addressed [10–13]. The data transmitted between mobile devices and edge servers are susceptible to various security threats, such as interception [14] and unauthorized access [15]. For example, without robust security measures, cyber attackers could potentially intercept sensitive data or manipulate the task execution process [16]. Most existing offloading algorithms focus primarily on performance metrics like latency and energy consumption, often overlooking crucial security considerations. This gap underscores the need for a comprehensive approach that integrates robust security measures into the offloading process to ensure data integrity and privacy [17].

In this paper, we explore security-aware task offloading in MEC systems using a DRL-based approach. Our primary objective is to minimize the task execution time and energy consumption while ensuring data security. To achieve this, we model system utility as a weighted sum of task execution latency and energy consumption. We have designed a task-offloading algorithm utilizing Proximal Policy Optimization (PPO) to achieve a near-optimal computational offloading strategy that minimizes system utility and incorporates security considerations into the decision-making process. Through this integration, our approach provides a more robust and efficient MEC system. The main contributions of our work can be summarized as follows:

- *Task Offloading for MEC Systems*: We undertake a thorough investigation of task offloading within MEC systems, focusing on the security aspects of data transmission between servers and mobile devices.
- *DRL-based Task-Offloading Algorithm*: We model system utility as a Markov Decision Process (MDP) and introduce a novel task-offloading algorithm using a DRL approach. This algorithm dynamically learns and adapts to the MEC environment to optimize task-offloading decisions.
- *Performance Evaluation*: Our results indicate that our proposal significantly outperforms traditional methods in minimizing task execution latency and energy consumption while maintaining high levels of data security.

The remainder of this paper is structured as follows. Section 2 reviews related work on task offloading in MEC systems. Section 3 details the system model and problem formulation. Section 4 describes the proposed DRL-based algorithm for security-aware task offloading. Section 5 validates the performance of the proposed offloading algorithm. Finally, the conclusion is presented in Section 6.

2. Related Work
2.1. Task Offloading in MEC

Task offloading in MEC systems has recently drawn significant attention from industry and academia. Lyu et al. [18] proposed an asymptotically optimal task-offloading approach for MEC employing a quantized dynamic programming algorithm to enhance scalability with minimal extra energy cost. Eshraghi et al. [19] investigated joint offloading decisions and resource allocation in mobile cloud networks and proposed the TORAUC algorithm, which optimizes offloading decisions and resource allocation to minimize system costs. Tang et al. [20] introduced a model-free DRL-based distributed algorithm for task offloading in MEC, incorporating LSTM, dueling DQN, and double-DQN techniques to minimize long-term costs, significantly reducing task drop rates and average latency compared to existing algorithms.

Wang et al. [21] developed a decentralized multi-user offloading framework, DEBO, for MEC. This framework optimizes user rewards under network latency by addressing unknown stochastic system-side information, achieving near-optimal performance with sub-linear regret across various scenarios. Liu et al. [22] proposed COFE, a dependent task-offloading framework for MEC and cloud systems, which adaptively assigns computation-intensive tasks with dependent constraints to improve the user experience, using a heuristic ranking-based algorithm to minimize the average makespan and reduce deadline violations. Wang et al. [23] explored multiobjective optimization in a multi-user and multi-server MEC scenario, focusing on joint task offloading, power assignment, and resource allocation. They developed an evolutionary algorithm to minimize response latency, energy consumption, and cost, significantly enhancing user offloading benefits. Fang et al. [24] introduced a dynamic offloading decision algorithm, named DODA-DT, for MEC that employs a DRL-based algorithm to reduce the task execution time and energy consumption across multiple devices under varying wireless conditions. Tan et al. [25] optimized the task offloading and allocation of physical resources in collaborative MEC networks using OFDMA, proposing a two-level alternation method that combines a heuristic algorithm for offloading and collaboration decisions with DRL for optimizing resource allocation.

2.2. Security-Aware Task Offloading in MEC

Task requests often involve sensitive data, making security and privacy concerns critical when offloading such data to edge servers for processing [26]. To address these challenges, Samy et al. [27] developed a blockchain-based architecture to enhance security in task offloading within MEC systems and implemented a DRL-based algorithm to optimize both energy and time costs in scenarios involving multiple users and tasks. Elgendy et al. [28] developed a multi-user resource allocation and task-offloading model that incorporates AES encryption for data security, optimizing system efficiency in terms of time and energy consumption. Wu et al. [29] investigated secure offloading for a wireless-powered MEC system, proposing a physical layer security-assisted scheme where a power beacon also acts as a cooperative jammer. This scheme maximizes secrecy energy efficiency by optimizing transmit power, time allocation, and task partitioning while satisfying secrecy and energy constraints. Asheralieva et al. [30] employed Lagrange coded computing to facilitate fast and secure offloading of request tasks in MEC systems. This method ensures efficient load and bandwidth allocation while promoting timely task completion. For a detailed comparison of our work with existing studies, please refer to Table 1.

Table 1. Comparison of existing works on task offloading.

Reference	Optimization	DRL-Based	Security	No. of Servers
[18]	Latency and energy	No	No	Single Server
[19]	Energy	No	No	Single Server
[20]	Latency	Yes	No	Multiple Servers
[21]	Latency	Yes	No	Multiple Servers
[22]	Latency	No	No	Multiple Servers
[23]	Latency and energy	No	No	Multiple Servers
[24]	Latency and energy	Yes	No	Single Server
[25]	Energy	Yes	No	Single Server
[27]	Latency and energy	Yes	Yes	Single Server
[28]	Latency and energy	No	Yes	Single Server
[29]	Energy	No	Yes	Single Server
[30]	Latency	Yes	Yes	Single Server
Our Work	Latency and energy	Yes	Yes	Multiple Servers

While the above studies have employed DRL [31], blockchain [32], and other methods to optimize task offloading and protect data security, there remains significant potential for further exploration in addressing the challenges of secure task offloading in MEC systems.

3. System Model and Problem Formulation

This section introduces the MEC system model for task offloading. Specifically, the system consists of multiple mobile devices, denoted by $\mathcal{M} = \{1, 2, \ldots, m, \ldots, M\}$, and multiple edge servers, represented by $\mathcal{N} = \{1, 2, \ldots, n, \ldots, N\}$. The set of tasks to be executed is indicated by $\mathcal{X} = \{1, 2, \ldots, x, \ldots, X\}$. The MEC system operates in episodes, and each is subdivided into time slots $\mathcal{T} = \{1, 2, \ldots, t, \ldots, T\}$ with a duration of Δ seconds [33]. Our focus is on the computational tasks from mobile devices, each of which is characterized as indivisible and capable of being processed either locally on the mobile device or offloaded to one of the edge servers. For offloaded tasks, data encryption is implemented to secure the data during transmission. Subsequent sections will detail the specific system models for the mobile device and edge server, as illustrated in Figure 1.

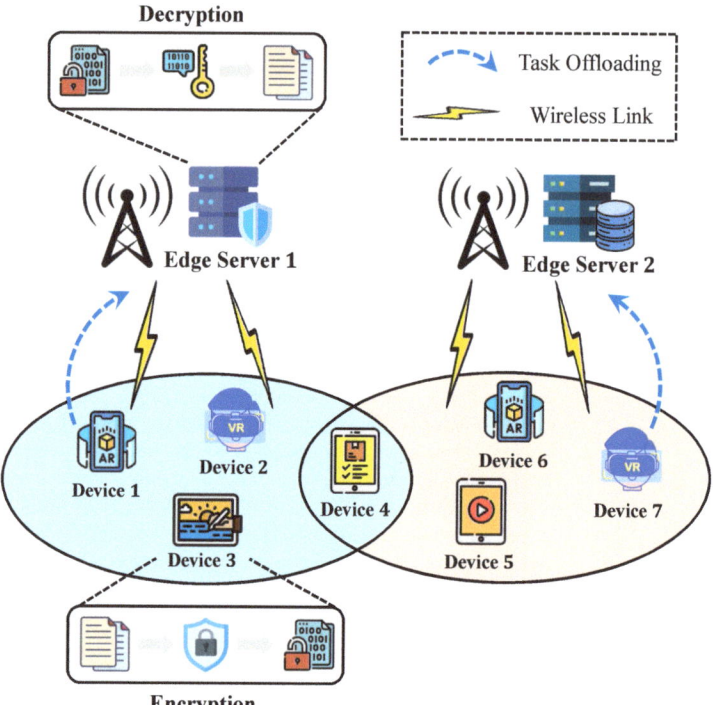

Figure 1. An illustration of MEC systems over wireless connections. Tasks are encrypted before offloading and decrypted upon reaching the edge server to ensure data security.

3.1. Communication Model

This subsection introduces the communication model used during task offloading. We assume that each device can only offload tasks to a single edge server that falls within its wireless coverage area at a given time slot [20]. The connectivity between a mobile device m and an edge server n at time t is represented by $\zeta_{m,n}(t)$, where $\zeta_{m,n}(t) = 1$ indicates that mobile device m is within the communication range of edge server n, and $\zeta_{m,n}(t) = 0$ otherwise. Task transmission utilizes Orthogonal Frequency Division Multiple Access (OFDMA). Accordingly, the transmission rate, denoted by $r_{m,n}(t)$, is defined as follows:

$$r_{m,n}(t) = b_m^n \log_2 \left(1 + \frac{p_m g_m}{b_m^n \sigma^2}\right), \tag{1}$$

where b_m^n is the channel bandwidth, g_m is the channel gain, p_m is the uplink transmission power of mobile device m, and σ^2 denotes the SINR in the wireless link.

During the task-offloading process, a mobile device consumes communication bandwidth b_m^n when offloading a task to an edge server. If the required bandwidth is less than the currently available bandwidth $B_n^{ava}(t)$, the task is offloaded immediately. Otherwise, the task waits until sufficient bandwidth becomes available.

3.2. Security Model

When offloading computational tasks to the edge server, the offloading data may be susceptible to various types of network attacks [34]. This paper proposes encrypting the offloaded data to ensure data security in edge task offloading. The Advanced Encryption Standard (AES) is utilized to encrypt the transmission of task data [35]. The AES is chosen for its robust security features, efficiency, and widespread acceptance as a standard for data encryption. Its symmetric encryption mechanism ensures fast encryption and decryption processes, which is critical for real-time task-offloading scenarios where low latency is essential.

For mobile devices requiring task offloading, a 128-bit AES key is first generated to encrypt the tasks before offloading them to the server. The edge server then uses the same key to decrypt the received encrypted data and execute the tasks. Upon completion, the server returns the task results to the mobile device. To formalize the encryption decision for the offloaded task, we introduce the variable $\alpha_m \in \{0,1\}$. Specifically, $\alpha_m = 0$ indicates that the offloaded task does not require encryption, while $\alpha_m = 1$ indicates that the offloaded task must be encrypted before transmission to the edge server.

3.3. Computing Model

Based on the communication and security models, we introduce the computation model that governs task-offloading requests on mobile devices within the MEC system. An arriving task x at time slot t is represented by $\Gamma_m^x(t) = \{I_m^x(t), \lambda_m^x(t), \ell_m^x(t)\}$, where $I_m^x(t)$ denotes the data size of the offloading task, $\lambda_m^x(t)$ specifies the CPU cycles required to complete the task, and $\ell_m^x(t)$ defines the task's execution deadline. The parameters $I_m^x(t)$ and $\lambda_m^x(t)$ are determined by specific application needs and are typically provided by the program vendor. Each mobile device selects the optimal execution destination for an arriving computation task, choosing either local processing or offloading to the edge server. We formulate two computational modes based on these operational dynamics: mobile device computing for local processing and edge server computing for offloaded tasks.

3.3.1. Mobile Device Computing

Transmission latency is negligible when a task request Γ_m^x is processed locally. Therefore, the focus is only on the local execution latency as well as the energy consumption, which are the primary concerns in this scenario. These metrics for mobile device m can be calculated as follows:

$$D_{m,x}^{local}(t) = \frac{\lambda_m^x(t)}{f_m}, \quad (2)$$

$$E_{m,x}^{local}(t) = \zeta_m \lambda_m^x(t), \quad (3)$$

where f_m represents the CPU frequency of the mobile device, and ζ_m denotes the energy consumption per CPU cycle.

3.3.2. Edge Server Computing

Edge server computing involves completely offloading the task to servers. To this end, the mobile device m first transmits the task request to the edge server n. Once the task is received, the edge server begins processing it. Once the task is completed, the results are sent back to the mobile device. Since the time required to return results is considerably shorter than the time needed for uploading tasks, we exclude the return time from our calculations [7]. In this context, task execution latency comprises both transmission latency and processing latency. The processing latency includes the computational latency at the edge server side, as well as the latency for data encryption and decryption, expressed as

$$D_{m,x}^{comp}(t) = \frac{\eta_{m,x}}{f_m} + \frac{\delta_{n,x}}{f_n} + \frac{\lambda_m^x(t)}{f_n}, \quad (4)$$

where $\eta_{m,x}$ and $\delta_{n,x}$ present the CPU cycles required for encrypting and decrypting the data, respectively. f_n represents the CPU frequency at the edge server.

Based on the data transmission rate defined in Equation (1), the transmission latency is calculated as follows:

$$D_{m,x}^{comm}(t) = \frac{I_m^x(t)}{r_{m,n}(t)}. \quad (5)$$

Combining Equations (4) and (5), the total execution latency for task offloading is expressed as

$$D_{m,x}^{edge}(t) = D_{m,x}^{comp}(t) + D_{m,x}^{comm}(t). \qquad (6)$$

For the offloading strategy, energy consumption primarily comprises the energy used for task transmission and the energy required for data encryption. These components are formulated as follows:

$$E_{m,x}^{comp}(t) = \xi_m \eta_{m,x}, \qquad (7)$$

$$E_{m,x}^{comm}(t) = p_m \frac{I_m^x(t)}{r_{m,n}(t)}. \qquad (8)$$

By integrating Equations (7) and (8), the total energy consumed for task offloading can be represented as follows:

$$E_{m,x}^{edge}(t) = E_{m,x}^{comp}(t) + E_{m,x}^{comm}(t). \qquad (9)$$

In summary, the total latency and energy consumption for task x on mobile device m are defined as follows:

$$D_{m,x}^{total}(t) = \left[(1 - \beta_{m,x}) D_{m,x}^{local}(t) + \beta_{m,x} D_{m,x}^{edge}(t)\right], \qquad (10)$$

$$E_{m,x}^{total}(t) = \left[(1 - \beta_{m,x}) E_{m,x}^{local}(t) + \beta_{m,x} E_{m,x}^{edge}(t)\right], \qquad (11)$$

where $D_{m,x}^{local}$ and $D_{m,x}^{edge}$ represent the local and remote execution latencies, and $E_{m,x}^{local}$ and $E_{m,x}^{edge}$ represent local and remote energy consumption, respectively. $\beta_{m,x}$ is a binary indicator, where $\beta_{m,x} = 0$ indicates local execution and $\beta_{m,x} = 1$ indicates remote execution.

3.4. Problem Formulation

In this paper, we aim to minimize the system costs related to task offloading in MEC systems by taking into account both the task completion time and energy consumption. To achieve this, we define the total system costs as follows:

$$\begin{aligned}
\min \quad & \frac{1}{|\mathcal{T}|} \sum_{t=1}^{T} \sum_{m=1}^{M} \left(D_{m,x}^{total}(t) + \lambda E_{m,x}^{total}(t) \right) \\
\text{s.t} \quad & 0 < f_n(t) \leq F_n^{ava}(t) \quad (C1) \\
& 0 < f_m(t) \leq F_m^{ava}(t) \quad (C2) \\
& 0 < b_m^n \leq B_n^{ava}(t) \quad (C3) \\
& D_{m,x}(t) \leq \ell_m^x(t) \quad (C4) \\
& \beta_{m,x} \in \{0,1\}, \forall m \quad (C5)
\end{aligned} \qquad (12)$$

where λ represents the weight coefficient of energy consumption, indicating the relative importance of execution latency and energy consumption across different tasks. Constraint (C1) ensures that the computing resources required for each task $f_n(t)$ do not exceed the mobile device's available resources. Constraint (C2) specifies that local computation for each task $f_m(t)$ remains within the mobile device's capabilities. Constraint (C3) guarantees that the bandwidth utilized for offloaded tasks does not surpass the edge server's available bandwidth. Constraint (C4) imposes time limits on task processing to ensure timely completion. Finally, Constraint (C5) ensures that the offloading decision β_m is binary, distinctly classifying tasks as either offloaded or executed locally.

4. DRL-Based Offloading Algorithm

To address the optimization challenge outlined in Section 3.4, efficient task offloading from mobile devices to edge servers is essential within MEC systems. Task offloading, however, is proven to be an NP-hard problem [34]. Recent advancements in Deep Reinforcement Learning (DRL) have demonstrated its superior capabilities in various model-free control problems, making it well suited for our task-offloading scenario. Motivated by these developments, we adopt the PPO algorithm [36] to solve the dynamic and complex decisions involved in task offloading. This section defines the task-offloading procedure as an MDP and explains the PPO algorithm and its implementation.

4.1. MDP Formulation

The results of task offloading are influenced by multiple factors, including local computing resources, the number of edge servers, and the current available resources on edge servers. In addition, the current offloading status is affected by the actions taken in the previous step. Therefore, the task-offloading process is typically considered to have MDP properties [7]. This subsection defines a discrete-time MDP to describe the edge-assisted task scheduling system. The three main elements of the MDP, i.e., state, action, and reward, are defined as follows.

State: The state of the system captures the characteristics of the network environment within the MEC system, including detailed information about mobile devices and edge servers. Specifically, the state is defined as

$$s_t = \{t, \Gamma_m^x(t), F_n^{ava}(t), F_m^{ava}(t)\}, \tag{13}$$

where t denotes the current time series, and $\Gamma_m^x(t)$ includes task request details such as the data volume $I_m^x(t)$ to be processed, the required computational resources $\lambda_m^x(t)$, and the maximum time constraint $\ell_m^x(t)$. Additionally, $F_n^{ava}(t)$ and $F_m^{ava}(t)$ indicate the currently available computational resources of the mobile devices and edge servers, respectively. This state formulation ensures that decision-making accounts for both detailed task requests and the availability of resources.

Action: The agent selects an action from a set of possible options according to the current system state. The action space is defined as

$$a_t = \{MD, ES_1, \ldots, ES_n, \ldots, ES_N\}, \tag{14}$$

where MD denotes processing the task locally, and ES_n refers to offloading the task to the n-th edge server.

Reward: At each time step, executing an action yields an immediate reward. The agent aims to maximize the cumulative rewards by adjusting its behavior based on these reward signals. This iterative learning approach continuously refines the agent's strategy for optimal task performance. The reward function is derived from the system cost in Equation (12) and is expressed as

$$r_t = D_{m,x}^{total}(t) - \lambda E_{m,x}^{total}(t). \tag{15}$$

4.2. Preliminaries of DRL

DRL trains agents to make decisions by performing actions within an environment to maximize cumulative rewards. In DRL, decision-making is typically modeled as an MDP, where each current state depends only on its preceding state. Within this framework, the agent observes the environment, selects an action, transitions to a new state, and receives a corresponding reward. The cumulative reward, denoted by G_t, is the sum of discounted future rewards, calculated as

$$G_t = \sum_{k=0}^{\infty} \gamma^k R_{t+k+1} \tag{16}$$

where γ denotes the discount factor, ranging from 0 to 1. R_{t+k+1} represents the reward received at $t+k+1$.

The expected cumulative reward from a given state s, known as the state value $V(s)$, is defined as

$$V(s) = \mathbb{E}\left[\sum_{k=0}^{\infty} \gamma^k R_{t+k+1} \mid S_t = s\right]. \tag{17}$$

Furthermore, the value of taking a specific action a in state s, known as the action-value function $Q(s,a)$, is expressed as

$$Q(s,a) = \mathbb{E}\left[\sum_{k=0}^{\infty} \gamma^k R_{t+k+1} \mid S_t = s, A_t = a\right]. \tag{18}$$

The Bellman optimality equation [7], which connects the values of state and state–action pairs, is given by

$$Q(S_t, A_t) = \mathbb{E}[R_{t+1} + \gamma V(S_{t+1})]. \tag{19}$$

Finally, the advantage function $A(s,a)$ is defined as

$$A(s,a) = Q(s,a) - V(s). \tag{20}$$

Policy gradient (PG) methods, such as REINFORCE, are policy-based DRL algorithms [37] that optimize a loss function to update policy parameters θ to maximize expected cumulative rewards. The policy gradient is defined by the following equation:

$$L(\theta) = -\mathbb{E}_{s \sim d^{\pi}, a \sim \pi_\theta}[\nabla_\theta \log \pi_\theta(a \mid s) A^{\pi}(s,a)], \tag{21}$$

where θ represents the parameters of the policy π, $s \sim d^{\pi}$ denotes states sampled from the distribution under policy π, $a \sim \pi_\theta$ indicates actions sampled from the policy, and $\nabla_\theta \log \pi_\theta(a \mid s)$ represents the gradient of the log-probability of selecting action a in state s.

Despite their effectiveness, PG methods face challenges such as high variance and inefficiency due to their reliance on complete state sequences via Monte Carlo sampling. These issues led to the development of more robust algorithms like Proximal Policy Optimization (PPO) [36], which builds on PG principles but incorporates advanced strategies to improve learning stability and efficiency.

PPO is an evolution of the Actor–Critic (AC) architecture, a sophisticated form of PG that employs two neural networks: the actor that dictates the policy and the critic that evaluates the action outcome based on the state value. This dual-network structure enables the continuous learning and adjustment of the policy using more stable and lower-variance feedback from the critic. In an AC framework, the actor updates its policy based on

$$L_{\text{actor}} = \frac{\pi_{\theta'}(A_t \mid S_t)}{\pi_\theta(A_t \mid S_t)} A^{\pi_\theta}, \tag{22}$$

where $\pi_{\theta'}(A_t \mid S_t)$ represents the new policy.

To further enhance the efficacy and stability of policy updates, PPO introduces an innovative clipping mechanism in the policy update step, known as PPO-clip. This mechanism ensures that adjustments to the policy do not deviate excessively from the previous policy, thus maintaining a balance between rapid learning and stability.

The PPO-clip algorithm adjusts the policy parameters θ to maximize the expected return while ensuring that the new policy remains close to the previous policy θ_{old}. The update is formulated as follows:

$$\theta_{new} = \arg\max_{\theta} \mathbb{E}_{s,a \sim \pi_{\theta_{old}}}[L(s, a, \theta_{old}, \theta)]. \tag{23}$$

The objective function L is defined by

$$L(s, a, \theta_{old}, \theta) = \min\left(\frac{\pi_\theta(a|s)}{\pi_{\theta_{old}}(a|s)} A^{\pi_{\theta_{old}}}(s, a),\right.$$
$$\left.\text{clip}\left(\frac{\pi_\theta(a|s)}{\pi_{\theta_{old}}(a|s)}, 1-\varsigma, 1+\varsigma\right) A^{\pi_{\theta_{old}}}(s, a)\right), \quad (24)$$

where ς is a hyperparameter that limits the extent of policy updates. For ease of representation, we denote the ratio of the new policy π_θ to the old policy $\pi_{\theta_{old}}$ for taking an action a in state s by $\rho(s, a) = \frac{\pi_\theta(a|s)}{\pi_{\theta_{old}}(a|s)}$. The clipping function is defined as

$$\text{clip}(x, 1-\varsigma, 1+\varsigma) = \begin{cases} 1-\varsigma & \text{if } x < 1-\varsigma \\ x & \text{if } 1-\varsigma \leq x \leq 1+\varsigma \\ 1+\varsigma & \text{if } x > 1+\varsigma \end{cases} \quad (25)$$

The advantage function $A^{\pi_{\theta_{old}}}(s, a)$ is calculated as

$$A^{\pi_{old}}(s, a) = \mathbb{E}_{\pi_{old}}\left[\sum_{k=0}^{\infty} \gamma^t r_{t+k+1} \mid s_t = s, a_t = a\right] - V^{\pi_{old}}(s). \quad (26)$$

The DRL agent is trained using an AC approach, which has been effectively applied in various domains. The PPO algorithm optimizes the actor network. During training, the critic network is updated by minimizing the Mean Squared Error (MSE) between its prediction and the target value function, defined by the following loss function:

$$L(\phi) = (r_t + \gamma V_\phi(s_{t+1}) - V_\phi(s_t))^2. \quad (27)$$

The loss function for the policy network includes a clipped objective to ensure that updates to the policy remain within an acceptable range. This is formally defined as

$$L(\theta) = \min(\rho \cdot A^{\pi_{old}}(s_t, a_t), \text{clip}(\rho, 1-\varsigma, 1+\varsigma) \cdot A^{\pi_{old}}(s_t, a_t)) \quad (28)$$

The advantage function, used for policy updates, is calculated as follows:

$$A^{\pi_{\theta_{old}}}(s_t, a_t) = Q^{\pi_{\theta_{old}}}(s_t, a_t) - V_\phi(s_t). \quad (29)$$

4.3. Complexity Analysis

In this section, we analyze the complexity of the PPO algorithm. This paper adopts an AC architecture to improve the stability of the training process. The complexity of the algorithm stems from the calculation of model parameters [38]. Since scheduling tasks are represented as vectors, fully connected networks are primarily used for model construction. Therefore, the computational complexity of these fully connected networks can be represented as $O\left(\sum_{l=1}^{L-1} n_l \cdot n_{l-1}\right)$, where n_l denotes the number of neurons in the lth hidden layer.

4.4. Task Offloading Using PPO

Figure 2 illustrates the proposed PPO-based task-offloading framework, which operates in two alternating phases: interaction and training. During the interaction phase, the system initializes the actor and critic networks and begins gathering experience data. At each time slot t, the agent selects mobile devices sequentially, utilizing observations to generate policies via the actor network. Each mobile device guided by these policies interacts with the environment, transitioning to subsequent states. The experience data, i.e., states, actions, and rewards, is preserved in the replay buffer. The interaction phase is determined once the buffer reaches capacity.

The training phase begins by sampling batches of data from the replay buffer, denoted by $b \in D$. In the initial learning round, these batches directly feed into the primary actor and critic networks without importance sampling. In subsequent rounds within the same learning episode, data are processed using the updated and original networks within the importance sampling module, supporting the training of new network configurations. Once an episode is complete, the buffer is cleared, and the interaction phase is re-initiated to refill the replay buffer with fresh experience data. This cyclical approach ensures the continuous learning and adaptation of the networks, optimizing the task-offloading process in MEC.

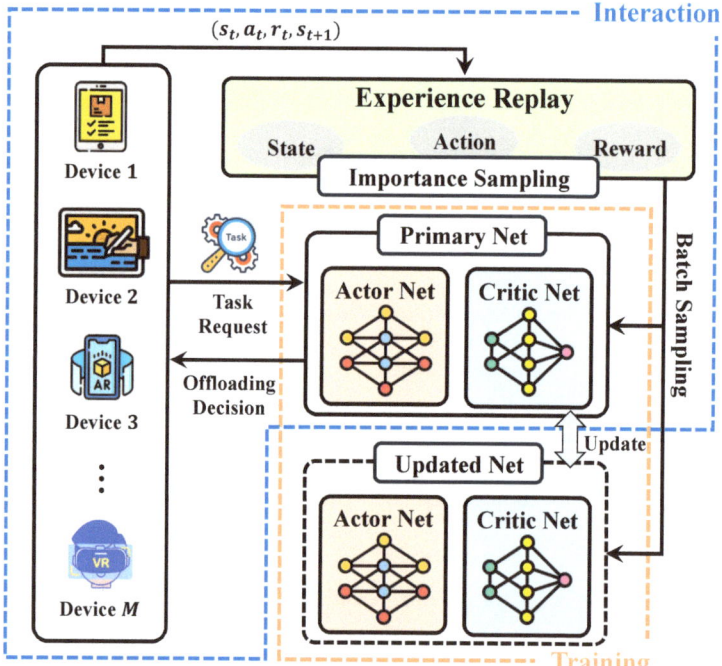

Figure 2. An illustration of PPO-based task offloading in the MEC system. The algorithm is divided into two main modules. The interaction module uses the actor network to interact with the environment, making specific offloading decisions, and collects experience data for storage in the experience buffer. The training module then samples these data from the experience buffer to update both the actor and critic networks. These modules operate alternately, continuing until the agent achieves convergence.

Training Workflow: Algorithms 1 and 2 further detail the algorithm update and data collection processes, respectively. Algorithm 1 begins with the initialization of the task scheduling environment, scheduling algorithm parameters, and the experience buffer D (Line 3 and Line 4). The agent interacts with the environment within each episode to generate experience data, which are then stored in buffer D (Line 6). Once the data in D reaches a preset threshold, the agent proceeds with the model update. This includes extracting a batch of experiences with sample size b from D for parameter updates (Line 7). The agent then calculates the advantage function and state value and uses this information to update the critic and actor networks using the SGD algorithm (Lines 8–11). At the end of each episode, the experience buffer D is cleared (Line 13). The above training process will be repeated until the model converges. Subsequently, the policy network π_θ can be deployed in the actual offloading system.

Algorithm 2 outlines the complete process by which mobile devices interact with the environment to generate training data. During the data collection phase, the experience buffer is initialized (Line 1). At each t, the edge server sorts the task requests from the mobile devices (Line 3). For each task request, the environment state s_t related to the current task offloading is constructed, and the policy network generates an $(N+1)$-dimensional offloading decision (Lines 5 and 6). The mobile device then executes the task based on this decision and receives the corresponding reward (Line 7). This information, including the state transition and reward, is compiled into a complete sample and stored in the experience buffer D (Line 8).

Algorithm 1 DRL-based task offloading.

1: **Input:** Task-offloading environment;
2: **Output:** Offloading strategy π_θ;
3: **Initialize:** Parameters θ and ϕ in actor network π_θ and critic network V_ϕ;
4: **Initialize:** Replay buffer D;
5: **for** $Episode = 1, 2, \ldots, Episode_{max}$ **do**
6:     Collect data via Algorithm 2 and store in D;
7:     **for** Each $b \in D$ **do**
8:         Compute advantage A according to Equation (29);
9:         Obtain state values $V(s_{t+1})$ and $V(s_t)$ from critic networks;
10:        Update parameters ϕ according to Equation (27);
11:        Update parameters θ according to Equation (28);
12:     **end for**
13:     Empty the replay buffer D.
14: **end for**

Algorithm 2 Data collection for DRL-based task offloading.

1: **Initialize:** Replay buffer D;
2: **for** Each time slot t **do**
3:     Sort the order of task requests;
4:     **for** Each mobile device **do**
5:         Observe the current environment state s_t;
6:         Compute action a_t using policy network π_θ with input s_t;
7:         Perform action a_t, transition to state s_{t+1}, and collect reward r_t;
8:         Record the transition (s_t, a_t, r_t, s_{t+1}) in buffer D.
9:     **end for**
10: **end for**

---

5. Performance Evaluation

In this section, we first outline the configuration of the MEC systems and the parameters of the algorithm. We then proceed to compare the proposed offloading algorithm against other approaches to validate its performance across various scenarios.

5.1. Experiment Settings

(1) Training Setup: We consider an experimental scenario with 30 mobile devices and 4 edge servers. Each mobile device is assigned a CPU capacity selected from the set $\{0.2, 0.4, 0.6, \ldots, 1.4\}$ GHz to simulate computational heterogeneity. In contrast, the CPU capacity for each MEC server is fixed at 10 GHz. Depending on the task, it is randomly determined whether the offloading process requires encrypted data transmission. For tasks requiring encryption, 100 megacycles are allocated for encryption and decryption processes. For the wireless transmission model, we set the communication bandwidth b_m^n to 2 MHz and the uplink transmission power p_m to 0.25 W. The Rayleigh fading channel g_m is modeled according to the methods described in [9], expressed as $g_m = A\left(3 * 10^8 / 4\pi f d\right)^2$, where A is the antenna gain, f is the carrier frequency set at 915 MHz, and d represents the distance between the user and the server. Table 2 outlines the main system parameters.

For the PPO-based offloading algorithm, the convergence of neural networks is highly dependent on the selection of hyperparameters. To identify the most appropriate hyperparameters, we employ Neural Network Intelligence (NNI) (https://github.com/microsoft/nni/ (accessed on 15 March 2024)), an automated learning tool, to conduct an exhaustive search. The optimal parameters identified through this method are then used for the final training of our algorithm. Specifically, the neural network configuration for the PPO algorithm includes two hidden layers, each with 128 neurons, in both the actor and critic networks. The batch size is set to 32. The learning rates are set at 0.003 for the actor and 0.001 for the critic, with a discount factor of 0.9. The buffer size is 10,000. We implement the algorithm using the PyTorch framework, updating the model with the Adam optimizer [39]. To compare the performance of the offloading algorithm under different encryption requirements, we denote the offloading process with data encryption as PPO-E and the offloading process without data encryption as PPO-WE.

Table 2. System parameter configurations.

Parameters	Value	Parameters	Value
Number of mobile devices	30	Number of edge servers	4
Task data size	{5, 10, 15, ..., 30} MB	System bandwidth	15 MHz
Background noise	−100 dBm	Computation capacity of device	{0.2, 0.4, 0.6, ..., 1.4} GHz
MEC server capacity	10 GHz	Transmission power of device	250 mW
Communication bandwidth	2 MHz	Carrier frequency	915 MHz

(2) **Baselines**: We compare the offloading performance of the proposed algorithm against four methods, described as follows:

- **Local Execution**: All tasks are executed locally on the device without offloading or data transmission, i.e., $\beta_{m,x} = 0$.
- **Full Offloading**: All tasks are offloaded to edge servers for execution, i.e., $\beta_{m,x} = 1$.
- **Offloading based on DQN without security (DQN-WS)**: This approach utilizes the DQN algorithm for task offloading but does not incorporate security measures for data transmission.
- **Offloading based on DQN with security (DQN-S)**: Similar to DQN-WS, this method employs the DQN algorithm but includes task encryption to secure data transmission.

For the DQN algorithm, we construct a two-layer neural network with 64 units in the first layer and 128 in the second. We utilize an experience replay buffer of size 10,000 and set the learning rate at 0.001 [40]. DRL-based algorithms, such as DQN and PPO, mainly use a trial-and-error learning method, continuously interacting with the environment to generate reward signals. These signals guide the agent in refining its decision-making model parameters, thereby enhancing performance.

5.2. Algorithm Convergence Comparison

We first assess the convergence of DRL-based models for task offloading, considering different data encryption conditions. The encryption status is controlled by the parameter α. Data transmission encryption is not used when $\alpha = 0$, making the process standard task offloading. When $\alpha = 1$, data transmission encryption is enforced. We evaluate the average rewards of the agents over 1000 episodes.

As shown in Figure 3, the PPO-based offloading algorithm outperforms the DQN algorithm in both encrypted and non-encrypted scenarios. Notably, in scenarios involving data transmission encryption, both DQN-E and PPO-E exhibit lower overall rewards compared to their non-encrypted counterparts, i.e., DQN-WE and PPO-WE, confirming that encryption imposes a performance penalty. Despite this, PPO-E achieves a reward nearly equivalent to its performance in the non-encrypted state. Specifically, by episode 100, PPO-E reaches a reward value of about −100, while DQN-E achieves only about

−190. This result highlights the PPO algorithm's superior sample efficiency, enabling it to learn and adapt more effectively with limited interaction samples. Moreover, the PPO algorithm's mechanism of limiting the magnitude of policy updates ensures stability and consistency in the learning process, reducing efficiency losses due to policy fluctuations. Overall, the performance superiority of the PPO algorithm in this task scheduling scenario, especially its significant advantage in sample efficiency, establishes it as a preferred solution for managing encrypted-task-offloading challenges in edge computing contexts.

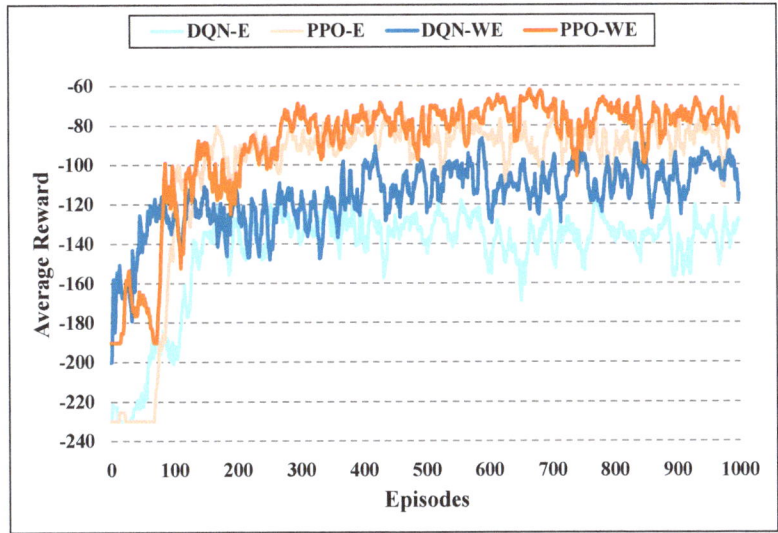

Figure 3. Training convergence of DRL agent in MEC systems.

5.3. Average System Performance Analysis

After offline training, the converged DRL network is saved for subsequent online task offloading. During online offloading, only the actor network is utilized for model inference to generate a specific offloading decision. Upon receiving these decisions, the terminal device transitions to the next offloading state s_{t+1}. To evaluate the actual performance of the algorithm, the actor network is adopted to infer multiple offloading tasks, and the average of these inferences is taken as the final performance metric. This assessment includes comparing average system cost, average latency, and average energy consumption across different offloading methods.

As shown in Figure 4, the proposed PPO-based offloading algorithm demonstrates superior performance. In non-encrypted scenarios, the average system cost using PPO-WE is 85, whereas the average system costs for local execution, full offloading, and DQN-WE are 238, 193, and 129, respectively. In encrypted scenarios, PPO-E reduces the average system cost by 31.9% compared to DQN-E. Note that in our experiments, the tasks are mainly compute-intensive. Therefore, the benefits of fully offloading tasks to edge servers far outweigh those of local processing, resulting in the average overhead of local computation exceeding that of the full offloading strategy. Figure 4 also compares the average execution latency and energy consumption, demonstrating that the proposed offloading algorithm achieves the lowest average latency and energy consumption compared to other methods. Specifically, PPO-WE reduces the average latency by 77.5%, 58.9%, and 28.1% compared to local execution, full offloading, and DQN-WE, respectively. In encrypted data transmission, PPO-E reduces average energy consumption by 38.2% compared to DQN-E. In summary, the proposed offloading algorithm outperforms other methods in the overall system cost, effectively enhancing the MEC performance.

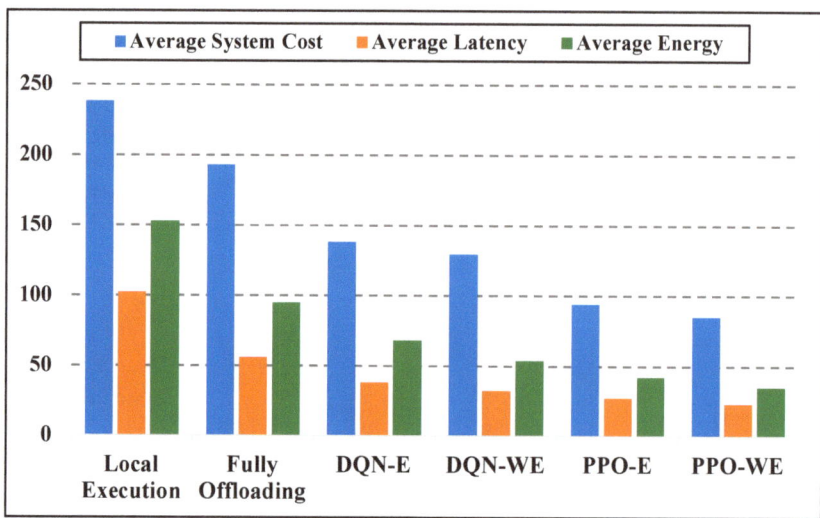

Figure 4. Performance comparison of different algorithms.

5.4. Impact of Number of Edge Servers

In MEC systems, mobile devices offload task requests to edge servers, which utilize their computing resources to process these tasks and return the results. However, a high volume of task requests can deplete the limited computing resources of edge servers, potentially leading to increased latency in task offloading. One way to address this issue is by increasing the number of edge servers, which provides additional computing resources to mobile devices and improves offloading performance. Therefore, the number of edge servers is critical to the overall offloading efficiency.

Figure 5 shows the average system cost for various edge servers while keeping the number of mobile devices fixed at 30. It can be observed that with only two edge servers, the limited resources result in the highest average system cost. With its efficient offloading strategy, the PPO algorithm effectively improves system performance under resource-constrained conditions. In both encrypted and non-encrypted scenarios, PPO-E and PPO-WE reduce the average system cost by 38.6% and 41.1%, respectively, compared to DQN-E and DQN-WE. Notably, when the number of edge servers increases from six to eight, the overall performance improvement of different methods is relatively small. This is because the computing resources of edge servers are no longer a bottleneck for task offloading, and mobile devices have sufficient resources to offload tasks. With eight servers, PPO-WE achieves the lowest average system cost, reducing it by 65.1% compared to DQN-WE. In summary, as the number of edge servers increases, the overall offloading performance of tasks improves significantly. The proposed algorithm effectively optimizes the decision-making process of task offloading, achieving a lower average system cost.

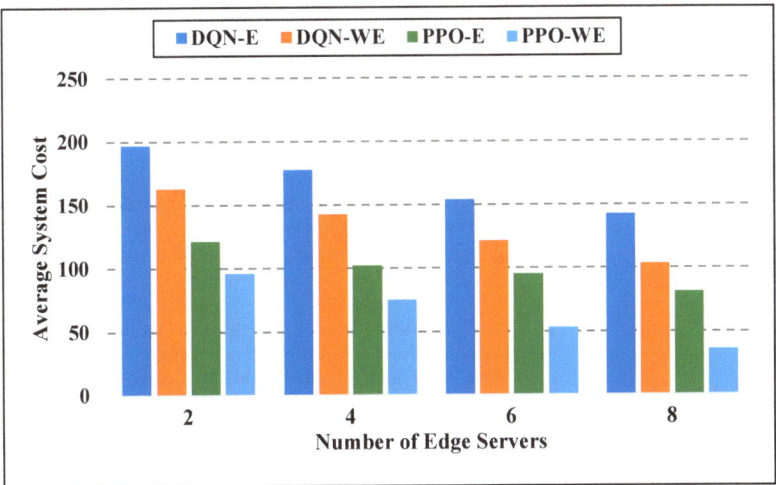

Figure 5. Average system cost with different numbers of edge servers.

6. Conclusions

This paper investigates the critical issue of secure task offloading in MEC systems, highlighting the limitations of current strategies that often neglect fundamental security aspects. To this end, we propose a security-aware task-offloading framework utilizing DRL. Specifically, we employ the AES encryption method to ensure the security of data transmission during task offloading. We formulate task offloading as an MDP and adopt the PPO algorithm to optimize task execution latency and energy consumption, thereby minimizing system utility while ensuring data security. Comprehensive performance evaluations demonstrate that the proposed framework effectively balances computational efficiency with security, providing a robust solution for MEC systems.

In future work, we will expand on the following points: (1) Security-Aware Collaborative Offloading for Multiple Mobile Devices: Given the heterogeneity in computational resources among different mobile devices, it is possible to offload computational tasks to devices with idle or stronger computational resources while ensuring security. This collaborative offloading strategy can enhance overall system efficiency and task processing capabilities. (2) Federated Reinforcement Learning-Based Task Offloading: To further enhance the security of the task-offloading process, we can leverage the privacy-preserving characteristics of federated learning. By deploying decision models across different devices, federated learning can improve the response time of the decision-making process while maintaining high levels of data security.

Author Contributions: Conceptualization, H.L. and D.Z.; data curation, H.L.; funding acquisition, D.Z.; investigation, H.L. and X.H.; methodology, H.L.; project administration, D.Z.; software, H.L.; supervision, D.Z.; validation, X.H.; writing— original draft, H.L.; writing—review and editing, X.H. and D.Z. All authors have read and agreed to the published version of the manuscript.

Funding: This work was supported in part by the National Natural Science Foundation of China under Grant 61872423 and in part by the Postgraduate Research and Practice Innovation Program of Jiangsu Province under Grant KYCX22_0956.

Data Availability Statement: Data are contained within the paper.

Conflicts of Interest: The authors declare no conflicts of interest.

Abbreviations

The following abbreviations are used in this paper:

$\mathcal{M}$	Number of mobile devices.
$\mathcal{N}$	Number of edge servers.
$\mathcal{T}$	Time slots in each episode.
Δ	Length of each time slot.
$\zeta_{m,n}(t)$	Connectivity status between mobile device m and edge server n at time t.
b_m^n	Channel bandwidth between mobile device m and edge server n.
g_m	Channel gain between mobile device and edge server.
p_m	Uplink transmission power of mobile device m.
σ^2	Signal-to-Interference-plus-Noise Ratio (SINR) in wireless link.
$\Gamma_m(t)$	Computational task request at time t for mobile device m.
$I_m(t)$	Data size of offloading task at time t for mobile device m.
$\lambda_m(t)$	CPU cycles required for the task requested by mobile device m at time t.
$\ell_m(t)$	Execution deadline for task requested by mobile device m at time t.
f_m	CPU frequency of mobile device m.
f_n	CPU frequency of edge server n.
ξ_m	Energy consumption per CPU cycle for mobile device m.
η	CPU cycles required to encrypt the data.
δ	CPU cycles required to decrypt the data.
β	Binary indicator of execution.

References

1. Wu, Q.; Chen, X.; Zhou, Z.; Chen, L. Mobile Social Data Learning for User-Centric Location Prediction with Application in Mobile Edge Service Migration. *IEEE Internet Things J.* **2019**, *6*, 7737–7747. [CrossRef]
2. Yin, X.; Liu, X. Multi-Task Convolutional Neural Network for Pose-Invariant Face Recognition. *IEEE Trans. Image Process.* **2018**, *27*, 964–975. [CrossRef] [PubMed]
3. Tang, Y.; Hou, J.; Huang, X.; Shao, Z.; Yang, Y. Green Edge Intelligence Scheme for Mobile Keyboard Emoji Prediction. *IEEE Trans. Mob. Comput.* **2024**, *23*, 1888–1901. [CrossRef]
4. Wang, J.; Du, H.; Niyato, D.; Kang, J.; Xiong, Z.; Rajan, D.; Mao, S.; Shen, X. A Unified Framework for Guiding Generative AI with Wireless Perception in Resource Constrained Mobile Edge Networks. *IEEE Trans. Mob. Comput.* **2024**. [CrossRef]
5. Wang, J.; Du, H.; Niyato, D.; Xiong, Z.; Kang, J.; Mao, S.; Shen, X.S. Guiding AI-Generated Digital Content with Wireless Perception. *IEEE Wirel. Commun.* **2024**. [CrossRef]
6. Mao, Y.; You, C.; Zhang, J.; Huang, K.; Letaief, K.B. A Survey on Mobile Edge Computing: The Communication Perspective. *IEEE Commun. Surv. Tutorials* **2017**, *19*, 2322–2358. [CrossRef]
7. Xu, D.; Su, X.; Wang, H.; Tarkoma, S.; Hui, P. Towards Risk-Averse Edge Computing with Deep Reinforcement Learning. *IEEE Trans. Mob. Comput.* **2024**, *23*, 7030–7047. [CrossRef]
8. Ding, Z.; Xu, J.; Dobre, O.A.; Poor, H.V. Joint Power and Time Allocation for NOMA–MEC Offloading. *IEEE Trans. Veh. Technol.* **2019**, *68*, 6207–6211. [CrossRef]
9. Bi, S.; Zhang, Y.J. Computation Rate Maximization for Wireless Powered Mobile-Edge Computing with Binary Computation Offloading. *IEEE Trans. Wirel. Commun.* **2018**, *17*, 4177–4190. [CrossRef]
10. Shirazi, S.N.; Gouglidis, A.; Farshad, A.; Hutchison, D. The Extended Cloud: Review and Analysis of Mobile Edge Computing and Fog from a Security and Resilience Perspective. *IEEE J. Sel. Areas Commun.* **2017**, *35*, 2586–2595. [CrossRef]
11. Zhang, T.; Xu, C.; Lian, Y.; Tian, H.; Kang, J.; Kuang, X.; Niyato, D. When Moving Target Defense Meets Attack Prediction in Digital Twins: A Convolutional and Hierarchical Reinforcement Learning Approach. *IEEE J. Sel. Areas Commun.* **2023**, *41*, 3293–3305. [CrossRef]
12. Zhang, T.; Xu, C.; Shen, J.; Kuang, X.; Grieco, L.A. How to Disturb Network Reconnaissance: A Moving Target Defense Approach Based on Deep Reinforcement Learning. *IEEE Trans. Inf. Forensics Secur.* **2023**, *18*, 5735–5748. [CrossRef]
13. Zhang, T.; Xu, C.; Zou, P.; Tian, H.; Kuang, X.; Yang, S.; Zhong, L.; Niyato, D. How to Mitigate DDoS Intelligently in SD-IoV: A Moving Target Defense Approach. *IEEE Trans. Ind. Inform.* **2023**, *19*, 1097–1106. [CrossRef]
14. Ranaweera, P.; Yadav, A.K.; Liyanage, M.; Jurcut, A.D. Service Migration Authentication Protocol for MEC. In Proceedings of the IEEE Global Communications Conference (GLOBECOM), Rio de Janeiro, Brazil, 4–8 December 2022; pp. 5493–5498.
15. Singh, J.; Bello, Y.; Hussein, A.R.; Erbad, A.; Mohamed, A. Hierarchical Security Paradigm for IoT Multiaccess Edge Computing. *IEEE Internet Things J.* **2021**, *8*, 5794–5805. [CrossRef]
16. Feng, S.; Xiong, Z.; Niyato, D.; Wang, P. Dynamic Resource Management to Defend Against Advanced Persistent Threats in Fog Computing: A Game Theoretic Approach. *IEEE Trans. Cloud Comput.* **2021**, *9*, 995–1007. [CrossRef]

17. Liu, Y.; Du, H.; Niyato, D.; Kang, J.; Xiong, Z.; Jamalipour, A.; Shen, X. ProSecutor: Protecting Mobile AIGC Services on Two-Layer Blockchain via Reputation and Contract Theoretic Approaches. *IEEE Trans. Mob. Comput.* **2024**. [CrossRef]
18. Eshraghi, N.; Liang, B. Joint Offloading Decision and Resource Allocation with Uncertain Task Computing Requirement. In Proceedings of the IEEE Conference on Computer Communications (INFOCOM), Paris, France, 29 April–2 May 2019; pp. 1414–1422.
19. Lyu, X.; Tian, H.; Ni, W.; Zhang, Y.; Zhang, P.; Liu, R.P. Energy-Efficient Admission of Delay-Sensitive Tasks for Mobile Edge Computing. *IEEE Trans. Commun.* **2018**, *66*, 2603–2616. [CrossRef]
20. Tang, M.; Wong, V.W. Deep Reinforcement Learning for Task Offloading in Mobile Edge Computing Systems. *IEEE Trans. Mob. Comput.* **2022**, *21*, 1985–1997. [CrossRef]
21. Wang, X.; Ye, J.; Lui, J.C. Online Learning Aided Decentralized Multi-User Task Offloading for Mobile Edge Computing. *IEEE Trans. Mob. Comput.* **2024**, *23*, 3328–3342. [CrossRef]
22. Liu, J.; Ren, J.; Zhang, Y.; Peng, X.; Zhang, Y.; Yang, Y. Efficient Dependent Task Offloading for Multiple Applications in MEC-Cloud System. *IEEE Trans. Mob. Comput.* **2023**, *22*, 2147–2162. [CrossRef]
23. Wang, P.; Li, K.; Xiao, B.; Li, K. Multiobjective Optimization for Joint Task Offloading, Power Assignment, and Resource Allocation in Mobile Edge Computing. *IEEE Internet Things J.* **2022**, *9*, 11737–11748. [CrossRef]
24. Fang, J.; Qu, D.; Chen, H.; Liu, Y. Dependency-Aware Dynamic Task Offloading Based on Deep Reinforcement Learning in Mobile-Edge Computing. *IEEE Trans. Netw. Serv. Manag.* **2024**, *21*, 1403–1415. [CrossRef]
25. Tan, L.; Kuang, Z.; Zhao, L.; Liu, A. Energy-Efficient Joint Task Offloading and Resource Allocation in OFDMA-Based Collaborative Edge Computing. *IEEE Trans. Wirel. Commun.* **2022**, *21*, 1960–1972. [CrossRef]
26. Wang, J.; Du, H.; Tian, Z.; Niyato, D.; Kang, J.; Shen, X. Semantic-Aware Sensing Information Transmission for Metaverse: A Contest Theoretic Approach. *IEEE Trans. Wirel. Commun.* **2023**, *22*, 5214–5228. [CrossRef]
27. Samy, A.; Elgendy, I.A.; Yu, H.; Zhang, W.; Zhang, H. Secure Task Offloading in Blockchain-Enabled Mobile Edge Computing with Deep Reinforcement Learning. *IEEE Trans. Netw. Serv. Manag.* **2022**, *19*, 4872–4887. [CrossRef]
28. Elgendy, I.A.; Zhang, W.; Tian, Y.C.; Li, K. Resource allocation and computation offloading with data security for mobile edge computing. *Future Gener. Comput. Syst.* **2019**, *100*, 531–541. [CrossRef]
29. Wu, M.; Song, Q.; Guo, L.; Lee, I. Energy-Efficient Secure Computation Offloading in Wireless Powered Mobile Edge Computing Systems. *IEEE Trans. Veh. Technol.* **2023**, *72*, 6907–6912. [CrossRef]
30. Asheralieva, A.; Niyato, D. Fast and Secure Computational Offloading with Lagrange Coded Mobile Edge Computing. *IEEE Trans. Veh. Technol.* **2021**, *70*, 4924–4942. [CrossRef]
31. Li, Y.; Aghvami, A.H.; Dong, D. Intelligent Trajectory Planning in UAV-Mounted Wireless Networks: A Quantum-Inspired Reinforcement Learning Perspective. *IEEE Wirel. Commun. Lett.* **2021**, *10*, 1994–1998. [CrossRef]
32. Liu, Y.; Wang, K.; Lin, Y.; Xu, W. LightChain: A Lightweight Blockchain System for Industrial Internet of Things. *IEEE Trans. Ind. Inform.* **2019**, *15*, 3571–3581. [CrossRef]
33. Gao, Z.; Yang, L.; Dai, Y. Fast Adaptive Task Offloading and Resource Allocation in Large-Scale MEC Systems via Multiagent Graph Reinforcement Learning. *IEEE Internet Things J.* **2024**, *11*, 758–776. [CrossRef]
34. Peng, K.; Xiao, P.; Wang, S.; Leung, V.C. SCOF: Security-Aware Computation Offloading Using Federated Reinforcement Learning in Industrial Internet of Things with Edge Computing. *IEEE Trans. Serv. Comput.* **2024**. [CrossRef]
35. Zhang, W.Z.; Elgendy, I.A.; Hammad, M.; Iliyasu, A.M.; Du, X.; Guizani, M.; El-Latif, A.A.A. Secure and Optimized Load Balancing for Multitier IoT and Edge-Cloud Computing Systems. *IEEE Internet Things J.* **2021**, *8*, 8119–8132. [CrossRef]
36. Zhan, Y.; Li, P.; Wu, L.; Guo, S. L4L: Experience-Driven Computational Resource Control in Federated Learning. *IEEE Trans. Comput.* **2022**, *71*, 971–983. [CrossRef]
37. Sutton, R.S.; McAllester, D.; Singh, S.; Mansour, Y. Policy Gradient Methods for Reinforcement Learning with Function Approximation. In *Advances in Neural Information Processing Systems (NIPS)*; MIT Press: Cambridge, MA, USA, 1999; Volume 12.
38. Samir, M.; Assi, C.; Sharafeddine, S.; Ghrayeb, A. Online Altitude Control and Scheduling Policy for Minimizing AoI in UAV-Assisted IoT Wireless Networks. *IEEE Trans. Mob. Comput.* **2022**, *21*, 2493–2505. [CrossRef]
39. Lu, H.; He, X.; Du, M.; Ruan, X.; Sun, Y.; Wang, K. Edge QoE: Computation Offloading with Deep Reinforcement Learning for Internet of Things. *IEEE Internet Things J.* **2020**, *7*, 9255–9265. [CrossRef]
40. Li, Y.; Aghvami, A.H.; Dong, D. Path Planning for Cellular-Connected UAV: A DRL Solution with Quantum-Inspired Experience Replay. *IEEE Trans. Wirel. Commun.* **2022**, *21*, 7897–7912. [CrossRef]

Disclaimer/Publisher's Note: The statements, opinions and data contained in all publications are solely those of the individual author(s) and contributor(s) and not of MDPI and/or the editor(s). MDPI and/or the editor(s) disclaim responsibility for any injury to people or property resulting from any ideas, methods, instructions or products referred to in the content.

Article

Edge Computing-Enabled Secure Forecasting Nationwide Industry $PM_{2.5}$ with LLM in the Heterogeneous Network

Changkui Yin [1,†], Yingchi Mao [1,*], Zhenyuan He [2], Meng Chen [3,*,†], Xiaoming He [4] and Yi Rong [1]

1. College of Computer Science and Software Engineering, Hohai University, Nanjing 210098, China; changkuiyin@163.com (C.Y.); rongyi1220@163.com (Y.R.)
2. Yuxin Electronic Technology Group Co., Ltd., Zhengzhou 450046, China; y12356777@163.com
3. Shenzhen Urban Transport Planning Center Co., Ltd., Shenzhen 518000, China
4. College of Internet of Things, Nanjing University of Posts and Telecommunications, Nanjing 210003, China; hexiaoming@njupt.edu.cn
* Correspondence: yingchimao@hhu.edu.cn (Y.M.); chenmeng9806@163.com (M.C.)
† These authors contributed equally to this work.

Abstract: The heterogeneous network formed by the deployment and interconnection of various network devices (e.g., sensors) has attracted widespread attention. $PM_{2.5}$ forecasting on the entire industrial region throughout mainland China is an important application of heterogeneous networks, which has great significance to factory management and human health travel. In recent times, Large Language Models (LLMs) have exhibited notability in terms of time series prediction. However, existing LLMs tend to forecast nationwide industry $PM_{2.5}$, which encounters two issues. First, most LLM-based models use centralized training, which requires uploading large amounts of data from sensors to a central cloud. This entire transmission process can lead to security risks of data leakage. Second, LLMs fail to extract spatiotemporal correlations in the nationwide sensor network (heterogeneous network). To tackle these issues, we present a novel framework entitled Spatio-Temporal Large Language Model with Edge Computing Servers (STLLM-ECS) to securely predict nationwide industry $PM_{2.5}$ in China. In particular, We initially partition the entire sensor network, located in the national industrial region, into several subgraphs. Each subgraph is allocated an edge computing server (ECS) for training and inference, avoiding the security risks caused by data transmission. Additionally, a novel LLM-based approach named Spatio-Temporal Large Language Model (STLLM) is developed to extract spatiotemporal correlations and infer prediction sequences. Experimental results prove the effectiveness of our proposed model.

Keywords: secure forecasting nationwide industry $PM_{2.5}$; heterogeneous network; LLM; edge computing; security risks of data leakage

1. Introduction

With the deployment and interconnection of diverse network devices (e.g., sensors and servers), the heterogeneous network has emerged as a widespread network scenario covering a wide range of geographic areas and integrating various types of information for more effective decision-making [1–4]. Recently, the Chinese government has deployed numerous sensors across national industry regions, forming a nationwide sensor network (heterogeneous network) to monitor and collect industry Particulate Matter 2.5 ($PM_{2.5}$), i.e., particulate matter with a diameter of 2.5 μm or less in industrial regions. Based on these data in the heterogeneous network, an important application is nationwide industry $PM_{2.5}$ prediction, which has important value for overhauling industrial production and human health [5,6].

Lately, we have viewed the birth of Large Language Models (LLMs) [7] and the revolutions that it has brought to Natural Language Processing (NLP) [8]. The core idea is to pretrain LLMs from billions of corpora, bringing about abundant intrinsic knowledge for facilitating downstream tasks. Until now, many efforts have attempted to use LLMs for time series forecasting on sensor networks. Most of these model a sensor network with small space granularity (e.g., Beijing, Shanghai, Yangtze River Delta, or Pearl River Delta) and train on a central server [9,10]. However, in our study we broaden our scope to collectively predict industry $PM_{2.5}$ in industrial regions of the Chinese mainland with enormous fine space granularity covering thousands of sensors. More data are generated due to the large number of sensors. If we continue to use the centralized training pattern, more data need to be uploaded to the central cloud. This increase in data transmission volume is bound to raise the security risks around data leakage.

Several studies have shown that spatiotemporal correlations exist among sensors in the nationwide sensor network [11]. In particular, the nationwide sensor network is quite complex. Assuming a sensor network with multiple interlinked sensors, industry $PM_{2.5}$ concentration on a given sensor is affected by its neighbors; these are identified as the spatial dependencies. The future industry $PM_{2.5}$ concentration of each sensor is substantially influenced by its history, termed the temporal dependencies. These two types of dependencies change dynamically over time and interact with each other. Collectively, we call them the spatiotemporal correlations. As a decoder-only structure, an LLM produces purely output sequences. Thus, if LLMs are employed directly on the sensor network, the spatiotemporal correlations between the sensors are ignored.

In summary, two urgent challenges necessitate solutions in nationwide industry $PM_{2.5}$ forecasting via LLM. First, handling large volumes of data on a central server heightens the related security risks. Second, LLMs struggle to contemplate spatiotemporal correlations among sensors. Motivated by these challenges, a novel LLM-based approach entitled Spatio-Temporal Large Language Model with Edge Computing Servers (STLLM-ECS) is developed to securely forecast nationwide industry $PM_{2.5}$ in ECS. In detail, we first represent the nationwide sensor network as an undirected graph. Our NodeSort method is then used to partition the graph into several subgraphs. We deploy an ECS on each subgraph accordingly. The sensor data of each subgraph are allocated to the corresponding ECS for training instead of to a central cloud. This means that the data do not need to be transmitted to the central cloud, avoiding the security risks triggered by data transmission. Next, for each subgraph we develop an LLM-based module named the Spatio-Temporal Large Language Model (STLLM) to learn the spatiotemporal correlations and infer the output sequences. STLLM fills multiple gaps in modeling spatiotemporal features via LLM. The idea of our proposed method is depicted in Figure 1. The contributions of our work are summarized below:

- To mitigate the security risks of centralized training due to data leakage during transmission, we present an edge-based distributed learning framework, STLLM-ECS, to securely forecast nationwide industry $PM_{2.5}$ in ECS. In detail, we develop a novel method named NodeSort to partition the nationwide sensor network graph into several subgraphs. The data and training tasks of each subgraph are then uploaded to an individual ECS rather than to a central cloud. This avoids the security risks around data leakage when transmitting data from sensors to the central cloud. In addition, we design an edge training strategy between neighbor subgraphs to speed up training and achieve the "training-during-inference" pattern. Meanwhile, the strategy facilitates sharing of similar industry $PM_{2.5}$ changes among neighboring subgraphs, thereby improving prediction accuracy.
- An LLM-based model called STLLM is presented. A spatiotemporal module (STM) is developed to capture spatiotemporal correlations, while GPT-2 [7] is adopted to produce output sequences. This is a novel hybrid framework that introduces a spatiotemporal feature extraction module into the LLM for industry $PM_{2.5}$ prediction. It effectively provides the LLM with the ability to model spatiotemporal features. In addition, considering the weak computing power of ECS, a pruning strategy is developed to further lighten model deployment on the ECS.

- We conduct extensive experiments on a nationwide industry $PM_{2.5}$ dataset comprising data from over 1000 sensors collected from across China's industrial regions. Our results indicate that the proposed STLLM-ECS is superior to all compared baselines.

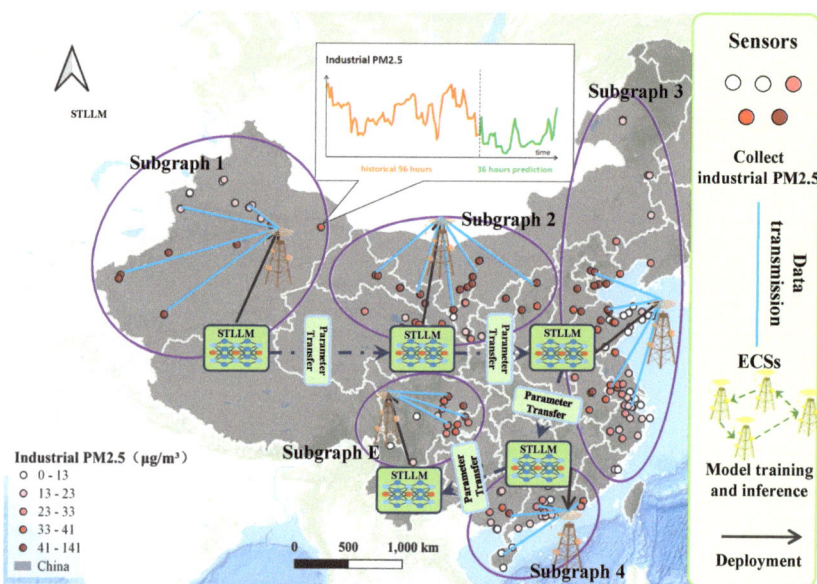

Figure 1. The architecture of STLLM-ECS for nationwide industry $PM_{2.5}$ prediction. A nationwide sensor network with over 1000 sensors located throughout China's industrial areas is first partitioned into E subgraphs. Each Edge Computing Server (ECS) covers a specific subgraph. Sensors installed on the subgraph record industrial $PM_{2.5}$ data, which are uploaded to the surrounding ECS. Meanwhile, an STLLM is deployed on each ECS. Each ECS is responsible for dealing with industry $PM_{2.5}$ data, training the STLLM, and inferring future industry $PM_{2.5}$ in the specific subgraph. Subsequently, the future industry $PM_{2.5}$ information is transmitted to the management department for factory rectification. To accelerate training, the parameter transfer strategy is used to initialize STLLM deployment on each ECS.

2. Related Work

2.1. Edge Computing

Presently, various concepts relevant to edge computing have been defined. One definition declares it to be a methodology that conducts computing at the edge of a network, i.e., ECS deployment to process computational tasks should occur near the data source [12]. In [13], the researchers classified ECS into three main categories. First, edge servers, which mainly contains Cloudlets, local cloud, etc. In contrast to traditional cloud computing, edge servers have weaker arithmetical power. Second, devices that coordinate among terminal devices. Compared to the edge servers, these have lower computing power, but are more portable. Third, communication technologies (e.g., opportunistic computing) in the device cloud accomplish resource migration and exploration among terminal devices. In addition, a vehicle cloud can be treated as a form of edge computing. In this scenario, the resources of the vehicle cloud are temporarily requisitioned. The edge, core cloud, and mobile users constitute the edge architecture. The computational tasks of mobile users can be offloaded from the central cloud and assigned to the edge for processing [14–16]. To date, edge applications have appeared in a variety of air pollution analysis tasks, including air pollution monitoring [17] and air pollution prediction in Beijing [18]. However, few works have focused on forecasting nationwide industry $PM_{2.5}$ in China using edge computing.

2.2. LLMs for Time Series Analysis

LLMs exhibit powerful capabilities in understanding the complex dependencies of heterogeneous textual data and offering plausible generation [19]. Representative LLMs include GPT [20], GPT-2 [7], and GPT-4 [21]. Their presence has revolutionized various fields, especially time series analysis. To date, several researchers have employed LLMs in time series analysis. For instance, Yu et al. [22] designed an explainable financial forecasting approach based on Open-LLaMA and GPT-4. In [23], LLM4TS was proposed for time series forecasting. Specifically, Chang et al. designed a two-stage fine-tuning strategy, with *Stage 1* consisting of supervised pretraining and *Stage 2* of fine-tuning according to specific tasks. Zhou et al. [24] conducted fine-tuning using a Frozen Pretrained Transformer (FPT) without adjusting its feedforward or self-attention layers. After fine-tuning, the FPT was deployed on different time series analysis tasks. Nevertheless, existing LLMs encounter two issues in industry $PM_{2.5}$ prediction. First, most LLM-based models use centralized training, requiring data to be transmitted from sensors to the central cloud. The large amount of data transmission increases the security risks around data leakage. Second, LLMs cannot extract the spatiotemporal correlations in the sensor network.

2.3. Air Pollution Forecasting

Air pollution forecasting methods are classified into two main categories, namely, physics-based and data-driven models.

Physics-based models: Such models treat the emission and diffusion of pollutants as a dynamic process which can be simulated by numerical functions. In order to achieve this, researchers must trace back the air pollution to its main causes, e.g., factories and vehicles [25,26]. However, it can be challenging to accurately collect these data sources.

Data-driven models: This type of model has become the most popular approach for air pollution prediction. This line of study adopts parameterized methods, e.g., deep neural networks, to mine the spatiotemporal correlations within air pollution data. In contrast to physics-based models, data-driven models are more flexible and demand less sophisticated domain knowledge. For example, Zheng et al. [27] designed a hybrid data-driven model which integrates predicted outcomes from different perspectives. Yi et al. [28] proposed a novel model called DeepAir which uses deep neural networks. Their experimental results proved that DeepAir is significantly superior to other shallow baselines in both long- and short-term forecasting. Several follow-ups have studied whether Graph Convolutional Network (GCN) approaches or attention-based approaches are more effective for capturing spatiotemporal correlations [29,30]. Unfortunately, these methods encounter a number of issues in the context of nationwide industry $PM_{2.5}$ prediction, including performance degradation and inefficiency.

3. Preliminaries

Currently, a large number of sensors are deployed in industrial regions throughout the country to monitor and collect time series $PM_{2.5}$ data. This allows critical spatial information (e.g., connectivity and distances) among sensors to be calculated. Given this spatial and temporal information, our proposed model has the capacity to forecast future industry $PM_{2.5}$. Three definitions are introduced below to facilitate the explanation of this process.

Definition I: Nationwide Sensor Network. The nationwide sensor network is treated as a undirected graph $\mathcal{G} = (\mathcal{V}, \mathcal{E})$, where $\mathcal{V}$ is a set of nodes that denote the sensors in nationwide industry regions. Assuming that N is the total number of nodes, we have $|\mathcal{V}| = N$ and $\mathcal{V} = (V_1, V_2, \ldots, V_N)$, with $\mathcal{E}$ as the set of edges, revealing whether specific nodes are connected.

Definition II: Subgraphs. In order to employ edge computing, it is necessary to partition $\mathcal{G}$ into some number of subgraphs depending on the number of deployed ECSs. Each ECS is deployed in the region where a subgraph is located and is responsible for processing the data of the nodes in the subgraph. Given E ECSs, the subgraphs are identified as $SG = (SG^1, SG^2, \ldots, SG^E)$, where $SG^j = (V_{j,1}, V_{j,2}, \ldots, V_{j,n_j})$, $j \in [1, E]$, n_j stands for the total number of nodes in subgraph j.

Definition III: Subgraph Representations. For brevity, $X_{t_k}^j = (x_{t_k,1}, x_{t_k,2}, \cdots, x_{t_k,n_j}) \in \mathbb{R}^{n_j \times F}$ is used to indicate the representations of subgraph j, where F denotes the features of the nodes (in our case, industry $PM_{2.5}$; thus, $F = 1$). Hence, $x_{t_k,i}$ is the industry $PM_{2.5}$ value of node i at timestep t_k.

Problem Formulation. For a subgraph j, given its subgraph representations of past P timesteps $\chi^j = (X_1^j, X_2^j, \cdots, X_P^j)$, we propose learning a mapping function $f_j(\cdot)$ which infers the industry $PM_{2.5}$ value of n_j nodes at the next Q timesteps. The problem can be formulated as follows:

$$(\chi^j, SG^j) \xrightarrow{f_j(\cdot)} \mathcal{Y}^j \quad (1)$$

where $\mathcal{Y}^j = (\hat{Y}_{t_{P+1}}^j, \hat{Y}_{t_{P+2}}^j, \cdots, \hat{Y}_{t_{P+Q}}^j)$ denotes the output sequences and SG^j is the topology of subgraph j.

4. STLLM-ECS Design

In this section, we describe the architecture of STLLM-ECS. First, a systematic review is presented, after which we detail the three main components of STLLM-ECS.

4.1. System Overview

To solve the above-mentioned challenges, STLLM-ECS is presented. The overview of STLLM-ECS is depicted in Figure 2. First, graph partitioning is proposed. In detail, we denote the entire nationwide sensor network as a graph. To allocate data and computing tasks to the ECSs, the graph ought to be partitioned into subgraphs. Unfortunately, the procedure of graph partitioning leads to information loss, as crucial edges in the graph are severed. In view of this, we propose the novel NodeSort method. It can evaluate node significance and retain the edges of significant nodes, effectively alleviating information loss. NodeSort follows the basic theory of PageRank [31], the universal algorithm for sorting web pages. Furthermore, we introduce Betweenness Centrality [32] to incorporate valuable information into PageRank. In contrast to traditional PageRank, NodeSort can better adapt to the characteristics of the nationwide sensor network and measure node importance.

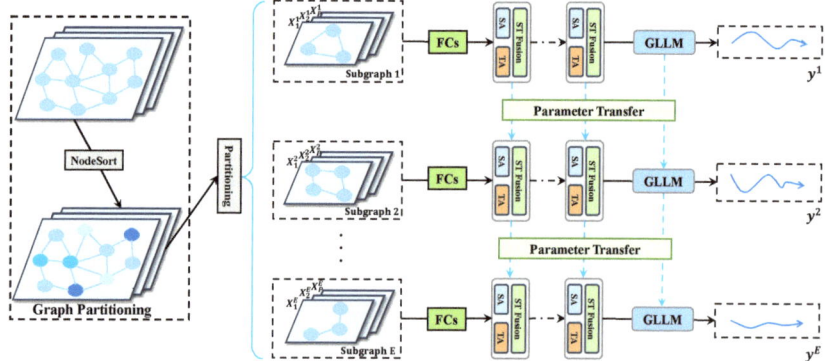

Figure 2. Overview of STLLM-ECS. SA is the spatial attention. TA is the temporal attention.

After graph partitioning, we allocate each subgraph to the corresponding ECS. For each subgraph, an intelligent method based on STM and Generative Large Language Model (GLLM) named STLLM is developed to capture spatiotemporal correlations and infer prediction sequences. In particular, spatial and temporal attention dynamically adjust model attention in both spatial and temporal dimensions, enabling us to identify complicated relationships in two dimensions. Thus, we introduce them into the STM to capture spatiotemporal correlations. Moreover, the LLM facilitates the generation of prediction sequences due to its extensive intrinsic knowledge acquired from pretraining. We introduce the LLM into the GLLM to generate future industry $PM_{2.5}$ predictions.

In addition, an edge training strategy is designed to reduce training time. In particular, considering the weak computational power of ECSs, pruning operations are adopted to make STLLM more lightweight and decrease the training workload.

4.2. Graph Partitioning Design

As mentioned above, the entire graph is partitioned into several subgraphs, which are then allocated to corresponding ECSs. To mitigate information loss during graph partitioning, we develop a novel method named NodeSort. The design details are as follows.

Similarly to other networks, e.g., road networks, node significance is a key factor in nationwide sensor networks. By measuring node significance, we can construct subgraphs centered on the most important nodes. As a result, the edges of the center nodes are preserved. These edges contain more information, which can help to reduce information loss. This type of method for effectively measuring node importance is indispensable. Therefore, we introduce PageRank with Betweenness Centrality to form NodeSort for implementation.

(1) *PageRank*: PageRank was initially applied to rank web pages based on their importance. Because PageRank can be defined on any digital graph, it has since been adopted in other domains, e.g., text summarization. Based on a random walk, given that the degree of node s is $\mathcal{D}$, the likelihood of industrial $PM_{2.5}$ diffusing from node s to other nodes is

$$LK_{s,t} = \begin{cases} 1/\mathcal{D}, & s \text{ links to } t \\ 0, & \text{otherwise,} \end{cases} \quad (2)$$

where s, t are set to $1, 2, \cdots, N$, $s \neq t$, $LK_{s,t}$ stands for the transition likelihood among nodes s and t, and $LK = [LK_{s,t}]_{N \times N} \in \mathbb{R}^{N \times N}$ denotes the transition matrix. In addition, two characteristics are present in LK, i.e., $LK_{s,t} \geq 0$ and $\sum_{s=1}^{N} LK_{s,t} = 1$.

Now, coming to the value of PageRank, we let $PR_{\text{Value}} = [PR(\text{Value}_1), PR(\text{Value}_2), \ldots, PR(\text{Value}_N)]$, where $PR(\text{Value}_n)$ represents the PageRank value of node n. Given a complete random walk model, each element in its transition matrix LK' is $1/N$. The PageRank method can be presented as follows:

$$\begin{aligned} PR_{\text{Value}} &= \beta \cdot LK \cdot PR_{\text{Value}} + (1-\beta) \cdot LK' \\ &= \beta \cdot LK \cdot PR_{\text{Value}} + \frac{1-\beta}{N} \end{aligned} \quad (3)$$

where $\beta \in [0,1]$ stands for the damping factor, denoted as the resistance from one node to others. Due to the static distribution property of Markov chains, we further adopt this algorithm to solve for the PR_{Value} of all nodes.

(2) *Betweenness Centrality*: Ulrik and Brandes [32] clarified the Betweenness Centrality as the sum of the shortest paths passing through the node, formulated as follows:

$$B_c(n) = \sum_{s \neq n \neq t \in V} \frac{\rho_{s,t}(n)}{\rho_{s,t}} \quad (4)$$

where $\rho_{s,t}(n)$ indicates the shortest path from node s to node t that passes through node n. The sum of the shortest paths from s to t is $\rho_{s,t}$, while V is the set of nodes in the nationwide sensor network. According to this definition, we can infer that nodes with large B_c have a tendency to become industrial $PM_{2.5}$ pollution centers, as they are the shortest paths for many routes.

(3) *NodeSort*: By leveraging PageRank, it is possible to acquire the importance of nodes in the nationwide sensor network. However, PageRank fails when exploited directly on the nationwide sensor network due to two factors. First, the distance among nodes is a crucial feature that can help to determine industrial $PM_{2.5}$ diffusion and propagation.

Although we have defined the transition matrix, the distance feature is neglected. Second, PageRank allocates the same weight to each node without considering discrepancies in node importance. In light of these factors, our novel NodeSort method is designed to adapt the characteristics of the nationwide sensor network and assess node importance more realistically. In particular, affected by Betweenness Centrality, those nodes potentially serving as industrial $PM_{2.5}$ pollution centers may be more vital. Thus, Betweenness Centrality is initially used to quantify node importance through weighting calculations. First, $LK_{s,t}$ is reconstructed as

$$LK'_{s,t} = \begin{cases} \frac{B_C(t)}{\sum_t B_C}, & s \text{ links to } t \\ 0, & \text{otherwise,} \end{cases} \quad (5)$$

where $B_C(t)$ denotes as the Betweenness Centrality of node t and $\sum_t B_C$ indicates the sum of Betweenness Centrality values of the nodes connected with t.

In PageRank, the damping factor is usually treated as a constant value of 0.85. In NodeSort, the distance is employed to compute this factor, whic is possible because the distance is strongly resistant to movement. Let β be a diagonal matrix $\beta' = (\beta_1, \beta_2, \ldots, \beta_N)$ in which β_t is defined as

$$\beta_t = \gamma \cdot \frac{1}{\sum_s \frac{1}{d_{s,t}}}, \quad (6)$$

with $d_{s,t}$ representing the distance among nodes s and t and γ as the scaling factor. The Markov chain is reconstructed as follows:

$$PR_{\text{Value}} = \begin{bmatrix} \beta_1 & & \\ & \ddots & \\ & & \beta_N \end{bmatrix} \cdot LK \cdot PR_{\text{Value}} + \frac{1}{N} \begin{bmatrix} 1-\beta_1 & & \\ & \ddots & \\ & & 1-\beta_N \end{bmatrix}. \quad (7)$$

Leveraging the the value vector PR_{Value} of NodeSort, the most important nodes in the nationwide sensor network are acquired. After that, some subgraphs are constructed depending on these nodes.

In summary, NodeSort is adopted to calculate the importance of nodes in the large-scale network. The top-E most important nodes are leveraged as central nodes to construct the subgraphs. Hence, the edges of important nodes are retained, which assists in more precise predictions.

4.3. STLLM Design

As shown in Figure 3, STLLM is composed of three parts: (1) Input Embedding Layer; (2) STM; and (3) GLLM. Specifically, STLLM is a pipeline structure. In the following, we illustrate how to apply each part to capture spatiotemporal correlations and predict industrial $PM_{2.5}$, taking the processing of subgraph j as an example.

(1) *Input Embedding Layer*: For subgraph j, as the deep neural networks fail to directly deal with industry $PM_{2.5}$ data, we need to change these data dimensions. It is necessary to transform the industry $PM_{2.5}$ data X_j of P historical timesteps for n_j nodes into higher-dimensional features. In detail, two layers of FCs are used to transform the dimensions from F to d_{model}, represented as $H_j \in \mathbb{R}^{P \times n_j \times d_{model}}$.

(2) *STM*: After obtaining the input embedding features, STM is deployed to capture spatiotemporal correlations among nodes of the subgraph, which is composed of L stacked Spatio-Temporal blocks (ST block). Each ST block comprises spatial attention, temporal attention, and the Spatio-Temporal Fusion (ST Fusion) mechanism. Spatial attention is proposed to capture spatial dependencies. Temporal attention is designed to extract

temporal dependencies. Depending on the impact of temporal and spatial dependencies on the prediction, we use ST Fusion for adaptive fusion without human intervention. Figure 3 illustrates the structure of STM. Specifically, let $H_j \in \mathbb{R}^{P \times n_j \times d_{\text{model}}}$ denote the input of L ST blocks. In the lth ST block, its input is the output of the $l-1$th ST block, denoted as $HST^{l-1} \in \mathbb{R}^{P \times n_j \times d_{\text{model}}}$. The spatial representations generated by spatial attention are $HS^l \in \mathbb{R}^{P \times n_j \times d_{\text{model}}}$, in which $hs^l_{t_k} \in \mathbb{R}^{n_j \times d_{\text{model}}}$ is the spatial representations at timestep t_k. The temporal representations generated by temporal attention are $HT^l \in \mathbb{R}^{P \times n_j \times d_{\text{model}}}$, in which $ht^l_n \in \mathbb{R}^{P \times d_{\text{model}}}$ is the temporal representations of node n. The spatiotemporal representations produced by ST fusion are indicated as $HST^l \in \mathbb{R}^{P \times n_j \times d_{\text{model}}}$. In addition, the residual connections are used to enable a larger receptive field and boost training speed. Hence, the output of the lth ST block can be expressed as $HST^l = HST^l + HST^{l-1}$. The details of spatial attention, temporal attention, and ST Fusion in the lth ST block are described below.

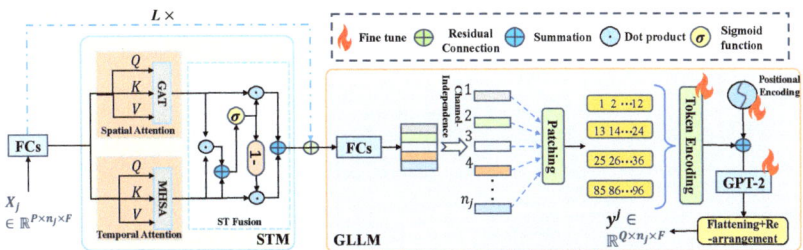

Figure 3. Framework of STLLM. STLLM is composed of STM and GLLM, in which STM contains L stacked ST blocks.

Spatial Attention: To extract spatial dependencies, spatial attention based on a one-layer graph attention network is designed. Through an attention mechanism, such a network can dynamically assign weights to sensors in the nationwide sensor network based on the relevance between sensors.

In the lth ST block at timestep t_k, let $hst^{l-1}_{t_k} \in \mathbb{R}^{n_j \times d_{\text{model}}}$ be the input of a one-layer graph attention network. The operation of a single hth head is expressed as

$$hs^{l,h}_{t_k} = \text{Softmax}\left(\alpha Q^S_h K^S_h\right) V^S_h, \qquad (8)$$

where $hs^{l,h}_{t_k} \in \mathbb{R}^{n_j \times \left(\frac{d_{\text{model}}}{N_h}\right)}$ refers to the spatial representations in the hth head. Query $Q^S_h \in \mathbb{R}^{n_j \times \left(\frac{d_{\text{model}}}{N_h}\right)}$, key $K^S_h \in \mathbb{R}^{n_j \times \left(\frac{d_{\text{model}}}{N_h}\right)}$, and value $V^S_h \in \mathbb{R}^{n_j \times \left(\frac{d_{\text{model}}}{N_h}\right)}$ are generated by linear mappings $hst^{l-1}_{t_k} W^S_Q$, $hst^{l-1}_{t_k} W^S_K$, and $hst^{l-1}_{t_k} W^S_V$, respectively, while W^S_Q, W^S_K, and $W^S_V \in \mathbb{R}^{d_{\text{model}} \times \left(\frac{d_{\text{model}}}{N_h}\right)}$ are the weight parameters for linear mapping, N_h is the number of heads, and α is considered as a scaling factor. Later on, the spatial representations $hs^l_{t_k} \in \mathbb{R}^{n_j \times d_{\text{model}}}$ at timestep t_k are obtained through the following concentration operation:

$$hs^l_{t_k} = \left[hs^{l,1}_{t_k}, hs^{l,2}_{t_k}, \ldots, hs^{l,N_h}_{t_k}\right] W^S_o \qquad (9)$$

where $W^S_o \in \mathbb{R}^{d_{\text{model}} \times d_{\text{model}}}$ is the trainable mapping matrix.

Temporal Attention: To capture temporal dependencies, we develop the temporal attention with one-layer Multi-Head Self-Attention (MHSA). The main reason for this is that the attention can dynamically allocate weights to different timesteps according to their significance.

Assuming that the input of the lth ST block in node n is $hst_n^{l-1} \in \mathbb{R}^{P \times d_{\text{model}}}$, the operation of a single hth head is expressed as follows:

$$ht_n^{l,h} = \text{Softmax}\left(\alpha Q_h^T \left(K_h^T\right)^T\right) V_h^T \tag{10}$$

where $ht_n^{l,h} \in \mathbb{R}^{P \times \left(\frac{d_{\text{model}}}{N_h}\right)}$ refers to the temporal representations generated by he one-layer MHSA operation on the hth head, $Q_h^T = hst_n^{l-1} W_Q^T, K_h^T = hst_n^{l-1} W_K^T$, and $V_h^T = hst_n^{l-1} W_V^T$ are query, key, and value, respectively, and W_Q^T, W_K^T, and $W_V^T \in \mathbb{R}^{d_{\text{model}} \times \left(\frac{d_{\text{model}}}{N_h}\right)}$ are the learnable parameters for linear mapping. The output results of each head are concatenated and further mapped to obtain the temporal representations $ht_n^l \in \mathbb{R}^{P \times d_{\text{model}}}$ of node n in the lth ST block, denoted as

$$ht_n^l = \left[ht_n^{l,1}, ht_n^{l,2}, \ldots, ht_n^{l,N_h}\right] W_o^T, \tag{11}$$

where $W_o^T \in \mathbb{R}^{d_{\text{model}} \times d_{\text{model}}}$ is the trainable mapping matrix.

ST Fusion: The industry $PM_{2.5}$ value of a node at a specific timestep is associated with its previous timesteps and other nodes. To adaptively fuse the temporal and spatial dependencies, we design ST Fusion as described in Figure 3. In the lth ST block, the outputs of spatial attention and temporal attention are separately denoted as $HT^l \in \mathbb{R}^{P \times n_j \times d_{\text{model}}}$ and $HS^l \in \mathbb{R}^{P \times n_j \times d_{\text{model}}}$, respectively. These two first conduct FC and layer normalization, then are fused together:

$$z = \sigma\left(\left(HS^l \odot HT^l\right) W_z^{ST} + HT^l W_z^T + b_z\right), \tag{12}$$

$$HST^l = HS^l \odot z + HT^l \odot (1-z), \tag{13}$$

where $HST^l \in \mathbb{R}^{P \times n_j \times d_{\text{model}}}$ denotes spatiotemporal representations generated by the lth ST block, z is the gate, σ represents the sigmoid function, $\odot$ is the element-wise product, and $W_z^{ST} \in \mathbb{R}^{d_{\text{model}} \times d_{\text{model}}}$, $W_z^T \in \mathbb{R}^{d_{\text{model}} \times d_{\text{model}}}$, and $b_z \in \mathbb{R}^{d_{\text{model}}}$ are trainable parameters.

(3) **GLLM**: After modeling the spatiotemporal correlations, we need to generate the output sequences depending on these features. Because the LLM has acquired rich intrinsic knowledge through pretraining and has been applied to downstream tasks, we design a novel LLM-based method named GLLM to infer industry $PM_{2.5}$ in the future, leveraging GPT-2 [7] as the backbone model. Concretely, GLLM is composed of channel-independence and patching, token and positional encoding, GPT-2, and the output layer. Next, we present these individual structures.

Channel-Independence and Patching: To adapt spatiotemporal representations for GPT-2, channel-independence and patching in the PatchTST method [33] are employed to tokenize these features. Specifically, we first use the FCs to restore the spatiotemporal features $HST^L \in \mathbb{R}^{P \times n_j \times d_{\text{model}}}$ generated by the Lth ST block, denoted as $\mathbb{R}^{P \times n_j \times F}$. Channel-independence then treats multi-node spatiotemporal representations ($P \times n_j \times F$) as multiple single nodes ($[P \times 1 \times F] \times n_j$) and a model is used to independently process them. Channel-blending models are intended to directly leverage cross-channel data, whereas channel-independence often indirectly extracts cross-channel interactions through weight sharing, thereby providing more precise predictions. The underlying reason for this is that channel-blending models often encounter data limitations and overfitting. In the context of applying channel-independence, the subsequent patching process groups adjacent timesteps into a singular patch-based token. This approach expands the input's historical span without increasing the token length, providing more valuable information for GPT-2.

Token Encoding and Positional Encoding: After obtaining a sequence of tokens through patching, token encoding is adopted to transform these tokens to ensure compatibility with the GPT-2 backbone model. In traditional NLP practice, token encoding is usually accomplished by exploiting a learnable lookup table to project tokens into a high-dimensional space. However, as we are patching for spatiotemporal features that denote vectors rather than scalars, we use a one-dimensional convolutional layer instead.

For positional encoding, we employ the structure in the transformer [34] to map the patch locations. During the training phase, token encoding and positional encoding need to be fine-tuned.

GPT-2: Furthermore, we use a pretrained GPT-2 with six layers as the backbone architecture of GLLM. To preserve the foundational knowledge acquired by pretraining, most parameters are frozen during the training phase, including those related to MHSA and FC layers. In addition to the low data requirements of this approach, retaining most of the non-training parameters tends to result in better predictive performance than training LLMs from scratch.

To enhance downstream tasks at minimal cost, we fine-tune the layer normalization, which is viewed as a common practice.

Output layer: After GPT-2, the output layer is adopted to produce industry $PM_{2.5}$ value in the future. Because the output of GPT-2 retains the form of patches, essentially a series of tokens, we utilize flattening, FC, and rearrangement operations, all of which must be fine-tuned during the training phase. In particular, assuming that the output token for a specific node n is produced, flattening is first used to straighten the tokens; FCs are then employed to modify the dimensions; finally, rearrangement is utilized to generate the unpatched time series for the next Q timesteps as the output of node n, denoted as $\mathbb{R}^{Q \times 1 \times F}$. We separately iterate the spatiotemporal representations of the channel-independent n_j nodes to obtain the industry $PM_{2.5}$ in the next Q timesteps, denoted as $\mathcal{Y}^j \in \mathbb{R}^{Q \times n_j \times F}$.

Eventually, we optimize the parameters of STLLM-ECS for subgraph j by minimizing the Mean Squared Error (MSE) loss function, represented as

$$\text{MSE} = \frac{\sum_{t_s=1}^{Q} \sum_{n=1}^{n_j} (y_{t_s,n} - \hat{y}_{t_s,n})^2}{Q \times n_j} + \frac{\lambda}{2}\|W\|^2, \tag{14}$$

where n_j is the total number of nodes in subgraph j and Q denotes the length of the predicted sequence. The predicted and observed values at timestep t_s on node n are $y_{t_s,n}$ and $\hat{y}_{t_s,n}$, respectively, while λ denotes the regularization and W is the learnable parameter.

4.4. Edge Training Strategy

Due to the similarity in terms of land use, we generally believe that there is an association between the industry $PM_{2.5}$ concentrations of adjacent subgraphs. For instance, during the weekday in industrial areas, the industry $PM_{2.5}$ concentrations not only affect the area but also spread to the surrounding areas; in other words, there are similar industry $PM_{2.5}$ features in the surrounding areas due to the diffusion of industry $PM_{2.5}$. As a result, transfer learning is introduced to the neighboring subgraphs through sharing trainable network parameters on each RSU, which aims to shorten the training time and improve the predictions' precision. In particular, assuming that the network parameters used to modeling subgraph j are transferred to its neighboring subgraph k, we first train the jth STLLM using the jth subgraph representations. After training, STLLM produces output sequences on the RSU. Meanwhile, the parameters of STM and the unfrozen parameters of GLLM are transferred to the kth RSU adjacent to the jth RSU for the initialization. The kth subgraph representations are then adopted to train based on the initialization. After multiple rounds of iteration, we obtain the optimized kth STLLM. In this way, when the jth STLLM is performing inference, the kth STLLM starts training. This "inference while training" mode further decreases the training time. Because the frozen GLLM parameter do not participate in training, we uniformly deploy these frozen model structures to each RSU before training. In addition, considering the limited computing power of the RSU, pruning operations are performed before uploading, i.e., cutting the heads of the MHSA and STBMHSA to implement dimensionality reduction and lightening.

5. Experiments

5.1. Experimental Settings

5.1.1. Dataset

STLLM-ECS was assessed on nationwide $PM_{2.5}$ concentration data from throughout China's industrial areas ranging from 1 January 2015 to 31 December 2018. We collected industrial $PM_{2.5}$ concentrations from 1065 sites covering industrial areas in 186 cities. The data collection frequency was one hour. In addition, the method used for data normalization was Z-score normalization. We split the dataset in chronological order, with the initial two years as the training set, the third year as the cross-validation set, and the fourth year as the test set.

5.1.2. Baselines

STLLM-ECS was compared with advanced baselines affiliated with the following four classes:

- *Classical statistics and shallow machine learning models*: **History Average (HA)** [35] was adopted to predict industrial $PM_{2.5}$ using the average of historical observed values. **Support Vector Regression (SVR)** [36] refers to vector autoregression.
- *Spatio-Temporal Graph Convolutional Networks (STGCNs)-based models*: Selected STGCNs (e.g., **Diffusion Convolutional Recurrent Neural Network (DCRNN)** [29] and **Spatio Temporal Graph Convolutional Network (STGCN)** [30]) were used as baselines. DCRNN and STGCN generalize well to nationwide industrial $PM_{2.5}$ prediction.
- *Attention-based models*: **Spatio-Temporal Graph Attention (ST-GRAT)** [34], **Graph Multi-Attention Network (GMAN)** [37], **ST-Transformer** [38], and **Airformer** [39] are transformer variants used for spatiotemporal prediction that can easily accommodate industrial $PM_{2.5}$ prediction.
- *LLM-based models*: Two LLM-based time series prediction models (e.g., **LLM4TS** [23] and **FPT** [24]) awere choosed for a comparison.

5.1.3. Evaluation Metrics

The performance of STLLM-ECS and the baselines are tested through four metrics divided into two groups: (a) Mean Absolute Error (MAE) and Root Mean Squared Error (RMSE) were used to evaluate the prediction accuracy; and (b) training time and GPU memory were utilized to assess model efficiency. In detail:

(1) *MAE*:

$$MAE = \frac{1}{Q \times n_j} \sum_{t_s=1}^{Q} \sum_{n=1}^{n_j} |y_{t_s,n} - \hat{y}_{t_s,n}|. \tag{15}$$

(2) *RMSE*:

$$RMSE = \sqrt{\frac{1}{Q \times n_j} \sum_{t_s=1}^{Q} \sum_{n=1}^{n_j} (y_{t_s,n} - \hat{y}_{t_s,n})^2}. \tag{16}$$

(3) Training time: The training time is composed of the Total Time (TT) and Average Time (AT); TT represents the overall cost of the entire training phase until the model converges, while AT is the average training time of the subgraphs. The training efficiency of a model can be measured through the training time. For instance, if the accuracy of two models is comparable, a shorter training time implies more efficient training.

(4) GPU M: The GPU M is the the memory usage of the GPU in the training phase, which can be used to evaluate the space overhead of the model. For example, lower GPU M means that fewer model parameters need to be trained. This shows that the model does not consume excessive GPU resources during training.

5.1.4. Parameter Settings

We reproduced HA through the statsmodels package in Python 3.8. The SVR was implemented using the sklearn package in Python. The remaining models were implemented using the PyTorch library. For STLLM-ECS, some parameters were set as follows.

In Graph Partitioning, the number of subgraphs was selected as 10. Hence, we employed ten Nvidia 3090 Ti GPU cards, Nvidia, CA, USA, to simulate ten RSUs. In addition, We set the scaling factor γ to 0.9.

In each STLLM, the predicted timesteps were set to 36 ($Q = 36$), i.e., predicting the nationwide industry $PM_{2.5}$ for 1065 sites throughout China. The referenced timesteps were 96 h ($P = 96$). We set the learning rate and batch size as 0.0002 and 32, respectively. Stochastic gradient descent was selected as the optimizer, with d_{model} as 64. In addition, hyperparameters need to be set for two parts, i.e., STM and GLLM. For STM, the initial number of heads in spatial and temporal attention N_h, the dimensions of each head d, and the number of ST blocks L were set as 4, 16, and 1, respectively. For GLLM, we selected a patch length of 12 and stride of 12 in patching. The number of GPT-2 layers L_{GPT} was 6.

In pruning, the initial number of heads for MHSA and STBMHSA was 16. After every two subgraphs, we reduced the number of heads in MHSA and STBMHSA through a pruning operation.

5.2. Experimental Results

5.2.1. Performance Comparisons

STLLM-ECS was contrasted with the above baselines for nationwide industry $PM_{2.5}$ prediction in the next 36 h, as shown in Table 1. GPUM is the GPU memory usage, while '-' indicates that the model does not run using the GPU.

Table 1. Industry $PM_{2.5}$ prediction accuracy comparison of STLLM-ECS and baselines on the nationwide sensor network. Bolding indicates the best results.

Model	GPUM	1–12 h		13–24 h		25–36 h		Average		TT	AT
		MAE	RMSE	MAE	RMSE	MAE	RMSE	MAE	RMSE		
HA	-	47.28	92.65	47.28	92.65	47.28	92.65	47.28	92.65	1.95 h	-
SVR	-	31.04	64.75	34.57	70.41	37.83	75.24	34.48	70.07	2.04 h	-
DCRNN	5.03 G	15.63	29.59	16.72	31.15	17.48	34.34	16.52	31.36	4.84 h	-
STGCN	4.78 G	15.37	30.28	15.98	31.24	16.82	32.36	16.06	31.29	3.89 h	-
ST-GRAT	5.33 G	16.36	31.27	18.01	36.43	19.86	40.24	18.08	35.98	5.61 h	-
GMAN	6.73 G	16.84	33.65	17.47	36.92	19.24	39.85	17.85	36.81	6.94 h	-
ST-Transformer	5.17 G	16.24	30.89	17.82	35.89	19.01	39.14	17.69	35.31	5.12 h	-
Airformer	4.21 G	15.58	29.37	16.96	34.27	18.41	38.12	16.98	33.92	3.98 h	-
LLM4TS	1.72 G	14.23	27.84	15.99	30.17	17.72	33.46	15.98	30.49	2.35 h	-
FPT	1.58 G	14.12	28.54	16.39	33.95	**16.03**	32.67	15.51	31.72	2.14 h	-
STLLM-ECS	2.24 G	**13.25**	**25.32**	**15.37**	**28.89**	16.93	**32.17**	**15.18**	**28.79**	2.67 h	0.27 h

(1) Prediction Accuracy Comparison: From Table 1, we can draw the following conclusions: (1) deep learning-based models outperform the classical statistical and shallow machine learning models (e.g., HA and SVR) due to lack of spatiotemporal feature extraction capability; (2) attention-based models (e.g., ST-GRAT, GMAN, ST-Transformer, and Airformer) are superior to STGCN-based models (e.g., DCRNN, and STGCN), as the attention-based network further improves the capacity to extract global and dynamic spatiotemporal features using spatiotemporal attention compared to STGCN-based models; (3) although the LLM-based models (e.g., LLM4TS and FPT) were originally applied other spatiotemporal analysis tasks such as traffic flow prediction, they generalize well to nationwide industry $PM_{2.5}$ prediction; and (4) compared with all baselines, STLLM-ECS demonstrates the best prediction accuracy, proving that STM can effectively extract spatiotemporal correlations and GLLM can generate prediction sequences thanks to the extensive intrinsic knowledge in the pretrained GPT-2.

(2) *Training Efficiency Comparison*: According to TT, AT, and GPUM, shown in Table 1, the following conclusions can be drawn. First, the TT of HA and ARIMA is lower than that of the other deep learning-based models due to their simple structures. Second, among the deep learning-based models, the LLM-based models (FPT and LLM4TS) have the lowest TT and GPUM. This is because most of the parameters in these models are frozen, and only a small portion of the parameters need to be trained. Third, except for FPT and LLM4TS, the TT of STLLM-ECS is the shortest. Meanwhile, the AT of STLLM-ECS does not exceed 0.5 h. This reveals that STLLM-ECS maintains satisfactory accuracy with small time overheads. Finally, due to its small-scale structure, the GPU memory overhead of STLLM-ECS is relatively small. The main reason for this is that the size of the processed subgraphs is small, allowing STLLM-ECS to maintain relatively low GPU memory usage even though the size of the national sensor network is large.

5.2.2. Case Study

A case study was conducted to visualize the fitting results of STLLM-ECS. The JiNanHuaGongChang site in Shandong and the TongZhouXinCheng site in Beijing were chosen for evaluation. We plotted the fitting curves for 500 continuous hours using HA, GMAN, and STLLM-ECS, as shown in Figure 4, observing the following conclusions. First, HA fails to learn the complex nonlinear relationships in industry $PM_{2.5}$ data. Second, compared with HA, GMAN can extract spatiotemporal correlations, improving the ability in fitting; however, GMAN cannot recognize sudden changes in industry $PM_{2.5}$ at the JiNanHuaGongChang and TongZhouXinCheng sites. Third, our proposed STLLM-ECS achieves the best fitting. One potential reason is that the pretrained GPT-2 contains rich intrinsic knowledge, which help to identify various patterns of change in industry $PM_{2.5}$.

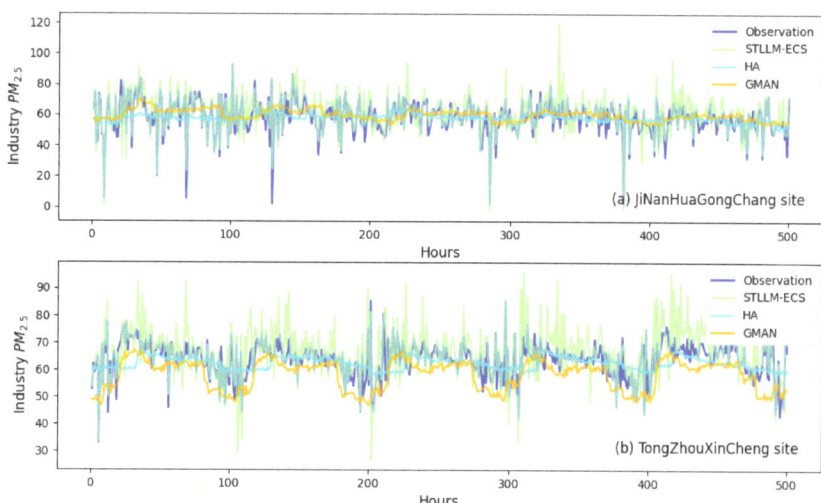

Figure 4. Results of the industry $PM_{2.5}$ prediction case study using the JiNanHuaGongChang and TongZhouXinCheng sites.

5.2.3. Effect of Hyperparameters

Figure 5 illustrates the MAE and RMSE of STLLM-ECS on 1065 sites under different hyperparameter settings for predicting the next 36 h. When one hyperparameter was adjusted, the other hyperparameters were kept at their default optimal values (e.g., $N_h = 4$, $d = 16$, $L = 1$, and $L_{GPT} = 6$). As shown in Figure 5a,b,d, the more complex model structures make it easier to underfit the data, while the simpler model structures make it easier to overfit. Figure 5c illustrates that the model with fewer ST blocks achieves the best prediction accuracy. This shows that stacking too many ST blocks leads to error accumulation.

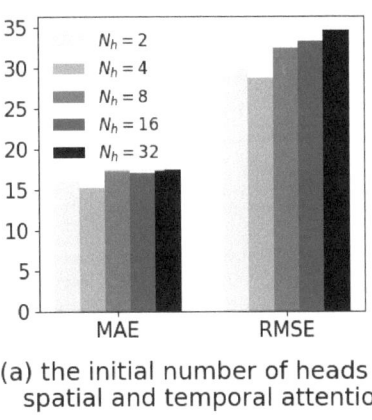
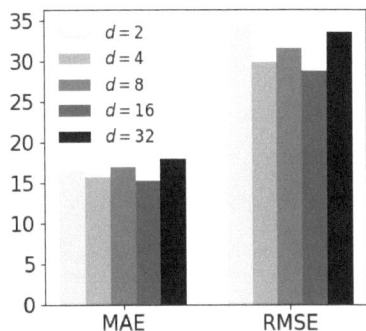

(a) the initial number of heads in spatial and temporal attention

(b) The dimensions of each head

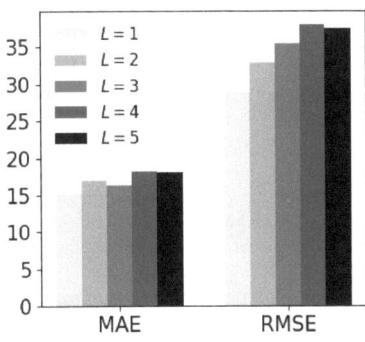
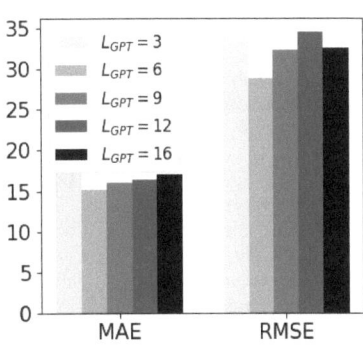

(c) The number of ST blocks

(d) The number of GPT-2 layers

Figure 5. Experimental results under different hyperparameter settings on the nationwide industry $PM_{2.5}$ dataset.

6. Conclusions

In this paper, we have proposed a novel framework entitled STLLM-ECS for securely predicting nationwide industry $PM_{2.5}$ in China. Specifically, the nationwide sensor network is first partitioned into several subgraphs. Each subgraph is been assigned an ECS. We then deploy STLLM on each ECS to extract spatiotemporal correlations and infer prediction sequences in the subgraphs. We conducted experiments on a nationwide sensor network throughout China's industrial areas. Our experimental results show that STLLM-ECS is superior to state-of-the-art baselines in prediction performance.

Author Contributions: Conceptualization, Z.H., M.C., and X.H.; Data curation, C.Y. and M.C.; Formal analysis, C.Y., Z.H., M.C. and X.H.; Funding acquisition, Y.M.; Investigation, C.Y. and Y.R.; Methodology, C.Y., Z.H., M.C., X.H. and Y.R.; Project administration, Y.M.; Resources, C.Y., Y.M. and X.H.; Software, C.Y. and M.C.; Supervision, Y.M.; Validation, Z.H., M.C. and Y.R.; Visualization, C.Y.; Writing—original draft, C.Y. and Z.H.; Writing—review and editing, Y.M., M.C., X.H. and Y.R. All authors have read and agreed to the published version of the manuscript.

Funding: This work was supported by Research on Distribution Room Condition Sensing Early Warning and Distribution Cable Operation and Inspection Smart Decision-Making Technology, No. 524609220092.

Data Availability Statement: Dataset available on request from the authors.

Conflicts of Interest: Author Zhenyuan He was employed by the company Yuxin Electronic Technology Group Co., Ltd. Author Meng Chen was employed by the company Shenzhen Urban Transport Planning Center Co., Ltd. The remaining authors declare that the research was conducted in the absence of any commercial or financial relationships that could be construed as a potential conflict of interest.

References

1. Liu, Y.; Wang, K.; Lin, Y.; Xu, W. LightChain: A lightweight blockchain system for industrial internet of things. *IEEE Trans. Ind. Inform.* **2019**, *15*, 3571–3581. [CrossRef]
2. Liu, Y.; Du, H.; Niyato, D.; Kang, J.; Xiong, Z.; Jamalipour, A.; Shen, X. ProSecutor: Protecting Mobile AIGC Services on Two-Layer Blockchain via Reputation and Contract Theoretic Approaches. *IEEE Trans. Mob. Comput.* **2024** . [CrossRef]
3. Dong, Y.; Hu, Z.; Wang, K.; Sun, Y.; Tang, J. Heterogeneous network representation learning. In Proceedings of the Twenty-Ninth International Joint Conference on Artificial Intelligence, Yokohama, Japan, 11–17 July 2020; Volume 20, pp. 4861–4867.
4. Zhang, T.; Xu, C.; Lian, Y.; Tian, H.; Kang, J.; Kuang, X.; Niyato, D. When Moving Target Defense Meets Attack Prediction in Digital Twins: A Convolutional and Hierarchical Reinforcement Learning Approach. *IEEE J. Sel. Areas Commun.* **2023**, *41*, 3293–3305. [CrossRef]
5. Hu, K.; Rahman, A.; Bhrugubanda, H.; Sivaraman, V. HazeEst: Machine learning based metropolitan air pollution estimation from fixed and mobile sensors. *IEEE Sens. J.* **2017**, *17*, 3517–3525. [CrossRef]
6. Han, Q.; Liu, P.; Zhang, H.; Cai, Z. A wireless sensor network for monitoring environmental quality in the manufacturing industry. *IEEE Access* **2019**, *7*, 78108–78119. [CrossRef]
7. Radford, A.; Wu, J.; Child, R.; Luan, D.; Amodei, D.; Sutskever, I. Language models are unsupervised multitask learners. *OpenAI Blog* **2019**, *1*, 9.
8. Otter, D.W.; Medina, J.R.; Kalita, J.K. A survey of the usages of deep learning for natural language processing. *IEEE Trans. Neural Netw. Learn. Syst.* **2020**, *32*, 604–624. [CrossRef]
9. Wang, J.; Du, H.; Tian, Z.; Niyato, D.; Kang, J.; Shen, X. Semantic-aware sensing information transmission for metaverse: A contest theoretic approach. *IEEE Trans. Wirel. Commun.* **2023**, *22*, 5214–5228. [CrossRef]
10. Zhang, Q.; Wu, S.; Wang, X.; Sun, B.; Liu, H. A PM2.5 concentration prediction model based on multi-task deep learning for intensive air quality monitoring stations. *J. Clean. Prod.* **2020**, *275*, 122722. [CrossRef]
11. Hu, Y.; Cao, N.; Guo, W.; Chen, M.; Rong, Y.; Lu, H. FedDeep: A Federated Deep Learning Network for Edge Assisted Multi-Urban PM2.5 Forecasting. *Appl. Sci.* **2024**, *14*, 1979. [CrossRef]
12. Shi, W.; Dustdar, S. The promise of edge computing. *Computer* **2016**, *49*, 78–81. [CrossRef]
13. Toczé, K.; Nadjm-Tehrani, S. A taxonomy for management and optimization of multiple resources in edge computing. *Wirel. Commun. Mob. Comput.* **2018**, *2018*, 7476201. [CrossRef]
14. Zhang, T.; Xu, C.; Zou, P.; Tian, H.; Kuang, X.; Yang, S.; Zhong, L.; Niyato, D. How to mitigate DDoS intelligently in SD-IoV: A moving target defense approach. *IEEE Trans. Ind. Inform.* **2022**, *19*, 1097–1106. [CrossRef]
15. Wang, J.; Du, H.; Niyato, D.; Kang, J.; Xiong, Z.; Rajan, D.; Mao, S.; Shen, X. A unified framework for guiding generative ai with wireless perception in resource constrained mobile edge networks. *IEEE Trans. Mob. Comput.* **2024**. [CrossRef]
16. Zhang, T.; Xu, C.; Shen, J.; Kuang, X.; Grieco, L.A. How to Disturb Network Reconnaissance: A Moving Target Defense Approach Based on Deep Reinforcement Learning. *IEEE Trans. Inf. Forensics Secur.* **2023**, *18*, 5735–5748. [CrossRef]
17. Su, X.; Liu, X.; Motlagh, N.H.; Cao, J.; Su, P.; Pellikka, P.; Liu, Y.; Petäjä, T.; Kulmala, M.; Hui, P.; et al. Intelligent and scalable air quality monitoring with 5G edge. *IEEE Internet Comput.* **2021**, *25*, 35–44. [CrossRef]
18. Wardana, I.N.K.; Gardner, J.W.; Fahmy, S.A. Collaborative Learning at the Edge for Air Pollution Prediction. *IEEE Trans. Instrum. Meas.* **2023**, *73*, 2503612. [CrossRef]
19. Wang, J.; Du, H.; Niyato, D.; Xiong, Z.; Kang, J.; Mao, S.; Shen, X.S. Guiding AI-generated digital content with wireless perception. *IEEE Wirel. Commun.* **2024**. [CrossRef]
20. Radford, A.; Narasimhan, K.; Salimans, T.; Sutskever, I. Improving Language Understanding by Generative Pre-Training. 2018. Available online: https://www.mikecaptain.com/resources/pdf/GPT-1.pdf (accessed on 25 June 2024)
21. Achiam, J.; Adler, S.; Agarwal, S.; Ahmad, L.; Akkaya, I.; Aleman, F.L.; Almeida, D.; Altenschmidt, J.; Altman, S.; Anadkat, S.; et al. Gpt-4 technical report. *arXiv* **2023**, arXiv:2303.08774.
22. Yu, X.; Chen, Z.; Ling, Y.; Dong, S.; Liu, Z.; Lu, Y. Temporal Data Meets LLM–Explainable Financial Time Series Forecasting. *arXiv* **2023**, arXiv:2306.11025.
23. Chang, C.; Peng, W.C.; Chen, T.F. Llm4ts: Two-stage fine-tuning for time-series forecasting with pre-trained llms. *arXiv* **2023**, arXiv:2308.08469.
24. Zhou, T.; Niu, P.; Sun, L.; Jin, R. One fits all: Power general time series analysis by pretrained lm. *Adv. Neural Inf. Process. Syst.* **2023**, *36*, 43322–43355.
25. Arystanbekova, N.K. Application of Gaussian plume models for air pollution simulation at instantaneous emissions. *Math. Comput. Simul.* **2004**, *67*, 451–458. [CrossRef]

26. Daly, A.; Zannetti, P. Air pollution modeling—An overview. *Ambient. Air Pollut.* **2007**, 15–28. Available online: https://www.researchgate.net/profile/Arideep-Mukherjee/post/What-are-the-models-for-modelling-air-pollution/attachment/5bc95d70cfe4a76455fbd37d/AS%3A683302050607104%401539923312818/download/Modeling.pdf (accessed on 25 June 2024).
27. Zheng, Y.; Yi, X.; Li, M.; Li, R.; Shan, Z.; Chang, E.; Li, T. Forecasting fine-grained air quality based on big data. In Proceedings of the 21th ACM SIGKDD International Conference on Knowledge Discovery and Data Mining, Sydney, NSW, Australia, 10–13 August 2015; pp. 2267–2276.
28. Yi, X.; Zhang, J.; Wang, Z.; Li, T.; Zheng, Y. Deep distributed fusion network for air quality prediction. In Proceedings of the 24th ACM SIGKDD International Conference on Knowledge Discovery & Data Mining, London, UK, 19–23 August 2018; pp. 965–973.
29. Li, Y.; Yu, R.; Shahabi, C.; Liu, Y. Diffusion convolutional recurrent neural network: Data-driven traffic forecasting. *arXiv* **2017**, arXiv:1707.01926.
30. Yu, B.; Yin, H.; Zhu, Z. Spatio-temporal graph convolutional networks: A deep learning framework for traffic forecasting. *arXiv* **2017**, arXiv:1709.04875.
31. Brin, S. The PageRank citation ranking: Bringing order to the web. *Proc. ASIS* **1998**, *98*, 161–172.
32. Brandes, U. A faster algorithm for betweenness centrality. *J. Math. Sociol.* **2001**, *25*, 163–177. [CrossRef]
33. Nie, Y.; Nguyen, N.H.; Sinthong, P.; Kalagnanam, J. A time series is worth 64 words: Long-term forecasting with transformers. *arXiv* **2022**, arXiv:2211.14730.
34. Park, C.; Lee, C.; Bahng, H.; Tae, Y.; Jin, S.; Kim, K.; Ko, S.; Choo, J. ST-GRAT: A novel spatio-temporal graph attention networks for accurately forecasting dynamically changing road speed. In Proceedings of the 29th ACM International Conference on Information & Knowledge Management, Virtual Event, 19–23 October 2020; pp. 1215–1224.
35. Bhatti, U.A.; Yan, Y.; Zhou, M.; Ali, S.; Hussain, A.; Qingsong, H.; Yu, Z.; Yuan, L. Time series analysis and forecasting of air pollution particulate matter (PM2.5): An SARIMA and factor analysis approach. *IEEE Access* **2021**, *9*, 41019–41031. [CrossRef]
36. Zhang, B.; Rong, Y.; Yong, R.; Qin, D.; Li, M.; Zou, G.; Pan, J. Deep learning for air pollutant concentration prediction: A review. *Atmos. Environ.* **2022**, *290*, 119347. [CrossRef]
37. Zheng, C.; Fan, X.; Wang, C.; Qi, J. Gman: A graph multi-attention network for traffic prediction. In Proceedings of the AAAI Conference on Artificial Intelligence, Hilton, NY, USA, 7–12 February 2020; Volume 34, pp. 1234–1241.
38. Yu, M.; Masrur, A.; Blaszczak-Boxe, C. Predicting hourly PM2.5 concentrations in wildfire-prone areas using a SpatioTemporal Transformer model. *Sci. Total Environ.* **2023**, *860*, 160446. [CrossRef] [PubMed]
39. Liang, Y.; Xia, Y.; Ke, S.; Wang, Y.; Wen, Q.; Zhang, J.; Zheng, Y.; Zimmermann, R. Airformer: Predicting nationwide air quality in china with transformers. In Proceedings of the AAAI Conference on Artificial Intelligence, Washington, DC, USA, 7–14 February 2023; Volume 37, pp. 14329–14337.

Disclaimer/Publisher's Note: The statements, opinions and data contained in all publications are solely those of the individual author(s) and contributor(s) and not of MDPI and/or the editor(s). MDPI and/or the editor(s) disclaim responsibility for any injury to people or property resulting from any ideas, methods, instructions or products referred to in the content.

Article

MOMTA-HN: A Secure and Reliable Multi-Objective Optimized Multipath Transmission Algorithm for Heterogeneous Networks

Shengyuan Qi [1,2,3,*], Lin Yang [1,2,3,*], Linru Ma [2], Shanqing Jiang [1,2,3], Yuyang Zhou [1,3] and Guang Cheng [1,3,*]

1. School of Cyber Science and Engineering, Southeast University, Nanjing 211189, China; sqjiang@njnet.edu.cn (S.J.); yyzhou@seu.edu.cn (Y.Z.)
2. National Key Laboratory of Science and Technology on Information System Security, Beijing 100101, China; malinru@163.com
3. Jiangsu Province Engineering Research Center of Security for Ubiquitous Network, Nanjing 211189, China
* Correspondence: syqi@seu.edu.cn (S.Q.); yanglin61s@126.com (L.Y.); chengguang@seu.edu.cn (G.C.)

Citation: Qi, S.; Yang, L.; Ma, L.; Jiang, S.; Zhou, Y.; Cheng, G. MOMTA-HN: A Secure and Reliable Multi-Objective Optimized Multipath Transmission Algorithm for Heterogeneous Networks. *Electronics* **2024**, *13*, 2697. https://doi.org/10.3390/electronics13142697

Academic Editor: Srinivas Sampalli

Received: 17 June 2024
Revised: 4 July 2024
Accepted: 7 July 2024
Published: 10 July 2024

Copyright: © 2024 by the authors. Licensee MDPI, Basel, Switzerland. This article is an open access article distributed under the terms and conditions of the Creative Commons Attribution (CC BY) license (https://creativecommons.org/licenses/by/4.0/).

Abstract: With the rapid development of heterogeneous network technologies, such as mobile edge computing, satellite communications, self-organizing networks, and the wired Internet, satisfying users' increasingly diversified and complex communication needs in dynamic and evolving network environments has become a critical research topic. Ensuring secure and reliable information transmission is essential for stable network operation in these complex environments. Addressing this challenge, this study proposed a secure and reliable multi-objective optimized multipath transmission algorithm for heterogeneous networks to enhance security and reliability during data transmission. The core principle of this algorithm was that multipath transmission can provide additional protection through redundant paths. This redundancy ensured that even if one path is attacked or fails, alternative paths can maintain data integrity and reachability. In this study, we employed the Optimized Non-dominated Sorting Genetic Algorithm II (ONSGA-II) to determine the range of the initial population and filter suitable paths by optimizing them according to different demand objectives. In the path selection process, we introduced an innovative deletion graph method, which ensures that redundant paths do not share any common links with the original paths, except when there are unique links. This approach enhances the independence of transmission paths and improves the security of the transmission process. It effectively protects against security threats such as single points of failure and link attacks. We have verified the effectiveness of the algorithm through a series of experiments, and the proposed algorithm can provide decision-makers with high-reliability and low-latency transmission paths in heterogeneous network environments. At the same time, we verified the performance of the algorithm when encountering attacks, which is superior to other classical algorithms. Even in the face of network failures and attacks, it can maintain a high level of data integrity and security.

Keywords: heterogeneous network; multi-objective optimization; multipath transmission; privacy protection; security; reliability

1. Introduction

Heterogeneous networks, a significant research direction in the field of networking, have demonstrated a vigorous development momentum. These networks are composed of various types of devices, communication technologies, and network structures [1]. The research scope is broad, encompassing mobile edge networks [2,3], satellite networks [4,5], self-organized networks [6,7], and the wired Internet [8,9]. The objective of constructing heterogeneous networks is to integrate diverse network resources to provide users with more flexible, efficient, and reliable communication services, thereby meeting increasingly diverse and complex communication needs. Despite the significant advantages of heterogeneous networks, their security still faces serious challenges. For instance, replay attacks, distributed denial-of-service (DDoS) attacks, and privacy breaches can lead to network disruptions, transmission failures, or even more severe consequences. Therefore, security management in heterogeneous networks remains a critical research area, with the secure transmission of network information being a primary focus.

To address security issues in heterogeneous networks, researchers have proposed various approaches, including strategies such as mobile target defense, privacy protection, and malicious traffic detection to counter complex network threats. Data encryption techniques are most commonly employed to secure data transmission. According to a Google report, encrypted data accounted for more than 80% of total network traffic as of 2024. Despite this high percentage, data breaches have become more frequent, primarily due to security vulnerabilities in network data transmission [10]. The main reasons for these vulnerabilities include the following: encryption and decryption algorithms typically require substantial computational resources, leading to high computational complexity and significant operational costs for nodes [11]; the rise of intelligent algorithms, such as semantic recognition, enables attackers to infer the overall content by obtaining only part of the data [12]. Clearly, avoiding malicious nodes during transmission is an effective method to prevent data leakage. Thus, there is a need to develop secure, resilient, and efficient detection techniques to manage malicious nodes within the network to defend against network attacks [13].

However, existing detection solutions are not yet adequate for defending against the latest internal and external threats. These models typically require monitoring both potential internal and external attacks [14–16] and heavily rely on the accuracy of malicious node detection. Existing studies indicate that the best malicious node detection methods achieve an accuracy of up to 80%, leaving a 20% uncertainty [17]. While it is feasible to develop algorithms that compute secure transmission routing paths to avoid data eavesdropping or interception by malicious nodes, these paths often require significantly more hops than optimal routes, reducing transmission efficiency and increasing costs. Additionally, the destination node must collect all transmitted packets to reconstruct the original data, which imposes very high reliability requirements on the network [18].

Over time, there has been a growing interest in the introduction of dynamic parameters in cyber adversarial environments, an approach that has allowed cybersecurity protection techniques to evolve from static protection to dynamic active defense. For example, Moving Target Defense (MTD) serves as a defense paradigm aimed at minimizing the inherent advantages of attackers over defenders [19,20]. MTD protocols increase the cost of an attack, limit the exposure of susceptible components, and deceive adversaries by developing mechanisms to continuously and unpredictably change system parameters [21,22]. However, even active defense techniques such as MTD still face significant challenges [23]. These methods have a high probability of escape failure because the dynamic scheduling links of such approaches and the system execution body itself can still be "bypassed or short-circuited" by exploiting high-risk vulnerabilities. Additionally, the diversity and dynamism introduced by MTD do not change the logical nature of software and hardware vulnerability backdoors, nor can they prevent coordinated attacks from internal and external sources [24].

Indeed, packet routing and communication security are two energy-consuming and critical network functions, making secure and reliable communication in heterogeneous networks a challenging task [25,26]. Many current approaches primarily detect threats and respond to them from a policy perspective. However, a more technical response from a network function perspective can also be effective. For example, the receiver could make sender know that the receiver has successfully received each packet or group of packets through an acknowledgment packet sent by the receiving node. However, this technique is impractical in a lossy environment—such as when the network is under attack from physical or information domains—because the acknowledgment messages themselves are at risk of being lost. Additionally, transmitting a large number of acknowledgment messages or waiting for their reception can significantly increase network overhead and communication delay [27]. Therefore, proposing path redundancy and path backup schemes from a transport perspective is particularly important to enhance reliability and protect against multiple network threats, such as Denial of Service (DoS) attacks, through multipath routing. However, in severely constrained environments, even multipath routing techniques may be difficult to implement, especially if their traditional principles remain unchanged (i.e., the involvement of all network nodes in the multipath routing process throughout the network lifecycle). Achieving secure and reliable data transmission in heterogeneous networks is thus a crucial and complex research area that warrants in-depth exploration. In this context, our study makes several significant contributions:

1. A generic secure and reliable multi-objective optimized multipath transmission algorithm for heterogeneous networks is proposed: We propose an algorithm capable of constructing multiple redundant transmission paths in heterogeneous networks composed of various sub-networks. By considering the unique characteristics and task requirements of heterogeneous networks, multiple optimization objectives are introduced into the path selection process. This allows the computation of multiple optimal paths that not only meet performance requirements such as delay and reliability but also effectively avoid potential security threats, ensuring efficient and secure transmission across different types of network environments.

2. Optimization of path planning decisions: Path planning decisions in this context represent a mixed-integer programming problem (MIPP), an NP-hard problem. Additionally, there are trade-offs between optimization objectives, and the dimensionality of the solution is variable, making it difficult for traditional algorithms to solve these problems in polynomial time. To address this, we propose optimizing the initial population range using the Optimized Non-dominated Sorting Genetic Algorithm II, which considers multiple objective functions, such as task reliability and delay. This approach filters out the optimal combination of paths to satisfy different demand objectives, ultimately obtaining the Pareto-optimal solution set for the optimization problem.

3. Innovative application of the deletion graph method: After calculating the primary path, we propose simplifying the topological map using the deletion graph method. Unless no other links are available, this method ensures that any redundant paths do not share common links with the original path. This approach enhances the security of the transmission process and improves transmission reliability. The deletion graph technique searches for redundant paths on the new pruned graph by gradually deleting all links on the original paths, ensuring that these paths are physically independent from the original paths.

4. Experimental validation and evaluation: We further validate the effectiveness of the proposed method through comparative analysis and experimental demonstration. The adaptability and robustness of the algorithm in complex and changing network environments are highlighted. The flexibility of the proposed algorithm in terms of optimization strategy is demonstrated by adopting a soft update strategy to dynamically adjust network weight parameters. This strategy allows for the collaborative optimization of the multi-objective problem under different priorities. Experimental results show that the proposed algorithm exhibits significant advantages in the face of malicious attacks and network failures, maintaining a high transmission success rate and low latency.

This study highlights the potential of multi-objective optimized multipath transmission algorithms in addressing the challenges of secure and reliable communication in heterogeneous networks. By leveraging advanced techniques like NSGA-II and the deletion graph method, the proposed solution offers a robust and adaptable framework capable of maintaining high levels of data integrity and security even in the face of network failures and attacks. The rest of this paper is organized as follows. Section 2 details the specific methods for achieving multi-objective optimization in multipath transmission for heterogeneous networks. In Section 3, we demonstrate the effectiveness of our proposed method through experimental validation. In Section 4, we review the state of the art in research on multi-objective optimization and multi-objective transmission. Finally, Section 5 provides a summary and discusses future research directions.

2. Methodology

2.1. System Model

This paper proposes a dual-network architecture for secure and reliable transmission in heterogeneous networks. The system model comprises heterogeneous transmission network resources, including satellite networks, the Internet, mobile networks, and self-organized networks, as illustrated in Figure 1. The network architecture employs a layered decoupling design to separate the transmission control layer from the network resource layer. This separation forms a flexible dual-network structure, corresponding to the transmission control network and the network resource network. The network resource layer is designed to ensure stability and reliability while allowing for network flexibility, scalability, and programmability of the forwarding plane. It provides redundant physical transmission channels, enhancing the robustness of the network. The transmission control layer is responsible for the reliable transmission of information. It utilizes innovative lightweight sharing algorithms, Delay Tolerant Networking (DTN), and other technological means to flexibly address diverse information transmission needs. The transmission control layer constructs a logically independent overlay network, with virtual nodes abstracted from the transmission control system. These virtual links correspond to the heterogeneous network access points in the network resource layer. Neighboring nodes are connected by multiple virtual links, forming redundant and reliable transmission paths.

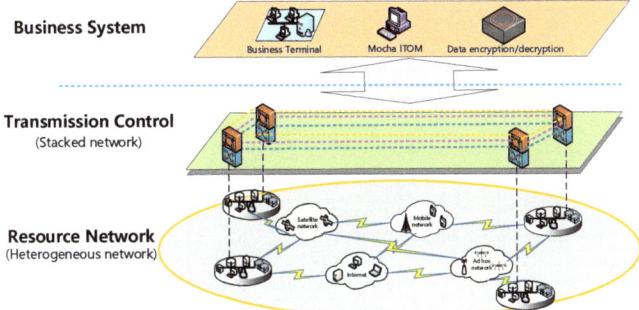

Figure 1. System architecture diagram.

By covering the network, the overall information of the network is shared with each other through lightweight consensus algorithms, and the transmission path is pre-calculated in the stacked network for information transmission in the physical network. The business system issues tasks and instructions at the upper level, while the transmission control layer encapsulates transmission-related functions into service-oriented entities, forming corresponding transmission control service entities. With the help of transmission control interfaces, resource collection and synchronization, path strategy control, and information transmission control are completed. We establish an identification system in the resource network layer to achieve automatic conversion of heterogeneous access protocol systems and consensus broadcasting between nodes, forming a unified resource status table for the entire network and providing support for transmission control services.

For the resource network layer, to address the characteristics of physical transmission network resources, such as heterogeneity and mobility, an overlay network based on overlay technology is constructed. This overlay network leverages various heterogeneous network resources to build a transmission control system, thus enabling the unified management and utilization of these diverse resources. By employing heterogeneous multi-means connections between disparate resource networks, the system ensures that at least two or more independent transmission channels are linked, thereby enhancing communication reliability and robustness.

The transmission control layer is the fundamental component of the system, responsible for establishing and managing physical information transmission channels across heterogeneous networks to support the operation of the secure transmission control overlay network. By interconnecting multiple heterogeneous network resources and utilizing dynamic networking functions, the transmission control system can effectively establish physical information transmission channels across heterogeneous networks. A consensus algorithm is used between transmission control systems to achieve information synchronization among distributed transmission control systems, thereby establishing a unified node resource and link state information table across the network. Based on this table, the system can execute redundant dynamic path calculations and path policy control through identification, ensuring the routing of heterogeneous networks is reachable and guaranteeing highly reliable information transmission.

The business system, as the user side, adapts to various types of service terminals and accepts operation and maintenance management. When accessing the transmission control system, the business system can perform encryption and decryption operations on the data as needed to enhance the security and reliability of system transmission. Concurrently, the business system can interact with the transmission control system to dynamically adjust the transmission strategy according to system demand and business requirements, guaranteeing the timely transmission and effective management of information.

The preceding network architecture proposes a secure and reliable multi-objective optimized multipath transmission algorithm for heterogeneous networks, aimed at safely and reliably delivering information from the source to the destination. The algorithm's framework is depicted in Figure 2. Firstly, the data acquisition module is responsible for obtaining the topological state of the network, the link state of each node, and the connectivity state of the links from the heterogeneous network. Then, this information will be fed into the path planning module, which generates a solution set of all feasible paths from the source to the destination. And the multi-objective optimization module processes this solution set to determine Path 1, which is then passed to the multipath computation module. This module generates a simplified topological graph and updates node states. The newly generated graph and updated node states are subsequently re-evaluated by the path planning module and the multi-objective optimization module to determine Path 2. Ultimately, the system outputs a multipath transmission solution from the source to the destination, ensuring secure and reliable data delivery.

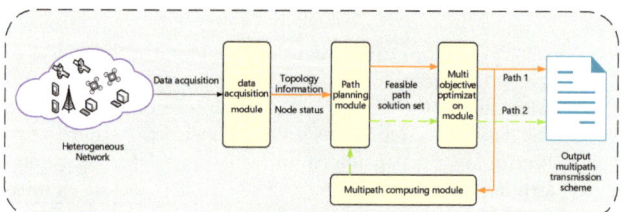

Figure 2. Algorithm framework diagram.

The specific implementation process is depicted in Algorithm 1. This algorithm computes multiple redundant transmission paths that satisfy the optimization objectives, utilizing network topology information and task requirements. The process involves the following steps: (1) Initialize the current network topology data and optimization parameters. (2) Obtain network topology information from the heterogeneous network, including the link status of each node and the connectivity status of the links. (3) Execute a variant of the algorithm based on depth-first search. This step recursively searches all feasible paths in the network, ensuring there are no duplicate vertices in each path within the set of paths. During the search, the algorithm records the length of the current path and ceases further searching when the path length exceeds the known maximum path length. This is achieved by optimizing the initial population size to reduce unnecessary computation. (4) Actively screen suitable paths using a multi-objective optimization algorithm to obtain the initial path. The objective is to maximize path reliability and minimize transmission delay. This study employs the optimized NSGA-II algorithm, which is based on the concepts of genetic algorithms and Pareto optimality, widely used in multi-objective optimization problems. The global search capability of the optimized NSGA-II algorithm helps circumvent the pitfall of local optimal solutions during the iteration process. (5) Utilize the multipath computation module to simplify the topology based on the first optimal transmission path. The core operation involves performing three distinct types of simplifications to the network topology graph to ensure that the newly generated path has no common links with the original path. (6) Re-run the depth-first search variant and multi-objective optimization steps with the pruned new topology graph to obtain the second path. (7) The final output comprises two paths that satisfy the optimization objectives.

Algorithm 1: Secure and Reliable Multi-Objective Optimization Multipath Transmission Algorithm for Heterogeneous Networks

Input: heterogeneous network $G(V, E)$, source node v_s, target node v_t, optimization parameters
Output: Multiple optimal transmission paths

1 **Initial**: the current network topology data and optimization parameters.
2 Obtain network topology information: the link status and connectivity status of each node.
3 Path search:
4   a. Run a variant algorithm based on Depth First Search (DFS) to recursively search for all feasible paths in the network.
5   b. Ensure that each path in the path set does not contain duplicate vertices.
6   c. When the path length exceeds the known maximum path length, stop further search.
7 Path filtering:
8   a. Using NSGA-II for multi-objective optimization, select the best path to maximize path reliability and minimize transmission delay.
9   b. The global search capability of NSGA-II avoids getting stuck in local optima during the iteration process.
10 Topology simplification:
11   a. Delete the network topology based on the first optimal transmission path.
12   b. Ensure that there is no common link between the new path and the original path.
13 Repeat path search and filtering:
14   a. Re input the deleted new topology map into the path search and multi-objective optimization module.
15   b. Obtain the second path.
16 **Return** multiple transmission paths that meet optimization objectives.

2.2. Multi-Objective Optimization Strategy

In this study, to address the conflicts among different optimization objectives, we propose using an optimized Non-dominated Sorting Genetic Algorithm II (NSGA-II) to solve multi-objective constrained optimal path problems. The NSGA-II is a powerful decision space exploration engine based on Genetic Algorithm (GA), primarily used to solve multi-objective optimization problems (MOOPs) [28]. Among the branches of multi-objective optimization problems, combinatorial optimization problems (COPs) are considered some of the most challenging and complex. Since most COPs are NP-hard, their computational complexity increases significantly as the problem size grows. Consequently, approximate methods such as metaheuristics are preferred over classical methods for solving such problems [29,30]. Multi-objective optimization involves finding the best possible solutions for multiple objectives within a given domain. A MOOP consists of a set of n decision variables, k objective functions, and a set of constraints comprising m inequality constraints and p equality constraints. The optimization objective is to find solutions that satisfy all constraints while optimizing the objective functions.

$$Min/Max\ y = f(x) = (f_1(x), f_2(x), \ldots, f_k(x)), k \geq 2 \tag{1}$$

$$Subject\ to\ g_i(x) \leq 0, i = 1, 2, \ldots, m \tag{2}$$

$$h_j(x) \leq 0, j = 1, 2, \ldots, m \tag{3}$$

Formally, $x = (x_1, x_2, \ldots, x_n) \in D$ is the n-dimensional decision vector in $X \subseteq R^n$, and y is the k-dimensional objective vector in R^k. f is defined as the mapping function, g_i is the i-th inequality constraint, and h_j is the j-th equality constraint. Thus, Equations (2) and (3) determine the set of all feasible solutions X, so it can also be written as a set of different feasible solutions $(x_1, x_2, \ldots, x_n) \in X$.

Suppose $x_1, x_2 \in X$ are two feasible solutions to a multi-objective problem. A solution x_1 can be regarded as superior to x_2 if the following condition is satisfied: x_1 is superior to x_2 in at least one of the objectives and no worse than the others. In this case, x_1 is said to dominate x_2.

$$\begin{cases} x_1 \prec x_2 \Leftrightarrow f_i(x_1) \leq f_i(x_2), \forall i \in \{1, 2, \ldots, m\} \\ \exists j : f_j(x_1) \leq f_j(x_2) \end{cases} \tag{4}$$

The j-th value of the objective function for the decision vector x is denoted by $f_j(x)$. The solution space is denoted by X, $\prec$ represents the dominance relation. Let $x \in \psi \subseteq X$, if all other solutions in ψ do not dominate x then x is nondominated with respect to the subset ψ. This means that x is nondominated with respect to ψ. Methods for identifying Pareto-optimal solutions include NSGA-II, the Pareto Adaptive Algorithm (APA), and others, which are employed in this study.

Optimization problems frequently exhibit not a single solution but a set of solutions, where improving one objective function necessarily entails a reduction in another. Such a solution is termed a nondominated or Pareto-optimal solution, and all Pareto-optimal solutions constitute a Pareto-optimal set (PS). In this context, a Pareto-optimal solution $x \in X$ is nondominated with respect to the entire solution space ψ. The set of all Pareto-optimal solutions constitutes the Pareto-optimal set (PS). The objective vector corresponding to the Pareto-optimal set is defined as the Pareto frontier, as illustrated in Figure 3.

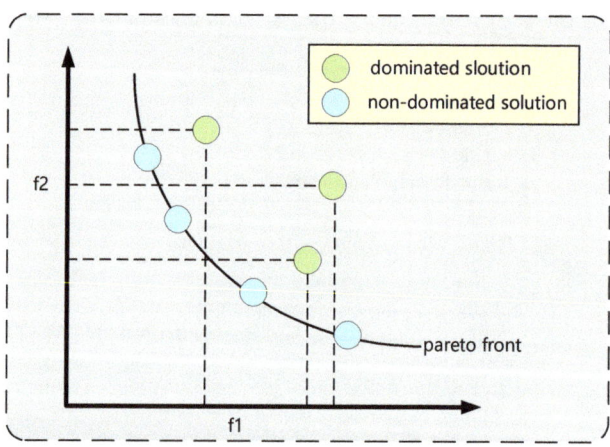

Figure 3. Pareto domination.

The NSGA-II is an enhanced iteration of the Non-dominated Sorting Genetic Algorithm (NSGA), widely utilized in multi-objective optimization problems due to its elitist properties, the absence of the necessity to share parameters, and its rapid computation speed [31]. NSGA-II effectively avoids falling into local optimal solutions during the iteration process through the use of the crowding distance operator as a diversity preservation mechanism and the ability to perform global searches based on the concepts of genetic algorithms and Pareto optimality. The optimization objectives proposed in this study include multiple goals, specifically maximizing reliability and minimizing delay. The objective of maximizing reliability is to optimize the reliability of the transmission path, thereby ensuring stability and resistance to interference during data transmission. The objective of minimizing delay is to optimize the delay of the transmission path, ensuring that data can be delivered to the target node rapidly and in a timely manner. Therefore, the objective function can be defined as follows:

$$\min F = \min\{\text{Rreliability}_{\max}, \text{delay}_{\min}\} \tag{5}$$

$$\min F = w_1 D + w_2(-R) \tag{6}$$

$$\begin{aligned} s.t. \quad & D = \sum t_i \\ & R = \prod r_i v_i \\ & r_i = \frac{\frac{1}{\lambda} \sum_{j=1}^{N} A_{j,i} c_e(v_j)}{E\left(\sum_{j=1}^{N} A_{j,i} S(v_i, v_j)\right)} \\ & t_i = \frac{e_i}{v} \\ & R \geq 0.99 \\ & D \leq 500 \end{aligned} \tag{7}$$

The reliability of the transmission path, R is computed as the cumulative product of the reliability of each node. The reliability of each node, r_i, is determined by node eigenvector centrality and node similarity. Eigenvector centrality represents the global importance of a node in the network topology, while the similarity between a node and its neighboring nodes measures the local importance of the network node. The delay of the transmission path, D is calculated as the sum of the delays of each link. The delay on each link segment, d_i contributes to the total path delay. In the process of multi-objective optimization, we limit the range of reliability and delay by setting optimization objective constraints. At the same time, based on the scenario in the algorithm, we prioritize reliability as the first optimization objective. When the reliability is greater than 0.99, we select paths with a delay of less than 500 as the selected object. In addition, this algorithm continuously collaborates on reliability and latency during the cross mutation screening process of offspring by using optimized NSGA-II algorithm, ultimately achieving Pareto-optimal solution. The optimization process is described as follows.

The algorithmic process effectively solves the multi-objective optimization problem in heterogeneous networks, ensuring the reliability and timeliness of information transmission (Algorithm 2). The elitist strategy of NSGA-II optimization retains the best individuals from the previous generation, allowing the algorithm to avoid local optimal solutions and improve global search capability. Additionally, the algorithm maintains population diversity by calculating the crowding distance of individuals in the objective space, enhancing the stability and convergence of the algorithm. By performing the non-dominated sorting of the population, the algorithm effectively identifies superior solutions. These characteristics enable the algorithm to excel in multi-objective optimization problems, improving computational efficiency while ensuring the diversity and comprehensiveness of the optimization results. Generating the initial population using heuristics accelerates the convergence process of the algorithm and enhances the quality of the solutions, thereby achieving efficient, secure, and reliable multipath information transmission.

Algorithm 2: Multi-objective optimization process of MOMTA-HN algorithm

Input : heterogeneous network $G(V, E)$, source node v_s, target node v_t, optimization parameters
Output: Optimal transmission paths

1 **Initial**: The network with the input parameters.
2 Initialize population: After determining the objective function, use heuristic methods to obtain a simple path between the source and destination to generate the initial population.
3 Non dominated sorting and selection: Perform non dominated sorting and selection on the initial population obtained from the path planning module.
4 Cross and mutation: Performing cross and mutation operations on the selected population to generate the next generation population.
5 Constraint check and repair: Check whether the generated population meets the constraint conditions and make necessary repairs.
6 Generate subpopulation: Generate the first generation subpopulation and update the evolutionary algebra.
7 Fast non dominated sorting: Perform fast non dominated sorting on each generation of population.
8 Repeat the above steps until the maximum evolutionary number is reached.
9 **Return** Pareto frontier solution.

2.3. Multipath Transmission Algorithm

This paper proposes a framework for multipath transmission algorithms based on hierarchical culling. The core operation involves performing three different types of simplification on the network topology graph. After the NSGA-II-based multi-constraint optimal path algorithm determines the first path that satisfies the multi-constraint requirements, the framework performs different simplification operations based on varying situations to obtain the second path.

2.3.1. The First Type of Simplification Operation

The core idea of the first type of simplification operation is to ensure the independence of the new paths by fine-grained management and deletion of the heterogeneous subnetworks where the source and destination nodes are located. As illustrated in Figure 4, new links are obtained by deleting different subnetworks and links. The red, yellow, blue, and purple clouds on the left represent different heterogeneous networks. The source and destination nodes are node S and node D, respectively. The first calculated path is S-E-I-K-N-D. Through the first type of graph deletion operation, we deleted the nodes and links that the purple heterogeneous network and the first path in the red and yellow heterogeneous networks passed through. Therefore, the second calculated path is S-A-B-G-L-D. The specific steps are as follows:

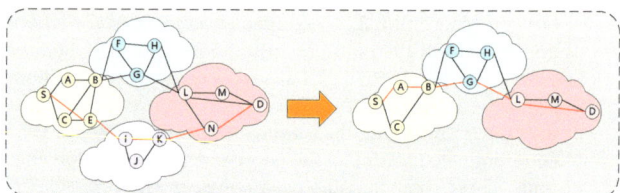

Figure 4. Schematic diagram of the first type of simplification operation.

Subnetwork lookup: Identify the subnetworks where the source and destination nodes are located separately. This step ensures that the network locations of the source and destination nodes are identified.

Path node subnetwork identification: Identify the subnetwork in which each node (other than the source and destination nodes) on the first path that satisfies the multi-constraint requirement is located. This step provides the basis for subsequent simplification operations by identifying the network locations of the intermediate nodes on the path.

Subnetwork compare and delete: Determine if the subnetwork where each node on the path is located is the same as the subnetwork where the source or destination node is located. If it is the same, delete the node and its associated links. Otherwise, delete all nodes within the subnetwork where the node is located and the links associated with each node in the subnetwork.

These operations result in a new network topology graph. At this point, the NSGA-II-based multi-constraint optimal path algorithm is used again to find a second path that satisfies the multi-constraint requirement. If the second path exists, the search is successful; otherwise, the second type of simplification operation is used.

2.3.2. The Second Type of Simplification Operation

The core idea of the second type of simplification operation is to delete every link on the first path that satisfies the multi-constraint requirement in the network topology. As illustrated in Figure 5, new links are obtained by deleting different subnetworks and links. The red, yellow, and purple clouds on the left represent different heterogeneous networks. The source and destination nodes are node S and node D, respectively. The first calculated path is S-E-I-K-N-D. Through the second type of graph deletion operation, we removed the nodes and links that the first path passed through in the red, yellow, and purple heterogeneous networks. Therefore, the second calculated path is S-B-J-L-D. The specific steps are as follows:

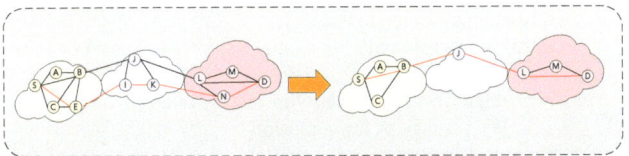

Figure 5. Schematic diagram of the second type of simplification operation.

Link deletion: In the network topology, delete each link on the first path that satisfies the multi-constraint requirement. This ensures that the new path does not intersect the first path in terms of physical links, thus improving the independence of the paths and the overall reliability of the system.

Path computation: After performing the second type of simplification operation, obtain a new network topology map. At this point, the NSGA-II-based multi-constraint optimal path algorithm is used again to find a second path that satisfies the multi-constraint requirement. If the second path exists, the search succeeds; otherwise, the third type of simplification operation is used.

2.3.3. The Third Type of Simplification Operation

The core idea of the third type of simplification operation is to find a new independent path by refining the link processing based on the link bottleneck on the first path. As illustrated in Figure 6, The red and yellow clouds on the left represent different heterogeneous networks. The source and destination nodes are node S and node D, respectively. The first calculated path is S-A-F-O-R-D. It can only go through link FO. At this point, FO is the only link of the network, and nodes O and F belong to the point cut set of the network, while link FO belongs to the edge cut set. When the link FO is deleted, the network topology will split into two disconnected subgraphs. In this situation, the first and second types of simplification methods become ineffective, necessitating the use of the third type of simplification. Based on link FO, the path is divided into two distinct subgraphs. Each subgraph will then re-determine the source and destination nodes and apply the second type of simplification again to find a second path that satisfies the multi-objective optimization requirements. Therefore, the second calculated path is S-E-F-O-T-D. The specific steps are as follows:

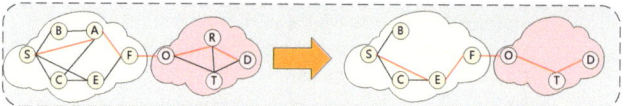

Figure 6. Schematic diagram of the third type of simplification operation.

Identify the link bottleneck: Locate the nodes on the first path where only two links are connected, i.e., the links that may have "link bottlenecks". These links are the weakest points in the path and require special handling.

Path splitting: Split the first path into two parts based on unique links. This step refines the path processing to ensure the new path avoids these bottleneck links.

Path computation: Apply the second simplification method again to find a second path that satisfies the multi-constraint requirements. This step ensures that a second path is found even in the presence of a link bottleneck.

The main purpose of the three types of simplification operations is to significantly improve the overall reliability of the two paths. The first type of simplification ensures that the nodes on the second path are in different subnets from the nodes on the first path. If the subnet of a node on the first path fails, the node on the second path can still transmit data normally, improving the system's fault tolerance. The second type of simplification ensures that the two paths do not share links. If a link on the first path fails, the data on the second path can still be transmitted normally, enhancing the system's redundancy and data transmission reliability. The third type of simplification provides an effective path scheduling scheme for cases where data can only be transmitted over specific segments of links on the first path. This operation ensures that even with a link bottleneck, a second path can be found that satisfies the multi-constraint requirements, thereby ensuring the high reliability and availability of the system.

The multipath transmission algorithm framework based on hierarchical culling, as proposed in this paper, offers an efficient and reliable multipath transmission scheme through three different types of simplification operations combined with the NSGA-II multi-objective optimization algorithm. This framework not only improves the independence of paths and the overall reliability of the system but also ensures the high efficiency and security of information transmission. It is particularly suitable for the multipath transmission requirements in complex heterogeneous network environments. By fine-grained management of the network topology graph and path planning, the algorithm effectively addresses various transmission challenges, providing robust technical support for achieving highly reliable network communication.

3. Experiment

3.1. Experiment Setup

To demonstrate the rationality and applicability of the proposed evaluation method, we selected the ChinaNet network from the Topology Zoo as the target for this experiment [32]. The Topology Zoo contains 261 real network topologies from around the world and is recognized by network researchers as a publicly available dataset for experimental testing, making it a valuable resource for network-related research and experiments, particularly for various network simulations.

As shown in Figure 7, the topology of the ChinaNet network, which we chose as the test network for this paper, contains 42 nodes and 66 edges. The topology graph reveals the presence of both centralized key nodes and edge nodes, thus allowing us to better characterize different styles within the network. When designing the experiments, we considered the connectivity between the topology nodes and the ease of operation. We chose ONOS 2.4.1 and Mininet to build the experimental environment. Mininet allows for the flexible setup of network topology based on specific requirements, while the ONOS controller can automatically disseminate flow tables and control the link relationships between nodes. In the subsequent attack experiments, we could easily select the nodes to attack. We replicated the ChinaNet network in Mininet and set various parameters such as IP address, MAC address, and bandwidth according to the actual network.

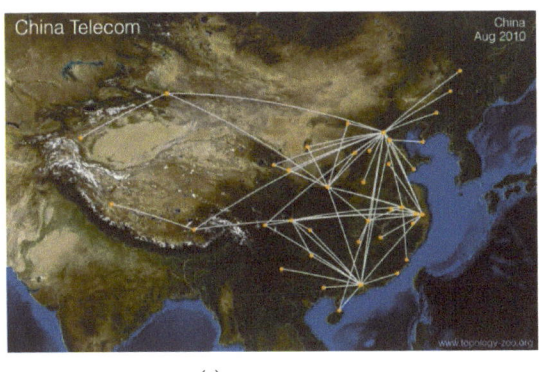

(a)

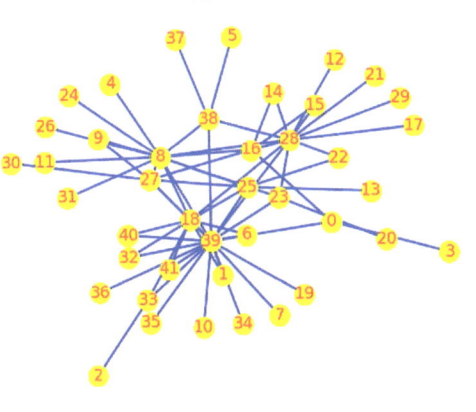

(b)

Figure 7. ChinaNet network topology. (a) Geographic map; (b) PYTHON generation graph.

As shown in Figure 8, based on the actual network configuration, we divided the network topology into different heterogeneous sub-networks according to a ratio of 2:3:1:4. Since nodes in different sub-networks exhibit varying information transmission performance, we define the common transmission delay of different heterogeneous networks as different unit times, i.e., the time it takes for data to traverse a link of length 1 in the topology, based on data from Google. The node types and their corresponding transmission unit delays are defined as follows: Dark blue nodes represent wired interconnection networks with a unit delay of 20 ms. Light blue nodes represent the mobile Internet with a unit delay of 5 ms. Yellow nodes represent satellite networks with a unit delay of 100 ms. Orange nodes represent drone self-organizing networks with a unit delay of 5 ms. To achieve efficient transmission across different heterogeneous networks, we must address the protocol conversion problem. When transmitting data across heterogeneous networks, the protocol fields of packets need to be converted to meet the requirements of the destination network. Traditional protocol conversion methods typically rely on complex protocol cross-reference tables, requiring each network node to refer to the table when transmitting data. This approach not only increases computational overhead but also introduces potential conversion errors and transmission delays.

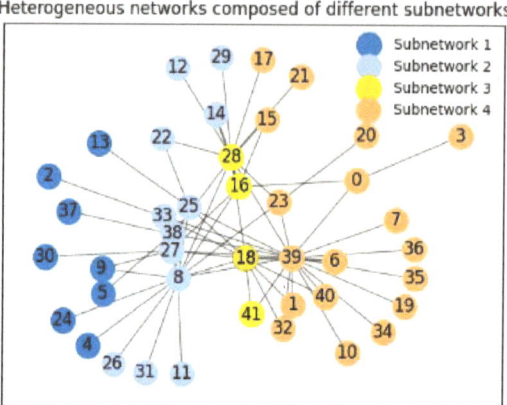

Figure 8. Heterogeneous network composition of ChinaNet network topology.

To address these issues, we propose a cross-layer protocol encapsulation approach. Specifically, we encapsulate the protocol fields required by different heterogeneous networks uniformly in the header of the transport system message at the application layer. This method allows a network node to parse the relevant fields in the message header to complete the protocol conversion without referring to a cross-reference table when a packet enters different heterogeneous networks. This approach simplifies the protocol conversion process, reduces computational overhead, and improves the efficiency and reliability of data transmission. Under this cross-layer protocol encapsulation architecture, data traversing different heterogeneous networks requires only one parsing operation to complete the protocol conversion, avoiding delays caused by multiple conversions. We define the uniform delay for cross-network protocol conversion as 50 ms, which includes the time for parsing message headers and performing protocol conversion. By introducing the cross-layer protocol encapsulation method, we effectively solve the protocol conversion problem between different heterogeneous networks and enhance the efficiency and reliability of data transmission.

To better evaluate the security and reliability of the MOMTA-HN algorithm under attack conditions, we designed a series of experiments to randomly attack different nodes in the network. In heterogeneous networks, attacks tend to be random and continuous, with nodes interacting and the network crashing at an accelerating rate. We used the transmission success rate as a metric to measure the performance of the algorithm. To ensure the fairness and statistical significance of the experimental results, we performed 1000 independent tests for each round of experiments.

The transmission success rate is calculated using the following formula:

$$P_{success} = \frac{N_{success}}{N_{total}} \quad (8)$$

where $P_{success}$ is the success rate, $N_{success}$ is the number of successful transmissions, and N_{total} is the total number of trials. For multipath transmission algorithms, the transmission success rate must be calculated by its complement. Suppose there are m paths in the network and the attack occurs randomly at any node on any path. After N attempts, the event of successful transmission on the i-th path is denoted as S_i, and the event of successful multipath transmission S is the case where at least one of all paths is successfully transmitted. If the success rate of each path independently is $P_1, P_2, \ldots, P_m$, then the multipath transmission success rate P_{multi} can be calculated by the following formula:

$$P_{multi} = 1 - \prod_{i=1}^{m}(1 - P_i) \quad (9)$$

where, $1 - P_i$ denotes the probability that the transmission of the i-th path fails, and thus $\prod_{i=1}^{m}(1 - P_i)$ denotes the probability that all paths fail, while its complement $1 - \prod_{i=1}^{m}(1 - P_i)$ is the probability that at least one path succeeds. In our experiments, we assume the existence of m independent transmission paths and evaluate the success rate of each path independently. Assuming that the number of successful transmissions of the i-th path in N experiments is NS_i, the success rate P_i of the i-th path is

$$P_i = \frac{NS_i}{N} \tag{10}$$

This allows us to systematically evaluate the performance of the MOMTA-HN algorithm in heterogeneous networks, particularly its robustness against malicious attacks. The experimental results demonstrate the advantages of the algorithm in complex network environments, as shown below.

3.2. Detailed Analysis and Comparison

Figure 9 presents a comparison of the MOMTA-HN algorithm with the SPFA and Dijkstra algorithms. Figure 9a depicts the comparison of reliability, while Figure 9b illustrates the comparison of delay. In the absence of attacks, we traversed the transmission paths between all nodes and computed the path transmission delay loss and the path reliability value for the three algorithms. The path reliability value is the product of the reliability of the different nodes. Minimum reliability is represented by the positive triangles in the figure. The minimum reliability for both the MOMTA-HN algorithm and the Dijkstra algorithm is 99.182%, while for the SPFA algorithm it is 99.004%. Maximum reliability is represented by the inverted triangles. The maximum reliability for all three algorithms is 99.999%. Mean reliability is represented by the star in the center of the box. The mean reliability values for the MOMTA-HN, Dijkstra, and SPFA algorithms are 99.69%, 99.666%, and 99.654%, respectively. Median reliability is represented by the tan solid line. The median reliability for all three algorithms is 99.6%.

When calculating the path transmission delay loss, we disregarded the time required for policy formulation and focused on the transmission time, derived by multiplying the link relative value by the transmission delay loss through different media, assuming constant external environmental conditions. Minimum delay is represented by positive triangles. The minimum transmission delay for all three algorithms is 10 ms. Maximum delay is represented by inverted triangles. The maximum transmission delay for both the MOMTA-HN and Dijkstra algorithms is 495 ms, while for the SPFA algorithm it is 425 ms. Mean delay is represented by the star in the middle of the box. The average transmission delays for the MOMTA-HN, Dijkstra, and SPFA algorithms are 311.66 ms, 239.5 ms, and 250.06 ms, respectively. Median delay is represented by the tan solid line. The median transmission delay for the MOMTA-HN algorithm is 325 ms, for Dijkstra it is 270 ms, and for SPFA it is 290 ms.

We can conclude through numerical analysis and comparison that the SPFA algorithm exhibited the lowest average delay (270 ms), while the MOMTA-HN algorithm exhibited the highest reliability. The MOMTA-HN algorithm selects the path with the highest reliability at the cost of slightly increased transmission delay as a result of multi-objective optimization. The algorithm enhances transmission security by calculating multiple redundant paths and ensuring that these redundant paths do not share any common links with the original paths in non-essential situations. Although the average delay of the MOMTA-HN algorithm is slightly higher than that of the SPFA algorithm, it has significant advantages in terms of network reliability. In particular, the MOMTA-HN algorithm is capable of selecting the path with the highest reliability for data transmission among multiple paths that can reach the destination during the process of multi-objective optimization. This strategy not only ensures the stability of data transmission but also improves the overall network quality of service and user experience to a certain extent.

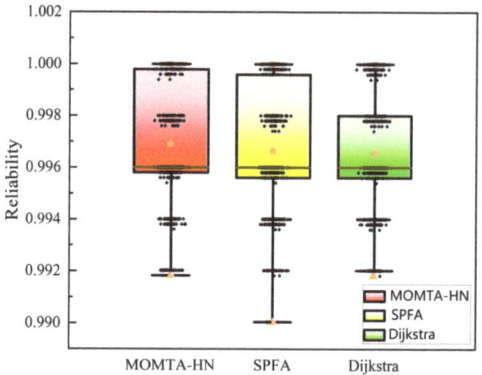

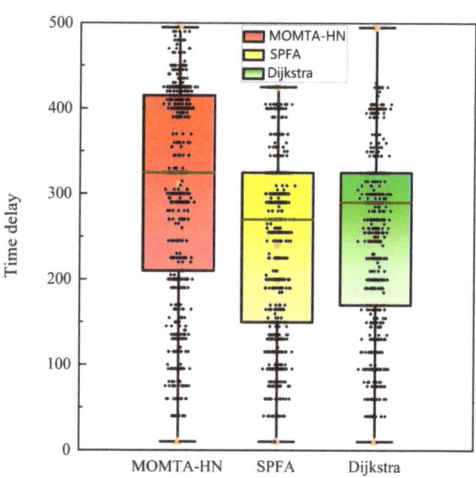

Figure 9. Comparison of results of different algorithms. (**a**) Reliability comparison of different algorithms; (**b**) delay comparison of different algorithms.

The following presents the results of transmission performance when encountering attacks, as evaluated by different algorithms.

As illustrated in Figure 10, this study presents the results of transmission success comparisons among the MOMTA-HN algorithm, the SPFA algorithm, and the Dijkstra algorithm when encountering attacks. The experiments comprise three scenarios to demonstrate the performance of each algorithm and their path selection strategies under different source and destination node configurations.

In Figure 10a, the source and destination nodes are node 9 and node 18, respectively. In this case, the MOMTA-HN algorithm performs the first type of simplification, which involves deleting all nodes of the sub-network where the first link transmitting node is located. This results in the generation of a new multipath for redundant transmission. The figure illustrates that the red line (MOMTA-HN) is considerably higher than the blue (SPFA) and green (Dijkstra) lines. Furthermore, the number of successful transmissions of the MOMTA-HN algorithm exceeds that of the other two algorithms at all stages of the attack. The MOMTA-HN algorithm effectively avoids single points of failure through first-class simplification, thereby enhancing the robustness and reliability of the network. In contrast, the SPFA and Dijkstra algorithms do not have the same nodes traversed by their calculated paths due to differing path computation principles. Consequently, the green and blue lines in Figure 11a do not overlap. This indicates that while all algorithms have analogous objectives in path selection, the MOMTA-HN algorithm is capable of greater flexibility in adjusting paths when the network is under attack, thus ensuring the success rate of transmission.

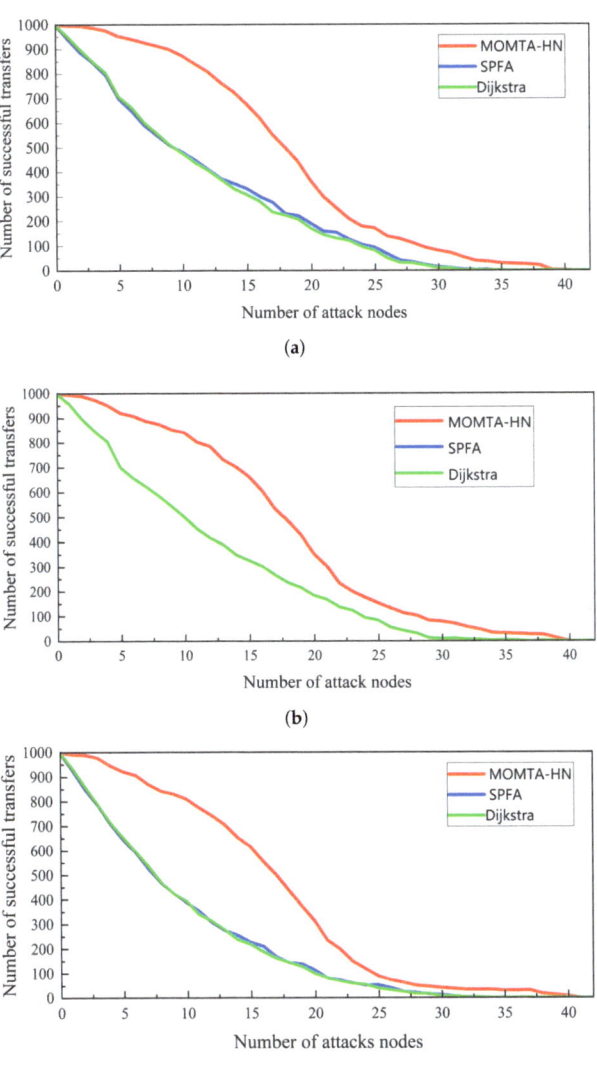

Figure 10. Transmission success rate of MOMTA-HN, SPFA, and Dijkstra algorithms encountering attacks with different types of simplifications. (**a**) Comparison of the number of successful transmissions from node 9 to node 18 encountering an attack; (**b**) comparison of the number of successful transmissions from node 18 to node 22 encountering an attack; (**c**) comparison of the number of successful transmissions from node 1 to node 9 encountering an attack.

In Figure 10b, the source and destination nodes are node 18 and node 22, respectively. The figure shows that the red line (MOMTA-HN) is significantly higher than the blue (SPFA) and green (Dijkstra) lines. The number of transmission successes of the MOMTA-HN algorithm is superior to those of the other two algorithms, both in the pre-attack period and in the later stages when there are fewer remaining nodes. At this juncture, the initial type of simplification employed by the MOMTA-HN algorithm is rendered ineffective, necessitating the implementation of a second type of simplification, namely the deletion of all nodes belonging to the initial link. With this simplification, the MOMTA-HN algorithm can recalculate the multipath for transmission. The SPFA and Dijkstra algorithms yield identical results in Figure 11b, resulting in the two lines overlapping.

In Figure 10c, the source and destination nodes are node 1 and node 9, respectively. The experimental results demonstrate that the red line (MOMTA-HN) is significantly higher than the blue (SPFA) and green (Dijkstra) lines. Furthermore, the number of successful transmissions of the MOMTA-HN algorithm outperforms the other two algorithms in both the pre-attack period and the later period when there are fewer remaining nodes. At this point, the first transmission path used for source and destination node transmission contains unique links. When both the Type I and Type II simplification methods of the MOMTA-HN algorithm prove ineffective, the algorithm employs a multipath computation strategy for Type III simplification methods, which it then compares with the other algorithms. This advanced simplification strategy enables the MOMTA-HN algorithm to identify and utilize new redundant paths, thereby preventing transmission interruptions caused by network attacks. The experimental results demonstrate that the MOMTA-HN algorithm is still capable of effectively guaranteeing the success rate of data transmission in this complex network environment, whereas the SPFA and Dijkstra algorithms are less adept at doing so.

The results of the above comparison experiments demonstrate that the MOMTA-HN algorithm exhibits a significantly higher success rate in information transmission than the SPFA and Dijkstra algorithms, particularly in the context of network attacks. The MOMTA-HN algorithm exhibits enhanced flexibility and reliability in path selection, and its multi-objective optimization strategy enables it to adapt to diverse network environments, ensuring the successful completion of transmission tasks. In contrast, the SPFA and Dijkstra algorithms demonstrate superior path selection capabilities under specific conditions. However, they lack the flexibility and robustness of the MOMTA-HN algorithm when confronted with network attacks and complex network environments.

As illustrated in Figure 11, this study presents a comprehensive comparison experiment among the MOMTA-HN algorithm, the multipath algorithm with the first type of simplification (MOMTA-I), and the multipath algorithm with the second type of simplification (MOMTA-II). The experiment is designed to evaluate the performance of these algorithms under attack scenarios, focusing on their ability to maintain successful transmissions.

In Figure 11a, the source and destination nodes are node 9 and node 18, respectively. At this juncture, the MOMTA-HN algorithm needs to perform only the first type of simplification, which involves deleting all nodes in the sub-network where the transmission node of the first link is located. This simplification aims to derive a second path for redundant transmission. The multipath algorithm that employs only the first type of simplification can also compute the same result. The deletion method of multipath algorithms using only the second type of simplification is simpler compared to the first type. After the optimization filtering of the multi-objective optimization algorithm, the second path calculated is identical for all the algorithms mentioned, causing the three lines in the figure to overlap. This scenario demonstrates that under certain conditions, both types of simplifications can achieve similar results.

In Figure 11b, the source and destination nodes are node 18 and node 22, respectively. In this scenario, the initial simplification approach of the MOMTA-HN algorithm proves ineffective, necessitating the use of the second type of simplification. This method involves deleting all nodes associated with the initial link to derive a second path for redundant transmission. The algorithm that performs only the first type of simplification is unable to compute the second path. However, the algorithm that performs only the second type of simplification can calculate the same second path as the MOMTA-HN algorithm after the required deletions, resulting in the two lines in the figure overlapping. This demonstrates the effectiveness of the second type of simplification when the first type fails.

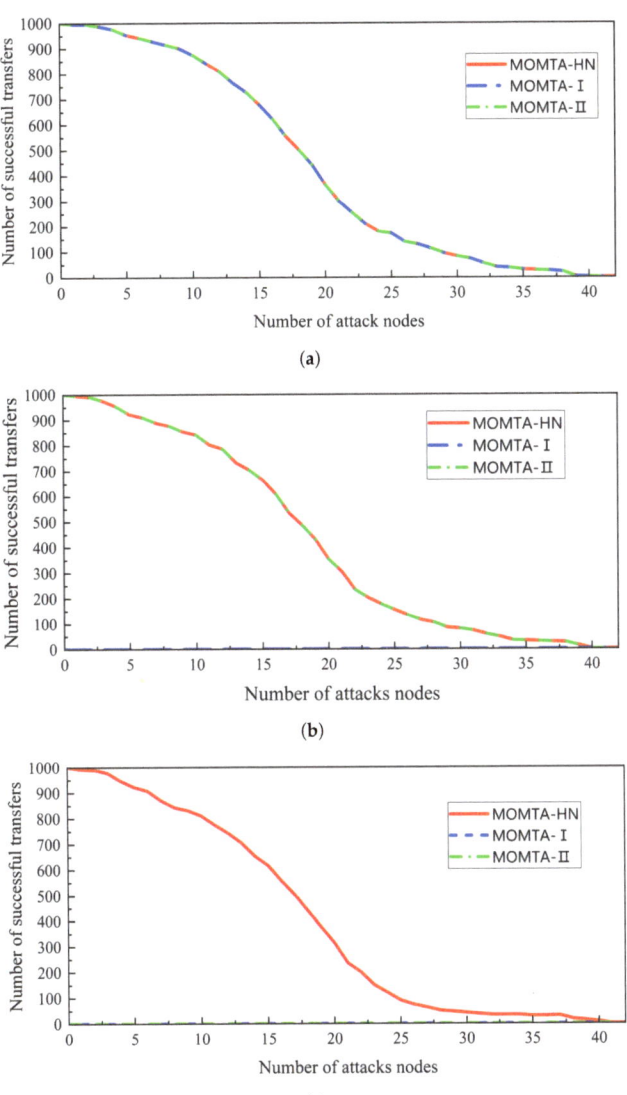

Figure 11. Transmission success rate of MOMTA-HN, MOMTA-I, and MOMTA-II encountering attacks with different types of simplifications. (**a**) Comparison of the number of successful transmissions from node 9 to node 18 encountering an attack; (**b**) comparison of the number of successful transmissions from node 18 to node 22 encountering an attack; (**c**) comparison of the number of successful transmissions from node 1 to node 9 encountering an attack.

In Figure 11c, the source and destination nodes are node 1 and node 9, respectively. At this juncture, both Type I and Type II simplification methods of the MOMTA-HN algorithm are ineffective in deriving a second path for redundant transmission. Consequently, Type III simplification is required. This advanced method involves a more sophisticated approach to ensure a new independent path is found, thereby enhancing the system's robustness. Both the algorithms that use only the first type of simplification and those that use only the second type are unable to compute the second path, causing the lines in the figure to overlap. This highlights the necessity of the third type of simplification in more complex scenarios where traditional methods fail.

The results of the preceding comparison experiments clearly demonstrate that the MOMTA-HN algorithm exhibits a markedly superior success rate in information transmission compared to the multipath algorithms employing only the first type of simplification (MOMTA-I) or the second type of simplification (MOMTA-II). The MOMTA-HN algorithm showcases enhanced flexibility and reliability in addressing network attacks. Its advanced multi-objective optimization strategy allows it to adapt dynamically to diverse network environments, ensuring the successful completion of transmission tasks. In contrast, while the SPFA and Dijkstra algorithms demonstrate effective path selection capabilities under specific conditions, they lack the flexibility and robustness of the MOMTA-HN algorithm when confronted with network attacks and complex network environments.

The MOMTA-HN algorithm's ability to utilize multiple types of simplifications allows it to maintain high transmission success rates even under adverse conditions. This capability is particularly crucial in heterogeneous network environments where attacks can occur unpredictably and affect various network segments differently. By effectively managing path redundancy and ensuring that redundant paths do not share critical links with the original paths, the MOMTA-HN algorithm significantly enhances the overall network reliability and security.

In conclusion, the experimental results validate the effectiveness of the MOMTA-HN algorithm in providing robust and reliable data transmission in heterogeneous networks. Its superior performance, especially in maintaining transmission success rates under attack conditions, underscores its potential as a highly adaptable and secure solution for complex network environments. This study demonstrates that incorporating multi-objective optimization and advanced simplification techniques can significantly improve network resilience and data transmission reliability, offering valuable insights for future research and development in network security and performance optimization.

4. Related Work

In recent years, the security of network transmission has gained critical importance due to the increasing complexity and variability of network environments. Particularly in the field of heterogeneous networks, researchers have been actively exploring methods to enhance the security and reliability of network transmission. This section reviews related work from the perspectives of multi-objective optimization and multipath transmission.

4.1. Multi-Objective Optimization

In traditional wireless sensor networks, the most important performance parameters are typically selected as optimization objectives, with other parameters used as constraints for optimization. However, these single-objective optimization techniques often struggle to perform effectively in real network environments [33]. Therefore, the use of multi-objective optimization (MOO) strategies is more aligned with practical needs. MOO strategies consider multiple performance metrics simultaneously, such as maximum reliability, minimum delay, and maximum network lifetime. This approach achieves a better performance balance and meets the complex demands of practical applications. In heterogeneous networks each subnetwork has different resources, mission objectives, and constraints due to the combination of various network resources. Multi-objective optimization strategies are particularly important to ensure that information reaches the desired destination safely and reliably. To achieve secure and reliable information transmission, researchers have proposed various multi-objective optimization strategies.

Cai et al. [34] proposed a multi-objective algorithm to address the information transmission problem when vehicles switch between different heterogeneous wireless networks while in high-speed motion. Their algorithm balances service delay and service cost of packet transmission by adding differential evolutionary variants to the multi-objective evolutionary algorithm, enhancing population diversity and promoting continuous evolution. Asha et al. [35] proposed a distributed energy-efficient cluster routing based on a clustering strategy to meet the network energy demands and maintain the quality of service (QoS) for heterogeneous wireless sensor-based IoT networks. They optimized network QoS parameters such as throughput and delay using a multi-objective squid optimization algorithm to ensure the best fitness value while optimizing these parameters. Song et al. [36] proposed a multitasking and multi-objective optimization algorithm for computational offload and relay communication in an air-ground integrated network consisting of UAVs, EVUs, and GSNs. The algorithm decomposes emergency communication message transmission into two multi-objective tasks, optimizing for maximum minimum link transmission rate and minimum weighted sum of delay and energy consumption. Federated learning and Dual Deep Q Network (DDQN) jointly optimize resource allocation to improve the model's generalization performance.

Pan et al. [37] addressed the resource scheduling problem for device-to-device (D2D) networks with UAV clusters. They considered the number of UAVs, their locations, transmit power, flight speed, communication channels, and device assignments to maximize D2D network capacity, minimize the number of deployed UAVs, and minimize the average energy consumption of all UAVs. Given the mixed integer programming problem (MIPP) and NP-hard nature of the problem, they proposed a non-dominated sorting genetic algorithm-III (NSGA-III-FDU) with a flexible solution dimensionality mechanism, a discrete part generation mechanism, and an adjustment mechanism for the number of drones. Guo et al. [38] discussed the use of multiple reconfigurable intelligent surface (RIS)-assisted satellite-UAV-terrestrial integrated network (IS-UAV-TN) heterogeneous network communication with co-optimization performance. They posed a multi-objective optimization problem for the collaborative UAV concerning obstacles and dynamic environments in the transmission path to maximize the system's achievable rate and minimize the UAV's energy consumption during a given mission. To facilitate online decision-making, they utilized Deep Reinforcement Learning (DRL) algorithms to achieve real-time interaction with the communication environment. Seifhosseini et al. [39] proposed a multi-objective cost-aware optimization algorithm for task scheduling in heterogeneous Internet of Things, which optimizes indicators such as execution time, cost, and reliability. They also verified the effectiveness of the algorithm through experiments in different scenarios. Seifhosseini et al. [40] considered the propagation cost in heterogeneous networks and solved the multi-objective key entity recognition problem by optimizing the maximum propagation scale and minimizing the heterogeneous propagation cost. By selecting strategies and hierarchical crossover operators, more complete Pareto solutions among candidates can be selected during the evolution process.

The above studies demonstrate that applying multi-objective optimization in heterogeneous networks not only improves the security and reliability of transmission but also offers new solutions for efficient transmission in complex network environments. Combining evolutionary algorithms, federated learning, and deep reinforcement learning, these studies have achieved efficient multi-objective optimization, thereby improving network performance and resource utilization.

4.2. Multipath Transmission

In recent years, researchers have been exploring ways to improve transmission security and reliability in heterogeneous network environments. Heterogeneous networks, such as satellite networks, the wired Internet, and mobile communication networks, face numerous challenges in data transmission due to their complex and variable characteristics. Multipath transmission protocols use multiple available paths to meet strict quality of service (QoS) constraints, achieving goals such as low latency while completing reliable transmission [41]. However, the traditional TCP protocol can only achieve single point-to-point transmission, and can only re-establish the connection after encountering threats such as attacks that cause transmission interruption. Therefore, researchers optimized TCP multipath transmission and proposed algorithms such as SCTP [42] and CMT [43] that can transmit the sender's data concurrently through different paths. However, these algorithms still have problems such as inappropriate packet scheduling, unnecessary packet retransmission, unnecessary congestion window (CWND) reduction, and receiver buffer blocking (RBB) [44]. In order to solve these problems, researchers further optimized the traditional TCP algorithm and proposed MPTCP [45] to use multiple paths to improve the resource utilization of the transmission path. MPTCP can not only transmit data packets through different paths according to different strategies, but also has a congestion control (CC) mechanism to manage network load and avoid congestion.

Okamoto et al. [46] proposed an SCTP extension to mitigate the impact of packet loss in lossy environments and limit redundant data transmission on different paths, thereby minimizing network congestion. Silva et al. [47] proposed a selective redundant multipath transmission (SRMT) strategy that uses the primary path to transmit data and the secondary path to transmit redundant data. Shailendra et al. [48] proposed an efficient SCTP multipath scheme (MPSCTP) that transmits packets on multiple paths simultaneously. MPSCTP solves the problems of packet reordering and invalid CWND growth and improves the efficiency of multipath transmission. MPSCTP was later enhanced to include full path delay, taking into account the data rate on each channel, thereby minimizing block delays on different channels.

Similar to SCTP, MPTCP is a connection-oriented multi-host standard protocol designed to distribute traffic between different routes and provide transparency at the application layer. In MPTCP, a session to be transmitted is usually divided into multiple different data substreams for transmission, and packet loss on different paths can be detected and reordered at the receiving end. Peng et al. [49] further optimized the MPTCP algorithm to address the problem that the system often misjudges random packet loss as congestion loss, and proposed a flow-based transmission model to improve the stability of the transmission system. Cai et al. [50] proposed a packet-differentiated OLIA (D-OLIA) based on packet loss, combining the delay jitter and CWND jitter eigenvalues to determine the type of packet loss, making up for the shortcomings of simply judging by delay or CWND. Oh and Lee [51] proposed a new heterogeneous network multipath transmission algorithm, which uses the MPTCP algorithm and the receiving end buffer scheduling strategy to estimate out-of-order packets and allocate packets accordingly based on the performance differences of each sub-flow, effectively balancing network throughput and delay performance. Wang et al. [52] studied how to minimize data transmission time in time-varying networks. The authors proposed a one-time solver that can solve the MDDT problem in polynomial time and verified the effectiveness of the proposed algorithm. Ouyang et al. [53] proposed an IMPNC transmission scheme to solve the problem of traditional TCP single-path transmission delay in low-orbit satellite networks. The scheme utilizes multiple paths for end-to-end redundant transmission and improves the algorithm to adapt to limited satellite bandwidth resources.

These studies demonstrate that multipath transmission has significant potential to improve network performance and reliability, especially in complex heterogeneous network environments. In conclusion, multi-objective optimization and multipath transmission techniques play a pivotal role in enhancing the security and reliability of network transmission. The multi-objective optimization strategy effectively addresses the actual needs in complex network environments by balancing multiple performance objectives. Furthermore, multipath transmission technology achieves higher data transmission efficiency and network reliability by utilizing multiple available paths. Consequently, we propose a multi-objective optimization multipath transmission algorithm for heterogeneous networks. The objective is to enhance transmission performance and security in heterogeneous network environments, better aligning with the needs of practical applications.

5. Conclusions

This paper presents a novel secure and reliable multi-objective optimized multipath transmission algorithm (MOMTA-HN) for heterogeneous networks. The primary objective of the algorithm is to provide highly secure and reliable transmission services, even when network attacks occur in heterogeneous networks. The proposed algorithm optimizes network task performance metrics, including reliability and delay, by considering multiple objective functions based on task requirements. Optimizing these objective functions ensures the smooth operation of transmission tasks and enhances the overall quality of service of the network. Furthermore, the algorithm leverages the refined population selection and ranking mechanism of the optimized Non-dominated Sorting Genetic Algorithm II (NSGA-II), effectively narrowing the initial population range and improving the convergence speed and optimization efficiency. This improvement enables the MOMTA-HN algorithm to find the optimal solution in a shorter period, demonstrating higher efficiency in practical applications. A significant innovation of the MOMTA-HN algorithm is the use of the pruned graph method to compute multiple paths for redundant transmission. The application of the pruned graph method makes the MOMTA-HN algorithm more flexible and secure in path selection. Conventional multipath transmission algorithms frequently encounter the issue of path sharing, which diminishes the dependability of transmission. In contrast, the MOMTA-HN algorithm ensures that there are no common links between the redundant paths and the original paths through the deletion graph technique, thereby enhancing network resilience and transmission reliability. Finally, this paper validates the efficacy and superiority of the MOMTA-HN algorithm through comprehensive simulation experiments and attack tests. The experimental results demonstrate that the MOMTA-HN algorithm not only maintains a high transmission success rate in the face of network attacks but also significantly improves the security and quality of service of the network. These results validate the practicality and reliability of the proposed algorithm in heterogeneous network environments. In future research, we will consider the impact of transmission bandwidth on transmission strategies in multi-objective optimization, further optimize the MOMTA-HN algorithm, and further improve the strategy of deleting graphs in the multipath transmission stage. And, we will validate it in more practical physical scenarios to further promote the development of heterogeneous network transmission technology.

Author Contributions: Conceptualization , S.Q., L.Y., Y.Z. and G.C.; Methodology, S.Q. and S.J.; Software, S.Q.; Formal analysis, S.J. and Y.Z.; Resources, L.Y. and L.M.; Writing—original draft, S.Q.; Writing—review & editing, S.J.; Supervision, G.C.; Project administration, L.M. and G.C.; Funding acquisition, L.Y. All authors have read and agreed to the published version of the manuscript.

Funding: This work was supported in part by the National Natural Science Foundation of China under Grant No. 62202097, in part by the China Postdoctoral Science Foundation under Grant No. 2024T170143 and Grant No. 2022M710677, and in part by the Jiangsu Funding Program for Excellent Postdoctoral Talent under Grant No. 2022ZB137.

Data Availability Statement: The data presented in this study are available in Topology zoo at http://www.topology-zoo.org/ (accessed on 6 July 2024). These data were derived from the following resources available in the public domain: http://www.topology-zoo.org/ (accessed on 6 July 2024).

Conflicts of Interest: The authors declare no conflicts of interest.

References

1. Shah, Z.; Ullah, I.; Li, H.; Levula, A.; Khurshid, K. Blockchain based solutions to mitigate distributed denial of service (ddos) attacks in the internet of things (iot): A survey. *Sensors* **2022**, *22*, 1094. [CrossRef] [PubMed]
2. Wang, J.; Du, H.; Niyato, D.; Kang, J.; Xiong, Z.; Rajan, D.; Mao, S.; Shen, X. A unified framework for guiding generative ai with wireless perception in resource constrained mobile edge networks. *IEEE Trans. Mob. Comput.* **2024**, 1–17. [CrossRef]

3. Chen, Y.; Hu, J.; Zhao, J.; Min, G. Qos-aware computation offloading in leo satellite edge computing for iot: A game-theoretical approach. *Chin. J. Electron.* **2023**, *33*, 1–12.
4. Karafolas, N.; Baroni, S. Optical satellite networks. *J. Light. Technol.* **2000**, *18*, 1792. [CrossRef]
5. Jiang, W. Software defined satellite networks: A survey. *Digit. Commun. Netw.* **2023**, *9*, 1243–1264. [CrossRef]
6. Chaoub, A.; Mämmelä, A.; Martinez-Julia, P.; Chaparadza, R.; Elkotob, M.; Ong, L.; Krishnaswamy, D.; Anttonen, A.; Dutta, A. Hybrid self-organizing networks: Evolution, standardization trends, and a 6G architecture vision. *IEEE Commun. Stand. Mag.* **2023**, *7*, 14–22. [CrossRef]
7. Li, J.; Chen, B.M.; Lee, G.H. So-net: Self-organizing network for point cloud analysis. In Proceedings of the IEEE Conference on Computer Vision and Pattern Recognition, Salt Lake City, UT, USA, 18–22 June 2018; pp. 9397–9406.
8. Esbin, B. Internet Over Cable: Defining the Future in Terms of the Past. *Commlaw Conspec.* **1999**, *7*, 37.
9. Ye, H.; Wang, S.; Li, D. Impact of International Submarine Cable on Internet Routing. In Proceedings of the IEEE INFOCOM 2023—IEEE Conference on Computer Communications, New York City, NY, USA, 17–20 May 2023; IEEE: Piscataway, NJ, USA, 2023; pp. 1–10.
10. Liu, J.; Gao, Q.; Wang, X.; Zhou, X.; Li, S.; Zhang, H.; Cui, X. FCMPR: A multi-path secure transmission method based on link security assessment and fountain coding. *Int. J. Intell. Netw.* **2024**, *5*, 275–285.
11. Panda, M. Performance analysis of encryption algorithms for security. In Proceedings of the 2016 International Conference on Signal Processing, Communication, Power and Embedded System (SCOPES), Paralakhemundi, India, 3–5 October 2016; IEEE: Piscataway, NJ, USA, 2016; pp. 278–284.
12. Li, Y.; Jiang, D.; Lian, R.; Wu, X.; Tan, C.; Xu, Y.; Su, Z. Heterogeneous latent topic discovery for semantic text mining. *IEEE Trans. Knowl. Data Eng.* **2021**, *35*, 533–544. [CrossRef]
13. Iftikhar, A.A.; Qureshi, K.N.; Altalbe, A.A.; Javeed, K. Security Provision by Using Detection and Prevention Methods to Ensure Trust in Edge-Based Smart City Networks. *IEEE Access* **2023**, *11* 137529–137547. [CrossRef]
14. Qureshi, K.N.; Iftikhar, A.; Bhatti, S.N.; Piccialli, F.; Giampaolo, F.; Jeon, G. Trust management and evaluation for edge intelligence in the Internet of Things. *Eng. Appl. Artif. Intell.* **2020**, *94*, 103756. [CrossRef]
15. Anwar, R.W.; Zainal, A.; Outay, F.; Yasar, A.; Iqbal, S. BTEM: Belief based trust evaluation mechanism for wireless sensor networks. *Future Gener. Comput. Syst.* **2019**, *96*, 605–616. [CrossRef]
16. Ahmed, A.; Qureshi, K.N.; Anwar, M.; Masud, F.; Imtiaz, J.; Jeon, G. Link-based penalized trust management scheme for preemptive measures to secure the edge-based internet of things networks. *Wirel. Netw.* **2022**, *30*, 4237–4259. [CrossRef]
17. Gao, B.; Maekawa, T.; Amagata, D.; Hara, T. Environment-adaptive malicious node detection in MANETs with ensemble learning. In Proceedings of the 2018 IEEE 38th International Conference on Distributed Computing Systems (ICDCS), Vienna, Austria, 2–5 July 2018; IEEE: Piscataway, NJ, USA, 2018; pp. 556–566.
18. Long, J; Chen, T; Ye, G; Zheng, K; Nguyen, Q.V.H; Yin, H. Physical trajectory inference attack and defense in decentralized poi recommendation. In Proceedings of the ACM on Web Conference 2024, Singapore, 13–17 May 2024; pp. 3379–3387.
19. Zhang, T.; Xu, C.; Lian, Y.; Tian, H.; Kang, J.; Kuang, X.; Niyato, D. When Moving Target Defense Meets Attack Prediction in Digital Twins: A Convolutional and Hierarchical Reinforcement Learning Approach. *IEEE J. Sel. Areas Commun.* **2023**, *41*, 3293–3305. [CrossRef]
20. Kim, D.S.; Kim, M.; Cho, J.H.; Lim, H.; Moore, T.J.; Nelson, F.F. Design and performance analysis of software defined networking based Web services adopting moving target defense. In Proceedings of the 2020 50th Annual IEEE-IFIP International Conference on Dependable Systems and Networks-Supplemental Volume (DSN-S), Valencia, Spain, 29 June–2 July 2020; IEEE: Piscataway, NJ, USA, 2020; pp. 43–44.
21. Zhou, D.; He, L.; Cao, Z.; Han, X. Stability Analysis of Dynamic Heterogeneous Redundant System with Mode Feedback Control. In Proceedings of the 2023 IEEE 11th International Conference on Information, Communication and Networks (ICICN), Xi'an, China, 17–20 August 2023; IEEE: Piscataway, NJ, USA, 2023; pp. 558–563.
22. Xu, J.; Guo, P.; Zhao, M.; Erbacher, R.F.; Zhu, M.; Liu, P. Comparing different moving target defense techniques. In Proceedings of the First ACM Workshop on Moving Target Defense, Scottsdale, AZ, USA, 7 November 2014; pp. 97–107.
23. Zhang, T.; Xu, C.; Shen, J.; Kuang, X.; Grieco, L.A. How to Disturb Network Reconnaissance: A Moving Target Defense Approach Based on Deep Reinforcement Learning. *IEEE Trans. Inf. Forensics Secur.* **2023**, *18*, 5735–5748. [CrossRef]
24. Potteiger, B.; Dubey, A.; Cai, F.; Koutsoukos, X.; Zhang, Z. Moving target defense for the security and resilience of mixed time and event triggered cyber–physical systems. *J. Syst. Archit.* **2022**, *125*, 102420. [CrossRef]
25. Zhang, T.; Xu, C.; Zou, P.; Tian, H.; Kuang, X.; Yang, S.; Zhong, L.; Niyato, D. How to mitigate DDoS intelligently in SD-IoV: A moving target defense approach. *IEEE Trans. Ind. Inform.* **2022**, *19*, 1097–1106. [CrossRef]
26. Sahraoui, S.; Henni, N. SAMP-RPL: Secure and adaptive multipath RPL for enhanced security and reliability in heterogeneous IoT-connected low power and lossy networks. *J. Ambient. Intell. Humaniz. Comput.* **2023**, *14*, 409–429. [CrossRef]
27. Zhou, Z.; Chen, L.; Hu, Y.; Zheng, F.; Liang, C.; Li, K. Q-Learning Based Multi-objective Optimization Routing Strategy in UAVs Deterministic Network. In Proceedings of the International Conference on Computer Engineering and Networks, Kunming, China, 25–27 June 2021; Springer: Berlin/Heidelberg, Germany, 2023; pp. 399–408.
28. Deb, K.; Agrawal, S.; Pratap, A.; Meyarivan, T. A fast elitist non-dominated sorting genetic algorithm for multi-objective optimization: NSGA-II. In Proceedings of the Parallel Problem Solving from Nature PPSN VI: 6th International Conference, Paris, France, 18–20 September 2000; Proceedings 6; Springer: Berlin/Heidelberg, Germany, 2000; pp. 849–858.

29. Verma, S.; Pant, M.; Snasel, V. A comprehensive review on NSGA-II for multi-objective combinatorial optimization problems. *IEEE Access* **2021**, *9*, 57757–57791. [CrossRef]
30. Ehrgott, M. Approximation algorithms for combinatorial multicriteria optimization problems. *Int. Trans. Oper. Res.* **2000**, *7*, 5–31. [CrossRef]
31. Srinivas, N.; Deb, K. Muiltiobjective optimization using nondominated sorting in genetic algorithms. *Evol. Comput.* **1994**, *2*, 221–248. [CrossRef]
32. Knight, S.; Nguyen, H.X.; Falkner, N.; Bowden, R.; Roughan, M. The internet topology zoo. *IEEE J. Sel. Areas Commun.* **2011**, *29*, 1765–1775. [CrossRef]
33. Singh, M.; Shrivastava, L. Multi-objective optimized multi-path and multi-hop routing based on hybrid optimization algorithm in wireless sensor networks. *Wirel. Netw.* **2024**, *30*, 2715–2731. [CrossRef]
34. Chai, Z.Y.; Cheng, Y.Y.; Chen, Z.P. Network access selection in heterogeneous Internet of vehicles based on improved multi-objective evolutionary algorithm. *J. Ambient. Intell. Humaniz. Comput.* **2024**, *15*, 673–682. [CrossRef]
35. Asha, A.; Srivastava, A.K.; Doohan, N.V.; Sharma, D.; Bist, A.S.; Neware, R.; Kumar, S. An optimized DEEC approach for efficient packet transmission in sensor based IoTs network. *Microprocess. Microsystems* **2023**, *96*, 104714. [CrossRef]
36. Song, X.; Cheng, M.; Lei, L.; Yang, Y. Multi-task and multi-objective joint resource optimization for UAV-assisted air-ground integrated networks under emergency scenarios. *IEEE Internet Things J.* **2023**, *10*, 20342–20357. [CrossRef]
37. Pan, H.; Liu, Y.; Sun, G.; Wang, P.; Yuen, C. Resource Scheduling for UAVs-aided D2D Networks: A Multi-objective Optimization Approach. *IEEE Trans. Wirel. Commun.* **2023**, *23*, 4691–4708. [CrossRef]
38. Guo, K.; Wu, M.; Li, X.; Song, H.; Kumar, N. Deep reinforcement learning and NOMA-based multi-objective RIS-assisted IS-UAV-TNs: Trajectory optimization and beamforming design. *IEEE Trans. Intell. Transp. Syst.* **2023**, *24*, 10197–10210. [CrossRef]
39. Seifhosseini, S.; Shirvani, M.H.; Ramzanpoor, Y. Multi-objective cost-aware bag-of-tasks scheduling optimization model for IoT applications running on heterogeneous fog environment. *Comput. Netw.* **2024**, *240*, 110161. [CrossRef]
40. Jiang, C.; Xie, J.; Ye, T. Network structure guided multi-objective optimization approach for key entity identification. *Appl. Soft Comput.* **2024**, *151*, 111115. [CrossRef]
41. Tomar, P.; Kumar, G.; Verma, L.P.; Sharma, V.K.; Kanellopoulos, D.; Rawat, S.S.; Alotaibi, Y. Cmt-sctp and mptcp multipath transport protocols: A comprehensive review. *Electronics* **2022**, *11*, 2384. [CrossRef]
42. Stewart, R.; Tüxen, M.; Nielsen, K. *RFC 9260: Stream Control Transmission Protocol*; Netflix, Inc.: Scotts Valley, CA, USA, 2022.
43. Iyengar, J.R.; Amer, P.D.; Stewart, R. Concurrent multipath transfer using SCTP multihoming over independent end-to-end paths. *IEEE/ACM Trans. Netw.* **2006**, *14*, 951–964. [CrossRef]
44. Wallace, T.D.; Shami, A. A review of multihoming issues using the stream control transmission protocol. *IEEE Commun. Surv. Tutorials* **2011**, *14*, 565–578. [CrossRef]
45. Ford, A.; Raiciu, C.; Handley, M.; Bonaventure, O. TCP Extensions for Multipath Operation with Multiple Addresses. Technical Report, 2013. Available online: https://www.rfc-editor.org/rfc/rfc6824.html (accessed on 6 July 2024)
46. Okamoto, K.; Yamai, N.; Okayama, K.; Kawano, K.; Nakamura, M.; Yokohira, T. Performance improvement of SCTP communication using selective bicasting on lossy multihoming environment. In Proceedings of the 2014 IEEE 38th Annual Computer Software and Applications Conference, Västerås, Sweden, 21–25 July 2014; IEEE: Piscataway, NJ, USA, 2014; pp. 551–557.
47. da Silva, C.A.G.; Ribeiro, E.P.; Pedroso, C.M. Preventing quality degradation of video streaming using selective redundancy. *Comput. Commun.* **2016**, *91*, 120–132. [CrossRef]
48. Shailendra, S.; Bhattacharjee, R.; Bose, S. An implementation of Min–Max optimization for multipath SCTP through bandwidth estimation based resource pooling technique. *AEU-Int. J. Electron. Commun.* **2013**, *67*, 246–249. [CrossRef]
49. Peng, Q.; Walid, A.; Low, S.H. Multipath TCP algorithms: Theory and design. *ACM Sigmetrics Perform. Eval. Rev.* **2013**, *41*, 305–316. [CrossRef]
50. Cai, Y.; Xiong, H.; Yu, S.; Chen, M.; Zhou, X. D-OLIA: The packet loss differentiation based opportunistic linked-increases algorithm for MPTCP in wireless heterogeneous network. In Proceedings of the 2021 31st International Telecommunication Networks and Applications Conference (ITNAC), Sydney, Australia, 24–26 November 2021; IEEE: Piscataway, NJ, USA, 2021; pp. 78–85.
51. Oh, B.H.; Lee, J. Constraint-based proactive scheduling for MPTCP in wireless networks. *Comput. Netw.* **2015**, *91*, 548–563. [CrossRef]
52. Wang, P.; Sourav, S.; Li, H.; Chen, B. One Pass is Sufficient: A Solver for Minimizing Data Delivery Time over Time-varying Networks. In Proceedings of the IEEE INFOCOM 2023—IEEE Conference on Computer Communications, New York City, NY, USA, 17–20 May 2023; IEEE: Piscataway, NJ, USA, 2023; pp. 1–10.
53. Ouyang, M.; Zhang, R.; Wang, B.; Liu, J.; Huang, T.; Liu, L.; Tong, J.; Xin, N.; Yu, F.R. Network Coding-Based Multi-Path Transmission for LEO Satellite Networks with Domain Cluster. *IEEE Internet Things J.* **2024**, *11*, 21659–21673. [CrossRef]

Disclaimer/Publisher's Note: The statements, opinions and data contained in all publications are solely those of the individual author(s) and contributor(s) and not of MDPI and/or the editor(s). MDPI and/or the editor(s) disclaim responsibility for any injury to people or property resulting from any ideas, methods, instructions or products referred to in the content.

Article

Efficient Inference Offloading for Mixture-of-Experts Large Language Models in Internet of Medical Things

Xiaoming Yuan [1,2,*,†], Weixuan Kong [1,†], Zhenyu Luo [1] and Minrui Xu [3]

1. Hebei Key Laboratory of Marine Perception Network and Data Processing, Northeastern University at Qinhuangdao, Qinhuangdao 066004, China; 202112001@stu.neuq.edu.cn (W.K.); 2272213@stu.neu.edu.cn (Z.L.)
2. State Key Laboratory of Integrated Services Networks, Xidian University, Xi'an 710071, China
3. School of Computer Science and Engineering, Nanyang Technological University, Singapore 639798, Singapore; minrui001@e.ntu.edu.sg
* Correspondence: yuanxiaoming@neuq.edu.cn
† These authors contributed equally to this work.

Abstract: Despite recent significant advancements in large language models (LLMs) for medical services, the deployment difficulties of LLMs in e-healthcare hinder complex medical applications in the Internet of Medical Things (IoMT). People are increasingly concerned about e-healthcare risks and privacy protection. Existing LLMs face difficulties in providing accurate medical questions and answers (Q&As) and meeting the deployment resource demands in the IoMT. To address these challenges, we propose MedMixtral 8x7B, a new medical LLM based on the mixture-of-experts (MoE) architecture with an offloading strategy, enabling deployment on the IoMT, improving the privacy protection for users. Additionally, we find that the significant factors affecting latency include the method of device interconnection, the location of offloading servers, and the speed of the disk.

Keywords: large language models; efficient inference offloading; mixture-of-experts; Internet of Medical Things

Citation: Yuan, X.; Kong, W.; Luo, Z.; Xu, M. Efficient Inference Offloading for Mixture-of-Experts Large Language Models in Internet of Medical Things. *Electronics* **2024**, *13*, 2077. https://doi.org/10.3390/electronics13112077

Academic Editor: Djuradj Budimir

Received: 1 May 2024
Revised: 20 May 2024
Accepted: 24 May 2024
Published: 27 May 2024

Copyright: © 2024 by the authors. Licensee MDPI, Basel, Switzerland. This article is an open access article distributed under the terms and conditions of the Creative Commons Attribution (CC BY) license (https://creativecommons.org/licenses/by/4.0/).

1. Introduction

In the medical field, the application of conversational large language models (LLM) has garnered widespread attention to meet the growing demand for personalized healthcare. However, LLMs deployed on the server side still face significant security challenges, such as data breaches and unauthorized access, within the network. Developing an IoMT device that can be deployed on consumer devices is crucial to safeguard user privacy.

The transformer architecture [1] has emerged as a foundational framework for most LLMs, due to its effectiveness for scalability and ability to outperform previous popular neural networks in accuracy. LLMs have been widely applied in various domains. By leveraging edge intelligence, the Internet of Medical Things (IoMT) [2] can collect and analyze medical information, enabling advice delivery through smartphones, wearable devices, and smart home sensors. Deployed in IoMT devices, LLMs can provide users with healthcare services, such as responding to common medical questions and offering health advice. Moreover, it can maximize the protection of user privacy and avoid privacy leaks in the network.

However, they present several significant challenges and limitations in healthcare applications. Given the complex nature of medical data and the specialized knowledge required in healthcare, direct applications of LLMs can pose risks such as misinterpretations and inaccuracies. In particular, general LLMs may struggle to grasp medical terminology and accurately interpret the specific context of medical texts, potentially leading to biased or incorrect medical advice. The data used in LLMs is sourced from different internet platforms, varying significantly in quality. While this approach allows LLMs to gather vast amounts of information quickly, it also impacts their performance in specific domains, including healthcare. To harness the full potential of LLMs in the medical domain, retraining existing general-purpose LLMs based on high-quality medical datasets is a viable approach. This enables LLMs to attain more accurate language understanding and better generation quality within specific domains. Furthermore, the selection of parameter scale has a profound impact on the performance of LLMs based on the transformer architecture, as a surplus of parameters can cause overfitting, while a shortage can restrict the LLM's performance in medical applications. The resource requirements of LLMs present a challenge in deploying medical LLMs on IoMT devices. LLMs commonly employ a strategy of distributing multiple models across different devices to enhance performance. This distributed approach necessitates communication between multiple devices to coordinate processing and enhance overall system efficiency. In this strategy, different levels of latency can significantly impact the inference speed of distributed LLMs.

To meet individuals' personalized healthcare needs, we aim to establish a new medical LLM specifically designed for deployment on IoMT devices. The literature includes several applications of LLMs in network communications. For example, Xu et al. [3] discuss their application in space–air–ground integrated networks, while [4] explore their use in 6G networks. To integrate theoretical results from these articles and achieve this goal, we use the latest mixture-of-experts (MoE) model from Mixtral, named Mixtral 8x7B [5], for fine-tuning in the medical domain, thus creating a new medical LLM, named MedMixtral 8x7B. Its MoE architecture can enhance performance, leading to higher accuracy in medical questions and answers (Q&As). To deploy MedMixtral 8x7B on IoMT devices, we utilize the methods proposed by [6], incorporating Accelerate's offloading techniques proposed by [7], which allows Mixtral 8x7B to require fewer VRAM and facilitate its deployment on IoMT devices. This ensures better protection of users' privacy data. We conducted extensive evaluations on MedMixtral 8x7B, demonstrating its advantages over strong general large models such as ChatGPT and Llama3 in various aspects of medical Q&As. The efficient offloading architecture saves memory, and research on inference latency suggests key strategies for reducing latency include enhancing disk speed, storing more model weights in the CPU's RAM rather than on disk, and opting for wireless communication.

The contributions of this paper are summarized as follows:

- To obtain efficient medical LLMs for healthcare applications, we fine-tune an LLM based on the MoE architecture, named MedMixtral 8x7B, using medical datasets to meet individuals' personalized healthcare needs.
- To deploy MedMixtral 8x7B on IoMT devices, we propose a novel offloading strategy, which allows the deployment of MedMixtral 8x7B in the IoMT with less resource requirement, thus enhancing the privacy protection for users.
- To assess latency's impact on LLM inference speed, we analyze both local and interconnection communication models. We highlight the critical role of latency in inference processes and propose several strategies to reduce it. These include enhancing disk speed, storing more model weights in the CPU's RAM rather than on disk, and opting for wireless communications.

2. Related Work

2.1. Large Language Models

LLMs, such as the ChatGPT series, have developed significantly in recent years, especially in model architecture, parameter scale, reinforcement learning, and so on. In 2018, OpenAI, in [8], proposes the methods of generative pre-training of a language model. The generative pre-trained transformer (GPT) is a unidirectional autoregressive model. Based on the GPT, OpenAI developed ChatGPT, which is one of the most influential LLM series. To address the issue of requiring fine-tuning layers in GPT-1, GPT-2 underwent training on a larger scale, possessing more parameters, and eliminating the need for fine-tuning layers. In 2019, OpenAI, in [9], proposes GPT-2, using this model, without fine-tuning for specific tasks, it enhances performance across tasks in a logarithm linear manner, and it can still achieve good results. To enhance contextual understanding and reduce computational overhead, OpenAI released GPT-3. In 2020, OpenAI, in [10], proposes GPT-3, which is trained by 1750B parameters, and achieves high performance on many NLP datasets. In 2022, OpenAI, in [11], designed the reward model (RM), and used reinforcement learning with proximal policy optimization (PPO) to update the GPT model. In 2023, OpenAI proposes GPT-4 [12], which is one of the highest-performing LLMs.

Although the ChatGPT series LLMs have high performance, the latest ChatGPT is not an open LLM. In addition to ChatGPT, many other companies and institutions have also proposed high-performance open LLMs. Zhao et al., in [13], survey the field of LLM, showing the development of LLMs. After the proposal of the transformers architecture, to enhance contextual understanding capability, Devlin et al., in [14], propose a new model, BERT, which is a simple and powerful model that has great results in natural language processing (NLP) tasks. To further improve the performance of BERT, Liu et al., in [15], propose RoBERTa, RoBERTa based on BERT, and introduce several improvements. RoBERTa employs dynamic masking, training with complete sentences without next sentence prediction (NSP) loss, large batch sizes, and larger byte-level byte pair encoding (BPE) for training.

Apart from extending BERT, there are also proposals for different architectures based on transformer. Google proposes the Text-to-Text Transfer Transformer (T5) model in [16]. T5-model modeling every text-related question as a "text-to-text" problem, using the same model, objective function, training, and decoding process for each NLP task, can lead to better performance.

In addition to different model architectures, there are also many models trained based on the traditional transformer architecture. Meta AI, in [17,18], proposes Llama, an open and efficient LLM. Llama is open and free for anyone, allowing individuals to learn about the structure of LLMs from Llama. Additionally, users can fine-tune the model based on Llama. Meta AI, in [19], proposes OPT, which is an open pre-trained transformer LLM. To satisfy the model requirements for the Chinese language, Zhang et al., in [20,21], propose CPM series LLMs, which are Chinese pre-trained LLMs. To meet the needs of generating computer programs, Nijkamp et al., in [22], propose CodeGen, which is a series of LLMs trained on natural language and programming language data, with 16.1B parameters. CodeGen series LLMs have advanced in generating computer programs through input–output examples or natural language descriptions. To fill the gap in open-source models with a large number of parameters, Le et al., in [23], propose BLOOM, which is an open LLM with 1760B parameters. To further expand the usability of multilingual language models, Zeng et al., in [24], propose GLM-130B, which is an English and Chinese pre-trained LLM with 130B parameters. To address the absence of open LLMs based on the MoE structure, Jiang et al. propose Mixtral 8x7B in [5], a model using the MoE architecture, where each token can use 47B parameters but only 13B are used for model inference.

Based on these LLMs, various domain-specific large models have emerged. Due to their conversational capabilities, LLMs are particularly well suited for applications in medical Q&As. Many medical LLMs have demonstrated remarkable abilities in the healthcare field. Luo et al., in [25], propose BioGPT. It is a medical LLM based on GPT-2. BioGPT is first pre-trained on a large-scale biomedical literature dataset, followed by fine-tuning and the adoption of new prompting strategies. It has particularly demonstrated good performance on BC5CDR, KD-DTI, and DDI end-to-end relation extraction tasks. Singhal et al., in [26], present MultiMedQA, providing benchmark datasets for performance evaluation of medical LLMs. Meanwhile, they first propose Flan-PaLM. Based on this, it is fine-tuned into the final product, Med-PaLM, through prompting strategies and other means. In the evaluation, Med-PaLM achieves accuracy comparable to that of real human doctors, yielding excellent results. Building upon this success, they further propose Med-PaLM2 [27]. Med-PaLM2 utilizes an improved base model and employs fine-tuning and prompting strategies specific to the medical domain, improving answer accuracy.

When it comes to medical Q&A tasks, although various types of LLMs are available, none are suitable for deployment on IoMT devices for privacy protection while being capable of handling such tasks. Typically, models with sufficient performance pose challenges when deployed on IoMT devices, while deployment on the server side introduces network security and privacy protection concerns. LLMs deployable on IoMT devices lack the necessary performance for medical Q&A tasks. To meet the growing demand for medical Q&As and privacy protection requirements from users, designing a high-performance medical LLM deployable on IoMT devices with privacy protection is crucial.

2.2. LLM Efficient Inference Offloading Methods

With the development of LLMs, the size of LLMs is increasing, leading to higher resource requirements for inference. Consequently, more and more scientists are researching ways to reduce resource demands and improve inference speed during LLM inference. Rasley et al., in [28], propose DeepSpeed, which is an optimization library for LLMs. It provides techniques for distributed training, especially memory optimization. Shoeybi et al., in [29], propose Megatron-LM, which is a library for deep learning, and provides a lot of optimization techniques for GPUs. Kwon et al., in [30], propose vLLM, which is a library that provides PagedAttention methods, assisting LLMs with efficient inference. Zhao et al., in [31], propose FSDP; while maintaining the simplicity of data parallelism, it breaks the barrier of slicing the model across multiple processes.

However, these methods do not significantly reduce the occupied VRAM in LLM inference to enable deployment on IoMT devices. Our work greatly improves reducing the occupied VRAM in LLM inference and LLM can be deployed in IoMT devices more easily.

2.3. AI Used in Communication

In the field of communication, the application of AI is rapidly increasing. Han et al., in [32,33], incorporate federated learning into communications yielding promising results. To enhance the management of base station power consumption, Piovesan et al., in [34], designed a machine learning algorithm to assess the power consumption of 5G base stations (BSs).To facilitate the transmission of AI/ML models, Ayed et al., in [35], designed the framework Accordion, which efficiently facilitates the transfer of AI/ML models. In addition to traditional AI, with the development of LLMs there is an increasing number of people applying LLMs in the field of communications. Du et al., in [36], explore using an LLM to assist FPGA wireless signal processing hardware development. Bariah et al., in [37], introduce the application of LLMs in future wireless networks and propose relevant theories along with insights into the challenges LLMs face in communication. Bariah et al., in [38], fine-tune several LLMs for the telecommunications domain language and use them for identifying the 3rd Generation Partnership Project (3GPP) standard working groups. Soman et al., in [39], analyze the capabilities and limitations of integrating LLMs into dialogue interfaces in the telecommunications domain. LLMs demonstrate their effectiveness in various communication applications. However, due to the significant resources required for deployment, there is little discussion about the communication issues of LLMs on IoMT devices. We integrate our offloading model to examine the communication of LLMs among consumer devices.

In mobile networks, Zhang et al. have investigated several security issues. Zhang et al. propose a collaborative mutation-based MTD (CM-MTD) [40] to address the challenges of poor coordination, high network resource consumption, and lack of consideration for future information in MTD. Zhang et al. propose a smart-driven host address mutation (ID-HAM) scheme [41], to address the issues of HAM lacking adaptive adversarial strategies, network states being time-varying, and the oversight of the survivability of existing connections. Zhang et al. propose an intelligent MTD scheme to defend against distributed denial-of-service in SD-IoV [42], to tackle the issues of MTD's inability to handle high-speed dynamic environments, lack of intelligence, and difficulty in tracking.

3. Methods

This section details the design of the communication model, the development of the MedMixtral 8x7B medical LLM, and the implementation of an efficient offloading strategy.

3.1. Communication Model Design

In this section, we investigate the inference offloading latency across IoMT devices, including interconnection communication latency and local communication latency. We model the two types of models separately and calculate the total communication latency at the end.

In e-healthcare, we propose a system model for the IoMT that enables users to utilize medical LLMs. As depicted in Figure 1, each model operates independently on one IoMT device in this system, while possessing the capability to function cooperatively with other models to enhance performance. For interconnection among IoMT devices, there is a set $\mathcal{N} = \{1, \ldots, n, \ldots, N\}$ of IoMT devices, which allows doctors and users to access e-healthcare services via wireless communication. In the interconnection communication model with $\mathcal{N}$, the interconnection communication latency between device n and device $n+1$ is denoted as l_n. The interconnection communication latency between device i and device j is denoted as l_{ij}. The interconnection communication latency is denoted as l_n^{com}; the l_n^{com} can be calculated as

$$l_n^{com} = d_n^p + d_n^{pr} + d_n^q + d_n^w, \tag{1}$$

where propagation delay is denoted as d_n^p, processing delay is denoted as d_n^{pr}, queueing delay is denoted as d_n^q, and waiting delay is denoted as d_n^w.

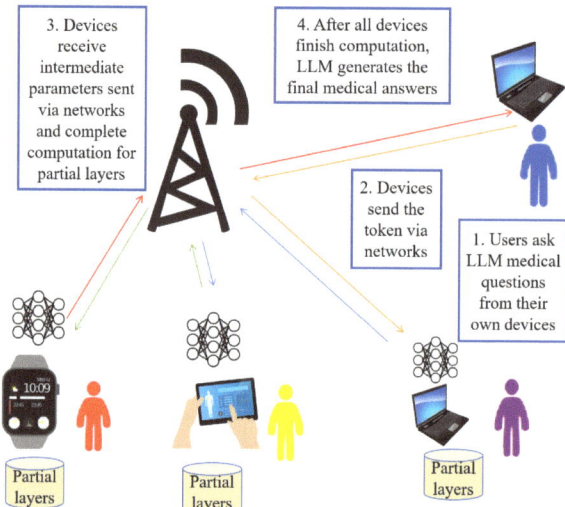

Figure 1. This is the communication model design. Users ask LLM medical questions from their own devices, then devices send the token via networks. Devices receive intermediate parameters sent via networks and complete computation for partial layers, and finally, all devices finish computation; LLM generates the final medical answers to the user.

3.1.1. Interconnection Communication Model

According to Equation (1), the values of d_n^{pr}, d_n^w, and d_n^q can be considered negligible compared to d_n^p. Therefore, the l_n^{com} can be approximately regarded as d_n^p. To obtain the d_n^p, we first need to obtain the signal-to-noise ratio (SNR). In wireless networks, the signal power between devices is denoted as S_n, and the noise power can be approximately regarded as white Gaussian noise, denoted as ω_n, and the SNR_n is calculated as

$$SNR_n = \frac{S_n}{\omega_n}, \qquad (2)$$

where $\omega_n = kTB_n$ is white Gaussian noise, k is the Boltzmann constant, T is the temperature in kelvin, and B_n is the channel bandwidth.

After obtaining the SNR_n, we still need to calculate the channel capacity for obtaining the d_n^p. According to Equation (2), the channel capacity C_n can be calculated as

$$C_n = B_n \log_2(1 + SNR_n), \qquad (3)$$

then, according to Equation (3), we calculate the d_n^p. The data volume of medical services is denoted as D_n. The d_n^p can be calculated as

$$d_n^p = \frac{D_n}{C_n}, \qquad (4)$$

and now, we obtain the value of d_n^p through the computation.

3.1.2. Local Communication Model

In the local communication model, the local communication latency in device n is denoted as l_n. The speed from the CPU's RAM to the GPU's VRAM is denoted as s_n^{cg}, the speed from the disk to the CPU's RAM is denoted as s_n^{dc}, the latency from the CPU's RAM to the GPU's VRAM is denoted as l_n^{cg}, the latency from the disk to the CPU's RAM is denoted as l_n^{dc}, the latency from the disk to the GPU's VRAM is denoted as l_n^{dg}, and the model weight for one layer is denoted as w_n.

The latency from the CPU's RAM to the GPU's VRAM l_n^{cg} is calculated as

$$l_n^{cg} = \frac{w_n}{s_n^{cg}}, \qquad (5)$$

the latency from the disk to the CPU's RAM l_n^{dc} for w is calculated as

$$l_n^{dc} = \frac{w_n}{s_n^{dc}}, \qquad (6)$$

when offloading w into a disk, they need to be first loaded into the CPU's RAM from the disk, then from the CPU's RAM to the GPU's VRAM for computation. The latency from the disk to the GPU's VRAM l^{dg} for w is calculated as

$$l_n^{dg} = \frac{w_n}{s_n^{cg}} + \frac{w_n}{s_n^{dc}}, \qquad (7)$$

and in an IoMT device, we denote by x the number of model layers offloading in the CPU's RAM in devices and denote by y the number of model layers offloading in the disk in devices. According to Equations (5)–(7), we can calculate l_n^{loc} as

$$l_n^{loc} = \frac{(x_n + y_n)w_n}{s_n^{cg}} + \frac{y_n w_n}{s_n^{dc}}, \qquad (8)$$

and now, we obtain the value of l_n^{loc} through the computation.

3.1.3. Total Communication Latency

In this section, we calculate the total communication latency. The total communication latency is denoted as l^{total} among the set of IoMT devices $\mathcal{N}$.

In the interconnection communication model, different layers are distributed across various devices. In the beginning, device i needs to send a token to the device that contains the first layer of the model, which is device 1. Then, it is required to transmit the token from the first computation device to the last computation device, which is device N. Finally, the device results are transmitted back to device i. To calculate l_n^{com} among all devices, we calculate the sum l_n^{com} of all devices in $\mathcal{N}$ and add the l_{i1}^{com} and l_{Ni}^{com}. In the local communication model, there are N devices; we calculate the sum l_n^{loc} of all devices in $\mathcal{N}$.

According to Equations (1) and (8), the total communication latency can be calculated as

$$l^{total} = \sum_{n \in \mathcal{N}}^{N} l_n^{loc} + \sum_{n \in \mathcal{N}}^{N-1} l_n^{com} + l_{i1}^{com} + l_{Ni}^{com}, \tag{9}$$

and now, we obtain the value of l^{total} through the computation.

3.2. MedMixtral 8x7B

With the increasing demands in healthcare, both patients and physicians are turning to medical Q&A services more frequently. Patients seek these services for timely advice, while physicians utilize them to manage their mounting workloads. Utilizing LLMs offers an approach to tackle this issue, given their capability to comprehend human language and facilitate Q&A interactions akin to those between individuals.

LLMs can specifically leverage a wealth of knowledge from the medical literature, databases, and clinical records, effectively processing and synthesizing this vast amount of information. As a result, LLMs can more accurately assess a patient's condition. For patients, an LLM can provide a preliminary diagnosis, and for physicians, it can reduce the risks of misdiagnosis. Furthermore, LLMs can provide patients with easily comprehensible medical explanations, treatment alternatives, and preventive measures. Therefore, LLMs can enhance patients' health literacy, increase patients' engagement, and subsequently, augment the public's foundational medical knowledge.

As depicted in Figure 2, we fine-tune an LLM based on the MoE architecture, with the pre-trained model being Mixtral 8x7B and the dataset named HealthCareMagic 8x7B. The MoE model is deployed on both memory and disk. We evaluate its performance on iCliniq. We choose to use the Mixtral 8x7b model due to its high performance. Mixtral 8x7b adopts a sparse mixture-of-experts (SMoE) architecture [43], functioning as a decoder-only model, where feedforward blocks are selected from a set of eight distinct parameter groups. For each token in the layers, the routers select two of these experts to deal with the token and aggregate outputs. The SMoE architecture enhances the model's parameters while reducing costs and latency by using only a fraction of the total parameters.

Specifically, Mixtral 8x7B has a total of 46.7B parameters. Compared to the GPT3.5 base model, Mixtral demonstrates comparable or superior performance across most benchmarks. As an SMoE model, it retains the strengths of a traditional MoE model while capitalizing on the advantages offered by an SMoE architecture.

We use the HealthCareMagic-100k dataset to fine-tune Mixtral 8x7B for medical-patient dialogue. In these conversations, patients often describe their conditions in non-standard ways. Self-made medical datasets can overuse specialized terminology and potentially introduce biased diagnoses, reducing data usefulness. Therefore, it is crucial to use real-world medical-patient dialogues from trusted sources to maintain data quality and reliability. The HealthCareMagic-100k dataset includes around 100,000 authentic doctor–patient dialogues from HealthCareMagic [44], with identifiers deleted and grammar errors corrected. This makes the HealthCareMagic-100k dataset an effective, information-rich, and comprehensive dataset, making it an excellent fit for medical Q&As.

The MedMixtral 8x7B model, which is fine-tuned on the HealthCareMagic-100k dataset, represents a novel medical LLM, enabling deployment on IoMT devices. By fine-tuning the pre-trained LLM with medical Q&A datasets, the MedMixtral 8x7B LLM can address medical inquiries and show exceptional performance in medical Q&A tasks.

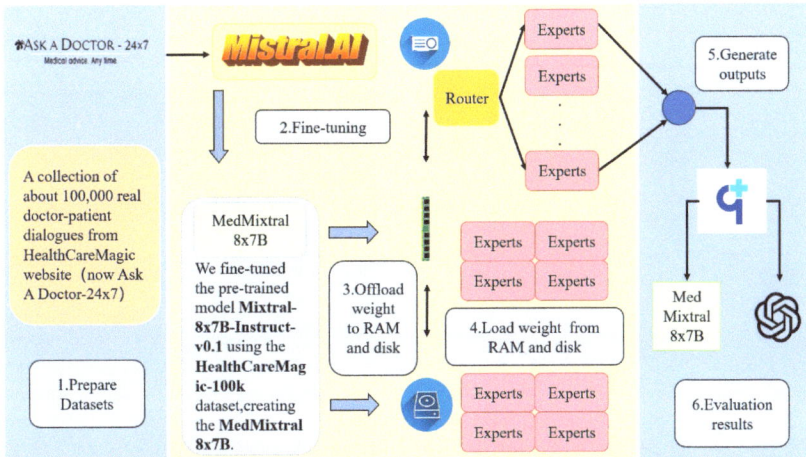

Figure 2. This is the MedMixtral 8x7B workflow. First, we prepare a dataset of about 100,000 samples from HealthCareMagic. Then, we fine-tune the Mixtral 8x7B model. After that, we design a strategy to offload the weights to both RAM and disk, aiming to alleviate the resource strain on IoMT deployments of LLMs. We obtain medical advice by asking the MedMixtral 8x7B model, and finally, evaluate our model's performance on iCliniq.

MedMixtral 8x7B demonstrates reduced bias and enhanced accuracy in medical Q&A tasks compared to traditional transformer-based LLMs. Figure 3 shows a medical Q&A example using MedMixtral 8x7B in the IoMT. The following paragraphs show some real and comprehensive answers of MedMixtral 8x7B to medical Q&As.

- Question1: Hello doctor, We have a 9-month-old baby girl. She has five brown marks, two of them are 2 cm size and the other three of 0.5 cm. They are irregular in shape. Initial two marks appeared when she was 3 months old and now when she is 9 months three more for added that are comparatively light and 0.5 cm of size. Are these birthmarks? Will they fade with the time? Do we need to take any precautions so that they do not increase or get added further? Can we also provide any medication to cure them?
- Answer1: Hello, The brown marks you are describing are commonly known as birthmarks. The two larger ones that appeared when your baby was three months old are likely to be called "cafe-au-lait" spots, while the smaller, lighter ones may be called freckles. Cafe-au-lait spots are harmless and may fade slightly with time, but they do not typically disappear completely. Freckles, on the other hand, may darken with sun exposure but can also be lightened with topical treatments. While these birthmarks are generally not a cause for concern, it is always a good idea to monitor any changes in their size, shape, or color. If you notice any new or unusual growths, or if the existing birthmarks become significantly larger or darker, it is recommended to consult a healthcare professional. In terms of precautions, it is important to protect your baby's skin from the sun, as UV radiation can darken the birthmarks and make them more noticeable. You can do this by dressing your baby in lightweight, long-sleeved clothing and a wide-brimmed hat, and by using a broad-spectrum sunscreen with an SPF of at least 30 on any exposed skin. As for medication, there is currently no cure or effective treatment for birthmarks. However, if the birthmarks are causing any discomfort, such as itching or irritation, your healthcare provider may recommend a topical cream or ointment to alleviate the symptoms. I hope this information is helpful. Please let me know if you have any further questions or concerns.
- Question2: Hello doctor, I have been going to a dentist about a tooth that is sore. They started a root canal but then did not finish. I have gone back several times and every

- time they open up the tooth and insert medicine. My tooth is in agony right now. I am just wondering if this is a standard procedure during a root canal? Should not the dentist remove the nerves so I am not in so much pain? Or is it the standard procedure to fight the infection first and then remove the nerves?
- Answer2: Hello, During a root canal procedure, the dentist typically removes the nerve tissue first in order to alleviate the pain caused by the infection. However, in some cases where the infection is severe, the dentist may choose to administer medication and apply a temporary filling to the tooth to eliminate the infection before completing the root canal. This is often done to make the procedure more manageable for the patient and to ensure the best possible outcome. The fact that your dentist has been repeatedly opening your tooth and applying medication suggests that they are trying to eliminate the infection before completing the root canal. While this approach can be somewhat uncomfortable, it is not uncommon and is often necessary to ensure the success of the procedure. I would recommend speaking with your dentist about your concerns and asking for more information about the approach they are taking. They may be able to provide you with additional pain relief measures or offer further insight into the procedure and what to expect.
- Question3: Hello doctor, I have been diagnosed with mild hereditary spherocytosis. My eyes still yellow. Is it unlikely hematologist who diagnosed me three years ago misdiagnosed? I do not doubt he knows his stuff. More about me getting worried. I lost weight a couple of months ago. I went very yellow in the eyes. I have always felt tired. I have had gallbladder out four years ago, I bruise easily, I do get little red skin dots at times, menstrual cycles can be irregular and spleen slightly enlarged.
- Answer3: Hello, While it is unlikely that your hematologist misdiagnosed you, the symptoms you have described could be indicative of other conditions such as liver disease or a more severe form of hereditary spherocytosis. The jaundice you mentioned, along with weight loss, fatigue, easy bruising, and enlarged spleen, are all potential symptoms of these conditions. It would be best to consult with your hematologist and possibly a gastroenterologist or liver specialist to rule out any other potential causes for your symptoms. They may want to perform additional tests, such as a liver function test or a bone marrow biopsy, to further evaluate your condition. It is important to remember that this advice is intended to be general in nature, and specific causes may not apply to your situation. Always consult with a healthcare professional for an accurate diagnosis. I hope this information helps, and please let me know if you have any further questions or concerns.
- Question4: Good evening, doctor. I have a severe toothache.It hurts so bad.It is difficult for me to eat.The pain is like a sharp knife cutting my teeth.What is the cause of it?
- Answer4: Good evening, I'm sorry to hear that you're experiencing tooth pain. The description you provided suggests that the pain is severe and sharp, which could indicate a few possible causes. The most common cause of tooth pain is tooth decay, which can cause a sharp pain when eating or drinking something sweet, hot or cold. Another possible cause is an infection or abscess in the tooth or gum, which can cause a persistent, throbbing pain. In some cases, tooth pain can also be caused by gum disease, injury, or a cracked tooth. It is important to see a dentist as soon as possible to determine the cause of the pain and to receive appropriate treatment. In the meantime, you can try taking over-the-counter pain relievers to help manage the pain. However, it is not recommended to apply pain relievers directly to the tooth or gums, as this can burn the gum tissue.

In the model fine-tuning process, we employed the LoRA fine-tuning method [45]. LoRA offers a fine-tuning approach that consumes less VRAM and memory while achieving performance close to full fine-tuning. In the fine-tuning setup, we set warmup steps to 0.03, max steps to 1000, learning rate to 2×10^{-4}, and logging steps to 1.

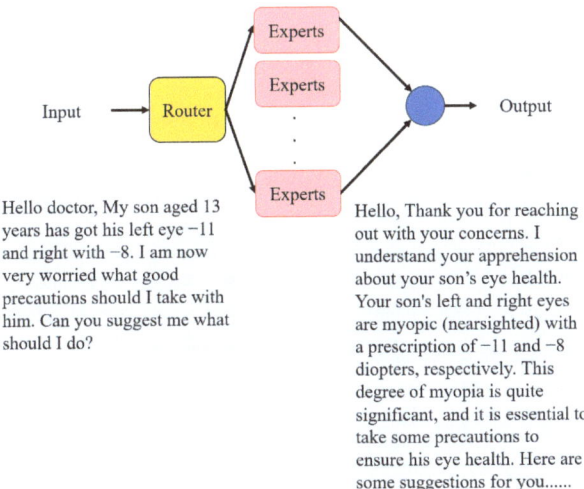

Figure 3. An instance of the process of MedMixtral 8x7B generating medical answers. After the input tokens enter the model, it is routed to the experts by the router. Then, the experts generate responses based on the input tokens.

3.3. Efficient Inference Offloading

The increasing adoption of LLMs is spurring demand for innovative LLM architectures with superior performance attributes. For instance, SMoE is one of the emergent architectures, where only specific model layers are activated for any given input, making it particularly useful for tasks such as NLP. In SMoE, this feature allows LLMs to generate tokens faster than before, even though it leads to an increase in model size due to the integration of multiple experts. Therefore, deploying high-performance LLMs demands considerable VRAM and high-performance GPUs to ensure optimal operation. We propose a novel strategy called efficient inference offloading to address the challenge of deploying MedMixtral 8x7B on IoMT devices.

Efficient Inference Offloading Algorithm

For the design of efficient inference offloading algorithms, we employ the least recently used (LRU) cache strategy [3] to dynamically adjust the number of experts per layer, based on VRAM size. In instances of limited VRAM availability, we augment the number of experts, whereas we decrease it when VRAM is abundant. Upon loading all experts of the current layer, we start the expert loading based on the 1–2 most probable experts derived from the inference results. These newly loaded experts do not replace any existing experts in the cache; however, if used in the inference of the subsequent layer, they replace the least recently used expert in the cache.

Meanwhile, we introduce an efficient strategy for loading model weights. First, an empty model framework is loaded into the CPU's RAM, minimizing the CPU's RAM consumption. Then, model weights are loaded into the CPU's RAM and stored on the disk as the configuration. The loaded weights are moved from the CPU's RAM to the disk, then the checkpoint is removed from the CPU's RAM. When loading the model weights, the loaded weights are moved from the disk to the CPU's RAM. Hooks are attached to each weight of the model, enabling the transfer of weights from the CPU's RAM to the GPU when needed, and back to the CPU's RAM after completing the associated computations.

We chose to offload certain parameters to the disk due to constraints in memory availability. Our offloading strategy prioritizes memory utilization, resorting to disk offloading only when memory resources are insufficient given the considerable size of parameters in LLMs. In SMoE, this feature allows LLMs to generate tokens faster than before, even though it leads to an increase in model size due to the integration of multiple experts. We paid particular attention to the performance of IoMT devices. Considering the limited memory capacity of IoMT devices in current scenarios, we specifically consider the option of offloading to the disk. Because we can offload to the disk, our flexible offloading strategy enables IoMT devices to support larger models without compromising performance.

4. Results

In this section, we first elaborate on our experimental environment by using a 36 vCPU AMD EPYC 9754 128-core Processor (AMD, Santa Clara, CA, USA) and NVIDIA GTX 3090 x2 (NVIDIA, Santa Clara, CA, USA).

4.1. MedMixtral 8x7B

MedMixtral 8x7B is a medical LLM designed for deployment on IoMT devices. By fine-tuning Mixtral 8x7B with medical datasets, the MedMixtral 8x7B proficiently addresses medical questions while demonstrating exceptional performance. The MedMixtral 8x7B consists of multiple experts, similar to conventional medical practice with multiple experts, which enhances the accuracy of medical diagnostics.

Comparative evaluations are conducted among our MedMixtral 8x7B, ChatGPT, Llama3 8B, and the original Mixtral 8x7b model. By utilizing the 4-bit quantized Mixtral 8x7B and MedMixtral 8x7B in this experiment, we observe from Table 1 that MedMixtral 8x7B consistently outperforms them in terms of Q&A accuracy.

The results indicate that our MedMixtral 8x7B shows significant improvements in the precision, recall, and F1 score metrics compared to the original Mixtral 8x7B metrics. Additionally, it slightly outperforms ChatGPT and Llama3 8B in all metrics. This demonstrates that our MedMixtral 8x7B exhibits superior performance in medical Q&As.

Table 1. Quantitative comparison among ChatGPT, Mixtral 8x7B, and MedMixtral 8x7B. According to the test results, our model MedMixtral 8x7B, which is fine-tuned on Mixtral 8x7B, outperforms other models in terms of precision, recall, and F1 score when answering medical questions on the test set. This indicates that our model has an advantage in the medical Q&A domain compared to Mixtral 8x7B, Llama3 8B, and ChatGPT.

	Precision	Recall	F1 Score
ChatGPT	0.837	0.8445	0.8406
Mixtral 8x7B	0.821	0.8434	0.8320
MedMixtral 8x7B	0.838	0.8447	0.8413
Llama 8B	0.799	0.8384	0.8179

4.2. Offloading Strategy

Figure 4 illustrates the occupied VRAM capacity as the number of offloaded experts changes. When no expert has been offloaded, the quantized Mixtral 8x7B model can be deployed with 18.4 GB VRAM. Conversely, in original offloading, it requires 20.1 GB VRAM. With two experts offloaded, the quantized Mixtral 8x7B model can be deployed with 14.5 GB VRAM, whereas in original offloading it demands nearly 16.3 GB VRAM. Upon offloading four experts, the quantized Mixtral 8x7B model can be deployed with 10.1 GB VRAM, whereas in original offloading it demands 11.9 GB, close to 12 GB VRAM. Furthermore, the model weights are loaded into both the CPU's RAM and disk, a strategy that conserves a certain amount of VRAM capacity while expanding the loadable model size.

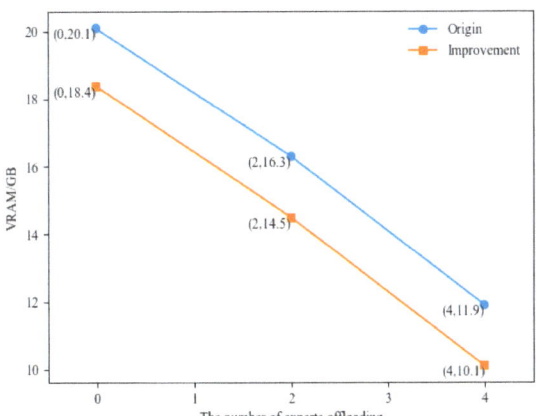

Figure 4. This is the trend in changes in VRAM usage with the number of offloading experts. Our strategy requires less VRAM capacity than the strategy method across all number of offloading experts scenarios.

4.3. Communication Latency

We conduct experiments to evaluate the interconnection communication latency associated with transferring intermediate parameters. In the experiment, we consider the communication latency l_n^{com} equals d_n^p and test its value.

Initially, we consider the interconnect via an SSH connection. The measured average l_n^{com} is recorded at 0.1039 s. Despite SSH having certain latency, it still has the advantage of facilitating distributed computing, upon network availability.

To reduce network latency, wireless networking emerges as a viable option for interconnection. In the test, the temperature is 290 K, and the B_n is 160 MHz. We measure an S_n of $10^{-3.90}$ mW. According to Equation (2), we calculate an ω_n of $10^{-9.19}$ mW in wireless networks. According to Equation (2), the SNR_n can be computed as $10^{5.29}$. After obtaining the SNR_n, according to Equation (3), we can calculate C_n as 2.796×10^9 bit/s. Converting 2.796×10^9 bits per second to megabytes per second gives 349.5 MB/s. The D_n is 64 bytes, according to Equation (4), we can calculate the minimum d_n^p as 1.748×10^{-7} s. Based on the results, we ascertain that the observed value of l_n^{com} is less than 0.001 s. The experiment meets expectations. Consequently, it can be inferred that the influence of using wireless on LLM is insignificant.

After testing interconnection communication latency, we test the local communication latency on the local device, We record the value of s_n^{dc} as 2.135 GBps and record the value of s_n^{cg} as 12.46 GBps. For the quantized LLM weights in the LLM, each layer is approximately 0.55 GB.

If the weight only loads from the CPU's RAM, according to Equation (5), the l_n^{cg} for each layer is approximately 0.044 s. However, if the weight loads from the disk, according to Equation (6), the l_n^{dc} for each layer is approximately 0.26 s. According to Equation (7), the l_n^{dg} for each layer is approximately 0.304 s. We assume that in the device, eight layers offload to CPU's RAM, and eight layers offload to disk, according to Equation (8), the l_n^{loc} can be calculated as 2.784 s. It is evident that the disk speed significantly influences the inference speed.

We find that opting for high-performance disks can significantly reduce latency. After using the high-performance NVMe drive, we boost the s_n^{dc} to 3.166 GBps. According to Equation (6), the l_n^{dc} is approximately calculated as 0.17 s. To calculate performance improvement, we denote the improvement performance as *Improvement*, while the original latency is denoted as *Original* and *Improved* is the improved latency. The formula is

$$Improvement = \left(\frac{Original - Improved}{Original}\right) \times 100\%. \qquad (10)$$

According to Equation (10), we can calculate that the performance improvement is approximately 32%.

Similarly, loading the majority of the model weights into the CPU's RAM leads to a substantial reduction in latency. However, in terms of the model's performance, the impact is only on latency and does not affect its inference capabilities.

Finally, we can calculate the l^{total}. We assume there are 32 IoMT devices similar to our device. Each device has one layer in the model. We use SSH connections and offload the weights to disk. According to Equation (9), we can approximately calculate the l^{total} as 13.16 s. If we offload the model weights to the CPU's RAM and use SSH connections, we can approximately calculate the l^{total} as 4.837 s. If we offload the model weights to the CPU's RAM and use the wireless connection, we can approximately calculate the l^{total} as 1.408 s.

5. Discussion and Limitations

The results demonstrate that our MedMixtral 8x7B, fine-tuned on the HealthCareMagic-100k dataset, excels in answering medical questions.

The robust performance of the MedMixtral 8x7B model is largely attributed to the extensive medical Q&A data provided by the HealthCareMagic-100k fine-tuning dataset. However, the model's remarkable performance cannot be solely attributed to its comprehensive learning of the dataset. The superior performance of MedMixtral 8x7B may also stem from the unique advantages of the MoE architecture in addressing medical Q&A issues. During the learning process, MedMixtral 8x7B, with its multiple experts, allows different experts to acquire diverse aspects of medical knowledge. When answering medical questions, the gate evaluates the input query and selects two suitable experts to respond. This method, which involves choosing a few experts rather than combining the opinions of all experts, reduces the model's bias and enhances accuracy.

Our model, fine-tuned on the HealthCareMagic-100k dataset, surpasses traditional models such as ChatGPT and Llama3 in terms of precision, recall, and F1 score. Moreover, MedMixtral 8x7B is compatible with our proposed efficient inference offloading architecture. Our efficient inference offloading algorithm dynamically adjusts the number of experts per layer based on available VRAM, thereby reducing resource consumption. By employing the LRU cache strategy and introducing model weight offloading techniques, MedMixtral 8x7B exhibits lower VRAM usage during deployment, making it a potential candidate for IoMT devices. Compared to other large LLMs, MedMixtral 8x7B offers superior or comparable medical Q&A capabilities with reduced resource consumption—utilizing VRAM typically required by models under 10B in size. Compared to other small LLMs deployable on IoMT devices, MedMixtral 8x7B provides a significant performance advantage in medical Q&As. Additionally, deploying MedMixtral 8x7B locally can effectively protect user privacy and mitigate network security risks.

In addition to addressing resource requirements, we examined the impact of latency on LLM inference speed. Through investigating local and interconnection communication models, we identified key factors affecting latency, including device interconnection methods, offloading locations, and disk speeds. We propose strategies to reduce latency, such as enhancing disk speed and utilizing wireless communication instead of SSH connections.

Our study highlights the potential of MedMixtral 8x7B in answering medical questions. Below, we discuss the limitations and outline directions for future research.

5.1. Hallucinations in LLMs within Medical Settings

Despite the promising results, our manual evaluation on consumer medical Q&A datasets indicates that the accuracy of existing LLMs remains insufficient. Models like ChatGPT and MedMixtral 8x7B may generate inaccurate answers in the medical domain, posing significant safety risks. In the future, we aim to enhance accuracy and safety by integrating techniques such as chain of thought (CoT), thereby narrowing the gap between these models and real-world clinicians, and facilitating quicker clinical adoption.

5.2. Expansion of the HealthCareMagic-100k Dataset

The HealthCareMagic-100k dataset encompasses a variety of medical Q&As from diverse sources, but it is not exhaustive. We plan to expand this dataset to include a broader range of medical Q&As. During this expansion, preprocessing data obtained from patients presents a challenge. Compared to multiple-choice tasks, preprocessing Q&A tasks is more complex. The varied tones and expressions in Q&A pairs affect LLM fine-tuning, requiring experimentation to determine which types of Q&As yield the best learning outcomes. We aim to preprocess the data accordingly for optimal results. Additionally, the HealthCareMagic-100k dataset is purely in English. In the future, we will seek to incorporate multilingual Q&As and evaluate multilingual capabilities.

5.3. Improving Evaluation Methods

We evaluated model performance on the iCliniq dataset, using metrics such as precision, recall, and F1 score, with BERTscore as our evaluation method. While BERTscore's advantage lies in its ability to assess answers' similarity to human responses, offering a more realistic measure than conventional test questions, its drawback is that it only measures similarity and not specific accuracy. Given the critical nature of medical Q&As, where errors can have severe consequences, we plan to incorporate additional evaluation methods, such as multiple-choice questions, to enhance the fairness and comprehensiveness of model assessments.

6. Conclusions

Through development and fine-tuning based on the HealthCareMagic-100k dataset, our MedMixtral 8x7B model has emerged as a new solution deployable in the medical Q&A domain, particularly on consumer devices such as IoMT devices. Its outstanding performance is attributed not only to the richness of the fine-tuned dataset but also to the utilization of the MoE architecture in the base model, which incorporates multiple experts to reduce bias and enhance accuracy.

Moreover, the integration of MedMixtral 8x7B with efficient inference offloading architectures makes it an excellent LLM deployable on medical IoMT devices. By dynamically adjusting resource allocation based on available VRAM and employing techniques like LRU cache and model weight offloading, MedMixtral 8x7B demonstrates remarkable medical Q&A capabilities while minimizing resource consumption. This gives it a significant advantage over larger language models and smaller deployable alternatives, while also maximizing user privacy protection and mitigating network attack concerns on IoMT devices.

Finally, strategies for reducing latency were explored, indicating that optimizing device interconnection methods, optimizing weight offloading locations, and enhancing disk speed all contribute to improving the overall efficiency and performance of MedMixtral 8x7B, enabling faster and more reliable inference. This positions it as one of the most suitable medical Q&A LLMs for deployment on IoMT devices.

Author Contributions: In this project, X.Y. and W.K. contributed to resource allocation, methodology development, software implementation, data validation, formal analysis, and original draft writing. X.Y. also contributed to supervision, and funding acquisition. Z.L. and M.X. contributed to conceptualization, formal analysis, investigation, and visualization. All authors have read and agreed to the published version of the manuscript.

Funding: This research was supported in part by the National Natural Science Foundation of China (62371116), in part by the Science and Technology Project of Hebei Province Education Department (ZD2022164), and in part by the Project of Hebei Key Laboratory of Software Engineering (22567637H).

Data Availability Statement: Data are contained within the article.

Acknowledgments: We would like to thank the editors and the anonymous reviewers for their insightful comments and constructive suggestions.

Conflicts of Interest: The authors declare no conflicts of interest.

Abbreviations

Symbol	Description in Device n
B_n	Channel bandwidth
C_n	Channel capacity
d_n^p	Propagation delay
d_n^{pr}	Processing delay
d_n^q	Queueing delay
d_n^w	Waiting delay
D_n	Data volume
k	Boltzmann constant
l_n^{cg}	Latency from the CPU's RAM to the GPU's VRAM
l_n^{com}	Interconnection communication latency
l_n^{dc}	Latency from the disk to the CPU's RAM
l_n^{dg}	Latency from the disk to the GPU's VRAM
l_n^{loc}	Local communication latency
$\mathcal{N}$	Set of IoMT devices
w_n	Model weight for one layer
s_n^{cg}	Speed from the CPU's RAM to the GPU's VRAM
s_n^{dc}	Speed from the disk to the CPU's RAM
S_n	Signal power
SNR_n	Signal-to-noise ratio
T	Absolute temperature in kelvin
l^{total}	Total communication latency
x_n	The number of model layers in device n
y_n	The number of model layers offloading in the disk in device n
ω_n	White Gaussian noise

References

1. Vaswani, A.; Shazeer, N.; Parmar, N.; Uszkoreit, J.; Jones, L.; Gomez, A.N.; Kaiser, Ł.; Polosukhin, I. Attention is all you need. In Proceedings of the Advances in Neural Information Processing Systems, Long Beach, CA, USA, 4–9 December 2017; pp. 5998–6008.
2. Amin, S.U.; Hossain, M.S. Edge intelligence and Internet of Things in healthcare: A survey. *IEEE Access* **2020**, *9*, 45–59. [CrossRef]
3. Xu, M.; Niyato, D.; Zhang, H.; Kang, J.; Xiong, Z.; Mao, S.; Han, Z. Cached Model-as-a-Resource: Provisioning Large Language Model Agents for Edge Intelligence in Space-air-ground Integrated Networks. *arXiv* **2024**, arXiv:2403.05826.
4. Xu, M.; Dusit, N.; Kang, J.; Xiong, Z.; Mao, S.; Han, Z.; Kim, D.I.; Letaief, K.B. When large language model agents meet 6g networks: Perception, grounding, and alignment. *arXiv* **2024**, arXiv:2401.07764.
5. Jiang, A.Q.; Sablayrolles, A.; Roux, A.; Mensch, A.; Savary, B.; Bamford, C.; Chaplot, D.S.; de las Casas, D.; Hanna, E.B.; Bressand, F.; et al. Mixtral of experts. *arXiv* **2024**, arXiv:2401.04088.
6. Eliseev, A.; Mazur, D. Fast inference of mixture-of-experts language models with offloading. *arXiv* **2023**, arXiv:2312.17238.
7. Gugger, S.; Debut, L.; Wolf, T.; Schmid, P.; Mueller, Z.; Mangrulkar, S.; Sun, M.; Bossan, B. Accelerate: Training and Inference at Scale Made Simple, Efficient and Adaptable. 2022. Available online: https://github.com/huggingface/accelerate (accessed on 6 March 2021).
8. Radford, A.; Narasimhan, K.; Salimans, T.; Sutskever, I. Improving Language Understanding by Generative Pre-Training. 2018. Available online: https://www.mikecaptain.com/resources/pdf/GPT-1.pdf (accessed on 11 June 2018).

9. Radford, A.; Wu, J.; Child, R.; Luan, D.; Amodei, D.; Sutskever, I. Language models are unsupervised multitask learners. *OpenAI Blog* **2019**, *1*, 9.
10. Brown, T.; Mann, B.; Ryder, N.; Subbiah, M.; Kaplan, J.D.; Dhariwal, P.; Neelakantan, A.; Shyam, P.; Sastry, G.; Askell, A.; et al. Language models are few-shot learners. *Adv. Neural Inf. Process. Syst.* **2020**, *33*, 1877–1901.
11. Ouyang, L.; Wu, J.; Jiang, X.; Almeida, D.; Wainwright, C.; Mishkin, P.; Zhang, C.; Agarwal, S.; Slama, K.; Ray, A.; et al. Training language models to follow instructions with human feedback. *Adv. Neural Inf. Process. Syst.* **2022**, *35*, 27730–27744.
12. Achiam, J.; Adler, S.; Agarwal, S.; Ahmad, L.; Akkaya, I.; Aleman, F.L.; Almeida, D.; Altenschmidt, J.; Altman, S.; Anadkat, S.; et al. Gpt-4 technical report. *arXiv* **2023**, arXiv:2303.08774.
13. Zhao, W.X.; Zhou, K.; Li, J.; Tang, T.; Wang, X.; Hou, Y.; Min, Y.; Zhang, B.; Zhang, J.; Dong, Z.; et al. A survey of large language models. *arXiv* **2023**, arXiv:2303.18223.
14. Devlin, J.; Chang, M.W.; Lee, K.; Toutanova, K. Bert: Pre-training of deep bidirectional transformers for language understanding. *arXiv* **2018**, arXiv:1810.04805.
15. Liu, Y.; Ott, M.; Goyal, N.; Du, J.; Joshi, M.; Chen, D.; Levy, O.; Lewis, M.; Zettlemoyer, L.; Stoyanov, V. Roberta: A robustly optimized bert pretraining approach. *arXiv* **2019**, arXiv:1907.11692.
16. Raffel, C.; Shazeer, N.; Roberts, A.; Lee, K.; Narang, S.; Matena, M.; Zhou, Y.; Li, W.; Liu, P.J. Exploring the limits of transfer learning with a unified text-to-text transformer. *J. Mach. Learn. Res.* **2020**, *21*, 1–67.
17. Touvron, H.; Lavril, T.; Izacard, G.; Martinet, X.; Lachaux, M.A.; Lacroix, T.; Rozière, B.; Goyal, N.; Hambro, E.; Azhar, F.; et al. LLaMA: Open and Efficient Foundation Language Models. *arXiv* **2023**, arXiv:2302.13971.
18. Touvron, H.; Martin, L.; Stone, K.; Albert, P.; Almahairi, A.; Babaei, Y.; Bashlykov, N.; Batra, S.; Bhargava, P.; Bhosale, S.; et al. Llama 2: Open foundation and fine-tuned chat models. *arXiv* **2023**, arXiv:2307.09288.
19. Zhang, S.; Roller, S.; Goyal, N.; Artetxe, M.; Chen, M.; Chen, S.; Dewan, C.; Diab, M.; Li, X.; Lin, X.V.; et al. Opt: Open pre-trained transformer language models. *arXiv* **2022**, arXiv:2205.01068.
20. Zhang, Z.; Han, X.; Zhou, H.; Ke, P.; Gu, Y.; Ye, D.; Qin, Y.; Su, Y.; Ji, H.; Guan, J.; et al. CPM: A large-scale generative Chinese pre-trained language model. *AI Open* **2021**, *2*, 93–99. [CrossRef]
21. Zhang, Z.; Gu, Y.; Han, X.; Chen, S.; Xiao, C.; Sun, Z.; Yao, Y.; Qi, F.; Guan, J.; Ke, P.; et al. Cpm-2: Large-scale cost-effective pre-trained language models. *AI Open* **2021**, *2*, 216–224. [CrossRef]
22. Nijkamp, E.; Pang, B.; Hayashi, H.; Tu, L.; Wang, H.; Zhou, Y.; Savarese, S.; Xiong, C. Codegen: An open large language model for code with multi-turn program synthesis. *arXiv* **2022**, arXiv:2203.13474.
23. Le Scao, T.; Fan, A.; Akiki, C.; Pavlick, E.; Ilić, S.; Hesslow, D.; Castagné, R.; Luccioni, A.S.; Yvon, F.; Gallé, M.; et al. Bloom: A 176b-Parameter Open-Access Multilingual Language Model. 2023. Available online: https://inria.hal.science/hal-03850124/ (accessed on 20 November 2023).
24. Zeng, A.; Liu, X.; Du, Z.; Wang, Z.; Lai, H.; Ding, M.; Yang, Z.; Xu, Y.; Zheng, W.; Xia, X.; et al. Glm-130b: An open bilingual pre-trained model. *arXiv* **2022**, arXiv:2210.02414.
25. Luo, R.; Sun, L.; Xia, Y.; Qin, T.; Zhang, S.; Poon, H.; Liu, T.Y. BioGPT: Generative pre-trained transformer for biomedical text generation and mining. *Briefings Bioinform.* **2022**, *23*, bbac409. [CrossRef] [PubMed]
26. Singhal, K.; Azizi, S.; Tu, T.; Mahdavi, S.S.; Wei, J.; Chung, H.W.; Scales, N.; Tanwani, A.; Cole-Lewis, H.; Pfohl, S.; et al. Large language models encode clinical knowledge. *arXiv* **2022**, arXiv:2212.13138.
27. Singhal, K.; Tu, T.; Gottweis, J.; Sayres, R.; Wulczyn, E.; Hou, L.; Clark, K.; Pfohl, S.; Cole-Lewis, H.; Neal, D.; et al. Towards expert-level medical question answering with large language models. *arXiv* **2023**, arXiv:2305.09617.
28. Rasley, J.; Rajbhandari, S.; Ruwase, O.; He, Y. Deepspeed: System optimizations enable training deep learning models with over 100 billion parameters. In Proceedings of the 26th ACM SIGKDD International Conference on Knowledge Discovery & Data Mining, Virtual Event, 6–10 July 2020; pp. 3505–3506.
29. Shoeybi, M.; Patwary, M.; Puri, R.; LeGresley, P.; Casper, J.; Catanzaro, B. Megatron-lm: Training multi-billion parameter language models using model parallelism. *arXiv* **2019**, arXiv:1909.08053.
30. Kwon, W.; Li, Z.; Zhuang, S.; Sheng, Y.; Zheng, L.; Yu, C.H.; Gonzalez, J.; Zhang, H.; Stoica, I. Efficient memory management for large language model serving with pagedattention. In Proceedings of the 29th Symposium on Operating Systems Principles, Koblenz, Germany, 23–26 October 2023; pp. 611–626.
31. Zhao, Y.; Gu, A.; Varma, R.; Luo, L.; Huang, C.C.; Xu, M.; Wright, L.; Shojanazeri, H.; Ott, M.; Shleifer, S.; et al. Pytorch fsdp: Experiences on scaling fully sharded data parallel. *arXiv* **2023**, arXiv:2304.11277.
32. Han, P.; Wang, S.; Leung, K.K. Adaptive gradient sparsification for efficient federated learning: An online learning approach. In Proceedings of the 2020 IEEE 40th International Conference on Distributed Computing Systems (ICDCS), Singapore, 29 November–1 December 2020; pp. 300–310.
33. Han, P.; Wang, S.; Jiao, Y.; Huang, J. Federated Learning While Providing Model as a Service: Joint Training and Inference Optimization. *arXiv* **2023**, arXiv:2312.12863.
34. Piovesan, N.; López-Pérez, D.; De Domenico, A.; Geng, X.; Bao, H.; Debbah, M. Machine learning and analytical power consumption models for 5G base stations. *IEEE Commun. Mag.* **2022**, *60*, 56–62. [CrossRef]
35. Ayed, F.; De Domenico, A.; Garcia-Rodriguez, A.; López-Pérez, D. Accordion: A communication-aware machine learning framework for next generation networks. *IEEE Commun. Mag.* **2023**, *61*, 104–110. [CrossRef]

36. Du, Y.; Liew, S.C.; Chen, K.; Shao, Y. The power of large language models for wireless communication system development: A case study on fpga platforms. *arXiv* **2023**, arXiv:2307.07319.
37. Bariah, L.; Zhao, Q.; Zou, H.; Tian, Y.; Bader, F.; Debbah, M. Large language models for telecom: The next big thing? *arXiv* **2023**, arXiv:2306.10249.
38. Bariah, L.; Zou, H.; Zhao, Q.; Mouhouche, B.; Bader, F.; Debbah, M. Understanding telecom language through large language models. In Proceedings of the GLOBECOM 2023—2023 IEEE Global Communications Conference, Kuala Lumpur, Malaysia, 4–8 December 2023; pp. 6542–6547.
39. Soman, S.; HG, R. Observations on LLMs for telecom domain: Capabilities and limitations. *arXiv* **2023**, arXiv:2305.13102.
40. Zhang, T.; Xu, C.; Lian, Y.; Tian, H.; Kang, J.; Kuang, X.; Niyato, D. When Moving Target Defense Meets Attack Prediction in Digital Twins: A Convolutional and Hierarchical Reinforcement Learning Approach. *IEEE J. Sel. Areas Commun.* **2023**, *41*, 3293–3305. [CrossRef]
41. Zhang, T.; Xu, C.; Shen, J.; Kuang, X.; Grieco, L.A. How to Disturb Network Reconnaissance: A Moving Target Defense Approach Based on Deep Reinforcement Learning. *IEEE Trans. Inf. Forensics Secur.* **2023**, *18*, 5735–5748. [CrossRef]
42. Zhang, T.; Xu, C.; Zou, P.; Tian, H.; Kuang, X.; Yang, S.; Zhong, L.; Niyato, D. How to mitigate DDoS intelligently in SD-IoV: A moving target defense approach. *IEEE Trans. Ind. Inform.* **2022**, *19*, 1097–1106. [CrossRef]
43. Fedus, W.; Zoph, B.; Shazeer, N. Switch transformers: Scaling to trillion parameter models with simple and efficient sparsity. *J. Mach. Learn. Res.* **2022**, *23*, 1–39.
44. Li, Y.; Li, Z.; Zhang, K.; Dan, R.; Jiang, S.; Zhang, Y. ChatDoctor: A Medical Chat Model Fine-Tuned on a Large Language Model Meta-AI (LLaMA) Using Medical Domain Knowledge. *Cureus* **2023**, *15*, e40895. [CrossRef]
45. Hu, E.J.; Shen, Y.; Wallis, P.; Allen-Zhu, Z.; Li, Y.; Wang, S.; Wang, L.; Chen, W. Lora: Low-rank adaptation of large language models. *arXiv* **2021**, arXiv:2106.09685.

Disclaimer/Publisher's Note: The statements, opinions and data contained in all publications are solely those of the individual author(s) and contributor(s) and not of MDPI and/or the editor(s). MDPI and/or the editor(s) disclaim responsibility for any injury to people or property resulting from any ideas, methods, instructions or products referred to in the content.

Article

CSIM: A Fast Community Detection Algorithm Based on Structure Information Maximization

Yiwei Liu [1], Wencong Liu [2], Xiangyun Tang [3], Hao Yin [4], Peng Yin [1,5], Xin Xu [1] and Yanbin Wang [6,*]

1. Defence Industry Secrecy Examination and Certification Center, Beijing 100089, China; yiweiliu_disecc@163.com (Y.L.); yinpeng@iie.ac.cn (P.Y.); xuxin@iie.ac.cn (X.X.)
2. School of Computer Science and Technology, Beijing Institute of Technology, Beijing 100081, China; 3120191093@bit.edu.cn
3. School of Information Engineering, Minzu University of China, Beijing 100081, China; xiangyunt@muc.edu.cn
4. Research Center of Cyberspace Security, PKU-Changsha Institute for Computing and Digital Economy, Changsha 410205, China; yinhao@icode.pku.edu.cn
5. School of Cyber Security, University of Chinese Academy of Sciences, Beijing 100085, China
6. College of Computer Science and Technology, Zhejiang University, Hangzhou 310027, China
* Correspondence: wangyanbin15@mails.ucas.ac.cn

Abstract: Community detection has been a subject of extensive research due to its broad applications across social media, computer science, biology, and complex systems. Modularity stands out as a predominant metric guiding community detection, with numerous algorithms aimed at maximizing modularity. However, modularity encounters a resolution limit problem when identifying small community structures. To tackle this challenge, this paper presents a novel approach by defining community structure information from the perspective of encoding edge information. This pioneering definition lays the foundation for the proposed fast community detection algorithm CSIM, boasting an average time complexity of only $O(n \log n)$. Experimental results showcase that communities identified via the CSIM algorithm across various graph data types closely resemble ground truth community structures compared to those revealed via modularity-based algorithms. Furthermore, CSIM not only boasts lower time complexity than greedy algorithms optimizing community structure information but also achieves superior optimization results. Notably, in cyclic network graphs, CSIM surpasses modularity-based algorithms in effectively addressing the resolution limit problem.

Keywords: networks; community detection; structure entropy; community structure information; modularity

Citation: Liu, Y.; Liu, W.; Tang, X.; Yin, H.; Yin, P.; Xu, X.; Wang, Y. CSIM: A Fast Community Detection Algorithm Based on Structure Information Maximization. *Electronics* **2024**, *13*, 1119. https://doi.org/10.3390/electronics13061119

Academic Editor: Christos J. Bouras

Received: 9 January 2024
Revised: 12 March 2024
Accepted: 13 March 2024
Published: 19 March 2024

Copyright: © 2024 by the authors. Licensee MDPI, Basel, Switzerland. This article is an open access article distributed under the terms and conditions of the Creative Commons Attribution (CC BY) license (https://creativecommons.org/licenses/by/4.0/).

1. Introduction

In various fields such as social media, computer science, biology, management science, and engineering, complex systems are often represented in the form of complex networks. These complex networks can be depicted as graphs in graph theory, where nodes in the graph represent entities in the system, and edges represent interactions between entities [1]. For example, in online social networks, nodes may represent users on the platform, and edges could signify friendship relationships or shared interests [2,3], and in a blockchain network, nodes represent participants such as individuals, companies, or servers that execute transactions, while edges represent the connections or interactions between these nodes, often symbolizing specific transactions. Due to varying degrees of connectivity between nodes of different types, these natural connections between nodes inherently facilitate the formation of communities. Communities are subsets of nodes within the network that are tightly connected internally but have sparse connections between them. Communities often reflect common characteristics among nodes, such as similar backgrounds in social networks or related functionalities in cellular metabolism [4–6].

Measuring the community structure within networks holds significant implications for understanding complex systems and characterizing organizational structures. Consequently, metrics for community structure have rapidly garnered widespread attention in computer science, leading to the introduction of several prominent measures such as modularity [7], modular density [8], surprise [9], and permanence [10], among others. Among these metrics, modularity, initially proposed by Newman and Girvan [11], stands out as the most renowned and widely applied. A specific class of community detection algorithms is designed to optimize modularity. For example, hierarchical clustering optimization has been utilized to optimize modularity [12], simulated annealing has been introduced into modularity optimization [13], extremum optimization methods have been employed for modularity optimization [14], the optimization of modularity using eigenvalues and eigenvectors of special matrices has been explored [15], and mathematical programming has been introduced for modularity optimization [16], among others. Among these, the Louvain algorithm [12] has become the most commonly used algorithm due to its low time complexity and high accuracy [17].

Despite the widespread application of modularity, it possesses inherent limitations, with the most notable being the resolution limit problem [18]. This refers to modularity optimization's inability to detect communities smaller than a certain threshold, presenting a challenge, particularly in networks with heterogeneous communities or when certain communities are substantially smaller than the overall network. In such instances, modularity-based community detection algorithms may overlook or merge smaller substructures, resulting in a loss of granularity in community delineation. This challenge stems from the inherent difficulty of the modularity function in striking an optimal balance between the number and size of communities, potentially merging or obscuring small-scale communities and impacting the accuracy and completeness of the detection process. In response to this challenge, researchers have proposed various modifications and alternative metrics [8,19]. However, these methods often address specific scenarios and come with high time complexity.

In 2015, Li et al. introduced an information-theoretic measure of network complexity termed the structure entropy of networks [20]. Structure entropy, defined for a graph, G, represents the average number of bits required to identify the codes of a node, v accessible from a step of random walk in G relative to a stationary distribution. They subsequently proposed an algorithm for community detection in networks by minimizing structure entropy, claiming that their approach achieves a more balanced community size compared to modularity optimization algorithms. While their research presents a promising avenue for community detection, the concept of structural entropy, derived from coded random walks, may pose challenges in terms of intuitiveness and comprehension for some researchers. Furthermore, their proposed algorithm exhibits higher time complexity compared to the widely used Louvain algorithm [12], hindering its widespread adoption and application in practical scenarios.

In summary, current research in community detection confronts several challenges that warrant attention and further exploration. Firstly, modularity-based algorithms such as Louvain, while renowned for their efficiency with low time complexity, are hindered by the resolution limit problem. This limitation poses a significant obstacle, particularly when dealing with networks exhibiting high heterogeneity or containing small-scale communities that may be overlooked or merged. Secondly, methods based on structural entropy have emerged as promising alternatives, boasting claims of achieving a harmonious balance between community size and quantity. However, the concept of structural entropy, derived from coded random walks, presents a steep learning curve and may prove less intuitive and accessible to researchers unfamiliar with its intricacies. Moreover, while some approaches, including those leveraging structural entropy, offer potential solutions to the resolution limit problem in certain contexts, they often come with higher algorithmic complexity. This increased computational overhead may limit their practical applicability, particularly in scenarios where computational resources are limited or where real-time processing is required.

In this paper, we aim to address the above challenging issues. Specifically, we define community structure information as the average amount of information that can be compressed per edge, given a known community structure, providing a more intuitive representation of the essence of structural entropy. Secondly, drawing inspiration from the Louvain algorithm, we introduce a fast community detection algorithm that optimizes the value of community structure information. Finally, we validate the practical effectiveness of the algorithm through experiments. The main contributions of this paper are summarized as follows:

- We introduce a novel approach to defining structural entropy by focusing on the encoding of edge information, named community structure information. This approach calculates the difference in the number of bytes required to encode an edge under unknown and known community structures, capturing the amount of information leaked via the community structure.
- We propose an algorithm, CSIM, for the approximate calculation of the maximum community structure information, which can be employed for community detection. Notably, for a social network with n nodes, the time complexity is the same as that of the Louvain algorithm, with both having an average time complexity of $O(n \log n)$.
- We conducted experiments on real-world network data, and the results demonstrate that the computational output of our proposed algorithm closely approximates the maximum value of community structure information. Furthermore, the community structure obtained through this algorithm aligns more closely with the ground truth community structure.

We organized the paper as follows. Section 2 presents an overview of related works on the measure of complex networks, community detection, and structure entropy. In Section 3, we provide the definition of community structure information from the perspective of encoding edge information and subsequently quantify the information leaked via the community structure. In Section 4, we introduce a novel community detection algorithm that maximizes community structure information, accompanied by proof of the algorithm's time complexity. In Section 5, we evaluate and analyze the performance of our algorithm using real-world network data. In Section 6, we discuss the contributions and implications of our study. Finally, we conclude our work in Section 7.

2. Related Work

In this section, we mainly focus on the related works on the metrics for structural information in complex network, community detection, and structure entropy.

2.1. Metrics for Structural Information

In the domain of information theory, the precise quantification of structural information poses a prominent challenge to computer and information science. Rashevsky [21] is acknowledged for pioneering the initial measurement of complex networks, inaugurating efforts to capture the intricacies of structural information. Over the years, researchers have introduced a myriad of metrics targeting the delineation of structural complexities across diverse network types, including notable measures like Shannon entropy, von Neumann entropy [22], parametric graph entropy [23], and Gibbs entropy [24], among others.

While these traditional information metrics have made significant contributions, many essentially represent variations of Shannon entropy tailored to distinct distribution types. Recognizing the necessity of innovative approaches, recent advancements have explored alternative perspectives on structural information [25].

Recognizing the importance of community structure in real-world networks, Newman [26] introduced modularity as a metric to assess the strength of community divisions within a network, becoming instrumental in uncovering underlying structures and patterns in complex systems. Drawing inspiration from random walks, Rosvall et al. [27] proposed a novel metric calculating the average bits per step, leveraging ergodic node visit frequencies within a network. This approach provides a nuanced understanding of structural information dynamics. Describing structural information, Li et al. [20,25] introduced the concept of K-dimensional structural entropy for graphs, defining it as the minimum bits required to encode a vertex accessible from a random walk step. This metric explores the multidimensional aspects of structural information, offering a more comprehensive characterization.

Additionally, Zhang et al. [28] proposed a novel metric of structural entropy for complex networks, drawing on nonextensive statistical mechanics to enhance comprehension of complex network structures and characteristics. Liu et al. [29] introduced A-entropy and B-entropy, metrics tailored to gauge self-reinforcing substructures within multi-agent systems. Zhang et al. [30] proposed betweenness structural entropy based on betweenness centrality, with the goal of shedding light on the structural organization and dynamics of complex systems represented by networks. Cai et al. [31] presented SP structure entropy, aiming to capture the complexity and organization of networks, especially those characterized by series-parallel components.

Recent advancements highlight a transition towards more diverse and nuanced methods for measuring structural information in complex networks, surpassing conventional entropy-based metrics. Drawing inspiration from these metrics, this paper introduces a novel approach to gauging structured information by encoding edge information perspectives.

2.2. Community Detection

Community detection, a crucial task in unveiling concealed structures within complex networks, traces its rich history back to 1955, when Weiss and Jacobson pioneered the analysis, leveraging relationships among members in government organizations to discern working groups [32]. In contemporary times, the prevalence of complex networks, spanning online social networks, online transaction networks [33], transportation networks, and biological information networks [34,35], has provided fertile ground for the evolution of community detection research.

Scholars from diverse disciplines have contributed myriad community detection algorithms, each offering unique perspectives. Notably, algorithms for detecting non-overlapping communities span various methodologies, including graph splitting [11,36], spectral analysis [37,38], modularity optimization [15,16,39–41], information theory [20,27], and others [42–44].

In recent years, traditional neural network approaches have been extended to handle graph data, enabling the swift advancement of graph neural networks for community detection. By directly applying filtering operations to the graph, graph neural networks acquire a concise representation of nodes through semi-supervised training methods [45]. This node representation plays a crucial role in tasks such as node classification and community detection [46]. Representative approaches include recurrent graph neural networks [47], spectral-based convolutional graph neural networks [48], spatial-based convolutional graph neural networks [49], graph autoencoders [50], and spatial-temporal graph neural networks [51].

Among these algorithms, the multilevel modularity optimization algorithm known as Louvain, proposed by Blondel et al. [12], stands out as the most renowned and widely adopted. This algorithm excels in both accuracy and efficiency, contributing significantly to the field. However, despite its widespread application, notable limitations persist, with the resolution limit problem [18] emerging as a prominent concern. Future research may explore novel algorithms that address these limitations and further enhance the efficacy of community detection in complex networks.

2.3. Structure Entropy

In 1953, Shannon [52] proposed addressing communication system issues through quantifying structural information. Over the past seventy years, this problem has remained a significant challenge in information science and computer science. In 2016, Li and Pan [25] introduced the concept of K-dimensional structural entropy as a measure of the structural information of networks, which has since garnered extensive research attention. This concept provides a deeper understanding of the multidimensional aspects of structural information, offering insights into the complexity of network structures. Minimizing K-dimensional structural entropy serves as a principle for detecting natural or ground truth structures in real-world networks [20].

Furthermore, the notion of graph resistance was introduced as a complementary concept to structural entropy, measuring a graph's resistance against strategic virus attacks that cause cascading failures [53]. Li et al. [54] applied structural entropy to decode topologically associated domains in Hi-C data with ultra-low resolution, demonstrating its applicability in deciphering complex genomic structures. Moreover, Liu et al. [55] proposed community-based structural entropy to express information leakage in community structures and used it to preserve the privacy of community structures, showcasing the versatility of structural entropy in diverse contexts.

In addition, Hirai et al. [56] introduced structural entropy as a measure to assess uncertainty in latent structures within data, aiming to provide insights into the reliability and stability of structural patterns. Wang et al. [57] introduced DS-entropy and applied it to perform label-specificity attacks, emphasizing the role of structural entropy in addressing security and privacy concerns in network data. Tian et al. [58] proposed a novel approach based on structural entropy in social IoT networks, aiming to protect sensitive information while enabling a meaningful analysis of network structure and clustering patterns. Liu et al. [59] presented a graph-generative algorithm based on structural entropy, demonstrating its utility in generating synthetic networks that preserve key structural characteristics.

In summary, the applications of structural entropy are increasingly widespread [60,61], spanning various domains including genomics, network security, privacy preservation, and network synthesis. Inspired by the aforementioned studies, this paper introduces a novel representation of structural information from the perspective of encoding edge information, further contributing to the diverse applications and advancements in structural entropy analysis.

3. Community Structure Information

In this section, we first address the problems with the definition of modularity. Building upon the research of these problems, we introduce the definition of community structure information to overcome the shortcomings of modularity.

3.1. The Problem of Modularity

Modularity stands as the most frequently employed metric for guiding community detection, utilized in methods like simulated annealing [62], extremal optimization [14], and greedy approaches [63]. Grounded in the idea that a random graph should lack a community structure, modularity is calculated as the difference between the actual density of edges in a community and the expected density of the edges that are constructed regardless of community structure [2]. The anticipated edge density is contingent on the chosen null model, which involves creating a copy of the original graph while maintaining the same degree distribution but devoid of any community structure. Elevated discrepancies indicate the potential existence of communities.

Suppose an undirected graph, $G = (V, E)$, consists of a node set, V, and an edge set, E. Let the number of edges between nodes i and j be denoted with A_{ij}, typically 0 or 1, although larger values are possible in networks allowing multiple edges. The quantities A_{ij} are the elements of the adjacency matrix. Simultaneously, the expected number of edges between nodes i and j, if edges are randomly placed, is $d_i d_j / 2L$, where d_i and d_j are the degrees of the nodes, and $L = 1/2 \sum_i d_i$ is the total number of edges in the network. Thus, the modularity Q is the sum of $A_{ij} - d_i d_j / 2L$ over all pairs of nodes i, j that fall in the same community. If $C = \{C_1, C_2, \ldots, C_S\}$ represents the community partition of G, then the modularity associated with C is determined as follows [64]:

$$Q_C = \frac{1}{2L} \sum_{i,j} (A_{ij} - \frac{d_i d_j}{2L}) \delta_{ij}, \quad (1)$$

where $\delta_{ij} = 1$ if $i, j \in C_s$ for some $1 \leq s \leq S$ and $\delta_{ij} = 0$ if not. This equation can be simplified to the following:

$$Q_C = \sum_{s=1}^{S} [\frac{l_s}{L} - (\frac{v_s}{2L})^2], \quad (2)$$

where S is the number of communities, l_s is the number of edges inside community C_s, L is the total number of edges in the network, and v_s is the total degree of the nodes in community C_s.

This definition introduces a novel perspective on measuring community detection, specifically the distinction between a real graph and a null model with the same degree distribution. However, certain issues in this definition warrant further consideration:

- The contribution term $\frac{l_s}{L} - (\frac{v_s}{2L})^2$ for community C_s in modularity is a linear function of l_s plus a quadratic function of v_s. This implies that the contribution of adding a new edge within community C_s to the Q_C value linearly diminishes with the scale of v_s. However, intuitively, this decay should be superlinear. For example, in two communities with the same number of nodes, where one is densely connected internally and the other is sparsely connected, the contribution of a new edge to the sparse community should be significantly greater than to the dense community.
- On the other hand, considering the addition of a new edge between C_s and other communities, although the term $\frac{l_s}{L} - (\frac{v_s}{2L})^2$ implies a penalty for the new edge, this penalty linearly increases with the scale of the community. This is counterintuitive because the penalty for small communities should be high, while for large communities, it should be low. This makes it easier for the optimization of Q_C to lead to the merging of small communities into larger ones.

These issues call for a new metric to measure community structure information. Next, we introduce the logarithmic function from information theory to address the aforementioned problems.

3.2. Community Structure Information

Complex networks represent the sum of all relationships among entities in a complex system. For a network graph, $G = (V, E)$, the relationships are the edges, E, and the individuals are the nodes, V, in $G = (V, E)$. Then, the total information of the graph, G, can be defined as the sum of information for all its edges. However, how much information does each edge carry? As illustrated in Figure 1, if we already know the degree of each node, for any edge $\{u, v\} \in E$, since nodes u and v are independent, the probability of $\{u, v\} \in E$ occurring is $(d_u/2L)(d_v/2L)$, where d_u and d_v represent the degrees of nodes u and v, respectively. Consequently, the information content of edge $\{u, v\} \in E$ is determined using $-\log_2[(d_u/2L)(d_v/2L)]$. Thus, the average information carried by one edge in G is expressed as follows:

$$\mathcal{H}(G) := -\frac{1}{|E|} \sum_{uv \in E} \log_2[(d_u/2L)(d_v/2L)]. \quad (3)$$

According to the definition, $\mathcal{H}(G)$ represents the average number of bits required to encode the edges or relationships in the graph, G. It is worth noting that in the construction of the edge u, v, the selection of nodes u and v is relatively independent. Therefore, the average number of bits required to encode one edge is equivalent to twice the number of bits required to encode one node:

$$\mathcal{H}(G) = -\frac{1}{L} \sum_{uv \in E} \log_2[(d_u/2L)(d_v/2L)]$$
$$= -2 \cdot \sum_{u \in V} \frac{d_u}{2L} \log_2 \frac{d_u}{2L}. \quad (4)$$

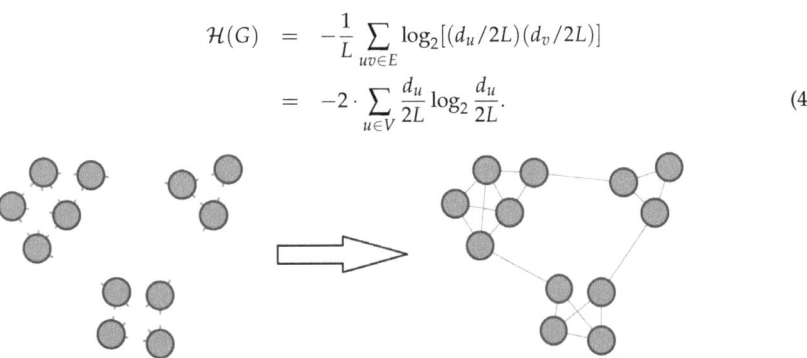

Figure 1. Example of encoding graph G when the community structure is unknown.

In the above definition, $\mathcal{H}(G)$ represents the average information required to encode edges when the community structure is not considered. Let $C = \{C_1, C_2, \ldots, C_S\}$ be a partition of the node set V, satisfying that for any $1 \leq s, t \leq S$, $V = C_1 \cup C_2 \ldots C_S$ and $C_s \cap C_t = \phi$, thus C divides G into S communities $\{C_1, C_2, \ldots, C_S\}$. With the information on the community structure, we know whether any two nodes are in the same community. In this case, the process of selecting two nodes to form an edge is divided into two steps. The first step is to identify the community to which the nodes belong, and the second step is to choose the corresponding nodes from the identified community. Let v_s be the total degree of all nodes in community C_s. For any edge $u, v \in E$, the execution of these two steps involves two scenarios:

(i) u and v belong to the same community C_s. In this case, we first identify community C_s with a probability of $v_s/2L$, and then we select u with a probability of d_u/v_s and v with a probability of d_v/v_s;

(ii) u and v belong to different communities, C_s and C_t, respectively. In this case, we first identify C_s and C_t with probabilities $v_s/2L$ and $v_t/2L$, respectively. Then, we independently select u from C_s with a probability of d_u/v_s and v from C_t with a probability of d_v/v_t.

Therefore, for cases (i) and (ii), the information content of edge $\{u, v\}$ is determined via $-\log_2[(v_s/2L)(d_u/v_s)(d_v/v_s)]$ and $-\log_2[(v_s/2L)(v_t/2L)(d_u/v_s)(d_v/v_t)]$, respectively. In the case of (ii), this expression can be simplified to $-\log_2[(d_u/2L)(d_v/2L)]$. Thus, if the community structure, C, of graph G is known, the average information content per edge can be expressed as follows:

$$\mathcal{H}_C(G) := \frac{1}{L}(\mathcal{H}_1(G) + \mathcal{H}_2(G)), \quad (5)$$

where

$$\mathcal{H}_1(G) = -\sum_{s=1}^{S} \sum_{uv \in E \& u, v \in C_s} \log_2[(v_s/2L)(d_u/v_s)(d_v/v_s)],$$

$$\mathcal{H}_2(G) = -\sum_{s=1}^{S} \sum_{uv \in E, u \in C_s \& v \notin C_s} \log_2[(d_u/2L)(d_v/2L)],$$

and $\mathcal{H}_1(G)$ and $\mathcal{H}_2(G)$ correspond to cases (i) and (ii), respectively.

The simplification of Equation (5) yields the following:

$$\mathcal{H}_C(G) = \sum_{s=1}^{S}[\frac{v_s}{2L}\mathcal{H}(C_s) - \frac{v_s - l_s}{L}\log_2\frac{v_s}{2L}]$$

$$= -\sum_{u \in V}\frac{d_u}{L}\log_2\frac{d_u}{2L} + \sum_{s=1}^{S}\frac{l_s}{L}\log_2\frac{v_s}{2L}$$

$$= \mathcal{H}(G) + \sum_{s=1}^{S}\frac{l_s}{L}\log_2\frac{v_s}{2L}, \quad (6)$$

where $\mathcal{H}(C_s) = -2\sum_{u \in C_s}\frac{d_u}{v_s}\log_2\frac{d_u}{v_s}$, and l_s represents the number of edges within community C_s. Figure 2 illustrates an example of encoding graph G with a known community structure. The value of $\mathcal{H}_C(G)$ reflects the average information required to encode an edge when the community structure C is known. In other words, the community structure, C, provides a certain amount of information, eliminating the uncertainty in encoding an edge. This reduction in uncertainty is represented by the absolute value of the second term in Equation (6).

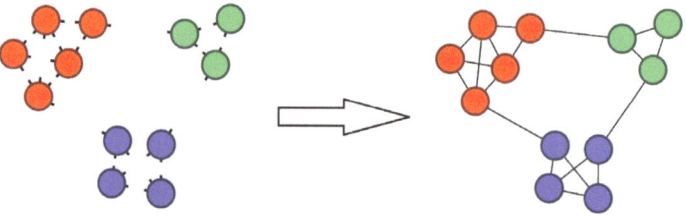

Figure 2. Example of an encoding graph G when the community structure is known.

We define the information provided via the community, C, as a measure of community structure information:

Definition 1. *Let $C = \{C_1, C_2, \ldots, C_S\}$ be the community structure (partition) of the graph, $G = (V, E)$. The community structure information of G relative to the community C is defined as follows:*

$$R_C(G) = \mathcal{H}(G) - \mathcal{H}_C(G) = -\sum_{s=1}^{S}\frac{l_s}{L}\log_2\frac{v_s}{2L}, \quad (7)$$

where S is the number of communities, l_s is the number of edges within community C_s, and v_s is the total degree of nodes in community C_s.

According to the definition, $R_C(G)$ reflects the information saved on average when encoding the edge information of graph G with knowledge of the community structure, C. The more pronounced the community structure, the greater the amount of saved information, and the closer the community structure, C, is to the ground truth community structure. Therefore, optimizing algorithms can be employed to find the maximum value of $R_C(G)$ for community detection.

4. Community Detection Algorithm, CSIM

In this section, we introduce a community detection algorithm based on the maximization of community structure information. Since community detection algorithms based on modularity have been extensively studied, and many excellent algorithms have been proposed [2,12,63], we drew inspiration from the ideas of these previous algorithms in designing our algorithm.

4.1. Preliminaries

Assuming the graph $G = (V, E)$ is the network under investigation, $C = \{C_1, C_2, \ldots, C_S\}$ represents any community partition of the node set V. Here, l_s and v_s denote the internal edge count and total node degree of community C_s, respectively, and $L = |E|$ is the total number of edges in graph G. The community structure, D, represents the configuration obtained by merging two communities, C_s and C_t, from the partition, C, into a single community. Without a loss of generality, let $s < t$. Then, D can be expressed as follows:

$$D = \{C_1, \ldots, C_{s-1}, C_{s+1}, \ldots, C_{t-1}, C_{t+1}, \ldots, C_S, C_s \cup C_t\}.$$

Then,

$$\begin{cases} R_C(G) = R_0 - \frac{l_s}{L} \log_2 \frac{v_s}{2L} - \frac{l_t}{L} \log_2 \frac{v_t}{2L} \\ R_D(G) = R_0 - \frac{l_s + l_t + l_{st}}{L} \log_2 \frac{v_s + v_t}{2L}, \end{cases} \quad (8)$$

where $R_0 = -\sum_{i \neq s,t} \frac{l_i}{L} \log_2 \frac{v_i}{2L}$, l_s, and l_t are the numbers of edges within communities C_s and C_t, respectively, and l_{st} is the number of edges between communities C_s and C_t.

Let $\Delta R_{s,t} = R_D - R_C$, and a derivation from Equation (8) leads to the following:

$$\Delta R_{s,t} = -\frac{l_{st}}{L} \log_2 \frac{v_s + v_t}{2L} + \frac{l_s}{L} \log_2 \frac{v_s}{v_s + v_t} + \frac{l_t}{L} \log_2 \frac{v_t}{v_s + v_t}. \quad (9)$$

As we aim to maximize $R_*(G)$, we merge communities C_s and C_t if $\Delta R_{s,t} > 0$; otherwise, we refrain from merging. It is noteworthy that, when $l_{st} = 0$, the following holds:

$$\Delta R_{s,t} = \frac{l_s}{L} \log_2 \frac{v_s}{v_s + v_t} + \frac{l_t}{L} \log_2 \frac{v_t}{v_s + v_t} < 0.$$

Therefore, in the algorithm aimed at maximizing $R_*(G)$, communities C_s and C_t are not merged when there are no inter-community edges between them.

4.2. CSIM

Inspired by the Louvain algorithm [12], we designed a fast hierarchical aggregation algorithm, CSIM. Assuming a graph to be undetected as $G = (V, E)$ and any node $v_i \in V$, the structure $\{C_1, C_2, \ldots, C_S\}$ represents the community partition when node v_i is removed from V. So, which community C_t is more suitable for placing v_i? An intuitive idea is to place v_i in the community C_t that maximizes the gain in $R_*(G)$ after placing v_i in each $1 \leq t \leq S$. This becomes a special type of community merging—merging a node as a standalone community with another community.

Let $C = \{\{v_i\}, C_1, C_2, \ldots, C_S\}$, $D = \{C_1, \ldots, \{v_i\} \cup C_t, \ldots, C_S\}$, and $\Delta R_{i,t} = R_D - R_C$. Then, according to Equation (9), we have the following:

$$\Delta R_{i,t} = -\frac{l_{it}}{L} \log_2 \frac{d_i + v_t}{2L} + \frac{l_t}{L} \log_2 \frac{v_t}{d_i + v_t}, \quad (10)$$

where l_{it} is the number of edges between node v_i and community C_t, and d_i is the degree of node v_i. Similarly, it can be observed that, if $l_{it} = 0$, then $\Delta R_{i,t} < 0$. In such a case, node v_i is not placed in community C_t.

Based on the above analysis, we designed a hierarchical clustering algorithm called CSIM, as shown in Algorithm 1. It mainly consists of two steps: node movement and node aggregation. Specifically, at the node movement step, each node is temporarily removed from its community and then assimilated into the neighboring community that maximizes the gain in $R_C(G)$. This process is repeated for all nodes, corresponding to lines 4 to 16 in the algorithm. Subsequently, the algorithm performs node aggregation, transforming the communities obtained from node movement into super-nodes. The total degree (weight) within each community becomes the self-loop weight of the super-node, and the number of edges (edge weight) between communities becomes the edge weight between super-nodes.

This results in the construction of a new graph, corresponding to lines 17 to 19 in the algorithm. These two steps are iteratively executed until $R_C(G)$ no longer increases.

Algorithm 1 Community Structure Information Maximization Algorithm: CSIM

Input: $G = (V, E), V = \{v_1, v_2, \ldots, v_n\}$;
Output: Community structure C and $R_C(G)$;
1: **do**
2:     Set each node as a community, namely $C_i = \{v_i\}$;
3:     $C' \leftarrow C$;
4:     **for** $v_i \in V$ **do**
5:         $\Delta_{max} = 0$;
6:         $C \leftarrow C \backslash v_i$;
7:         **for** $C_t \in C$ **do**
8:             **if** $l_{it} > 0$ **then**
9:                 Calculate the value of $\Delta R_{i,t}(G)$;
10:                **if** $\Delta R_{i,t}(G) > \Delta_{max}$ **then**
11:                    $\Delta_{max} = \Delta R_{i,t}(G), t^* = t$;
12:                **end if**
13:             **end if**
14:             $C \leftarrow$ put node v_i into C_{t^*} of C;
15:         **end for**
16:     **end for**
17:     **if** $R_C(G) - R_{C'}(G) > 0$ **then**
18:         $G \leftarrow$ Aggregate communities into super-nodes, and keep track of the members of each super-node;
19:     **end if**
20: **while** $R_C(G) - R_{C'}(G) > 0$
21: $C \leftarrow$ Extract the super nodes in C';
22: **Return:** C and $R_C(G)$

Now, let us analyze the time complexity of this algorithm. In the first iteration, CSIM executes approximately L times to calculate $\Delta R_{i,t}(G)$. In the subsequent iterations, the nodes aggregated into super-nodes reduce the number to approximately $\log n$. Thus, in the second iteration, CSIM executes a maximum of $\log^2 n \, \Delta R_{i,t}(G)$ operations in the worst case, and in the third iteration, the number of super-nodes is roughly $\log(\log n)$, and so on. Similar to the Louvain algorithm [12], CSIM has an average time complexity of $O(n \log n)$, which outperforms the greedy hierarchical aggregation algorithm proposed in [20], where the average time complexity is $O(n \log^{O(1)} n)$. In the experimental section, we further compare the performance of these two algorithms in optimizing $R_C(G)$.

5. Experiment

For this section, we conducted an experimental analysis of our algorithm with three main objectives: (1) that, compared to modularity-based optimization algorithms, our proposed algorithm can discover finer community partitions that are closer to the ground truth community structure; (2) that, in comparison to the greedy algorithm proposed in [20], our designed algorithm not only has lower complexity but also demonstrates advantages in optimizing the maximum value of community structure information; and (3) that our algorithm does not suffer from resolution limit issues on special cyclic graphs compared to modularity-based algorithms.

5.1. Experimental Settings

Datasets with ground truth community structure. The experiments with community-structured data utilized graph data discussed by Fortunato and Barthelemy [18]. Table 1 provides an overview of this data, where $|V|$ and $|E|$ correspond to the number of nodes and edges in the network graph. There are a total of five datasets, datasets *Yeast*, *E. coli*, *Elect. circuit* and *Social* from link www.weizman.ac.il/mcb/UriAlon (accessed on 20 November 2021), dataset *C. elegans* from link http://cdg.columbia.edu (accessed on 5 November 2021). The types listed in Table 1 cover various real-world domains, including human society, animals, microorganisms, and electronic circuits. The *Yeast* and *E. coli* represent transcriptional regulatory networks of microorganisms, where nodes represent operons, i.e., sets of genes transcribed onto the same mRNA. If operon A activates operon B, an edge is placed between nodes A and B. In this data, yeast has 688 nodes and 1079 edges, while *E. coli* has 423 nodes and 519 edges. The *Elect. circuit* represents an electronic circuit network, where nodes are electronic components (capacitors, diodes, etc.), and edges represent wires. The *Social* represents a social network, where 67 nodes represent a surveyed group of people, and 182 edges denote positive emotions transferred from one person to another (based on questionnaires). The *C. elegans* represents the neural network of the *C. elegans* roundworm, where nodes are neurons, and edges represent synaptic or gap connections. The networks can be both undirected and directed, and we uniformly treated them as undirected.

Table 1. Overview of graph data with ground truth community structure.

Data G	$|V|$	$|E|$	Type	Description
Yeast	688	1079	Microorganism	Transcriptional regulatory network in brewing yeast
E. coli	423	519	Microorganism	Transcriptional regulatory network in *Escherichia coli*
Elect. circuit	512	819	Electronic	Electronic circuit network of electronic components
Social	67	182	Social network	Social network of positive emotions among individuals
C. elegans	306	2345	Animal	Neural network of *Caenorhabditis elegans*

Datasets without a ground truth community structure. In comparing our algorithm with the experiments of the paper [20] in seeking the maximum value of community structure information, we introduced some classic datasets, as shown in Table 2, in addition to the data in Table 1. There are a total of seven datasets, datasets *Karate*, *Dolphin*, and *Facebook* from link http://konect.cc/networks/ (accessed on 26 November 2021), datasets *Jazz*, *Email*, and *PGP* from link https://deim.urv.cat/~alexandre.arenas/data/welcome.htm (accessed on 26 November 2021), dataset *Jazz* from link https://networkrepository.com/power-US-Grid.php (accessed on 26 November 2021). The *Karate* data are from the well-known Zachary Karate Club network. The data were collected by Wayne Zachary from a university's karate club. In this network, each node represents a club member, and each edge represents a relationship between two club members. The *Dolphin* data represents a social network of bottlenose dolphins living near the New Zealand fjord. Edges in the network represent frequent interactions. The *Jazz* data represent a collaboration network among jazz musicians. The nodes represent jazz musicians, and the edges represent musicians who play together in a band. The *Email* data represent a communication network among members of the University of Rovira i Virgili, where edges indicate communication between members. The Facebook data represent a friend network among some users on Facebook. Each node represents a user, and the edges represent friendships between users. The *Power grid* data represents the high-voltage power grid in the western United States. The nodes represent transformers, substations, and generators, while the edges represent high-voltage transmission lines. The *PGP* data represent a user network for the Pretty-Good-Privacy algorithm used in secure information exchange, where the edges represent instances of secure information exchanges between users. All of these networks are considered undirected.

Benchmark. In this experiment, four community detection algorithms were considered. Two were based on maximizing modularity, and two were based on maximizing community structure information. The four algorithms are described as follows: (1) Louvain [12] is a heuristic algorithm based on modularity maximization, with average time complexity of $O(n \log n)$; (2) Q_greedy [63] is a greedy hierarchical clustering algorithm that optimizes modularity through hierarchical merging, with an average time complexity of $O(n \log^{O(1)} n)$; (3) CISM is a heuristic algorithm designed by us based on maximizing community structure information, with an average time complexity of $O(n \log n)$; and (4) R_greedy [20] is a hierarchical clustering method based on $R_C(G)$, achieving the maximization of community structure information through hierarchical community merging, with a time complexity of $O(n \log^{O(1)} n)$. In the experiment, the $R_C(G)$ values and modularity Q values of the four algorithms were obtained from the corresponding community detection algorithms. Additionally, the datasets in Table 1 do not have completely ground truth community structures, and the ground truth structure was obtained using the method proposed by Fortunato [18], which involves two rounds of modularity optimization. The network graph was initially partitioned, and then the communities with significant substructures underwent a second round of partitioning until each community had no obvious substructure.

Table 2. Overview of graph data without ground truth community structure.

Data G	$|V|$	$|E|$	Type	Description
Karate	34	78	Social network	Social network among members of karate clubs
Dolphin	62	159	Animal	Social network of associations among dolphins
Jazz	198	2742	Social network	A collaboration network among jazz musicians
Email	1133	5451	Communication	Email communication network among members of a university in Spain
Facebook	2888	2981	Online social	Friendship network among selected users on Facebook
Power grid	4941	6594	Infrastructure	Topological network of the power grid in the western United States
PGP	10,680	24,316	Online social	Interacting network among PGP users

Evaluation index: NMI. Mutual information is one of the most commonly used metrics in information theory. It measures the shared information between two random variables and is typically employed to express the similarity between two variables [65]. If we consider community partitions as variables, mutual information can be used to assess the similarity between the detected community partition and the ground truth community partition. Let $C = \{C_1, C_2, \ldots, C_S\}$ be the ground truth community partition of the graph $G = (V, E)$, and let $C' = \{C'_1, C'_2, \ldots, C'_T\}$ be the artificial partition discovered using the community detection algorithm. Denote that

$$H(C) = -\sum_{i=1}^{S} \frac{|C_i|}{|V|} \log \frac{|C_i|}{|V|}, \text{ and } H(C|C') = -\sum_{i=1}^{S} \sum_{j=1}^{T} \frac{|C_i \cap C'_j|}{|V|} \log \frac{|C_i \cap C'_j|/|V|}{|C'_j|/|V|},$$

where $|C_i|$ represents the number of nodes in community C_i, $|C_i \cap C'_j|$ represents the number of nodes in the intersection of communities C_i and C'_j, and $|V|$ represents the total number of nodes. Then, mutual Information is defined as $I(C, C') = H(C) - H(C|C')$. Normalizing the mutual information yields normalized mutual information (NMI) [66]:

$$\text{NMI}(C, C') = \frac{I(C, C')}{\max\{H(C), H(C')\}}. \tag{11}$$

The range of NMI is $[0, 1]$, making it suitable for assessing the similarity between two community partitions. A higher NMI indicates a closer proximity between the detected and ground truth community structures, reflecting better detection performance. When NMI equals 1, the detected and ground truth communities are in perfect agreement.

5.2. Experimental Analysis

Comparison with optimized modularity. This experiment will use the datasets in Table 1 to validate that, compared to optimizing modularity, detecting communities by optimizing community structure information yields community partitions closer to the ground truth community structure. We used the normalized mutual information (NMI) mentioned in the experimental settings to measure the similarity between the detected community partition and the ground truth community partition. The NMI values ranged from 0 to 1, with values closer to 1 indicating a higher similarity to the ground truth partition and, thus, a better detection result. To achieve this, we first obtained community partitions of the graph data using the four detection algorithms and then calculated their NMI values with the ground truth partition. Figure 3 shows the histogram of NMI values between the partitions obtained via different algorithms and the ground truth partition on different datasets. From the figure, it is evident that the NMI values of the results from optimizing community structure information (algorithms CSIM and R_greedy) were significantly higher than those from optimizing modularity (Louvain and Q_greedy). In particular, the performance of algorithms CSIM and R_greedy was even close to 1 on the *E. coli*, *Social*, and *Yeast* datasets, indicating that the partitions detected via these two algorithms were nearly identical to the ground truth partition. This implies that maximizing $R_C(G)$ not only approximates the number of ground truth communities but also ensures high consistency among the members within the communities. Additionally, concerning the optimization of community structure information, the results obtained via the CSIM algorithm were slightly better than those obtained via R_greedy.

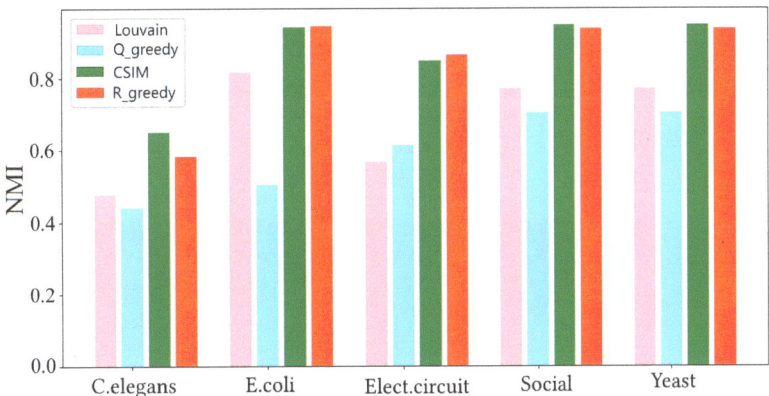

Figure 3. The NMI values between the partitions detected via the four algorithms and the ground truth partitions.

Comparison of optimized community structure information. This experiment verified the advantage of our proposed algorithm in optimizing community structure information. Tables 1 and 2 together consist of 12 graph datasets, involving network data from various real-world domains, including offline social domains, online social domains, animal domains, infrastructure, microbial domains, electronic circuits, etc. We conducted community detection using CSIM and R_greedy on these 12 datasets, outputting the maximum value of the optimized $R_C(G)$ for each algorithm. The results are presented in Table 3. We have highlighted in black and bold text the maximum $R_C(G)$ value for each dataset. It can be observed that, except for the *E. coli* dataset, for all the other datasets, the CSIM algorithm obtained larger $R_C(G)$ values compared to R_greedy. On the other hand, although R_greedy achieved a slightly larger value than CSIM on the E. coli dataset, their values were very close. This suggests that the CSIM algorithm is more effective than R_greedy in optimizing $R_C(G)$. Combining our discussion on time complexity in Section 4, it can be concluded that the CSIM algorithm excels in both efficiency and effectiveness compared to R_greedy.

Table 3. A comparison between the CSIM algorithm and R_greedy in optimizing the value of community structure information.

Data G	$R_C(G)$ via CSIM	$R_C(G)$ via R_greedy
Yeast	3.849	3.847
E. coli	4.005	4.032
Elect. circuit	4.117	4.097
Social	2.494	2.488
C. elegans	1.565	1.548
Karate	1.352	1.298
Dolphin	1.750	1.743
Jazz	1.434	1.308
Email	2.676	2.475
Facebook	2.723	2.723
Power grid	7.019	6.996
PGP	6.647	6.476

Comparison of resolution limits. This experiment verified the advantage of community structure information over modularity in addressing the resolution limit problem. Fortunato et al. [18] provided an example illustrating the resolution limit problem when optimizing modularity on a cyclic network composed of completely identical subgraphs connected with single edges. In contrast, optimizing community structure information does not suffer from this issue. We consider subgraphs of the cyclic network complete graphs with three nodes, as shown in Figure 4. The portions enclosed in dashed circles represent the community structures detected by optimizing the two metrics. When assuming that the community structure in Figure 4a is A, and that the community structure in Figure 4b is B, it is evident that A is the ground truth community structure. According to the definition of modularity, the modularity value in the ground truth community structure, $Q_A = 0.65$, is less than the value obtained by maximizing modularity, $Q_B = 0.675$. On the other hand, the community structure information value in the ground truth community structure, $R_A = 2.4914$, is significantly greater than its value, $R_B = 2.0317$, under community structure B. This implies that community structure information has an advantage in addressing the resolution limit problem.

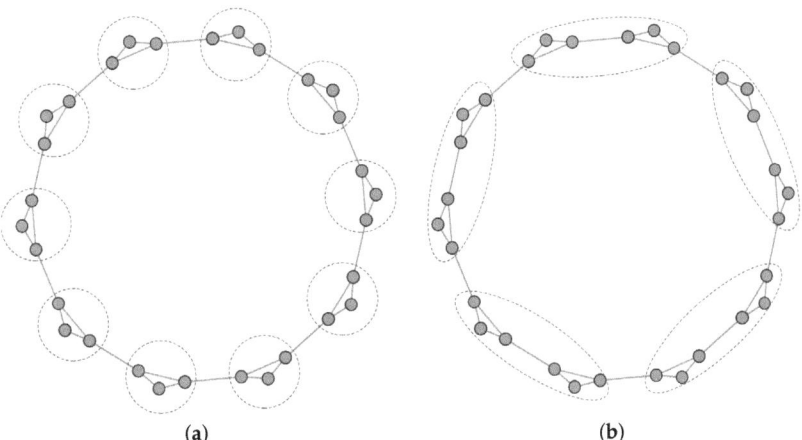

Figure 4. Comparison of modularity and community structure information in detecting community structure. (**a**) Community structure detected by optimizing community structure information. (**b**) Community structure detected by optimizing modularity.

6. Discussion

Here, we discuss the contributions of our study to theory and practice, as well as the implications of the study.

6.1. Analysis of Contribution

In the preceding three sections, we presented the definition of community structure information, devised the CSIM algorithm based on this information, and validated the superior performance of the CSIM algorithm. Next, we explore the key factors contributing to the outstanding performance of the CSIM algorithm, focusing on theoretical foundations, algorithm design, and algorithm execution.

Theoretical foundations. In contrast to modularity, which focuses on the probability of two nodes being connected by an edge [64], our definition of community structure information was inspired by Shannon's conception of information entropy, and it directly focuses on the amount of information conveyed via the connection of two nodes [52]. It reflects the community structure by compressing the amount of edge information conveyed via the community structure, which better captures the essence of the community structure. Furthermore, compared to structural entropy [25], defining community structure information from the perspective of edge information compression is more intuitive and straightforward than using random walks.

Algorithm design. In the design of the CSIM algorithm, we drew inspiration from the widely used Louvain algorithm and adopted a heuristic clustering method based on node aggregation and graph reconstruction [12]. This approach significantly reduces the algorithmic complexity of optimizing community structure information [20], bringing it down to $O(n \log n)$, thus enabling the algorithm to be applied to large-scale social networks. Moreover, similar to the Louvain algorithm, the CSIM algorithm also outperforms greedy hierarchical clustering algorithms in optimizing community structure information, striking a balance between efficiency and effectiveness.

Algorithm execution. At the algorithm execution level, due to the concept of community structure information being theoretically more reflective of the essence of community structure, the CSIM algorithm, which optimizes community structure information, can achieve a balance between community size and quantity [20]. Unlike algorithms optimizing modularity [18], it does not overlook or merge small-scale communities. Consequently, the communities detected via the CSIM algorithm are closer to the ground truth communities, and to some extent, the CSIM algorithm addresses the resolution limit problem.

6.2. Implications

Although community detection has been studied for many years, this research has provided important theoretical guidance and practical applications for this field. Firstly, defining community structure information from the perspective of encoding edge information is likely to change the traditional definition, which relies on edge density. This is conducive to a deeper exploration of the essence of community structure, including its application in areas such as graph compression, machine learning, and graph neural networks. Secondly, the CSIM algorithm, based on the theory of community structure information, offers advantages in both algorithm complexity and balancing community size and quantity. It can replace traditional algorithms like Louvain, especially for graphs with imbalanced community structures or a large number of small communities. Lastly, the related theory and algorithms can be further expanded for applications such as overlapping community detection and multi-graph analysis, promoting advancements in the field. Overall, this research provides a more intuitive, efficient, and effective method for identifying community structures in complex networks, contributing to the advancement of community detection.

7. Conclusions

This paper has investigated the direction of community structure detection in complex networks. Despite the widespread research and application of community structure detection algorithms in fields such as social media, computer science, and biology, challenges persist, including the lack of an essential definition of community structure, high algorithmic complexity, and the unreasonable structural characteristics of detected communities. In addressing these issues, we introduced, for the first time, the definition of community structure information from the perspective of encoding edge information. This information reflects the essence of community structure by compressing the amount of edge information conveyed via the community structure, thereby better expressing the intrinsic characteristics of the community structure. By maximizing community structure information, we further proposed the CSIM community detection algorithm, which achieves a balance between community size and quantity to identify the most natural community structure. Additionally, inspired by the heuristic clustering Louvain algorithm, we reduced the complexity of CSIM to $O(n \log n)$, enabling its application to large-scale complex networks. Our experimental results show that communities detected by optimizing community structure information are closer to ground truth communities, and they effectively address the resolution limit problem, especially in cyclic graphs.

Future research can delve deeper into the rationale behind the definition of community structure information and provide theoretical validation for the benefits of optimizing it. This will involve investigating its role in striking a balance within a community structure and overcoming the resolution limit problem. Additionally, the application of community structure information will be extended to domains like machine learning and graph neural networks, with the aim of enhancing existing algorithms for tasks such as node or graph classification. Furthermore, diverse forms of community structure information will be explored, including its utilization in identifying communities within multigraphs or those with overlapping structures. Tailoring the granularity of community detection to specific requirements will be a key focus, thereby broadening the scope of its applicability.

Author Contributions: Conceptualization, Y.L. and Y.W.; methodology, Y.L. and W.L.; software, H.Y. and X.T.; validation, W.L., P.Y., and X.X.; writing—original draft preparation, Y.L. and W.L.; writing—review and editing, Y.L., Y.W., and H.Y. All authors have read and agreed to the published version of the manuscript.

Funding: This research was supported in part by the Defense Industrial Technology Development Program (No. JCKY2021602B002 and JCKY2021906A001) and the National Natural Science Foundation of China (No. 62302539).

Data Availability Statement: The data used in this paper are publicly available, and the corresponding links to the datasets can be found in the footnotes of the paper.

Conflicts of Interest: The authors declare no conflicts of interest. The funders had no role in the design of the study or the decision to publish the results.

References

1. Zhang, T.; Xu, C.; Lian, Y.; Tian, H.; Kang, J.; Kuang, X.; Niyato, D. When Moving Target Defense Meets Attack Prediction in Digital Twins: A Convolutional and Hierarchical Reinforcement Learning Approach. *IEEE J. Sel. Areas Commun.* **2023**, *41*, 3293–3305. [CrossRef]
2. Fortunato, S. Community detection in graphs. *Phys. Rep.* **2010**, *486*, 75–174. [CrossRef]
3. Zhang, T.; Xu, C.; Shen, J.; Kuang, X.; Grieco, L.A. How to Disturb Network Reconnaissance: A Moving Target Defense Approach Based on Deep Reinforcement Learning. *IEEE Trans. Inf. Forensics Secur.* **2023**, *18*, 5735–5748. [CrossRef]
4. Traud, A.L.; Mucha, P.J.; Porter, M.A. Social Structure of Facebook Networks. *Phys. A Stat. Mech. Its Appl.* **2012**, *391*, 4165–4180. [CrossRef]
5. Ravasz, E.; Somera, A.L.; Mongru, D.A.; Oltvai, Z.N.; Barabasi, A. Hierarchical Organization of Modularity in Metabolic Networks. *Science* **2002**, *297*, 1551–1555. [CrossRef]
6. Zhang, T.; Xu, C.; Zou, P.; Tian, H.; Kuang, X.; Yang, S.; Zhong, L.; Niyato, D. How to Mitigate DDoS Intelligently in SD-IoV: A Moving Target Defense Approach. *IEEE Trans. Ind. Inform.* **2023**, *19*, 1097–1106. [CrossRef]
7. Newman, M.E.J.; Girvan, M. Finding and evaluating community structure in networks. *Phys. Rev. E* **2004**, *69*, 026113. [CrossRef] [PubMed]
8. Li, Z.; Zhang, S.; Wang, R.S.; Zhang, X.S.; Chen, L. Quantitative function for community detection. *Phys. Rev. E* **2008**, *77*, 036109. [CrossRef] [PubMed]
9. Aldecoa, R.; Marín, I. Deciphering network community structure by surprise. *PLoS ONE* **2011**, *6*, e24195. [CrossRef] [PubMed]
10. Chakraborty, T.; Srinivasan, S.; Ganguly, N.; Mukherjee, A.; Bhowmick, S. On the permanence of vertices in network communities. In Proceedings of the 20th ACM SIGKDD International Conference on Knowledge Discovery and Data Mining, New York, NY, USA, 24–27 August 2014; pp. 1396–1405.
11. Girvan, M.; Newman, M.E. Community structure in social and biological networks. *Proc. Natl. Acad. Sci. USA* **2002**, *99*, 7821–7826. [CrossRef] [PubMed]
12. Blondel, V.D.; Guillaume, J.; Lambiotte, R.; Lefebvre, E. Fast unfolding of communities in large networks. *J. Stat. Mech. Theory Exp.* **2008**, *2008*, 10008. [CrossRef]
13. Guimera, R.; Amaral, L.A.N. Functional cartography of complex metabolic networks. *Nature* **2005**, *433*, 895–900. [CrossRef]
14. Duch, J.; Arenas, A. Community detection in complex networks using extremal optimization. *Phys. Rev. E* **2005**, *72*, 027104. [CrossRef]
15. Newman, M.E. Finding community structure in networks using the eigenvectors of matrices. *Phys. Rev. E* **2006**, *74*, 036104. [CrossRef] [PubMed]
16. Agarwal, G.; Kempe, D. Modularity-maximizing graph communities via mathematical programming. *Eur. Phys. J. B* **2008**, *66*, 409–418. [CrossRef]
17. Lancichinetti, A.; Fortunato, S. Community detection algorithms: A comparative analysis. *Phys. Rev. E* **2009**, *80*, 056117. [CrossRef] [PubMed]
18. Fortunato, S.; Barthelemy, M. Resolution limit in community detection. *Proc. Natl. Acad. Sci. USA* **2007**, *104*, 36–41. [CrossRef] [PubMed]
19. Yang, L.; Cao, X.; He, D.; Wang, C.; Wang, X.; Zhang, W. Modularity Based Community Detection with Deep Learning. In Proceedings of the Twenty-Fifth International Joint Conference on Artificial Intelligence (IJCAI-16), New York, NY, USA, 9–15 July 2016; Volume 16, pp. 2252–2258.
20. Li, A.; Li, J.; Pan, Y. Discovering natural communities in networks. *Phys. A Stat. Mech. Its Appl.* **2015**, *436*, 878–896. [CrossRef]
21. Rashevsky, N. Life, Information Theory, and Topology. *Bull. Math. Biophys.* **1955**, *17*, 229–235. [CrossRef]
22. Braunstein, S.L.; Ghosh, S.; Severini, S. The laplacian of a graph as a density matrix: A basic combinatorial approach to separability of mixed states. *Ann. Comb.* **2006**, *10*, 291–317. [CrossRef]
23. Dehmer, M. Information processing in complex networks: Graph entropy and information functionals. *Appl. Math. Comput.* **2008**, *201*, 82–94. [CrossRef]
24. Anand, K.; Bianconi, G. Entropy measures for networks: Toward an information theory of complex topologies. *Phys. Rev. E Stat. Nonlinear Soft Matter Phys.* **2009**, *80*, 045102. [CrossRef] [PubMed]
25. Li, A.; Pan, Y. Structural Information and Dynamical Complexity of Networks. *IEEE Trans. Inf. Theory* **2016**, *62*, 3290–3339. [CrossRef]
26. Newman, M.E. Detecting community structure in networks. *Eur. Phys. J. B* **2004**, *38*, 321–330. [CrossRef]
27. Rosvall, M.; Bergstrom, C.T. Maps of random walks on complex networks reveal community structure. *Proc. Natl. Acad. Sci. USA* **2008**, *105*, 1118–1123. [CrossRef] [PubMed]

28. Zhang, Q.; Li, M.; Deng, Y. A new structure entropy of complex networks based on nonextensive statistical mechanics. *Int. J. Mod. Phys. C* **2016**, *27*, 1650118. [CrossRef]
29. Liu, Y.; Liu, J.; Wan, K.; Qin, Z.; Zhang, Z.; Khoussainov, B.; Zhu, L. From local to global norm emergence: Dissolving self-reinforcing substructures with incremental social instruments. In Proceedings of the International Conference on Machine Learning, PMLR, Virtual, 18–24 July 2021; pp. 6871–6881.
30. Zhang, Q.; Li, M. A betweenness structural entropy of complex networks. *Chaos Solitons Fractals* **2022**, *161*, 112264. [CrossRef]
31. Cai, M.; Liu, J.; Cui, Y. A Network Structure Entropy Considering Series-Parallel Structures. *Entropy* **2022**, *24*, 852. [CrossRef] [PubMed]
32. Weiss, R.S.; Jacobson, E. A method for the analysis of the structure of complex organizations. *Am. Sociol. Rev.* **1955**, *20*, 661–668. [CrossRef]
33. McCorry, P.; Möser, M.; Shahandasti, S.F.; Hao, F. Towards bitcoin payment networks. In Proceedings of the Australasian Conference on Information Security and Privacy, Melbourne, Australia, 4–6 July 2016; Springer: Cham, Switzerland, 2016; pp. 57–76.
34. Vidal, M.; Cusick, M.E.; Barabási, A.L. Interactome networks and human disease. *Cell* **2011**, *144*, 986–998. [CrossRef]
35. Barabási, A.L.; Gulbahce, N.; Loscalzo, J. Network medicine: A network-based approach to human disease. *Nat. Rev. Genet.* **2011**, *12*, 56–68. [CrossRef]
36. Gregory, S. *Local Betweenness for Finding Communities in Networks*; University of Bristol: Bristol, UK, 2008.
37. Shi, J.; Malik, J. Normalized cuts and image segmentation. *IEEE Trans. Pattern Anal. Mach. Intell.* **2000**, *22*, 888–905.
38. Von Luxburg, U. A tutorial on spectral clustering. *Stat. Comput.* **2007**, *17*, 395–416. [CrossRef]
39. Brandes, U.; Delling, D.; Gaertler, M.; Gorke, R.; Hoefer, M.; Nikoloski, Z.; Wagner, D. On modularity clustering. *IEEE Trans. Knowl. Data Eng.* **2007**, *20*, 172–188. [CrossRef]
40. Chen, M.; Kuzmin, K.; Szymanski, B.K. Community detection via maximization of modularity and its variants. *IEEE Trans. Comput. Soc. Syst.* **2014**, *1*, 46–65. [CrossRef]
41. Zhuang, D.; Chang, J.M.; Li, M. DynaMo: Dynamic community detection by incrementally maximizing modularity. *IEEE Trans. Knowl. Data Eng.* **2019**, *33*, 1934–1945. [CrossRef]
42. Fortunato, S.; Hric, D. Community detection in networks: A user guide. *Phys. Rep.* **2016**, *659*, 1–44. [CrossRef]
43. Jin, D.; Yu, Z.; Jiao, P.; Pan, S.; He, D.; Wu, J.; Philip, S.Y.; Zhang, W. A survey of community detection approaches: From statistical modeling to deep learning. *IEEE Trans. Knowl. Data Eng.* **2021**, *35*, 1149–1170. [CrossRef]
44. Ruggeri, N.; Contisciani, M.; Battiston, F.; De Bacco, C. Community detection in large hypergraphs. *Sci. Adv.* **2023**, *9*, eadg9159. [CrossRef]
45. Bronstein, M.M.; Bruna, J.; LeCun, Y.; Szlam, A.; Vandergheynst, P. Geometric deep learning: Going beyond euclidean data. *IEEE Signal Process. Mag.* **2017**, *34*, 18–42. [CrossRef]
46. Qu, L.; Zhu, H.; Duan, Q.; Shi, Y. Continuous-time link prediction via temporal dependent graph neural network. In Proceedings of the Web Conference 2020, Taipei, Taiwan, 20–24 April 2020; pp. 3026–3032.
47. Dai, H.; Kozareva, Z.; Dai, B.; Smola, A.; Song, L. Learning steady-states of iterative algorithms over graphs. In Proceedings of the International Conference on Machine Learning, PMLR, Stockholm, Sweden, 10–15 July 2018; pp. 1106–1114.
48. Kipf, T.N.; Welling, M. Semi-supervised classification with graph convolutional networks. *arXiv* **2016**, arXiv:1609.02907.
49. Veličković, P.; Cucurull, G.; Casanova, A.; Romero, A.; Lio, P.; Bengio, Y. Graph attention networks. *arXiv* **2017**, arXiv:1710.10903.
50. Yu, W.; Zheng, C.; Cheng, W.; Aggarwal, C.C.; Song, D.; Zong, B.; Chen, H.; Wang, W. Learning deep network representations with adversarially regularized autoencoders. In Proceedings of the 24th ACM SIGKDD International Conference on Knowledge Discovery & Data Mining, London, UK, 19–23 August 2018; pp. 2663–2671.
51. Guo, S.; Lin, Y.; Feng, N.; Song, C.; Wan, H. Attention based spatial-temporal graph convolutional networks for traffic flow forecasting. In Proceedings of the AAAI Conference on Artificial Intelligence, Honolulu, HI, USA, 27 January–1 February 2019; Volume 33, pp. 922–929.
52. Shannon, C. The lattice theory of information. *Trans. IRE Prof. Group Inf. Theory* **1953**, *1*, 105–107. [CrossRef]
53. Li, A.; Zhang, X.; Pan, Y. Resistance maximization principle for defending networks against virus attack. *Phys. A Stat. Mech. Appl.* **2017**, *466*, 211–223. [CrossRef]
54. Li, A.; Yin, X.; Xu, B.; Wang, D.; Han, J.; Wei, Y.; Deng, Y.; Xiong, Y.; Zhang, Z. Decoding topologically associating domains with ultra-low resolution Hi-C data by graph structural entropy. *Nat. Commun.* **2018**, *9*, 3265. [CrossRef] [PubMed]
55. Liu, Y.; Liu, J.; Zhang, Z.; Zhu, L.; Li, A. REM: From structural entropy to community structure deception. *Adv. Neural Inf. Process. Syst.* **2019**, *32*, 12938–12948.
56. Hirai, S.; Yamanishi, K. Detecting latent structure uncertainty with structural entropy. In Proceedings of the 2018 IEEE International Conference on Big Data (Big Data), Seattle, WA, USA, 10–13 December 2018; IEEE: Piscataway, NJ, USA, 2018; pp. 26–35.
57. Wang, H.; Liu, Y.; Yin, P.; Zhang, H.; Xu, X.; Wen, Q. Label specificity attack: Change your label as I want. *Int. J. Intell. Syst.* **2022**, *37*, 7767–7786. [CrossRef]
58. Tian, Y.; Zhang, Z.; Xiong, J.; Chen, L.; Ma, J.; Peng, C. Achieving graph clustering privacy preservation based on structure entropy in social IoT. *IEEE Internet Things J.* **2021**, *9*, 2761–2777. [CrossRef]

59. Liu, W.; Liu, J.; Zhang, Z.; Liu, Y.; Zhu, L. Residual Entropy-based Graph Generative Algorithms. In Proceedings of the 21st International Conference on Autonomous Agents and Multiagent Systems, Auckland, New Zealand, 9–13 May 2022; pp. 816–824.
60. Wan, K.; Liu, J.; Liu, Y.; Zhang, Z.; Khoussainov, B. Attacking community detectors: Mislead detectors via manipulating the graph structure. In Proceedings of the International Conference on Mobile Computing, Applications, and Services, Virtual, 23–24 November 2021; Springer: Cham, Switzerland, 2021; pp. 112–128.
61. Zhang, S.; Liu, J.; Liu, Y.; Zhang, Z.; Khoussainov, B. Improving togetherness using structural entropy. In Proceedings of the International Conference on Mobile Computing, Applications, and Services, Virtual, 23–24 November 2021; Springer: Cham, Switzerland, 2021; pp. 85–98.
62. Reichardt, J.; Bornholdt, S. Statistical mechanics of community detection. *Phys. Rev. E* **2006**, *74*, 016110. [CrossRef]
63. Clauset, A.; Newman, M.E.J.; Moore, C. Finding community structure in very large networks. *Phys. Rev. E* **2004**, *70*, 066111. [CrossRef]
64. Newman, M.E.J. Modularity and community structure in networks. *Proc. Natl. Acad. Sci. USA* **2006**, *103*, 8577–8582. [CrossRef] [PubMed]
65. Cover, T.M.; Thomas, J.A. *Elements of Information Theory*; John Wiley & Sons: Hoboken, NJ, USA, 2012.
66. Vinh, N.X.; Epps, J.; Bailey, J. Information theoretic measures for clusterings comparison: Variants, properties, normalization and correction for chance. *J. Mach. Learn. Res.* **2010**, *11*, 2837–2854.

Disclaimer/Publisher's Note: The statements, opinions and data contained in all publications are solely those of the individual author(s) and contributor(s) and not of MDPI and/or the editor(s). MDPI and/or the editor(s) disclaim responsibility for any injury to people or property resulting from any ideas, methods, instructions or products referred to in the content.

Article

FedScrap: Layer-Wise Personalized Federated Learning for Scrap Detection

Weidong Zhang [1,2], Dongshang Deng [2] and Lidong Wang [3,*]

[1] School of Metallurgical Engineering, Anhui University of Technology, Ma'anshan 243002, China; wdzhang@ahut.edu.cn
[2] School of Computer Science and Technology, Anhui University of Technology, Ma'anshan 243002, China; dsdeng@ahut.edu.cn
[3] Anhui Institute of Electronic Products Supervision and Inspection, Anhui Information Security Testing Evaluation Center, Hefei 230051, China
* Correspondence: wangld@ahjxw.gov.cn

Citation: Zhang, W.; Deng, D.; Wang, L. FedScrap: Layer-Wise Personalized Federated Learning for Scrap Detection. *Electronics* **2024**, *13*, 527. https://doi.org/10.3390/electronics13030527

Academic Editors: Tao Zhang, Xiangyun Tang, Jiacheng Wang and Jiqiang Liu

Received: 10 January 2024
Revised: 18 January 2024
Accepted: 24 January 2024
Published: 28 January 2024

Copyright: © 2024 by the authors. Licensee MDPI, Basel, Switzerland. This article is an open access article distributed under the terms and conditions of the Creative Commons Attribution (CC BY) license (https://creativecommons.org/licenses/by/4.0/).

Abstract: Scrap steel inspection is a critical entry point for connecting the smelting process to the industrial internet, with its security and privacy being of vital importance. Current advancements in scrap steel inspection involve collecting scattered data through the industrial internet, then utilizing them to train machine learning models for distributed classification. However, this detection method exposes original scrap steel data directly to the industrial internet, making it susceptible to interception by attackers, who can potentially obtain sensitive information. This paper presents a layer-wise personalized federated framework for scrap steel detection, termed FedScrap, which leverages federated learning (FL) to coordinate decentralized and heterogeneous scrap steel data while ensuring data privacy protection. The key challenge that FedScrap confronts is the heterogeneity of scrap steel data distributed across the network, which complicates the task of effectively integrating these data into a single detection model constructed via FL. To address this challenge, FedScrap employs a self-attention mechanism to aggregate personalized models for each layer of every client, focusing on the most relevant models to their specific data. By assigning higher attention scores to more relevant models, it achieves more accurate aggregation weights during the model aggregation process. To validate the efficacy of the proposed method, a dataset of scrap images was collected from a steel mill, and the results demonstrate that FedScrap achieves accurate classification of distributed scrap data with an impressive accuracy rate of 90%.

Keywords: scrap steel detection; federated learning; data heterogeneity; network security

1. Introduction

The classification of scrap steel signifies the preliminary phase of the steelmaking process and serves as a crucial component in the integration of heterogeneous industrial internets [1,2]. Currently, the development of scrap steel classification involves utilizing the industrial internet to gather scattered data on scrap steel, subsequently inputting this data into artificial neural networks for classification of the scrap. Although the centralized training via the low-power network [3] facilitates collaboration among scrap data located in various places, it may also give rise to network security and data privacy concerns [4]. The reason is that raw data transmitted directly through the industrial internet may be intercepted by attackers, who could obtain sensitive information to launch network attacks [5,6]. Therefore, a distributed scrap inspection method that can protect the original data is essential.

The emergence of federated learning (FL) makes distributed steel scrap inspection possible. FL trains a machine learning model locally among dispersed scrap data owners, whose parameters are collected to aggregate a shared scrap detection model, which is then fed back to the data owners [7]. Therefore, FL is extremely sensitive to perturbations of parameters, and a key factor causing perturbations is the distribution of data. The industrial internet is emblematic of a multi-user multiple-input single-output (MU-MISO) heterogeneous network [8]. Its scrap steel data are drawn from numerous recycling points, each with its own distinctive data distribution patterns. For example, industrial scrap recycling prefers a single scrap elimination, while social scrap recycling has a wide variety. The difference of distribution is widely known as the non-independent and identically distributed (Non-IID) problem in FL [9–11]. This kind of Non-IID data makes the model trained by each client biased towards its own data distribution, and the single shared model aggregated by the server cannot represent a unified global distribution, which cannot be generalized to the clients.

In response to the above problems, Personalized Federated Learning (PFL) was proposed to learn a personalized model for the client that has better performance on local data while still benefiting from collaborative training. One way to implement PFL is to cluster clients with similar data distributions, and the model parameters of similar clients are aggregated as their personalized models [12–19]. For example, Yan et al. [12] proposed ICFL, which can dynamically determine the cluster structure of clients during each training round and aggregate a personalized model for each cluster. In [13], Wang et al. proposed CPFL, which uses Earth mover's distance to measure the distribution similarity between client data, thereby clustering clients to combat the Non-IID problem. Long et al. [15] proposed multicenter FL, which forms multiple personalized models through clustering based on distributed similarity of data and optimizes them individually.

The above methods essentially make the client model differentiated and aggregated in the direction of autocorrelation through clustering, and generates the personalized model of client processing Non-IID. However, these cluster-based methods are lacking in the following aspects: (i) The number of partitioned clusters needs to be manually determined, which usually requires first determining the similarity between the data distributions of the clients. (ii) The collaboration between clients of different clusters is interrupted, resulting in a change in the base of model aggregation, but there are few ways to adjust the aggregation weights to accommodate this change. (iii) The object of clustering is the entire model, without considering the similarity relationship between clients at the level of the fine-grained model.

In this paper, we propose a FL framework based on self-attention for scrap classification, which aims to provide a privacy protection and model training platform for distributed scrap recycling with heterogeneous data. The core of self-attention is the self-clustering of clients at the level of granularity in the model, which aggregates a most relevant personalized model for each client, and the weight of the aggregation is adaptively adjusted according to the similarity of the model between clients. In this way, the decentralized scrap recycling sites can combine other inconsistently distributed data to collaboratively train a scrap classification model to meet their personalized needs, without worrying about data privacy leakage. Finally, we collected a scrap classification dataset from steel mills, including 6 scrap varieties, for a total of 1000 samples. The dataset is divided into 10 client datasets with Non-IID characteristics according to the Diliclet distribution. Specifically, the main contributions of our approach are as follows:

- We have developed a federated steel scrap classification framework based on self-clustering, which allows each client to autonomously aggregate a personalized scrap steel classification model most relevant to them through the self-attention mechanism.
- We propose a model aggregation method based on the self-attention mechanism, which calculates the attention weights between models after serializing the client models, and aggregates personalized models according to the weights.
- We compare the proposed method with multiple personalized FL methods using multiple deep learning models on the dataset collected by ourselves. The experimental results show that the proposed method can effectively improve the classification accuracy of scrap steel under Non-IID distribution.

The structure of this article is as follows: Section 1 provides background and a description of the problem, Section 2 introduces existing methods, Section 3 models the federated scrap steel detection problem, Section 4 presents our solution to the problem, Section 5 validates the effectiveness of the method through experiments, and Section 6 concludes the paper.

2. Related Work

2.1. Scrap Steel Classification

At present, the mainstream classification of scrap steel is to establish a classification model through Deep Learning (DL). In [20], Tu et al. proposed an automatic classification and grading of scrap based on hierarchical learning, which firstly removes complex background information from scrap picture data through the attention mechanism, and then uses a segmentation network to segment the scrap picture. Gao et al. [2] proposed a 3D vision-based scrap steel grading approach, which can detect the edge of thickness features in pictures through machine vision, and use the detected features to classify and grade scrap. Smirnov et al. [21] compared the accuracy of various CNN models for the classification of scrap in railway carriages. Xu et al. [1] used a high-resolution sensor-based image acquisition of scrap steel and proposed a deep learning model based on attention mechanism CSBFNet to classify scrap steel. Williams et al. [22] combined magnetic induction spectroscopy and machine learning technology to develop a scrap classification framework, using magnetic induction spectroscopy to establish the physical characteristics of scrap data as the input of the depth model to classify scrap. DazRomero et al. [23] used principal component analysis to filter scrap out of the environment, and then used deep network DenseNet to classify it.

The classification of non-ferrous metals is also on the agenda. Picn et al. [24] proposed to combine hyperspectral and spatial characteristics of materials to form feature vectors to identify non-ferrous metals. Chen et al. [25] used transfer learning to classify data of small samples of non-ferrous metals on the basis of traditional image recognition techniques. Han et al. [26] also proposed a scrap classification method based on computer image recognition.

The above scrap classification methods use deep learning methods to classify scrap, or based on machine vision on the physical and chemical properties of materials, it can be predicted that deep learning has great prospects in the application of scrap classification.

2.2. Personalized Federated Learning

FL aims to use the local data distributed in each terminal device to jointly train a unified model, and upload model parameters instead of uploading local data to protect user data privacy [7,27,28]. However, in steel scrap classification scenarios, different environments and different user characteristics need to be considered, resulting in data with Non-IID characteristics in distribution, which seriously affects the accuracy of steel scrap classification in FL.

For Non-IID problems, FL has already developed a personalized method to solve them. Existing solutions are extensively discussed in [29] by Tan et al. Li et al. [30] proposed FedProx. On the basis of minimizing the global experience loss, the ℓ_2-norm constraint is introduced to the loss function of the local training, so that the local update should not be too far away from the initial global model. Sai et al. [31] proposed a new algorithm (SCAFFOLD), which uses control variates (variance reduction) to correct for the "client-drift" in its local updates, and could taken advantage of similarity in the client's data yielding even faster convergence. In [13], Wang et al. use the parameters in the local training process as the cognitive basis and calculate Earth mover's distance to quantify the differences between different models. Presotto et al. [32] proposed a federated clustering algorithm FedCLAR, which grouped clients based on the similarity of client models, so as to better identify and distinguish client data with different distributions. Yan et al. [12] proposed ICFL, which can dynamically determine the cluster structure of clients during each training round and aggregate a personalized model for each cluster. Long et al. [15] proposed multicenter FL, which forms multiple personalized models through clustering based on distributed similarity of data and optimizes them individually.

We focused on the clustering-based personalized FL, and found that the existing clustering methods rely on artificial preset cluster number, there is a lack of cooperation between clients of different clusters, and the model aggregation of clients within clusters does not consider the correlation between data distributions in a fine-grained manner. This inspired us to develop an end-to-end self-clustering approach to cluster a personalized model for each client that is most relevant to them.

3. Problem Statement

3.1. Federated Learning

There are N clients, and each client has its own local scrap steel data $D_i (i \in [1, N])$ and the loss on jth sample $(x_{i,j}, y_{i,j})$ is $l(x_{i,j})$. Moreover, the total loss of the client on its local data is $F_i(w) = \frac{1}{|D_i|} \sum_{j=1}^{|D_i|} l(x_{i,j})$, where w is the model parameter, and $|D_i|$ is the length of the dataset. The overall loss after aggregation by the FL server is:

$$F(w) = \frac{\sum_{i=1}^{N} |D_i| F_i(w)}{|D|}, \qquad (1)$$

where $|D| = \sum_{i=1}^{N} |D_i|$ is the total size of all client datasets.

Suppose $F^* = \sum_{i=1}^{N} \alpha_i F_i(w^*)$ is the smallest overall loss, where w^* is the optimal parameter that causes the model to converge and α_i is the learning rate of gradient descent algorithm. Let $\Delta = |F^* - \sum_{i=1}^{N} \alpha_i F_i^*|$, F_i^* be the optimal loss, then:

$$\Delta = |\sum_{i=1}^{N} \alpha_i F_i(w^*) - \sum_{i=1}^{N} \alpha_i F_i^*|, \qquad (2)$$

where Δ is the difference between the optimal model of the client and the optimal model aggregated by the server, and its value can reflect the deviation of the aggregate model in the global data distribution.

Generally, the value of α_i is the proportion of each client to the total data. In this case, if the distribution of the clients' data is Non-IID, then $F_i(w^*) \neq F_i^*$ and $\Delta \neq 0$, resulting in the global model of server aggregation deviating from the global distribution.

In summary, the optimization objective of scrap steel classification based on FL can be summarized as follows:

$$w^* = \arg\min_{w} F(w) \qquad (3)$$

$$s.t. \quad D_i \sim X(i), X(i) \neq X(j),$$
$$i \neq j, \qquad (4)$$
$$\Delta < \delta,$$

where $X(\cdot)$ represents the distribution of the data and δ represents an upper bound on the difference between the loss at the convergence point and the optimal loss.

3.2. Personalized FL-Based Scrap Steel Classification

In the Non-IID scenario, the global model w^* obtained by the federated average algorithm may be a local optimal minimum point for the client, which cannot meet the optimization requirements of each client [10,33]. Existing work proposes personalized FL, where customers optimize their local goals while participating in server collaborative training:

$$w_1^*, \ldots, w_N^* = \arg\min \Phi(F(w_1), \ldots, F(w_N)), \qquad (5)$$

where $\Phi(\cdot)$ is set to $\sum_{i=1}^{N} a_i \cdot F(w_i)$ and a_i is the aggregation weights for w_i.

On the basis of PFL, this paper proposes federated steel scrap classification based on self-attention hierarchical aggregation. The optimization goal can be summarized as follows:

$$w_1^*, ..., w_N^* = \arg\min \Phi(w_1, ..., w_N)$$
$$s.t. \quad D_i \sim X(i), X(i) \neq X(j), i \neq j. \tag{6}$$

where D_i is the local dataset of client i, with different distributions ($X(i) \neq X(j)$), and $\Phi(\cdot)$ is a different aggregation function for different clients' models, as calculated by:

$$\Phi(w_i) = \sum_{j=1}^{N} \alpha_{i,j} \cdot w_j \tag{7}$$
$$= \sum_{j=1}^{N} \frac{\|w_i - w_j\|_2}{\sum_{j=1}^{N} \|w_i - w_j\|_2} \cdot w_j,$$

where $\alpha_{i,j}$ is the aggregation weight between w_i and w_j and $\|w_i - w_j\|_2$ is the L2-norm between w_i and w_j, which signifies their correlation. Through this method of aggregation, similar clients are allocated greater aggregate weights, enabling the personalized model aggregated for the clients to benefit more from those that are more closely related to themselves.

4. Overview and Implementation

4.1. Overview

The overall process of FedScrap is illustrated in Figure 1, which consists of two main parts: the model training on the client side and the model aggregation on the server side, as detailed below.

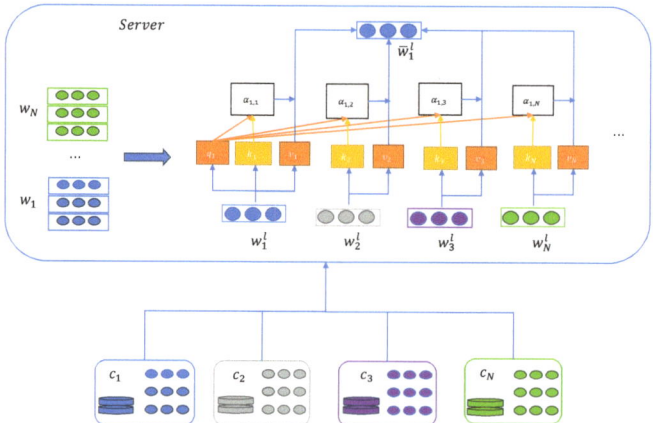

Figure 1. Overview of FedScrap. The dots in different colors represent different client's Scrap steel classification models, which are trained locally using pre-processed waste steel data. The server model aggregation is achieved by layer-by-layer aggregating a personalized model relevant to each client through the self-attention mechanism.

1. Preprocessing of scrap data and local training of classification models. Due to the complex scrap detection environment, which contains a large number of stacked scrap and background information, clients need to preprocess its scrap data and extract scrap features conducive to classification. Then, clients build their own neural network models with the same structure (such as resnet18, etc.) for training on the processed data.

2. Personalized aggregation of parameters based on self-attention. The server receives the model parameters trained by the clients and aggregates the personalized model for each client using self-attention. The core of self-attention is to measure the model similarity between clients, which can represent the distributed similarity between clients' data, and then assign greater aggregate weight to those clients' models that are more relevant to them when aggreging models for clients.

4.2. Implementation and Algorithm Description

4.2.1. Preprocessing of Scrap Data and Local Training of Classification Models

The scrap recycling sites collects the image data of scrap steel, and decomposes the scrap steel data in JPG format into RGB three primary color pixels through the image data processing function in python. The converted scrap data are unified into input data in the same format by pre-processing operations, such as cutting, de-noising, and normalization. The processed data are called the client's local data D_i, where D is the abbreviation for the dataset and client i is the i-th scrap recycling sites.

After processing the data, the clients locally build a deep learning model with the same structure to learn the features of the data. Different types of models have different feature extraction capabilities, but generally have input layers that are in contact with the data, fully connected layers for decision making, and a backbone network to extract features. The backbone network adopted in this paper is the residual network ResNet structure, which has the advantage of extracting the original features of the data and preventing the gradient disappearance caused by data heterogeneity. For ease of description, the overall model of the i-th client is denoted as w_i.

In order to speed up the training of the model, the scrap data are divided into small batch data and then iteratively fed into the network model for training. The training method adopts stochastic gradient descent (SGD) algorithm, which is a fast iterative training algorithm for small batch data. SGD calculates the error loss $F(w_i)$ between the sample label estimated by the network model and the real label through forward propagation, and inversely solves the gradient of the model parameters, i.e., $\nabla F(w_i)$, to update the parameters so as to reduce the loss. In general, the client's scrap classification model parameter w_i was updated in round t as follows:

$$w_i^t = w_i^{t-1} + \eta_i \nabla F(w_i^t), \qquad (8)$$

where $\nabla F(w_i^t)$ and η_i represent the model gradient and the step size of gradient descent, respectively. After local training, we upload the parameters or gradient values of the steel scrap classification model to the server for model aggregation.

4.2.2. Personalized Model Aggregation Based on Self-Attention

The server receives the model parameters uploaded by the clients and aggregates them into a global shared unified model according to the aggregation strategy, as follows:

$$w = \sum_{i=1}^{N} \alpha_i w_i, \qquad (9)$$

where α_i is the aggregation weight. The traditional aggregation strategy is to weight the model according to the data volume of the clients, i.e., $\alpha_i = |D_i| / \sum_{i=1}^{N} |D_i|$, but this approach involves the sensitive information of the data volume $|D_i|$, and does not take into account the model bias caused by the data distribution.

In this paper, we proposes a personalized model aggregation strategy based on layer-wise self-clustering, which aims to customize a most relevant model for each client to adapt to its data distribution. According to representation learning, the features presented by two models with the same structure after training with different data show decreasing similarity at each layer of the model. In order to examine the fine-grained features between clients, we quantified the layer-wised correlation of model parameters between clients, which is calculated by $d_{i,j}^l = \|w_i^l - w_j^l\|_2$. That is, $d_{i,j}^l$ reflects the degree of similarity between the layers of the model between the two clients, which is determined by the internal relationship of the data distribution between the clients.

On this basis, we aggregate a personalized model for each client individually. Specifically, the server takes each client as a cluster center to aggregate the models of other clients, and the weights of the aggregation are dynamically assigned according to the similarity of the parameters between them, that is:

$$\alpha_{i,j}^l = \frac{d_{i,j}^l}{\sum_{j \in N} d_{i,j}^l}, \tag{10}$$

$$\sum_{j=1}^{N} \alpha_{i,j}^l = 1. \tag{11}$$

In order to improve the ability of the aggregation model to process heterogeneous data, a larger aggregation weight $\alpha_{i,j}^l$ is assigned between clients with similar data, which makes the i-th client more "concerned" about the model parameters of the j-th client at layer j. In other words, there is more cooperation between similar clients, which is mutually desirable and satisfies each other's needs.

Then, the server repeats the aggregate weight $\alpha_{i,j}^l$ between the two clients and customizes the aggregate model for each client based on the weight, that is:

$$w_i^l = \sum_{j \in N} \alpha_{i,j}^l w_j^l, \tag{12}$$

where w_i^l is the model parameter of layer l aggregated by the server for client i. In a Non-IID environment, calculating the model similarity between clients layer by layer can facilitate effective cooperation among multiple parties, but a significant problem with this is the complexity of the calculations, which require frequent and repeated access to each client's parameters at each layer of the model. Therefore, it is necessary to develop a model aggregation method capable of parallel computation.

In this paper, the idea of self-attention is adopted, which can calculate the attention weight of serialized data in parallel, so as to extract the correlation within the sequence data. In this way, the more relevant content of each client is deeply extracted into the server model, reducing the aggregation of personalized features while preserving shared features. Specifically, the personalized federated scrap detection process based on self-attention is as follows:

1. Serialize the model parameters for each client of the same layer into an input vector, denoted as $w^l = [w_1^l, w_2^l, ..w_N^l]$ for any $l \in L$.
2. Multiply each vector w by three coefficients a^q, a^k, and a^v to get three vectors: query, key, and value, that is, $Q = A^q \cdot w^l$, $K = A^k \cdot w^l$ and $V = A^v \cdot w^l$, where $A = [a_1, a_2, ..., a_N]$.
3. The attention score (similarity score) is calculated for the clients by matrix multiplication, i.e., $\alpha^l = Q \cdot K$, where $\alpha_{i,j}^l = a^q \cdot w_i^l \cdot a^k \cdot w_j^l$, which reflects the degree of similarity between the parameters.
4. The attention scores were normalized using softmax and other methods, i.e., $\hat{\alpha}^l = softmax(\alpha^l)$.
5. Finally, the aggregated parameters are obtained by multiplying the normalized attention score by the parameter vector, i.e., $\hat{w}^l = \hat{\alpha}^l \cdot w^l$, where $\hat{w}_i^l = \sum_{j=1}^{N} \hat{\alpha}_{i,j}^l \cdot w_i^l$.

The aggregation algorithm of federated scrap detection is shown in Algorithm 1.

Algorithm 1 Personalized model aggregation based on self-attention

1: **for** $i \in N$ **do**
2:    The client local model training: $w_i^t = w_i^{t-1} + \eta_i \nabla F(w_i^t)$.
3:    The client uploads its local model parameter w_i^t.
4: **end for**
5: **for** $l \in L$ **do**
6:    The server serializes the model parameters of the clients: $w^l = [w_1^l, w_2^l, ..w_N^l]$.
7:    Parameter vector coefficients: $Q = A^q \cdot w^l$, $K = A^k \cdot w^l$ and $V = A^v \cdot w^l$.
8:    The server calculates the attention score for the clients: $\alpha^l = Q \cdot K$.
9:    Attention score normalization: $\hat{\alpha}^l = softmax(\alpha^l)$.
10:    Aggregate model parameters according to attention scores: $\hat{w}_i^l = \sum_{j=1}^{N} \hat{\alpha}_{i,j}^l \cdot w_i^l$.
11: **end for**
12: The server sends the aggregated model parameters $\hat{w}_i$ to all clients.

5. Evaluation

5.1. Set Up

In order to effectively evaluate the performance of the method proposed in this paper, we conduct experimental verification on a self-built FL framework with ten clients. The framework is deployed on a server with 56 NVIDIA GeForce RTX 3090 Ti graphic cards.

Since there is no open source scrap detection dataset at present, we collected a batch of scrap image data from a steel mill in China, which has six common types of scrap, including silicon steel sheet, rebar, steel slag hot pressed block, heavy scrap, square pressed block, and messy scrap, as shown in the Figure 2, and the total sample size was about 1000 images.

(a) silicon steel sheet   (b) rebar   (c) steel slag hot pressing block

(d) heavy scrap   (e) square pressing block   (f) messy scrap

Figure 2. Examples of different scrap types in self-built datasets.

In terms of the depth algorithm for extracting data features, we use three common models for verification, and the three model pairs are shown in Table 1.

Table 1. Models used to extract data features.

Models	Mechanism	Parameters	Layers	Activation Function
LeNet-5	Convolutional Layers	60 k	7	ReLU
ResNet-18	Convolutional Layers	11.7 M	18	ReLU
ViT-12	Self-Attention	86.57 M	12	ReLU/Layer Normalization

In order to compare the performance of the proposed layer-based method in terms of model prediction accuracy, client's local model accuracy, etc., the comparison method in this paper is as follows:

1. FedAvg [7], an FL classic algorithm that collects and averages model parameters across clients.
2. FedProx [30], an FL method that restricts the client's update direction to enhance the performance of the global model, has a hyperparameter μ for the constraint we set to 0.01.
3. ICFL [12], a clustering FL algorithm that automatically clusters clients and aggregates clustering models according to the correlation between clients without setting the number of clusters.
4. CPFL [13], a clustering FL algorithm that individually aggregates the personalized models associated with them for each client.

The comparison methods use the same dataset, network model, and hyperparameter settings.

5.2. Overall Accuracy Comparison

We divide the self-built dataset into ten clients using the Dilliclet distribution, with a Dilliclet coefficient α of 0.01, and each client has a different number or category of scrap data. Then, resnet and Vit models are used to train and test the accuracy of several comparison methods on each client. First, we averaged the accuracy of the client to observe the global average accuracy of the whole and evaluate the performance of each method. The result records are shown in Table 2, where $\pm$ represents the standard deviation between the accuracy of the clients.

Table 2. Overall accuracy comparison of methods on different models (the unit of accuracy is %).

Methods Models	Local	FedAvg	FedProx	CPFL	ICFL	FedScrap
ResNet-18	77.868 ± 14.88	97.655 ± 6.3	98.834 ± 2.06	99.583 ± 1.32	99.322 ± 1.43	99.655 ± 1.09
VIT	89.857 ± 15.7	98.199 ± 3.57	94.735 ± 10.38	97.776 ± 3.82	97.164 ± 3.35	98.985 ± 1.74
LeNet	80.593 ± 18.89	98.797 ± 10.99	95.5 ± 9.78	89.819 ± 15.6	94.468 ± 7.24	97.899 ± 2.4

The results indicate that under the Non-IID data distribution, the unprocessed local scrap steel classification model exhibits extremely low accuracy performance, and there is a substantial variance in accuracy across clients. This suggests that while some clients achieve high accuracy, others remain at very low levels, which is clearly unsatisfactory. Traditional FL methods such as FedAvg and FedProx can enhance classification accuracy; however, their performance is highly unstable across different models, exhibiting considerable variance. This is primarily due to their reliance on a single shared model maintained on the server to address the data from all clients. Cluster-based PFL methods significantly mitigate this issue, achieving a high average accuracy with reduced variance. Our proposed FedScrap outperforms these methods, demonstrating high robustness across various models. Both our accuracy and variance are superior to those of the comparative methods, which is attributed to the personalized models tailored for each client, absorbing the most relevant knowledge for their respective contexts.

For a more intuitive comparison, we plotted the test results of different models, as shown in Figure 3.

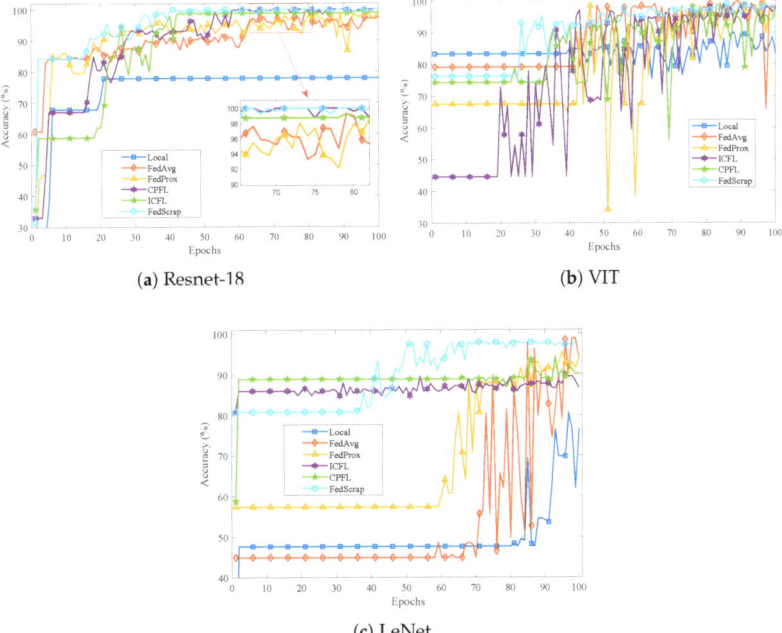

Figure 3. Accuracy comparison of methods on different models.

The analysis reveals that in scenarios characterized by an imbalance in scrap types, the classification model trained exclusively on local data exhibits low overall accuracy. This shortcoming arises because certain client-specific samples are too limited to yield effective training outcomes. Consequently, there is a pressing need for FL to collaborate with these dispersed clients and enhance the model's performance. The yellow curve, depicting conventional FL, demonstrates a notable enhancement in model accuracy. However, the accuracy fluctuates markedly and convergence is achieved gradually. This volatility is attributed to the data heterogeneity resulting from the unbalanced distribution of scrap types, which challenges a single global model's capacity to cater to the diverse needs of all clients.

Although existing cluster-based personalized methods can marginally elevate model accuracy, they are accompanied by significant fluctuations in the early stages, suggesting a slow convergence rate. This delay is rooted in the initial step of identifying cluster centers, followed by the aggregation of personalized models around these centers. The choice of cluster centers is critical and can significantly impact the model's convergence. In contrast to these approaches, our proposed FedScrap method treats each client as a clustering center, effectively positioning them as individual servers. This strategy facilitates the aggregation of highly relevant personalized models that have absorbed sufficient bespoke knowledge from similar clients, thereby aligning closely with their respective data distributions. As a result, FedScrap not only enhances model precision, but also ensures a smooth convergence process.

5.3. Comparison of Accuracy Differences between Methods among Clients

To more finely compare the individual variations of each method at the client level and to identify the reasons why the accuracy variances of other methods are not sufficiently impressive, we have recorded and plotted the accuracy box plots for each client. The results are shown in Figure 4, where the three box plots represent the three backbone network models used.

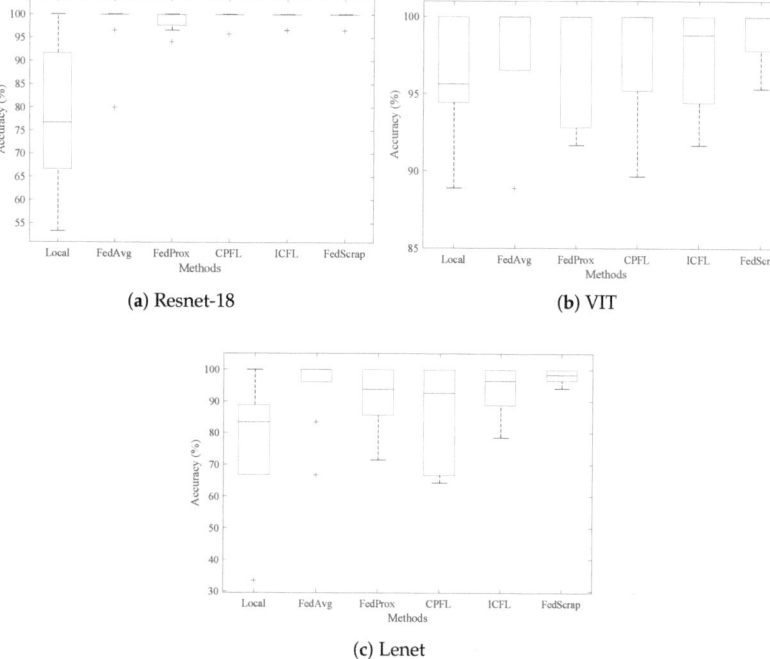

Figure 4. Accuracy comparison of different methods on boxplots.

It can be observed that the three graphs depict a similar pattern of performance: local performs the worst, with an accuracy of merely 50%, while FedScrap exhibits the best performance, consistently maintaining accuracy above 90%, and the other methods each have their strengths but also suffer from notable drawbacks.

Due to the impact of data Non-IID, there are certain differences in the types of scrap metal among clients. Some clients have extremely limited samples for certain types of scrap metal, resulting in poor accuracy, while those with better data resources perform well. Although FedAvg and FedProx, as representatives of a single global model, have combined client training, the differentiated data lead to poor performance on some clients. The cluster-based methods CPFL and ICFL group clients based on their similarity, maintaining a shared model within each group. However, this breaks the close connection between clients, leading to a decline in average accuracy.

Unlike these methods, FedScrap not only fully considers the relevance of data between clients but also uses this relevance to strengthen the connection between clients. As a result, the personalized models tailored for each client can absorb useful information from other clients based on their own data distribution. These aspects contribute to FedScrap's average accuracy among clients reaching up to 97%, with a standard deviation of only about 2%.

6. Conclusions

This paper introduced FedScrap, a layer-wised personalized FL framework for scrap detection. Utilizing the self-attention mechanism, FedScrap coordinates distributed scrap data to train a robust scrap classification model. The framework addressed the challenge of non-independent co-distribution in distributed scrap data by employing the self-attention concept to aggregate a personalized model for each client that is most relevant to its specific data. We also collected scrap pictures from a steel mill and labeled them to make scrap classification dataset, and carried out verification experiment on this dataset. Experimental results show that FedScrap accurately classifies distributed scrap data with an impressive accuracy rate of 90%.

Author Contributions: Conceptualization, W.Z. and L.W.; methodology, W.Z.; software, L.W.; validation, D.D. and L.W.; formal analysis, D.D.; investigation, L.W.; resources, L.W.; data curation, W.Z.; writing—original draft preparation, W.Z.; writing—review and editing, W.Z. and D.D.; visualization, D.D.; supervision, L.W.; project administration, W.Z.; funding acquisition, L.W. All authors have read and agreed to the published version of the manuscript.

Funding: This research was funded by the National Nature Science Foundation of China, grant number 62172003.

Data Availability Statement: The data can be shared up on request.

Conflicts of Interest: The authors declare no conflicts of interest.

References

1. Xu, W.; Xiao, P.; Zhu, L.; Zhang, Y.; Chang, J.; Zhu, R.; Xu, Y. Classification and rating of steel scrap using deep learning. *Eng. Appl. Artif. Intell.* **2023**, *123*, 106241. [CrossRef]
2. Gao, Z.; Lu, H.; Lei, J.; Zhao, J.; Guo, H.; Shi, C.; Zhang, Y. An RGB-D-Based Thickness Feature Descriptor and Its Application on Scrap Steel Grading. *IEEE Trans. Instrum. Meas.* **2023**, *72*, 5031414. [CrossRef]
3. Zhang, R.; Xiong, K.; Lu, Y.; Fan, P.; Ng, D.W.K.; Letaief, K.B. Energy efficiency maximization in RIS-assisted SWIPT networks with RSMA: A PPO-based approach. *IEEE J. Sel. Areas Commun.* **2023**, *41*, 1413–1430. [CrossRef]
4. Zhang, T.; Xu, C.; Lian, Y.; Tian, H.; Kang, J.; Kuang, X.; Niyato, D. When Moving Target Defense Meets Attack Prediction in Digital Twins: A Convolutional and Hierarchical Reinforcement Learning Approach. *IEEE J. Sel. Areas Commun.* **2023**, *41*, 3293–3305. [CrossRef]
5. Zhang, T.; Xu, C.; Shen, J.; Kuang, X.; Grieco, L.A. How to Disturb Network Reconnaissance: A Moving Target Defense Approach Based on Deep Reinforcement Learning. *IEEE Trans. Inf. Forensics Secur.* **2023**, *18*, 5735–5748. [CrossRef]
6. Zhang, T.; Xu, C.; Zou, P.; Tian, H.; Kuang, X.; Yang, S.; Zhong, L.; Niyato, D. How to mitigate DDOS intelligently in SD-IOV: A moving target defense approach. *IEEE Trans. Ind. Inform.* **2022**, *19*, 1097–1106. [CrossRef]
7. McMahan, B.; Moore, E.; Ramage, D.; Hampson, S.; y Arcas, B.A. Communication-efficient learning of deep networks from decentralized data. In Proceedings of the Artificial Intelligence and Statistics, Lauderdale, FL, USA, 20–22 April 2017; pp. 1273–1282.
8. Zhang, R.; Xiong, K.; Lu, Y.; Gao, B.; Fan, P.; Letaief, K.B. Joint coordinated beamforming and power splitting ratio optimization in MU-MISO SWIPT-enabled HetNets: A multi-agent DDQN-based approach. *IEEE J. Sel. Areas Commun.* **2021**, *40*, 677–693. [CrossRef]
9. Zhao, Y.; Li, M.; Lai, L.; Suda, N.; Civin, D.; Chandra, V. Federated learning with non-IID data. *arXiv* **2018**, arXiv:1806.00582.
10. Xu, J.; Tong, X.; Huang, S.L. Personalized Federated Learning with Feature Alignment and Classifier Collaboration. In Proceedings of the Eleventh International Conference on Learning Representations, Kigali, Rwanda, 1–5 May 2022.
11. Cheng, D.; Zhang, L.; Bu, C.; Wang, X.; Wu, H.; Song, A. ProtoHAR: Prototype Guided Personalized Federated Learning for Human Activity Recognition. *IEEE J. Biomed. Health Inform.* **2023**, *24*, 3900–3911. [CrossRef]
12. Yan, Y.; Tong, X.; Wang, S. Clustered Federated Learning in Heterogeneous Environment. *IEEE Trans. Neural Netw. Learn. Syst.* **2023**, 1–14. [CrossRef]
13. Wang, J.; Xu, G.; Lei, W.; Gong, L.; Zheng, X.; Liu, S. Cpfl: An effective secure cognitive personalized federated learning mechanism for industry 4.0. *IEEE Trans. Ind. Inform.* **2022**, *18*, 7186–7195. [CrossRef]
14. Li, B.; Chen, S.; Yu, K. FeDDkw–Federated Learning with Dynamic Kullback–Leibler-divergence Weight. In *ACM Transactions on Asian and Low-Resource Language Information Processing*; Association for Computing Machinery: New York, NY, USA, 2023.
15. Long, G.; Xie, M.; Shen, T.; Zhou, T.; Wang, X.; Jiang, J. Multi-center federated learning: Clients clustering for better personalization. *World Wide Web* **2023**, *26*, 481–500. [CrossRef]
16. Ghosh, A.; Chung, J.; Yin, D.; Ramchandran, K. An efficient framework for clustered federated learning. *Adv. Neural Inf. Process. Syst.* **2020**, *33*, 19586–19597. [CrossRef]
17. Duan, M.; Liu, D.; Ji, X.; Wu, Y.; Liang, L.; Chen, X.; Tan, Y.; Ren, A. Flexible clustered federated learning for client-level data distribution shift. *IEEE Trans. Parallel Distrib. Syst.* **2021**, *33*, 2661–2674. [CrossRef]
18. Vahidian, S.; Morafah, M.; Wang, W.; Kungurtsev, V.; Chen, C.; Shah, M.; Lin, B. Efficient distribution similarity identification in clustered federated learning via principal angles between client data subspaces. In Proceedings of the AAAI Conference on Artificial Intelligence, Washington, DC, USA, 7–14 February 2023; pp. 10043–10052.
19. Xu, B.; Xia, W.; Zhao, H.; Zhu, Y.; Sun, X.; Quek, T.Q. Clustered federated learning in Internet of Things: Convergence analysis and resource pptimization. *IEEE Internet Things J.* **2023**, *11*, 3217–3232. [CrossRef]
20. Tu, Q.; Li, D.; Xie, Q.; Dai, L.; Wang, J. Automated Scrap Steel Grading via a Hierarchical Learning-Based Framework. *IEEE Trans. Instrum. Meas.* **2022**, *71*, 5022313. [CrossRef]
21. Smirnov, N.V.; Trifonov, A.S. Deep Learning Methods for Solving Scrap Metal Classification Task. In Proceedings of the 2021 International Russian Automation Conference (RusAutoCon), Sochi, Russia, 5–11 September 2021; pp. 221–225.
22. Williams, K.C.; O'Toole, M.D.; Peyton, A.J. Scrap metal classification using magnetic induction spectroscopy and machine vision. *IEEE Trans. Instrum. Meas.* **2023**, *72*, 2520211. [CrossRef]

23. Diaz-Romero, D.J.; Van den Eynde, S.; Sterkens, W.; Engelen, B.; Zaplana, I.; Dewulf, W.; Goedemé, T.; Peeters, J. Simultaneous mass estimation and class classification of scrap metals using deep learning. *Resour. Conserv. Recycl.* **2022**, *181*, 106272. [CrossRef]
24. Picón, A.; Ghita, O.; Whelan, P.F.; Iriondo, P.M. Fuzzy Spectral and Spatial Feature Integration for Classification of Nonferrous Materials in Hyperspectral Data. *IEEE Trans. Ind. Inform.* **2009**, *5*, 483–494. [CrossRef]
25. Chen, S.; Hu, Z.; Wang, C.; Pang, Q.; Hua, L. Research on the process of small sample non-ferrous metal recognition and separation based on deep learning. *Waste Manag.* **2021**, *126*, 266–273. [CrossRef]
26. Han, S.D.; Huang, B.; Ding, S.; Song, C.; Feng, S.W.; Xu, M.; Lin, H.; Zou, Q.; Boularias, A.; Yu, J. Toward fully automated metal recycling using computer vision and non-prehensile manipulation. In Proceedings of the 2021 IEEE 17th International Conference on Automation Science and Engineering (CASE), Lyon, France, 23–27 August 2021; pp. 891–898.
27. Yang, Q.; Liu, Y.; Chen, T.; Tong, Y. Federated machine learning: Concept and applications. *ACM Trans. Intell. Syst. Technol. (TIST)* **2019**, *10*, 1–19. [CrossRef]
28. Li, T.; Sahu, A.K.; Talwalkar, A.; Smith, V. Federated learning: Challenges, methods, and future directions. *IEEE Signal Process. Mag.* **2020**, *37*, 50–60. [CrossRef]
29. Tan, A.Z.; Yu, H.; Cui, L.; Yang, Q. Towards personalized federated learning. *IEEE Trans. Neural Netw. Learn. Syst.* **2022**, *34*, 9587–9603. [CrossRef] [PubMed]
30. Li, T.; Sahu, A.K.; Zaheer, M.; Sanjabi, M.; Talwalkar, A.; Smith, V. Federated optimization in heterogeneous networks. *Proc. Mach. Learn. Syst.* **2020**, *2*, 429–450.
31. Karimireddy, S.P.; Kale, S.; Mohri, M.; Reddi, S.; Stich, S.; Suresh, A.T. Scaffold: Stochastic controlled averaging for federated learning. In Proceedings of the International Conference on Machine Learning, Online, 13–18 July 2020; pp. 5132–5143.
32. Presotto, R.; Civitarese, G.; Bettini, C. Fedclar: Federated clustering for personalized sensor-based human activity recognition. In Proceedings of the 2022 IEEE International Conference on Pervasive Computing and Communications (PerCom), Biarritz, France, 11–15 March 2022; pp. 227–236.
33. Zhang, J.; Hua, Y.; Wang, H.; Song, T.; Xue, Z.; Ma, R.; Guan, H. FedALA: Adaptive local aggregation for personalized federated learning. In Proceedings of the AAAI Conference on Artificial Intelligence, Washington, DC, USA, 7–14 February 2023; pp. 11237–11244.

Disclaimer/Publisher's Note: The statements, opinions and data contained in all publications are solely those of the individual author(s) and contributor(s) and not of MDPI and/or the editor(s). MDPI and/or the editor(s) disclaim responsibility for any injury to people or property resulting from any ideas, methods, instructions or products referred to in the content.

MDPI AG
Grosspeteranlage 5
4052 Basel
Switzerland
Tel.: +41 61 683 77 34

Electronics Editorial Office
E-mail: electronics@mdpi.com
www.mdpi.com/journal/electronics

Disclaimer/Publisher's Note: The title and front matter of this reprint are at the discretion of the Guest Editors. The publisher is not responsible for their content or any associated concerns. The statements, opinions and data contained in all individual articles are solely those of the individual Editors and contributors and not of MDPI. MDPI disclaims responsibility for any injury to people or property resulting from any ideas, methods, instructions or products referred to in the content.

www.ingramcontent.com/pod-product-compliance
Lightning Source LLC
LaVergne TN
LVHW072251110526
838202LV00106B/2373